Handbook of Qualitative Research in Communication Disorders

This volume provides a comprehensive and in-depth handbook of qualitative research in the field of communication disorders. It introduces and illustrates the wide range of qualitative paradigms that have been used in recent years to investigate various aspects of communication disorders.

The first part of the book introduces in some detail the concept of qualitative research and its application to communication disorders, and describes the main qualitative research approaches. The contributions are forward-looking rather than merely giving an overview of their topic. The second part illustrates these approaches through a series of case studies of different communication disorders using qualitative methods of research.

This book is an essential resource for senior undergraduate and graduate students, researchers, and practitioners in communication disorders and related fields.

Martin J. Ball is Hawthorne-BoRSF Endowed Professor at the University of Louisiana at Lafayette. He is co-editor of the journal *Clinical Linguistics and Phonetics* (Taylor & Francis), and the book series *Communication Disorders Across Languages* (Multilingual Matters). His main research interests include sociolinguistics, clinical phonetics and phonology, and the linguistics of Welsh. He is an honorary Fellow of the Royal College of Speech and Language Therapists, and a Fellow of the Royal Society of Arts.

Nicole Müller is Hawthorne-BoRSF Endowed Professor of Communicative Disorders at the University of Louisiana at Lafayette. Her main research interests include: clinical discourse studies and pragmatics, specifically as applied to Alzheimer's Disease; communication disorders and multilingualism; and functional grammar.

Ryan L. Nelson is Assistant Professor, Hawthorne-BoRSF Endowed Professor of Communicative Disorders at the University of Louisiana at Lafayette. His main research interests include childhood language disorders, literacy construction and usage, and qualitative research methodologies.

LANGUAGE AND SPEECH DISORDERS BOOK SERIES

Series Editors:
Martin J. Ball, *University of Louisiana at Lafayette*
Jack S. Damico, *University of Louisiana at Lafayette*

This new series brings together course material and new research for students, practitioners, and researchers in the various areas of language and speech disorders. Textbooks covering the basics of the discipline will be designed for courses within communication disorders programs in the English-speaking world, and monographs and edited collections will present cutting-edge research from leading scholars in the field.

PUBLISHED

Recovery from Stuttering, Howell
Handbook of Vowels and Vowel Disorders, Ball & Gibbon (Eds.)
Handbook of Qualitative Research in Communication Disorders, Ball, Müller, & Nelson (Eds.)

FORTHCOMING

Applying English Grammatical Analysis: Clinical Language Assessment and Intervention, Jin & Cortazzi
Electropalatography for Speech Assessment and Intervention, McLeod, Wood, & Hardcastle

For continually updated information about published and forthcoming titles in the *Language and Speech Disorders* book series, please visit **www.psypress.com/language-and-speech-disorders**

Handbook of
Qualitative Research
in Communication
Disorders

Edited by

Martin J. Ball, Nicole Müller,
and Ryan L. Nelson

Psychology Press
Taylor & Francis Group
NEW YORK AND LONDON

First published 2014
by Psychology Press
711 Third Avenue, New York, NY 10017

Simultaneously published in the UK
by Psychology Press
27 Church Road, Hove, East Sussex BN3 2FA

Psychology Press is an imprint of the Taylor & Francis Group, an informa business

Library of Congress Cataloging in Publication Data
A catalog record for this book has been requested

ISBN: 978-1-84872-642-0 (hbk)
ISBN: 978-1-84872-643-7 (pbk)
ISBN: 978-0-203-79887-4 (ebk)

Typeset in Minion
by EvS Communication Networx, Inc.

Printed and bound in the United States of America
by Edwards Brothers Malloy

Contents

**Part III
Epilogue**

Contributors

Kathleen Abendroth, Fluvanna County Public Schools, Palmyra, USA

Elizabeth Armstrong, Edith Cowan University, Australia

Peter Auer, University of Freiburg, Germany

Martin J. Ball, University of Louisiana at Lafayette, USA

Bonnie Brinton, Brigham Young University, USA

Sarah D'Agostino, National Stuttering Association, USA

Holly W. Damico, University of Louisiana at Lafayette, USA

Jack S. Damico, University of Louisiana at Lafayette, USA

Judith Felson Duchan, State University of New York at Buffalo, USA

Alison Ferguson, University of Newcastle, Australia

Martin Fujiki, Brigham Young University, USA

Juliet Goldbart, Manchester Metropolitan University, UK

Charles Goodwin, University of California, Los Angeles, USA

Jacqueline Guendouzi, Southeastern Louisiana University, USA

Marie-Christine Hallé, Université de Montréal, Canada

Carol Scheffner Hammer, Temple University, USA

Deborah Hersh, Edith Cowan University, Australia

Jacqueline J. Hinckley, University of South Florida, USA

Louise Keegan, Appalachian State University, USA

Dana Kovarsky, University of Rhode Island, USA

Tobias Kroll, Texas Tech University Health Sciences Center, USA

Guylaine Le Dorze, Université de Montréal, Canada

Karen Lynch, Southeastern Louisiana University, USA

Julie Marshall, Manchester Metropolitan University, UK

Zaneta Mok, La Trobe University, Australia

Nicole Müller, University of Louisiana at Lafayette, USA

Ryan L. Nelson, University of Louisiana at Lafayette, USA

Claire Penn, University of the Witwatersrand, South Africa

Michael R. Perkins, University of Sheffield, UK

Nancye Roussel, University of Louisiana at Lafayette, USA

Ben Rutter, University of Sheffield, UK

Nina Simmons-Mackie, Southeastern Louisiana University, USA

John A. Tetnowski, University of Louisiana at Lafayette, USA

Mitchell Trichon, St John's University, New York, USA

Ray Wilkinson, University of Sheffield, UK

Foreword

CHARLES GOODWIN

"No man is an island, entire of himself"

John Donne, *Devotions Upon Emergent Occasions*, Devotion XVIII

By their very nature *festschrifts* seem to embody a retrospective orientation. They attempt to both celebrate and do justice to a distinguished career, one that has created new possibilities for thinking and acting which we now use as resources for our own work. This is certainly true for Jack Damico, and I am most honored to be able to contribute something to both this volume and the community of thinking and practice that intersects at his work.

However, this volume has an equally important prospective orientation. With its extraordinary group of contributors, it is a call for a future that will move in new and most important directions. What is presented here has profound implications theoretically for how we conceptualize human language and action, and practically for how we care for each other, how we do research on impairments to both language and the body, and how health care should be organized.

I personally grapple with the issues that are the focus of this volume from two equally important perspectives. On the one hand, my professional life, indeed passion, has focused on how talk, the human ability to say something meaningful, is organized through the co-operative actions of multiple participants (for example, both a speaker and different kinds of hearers) within situated human interaction. On the other hand, my father, Chil, suffered a stroke that left him with a catastrophically impaired lexicon (basically significant variants of *Yes, No,* and *And* and meaningful gestures such as numbers). Chil's aphasia was a living presence in our family for over 20 years.

Within a framework that focuses on linguistic competence, it seems reasonable to conceptualize the speaker as an entity, frequently an isolated individual, capable of constructing syntactically complex sentences, with part of that ability emerging from powerful forms of organization within the human brain. Chil, with a vocabulary that could quite literally be counted on the fingers of one hand and virtually no syntax, absolutely failed to meet this standard. We later learned that at the time of his stroke Chil's neurologists expected him to spend the rest of his life lying in bed in a state of profound isolation.

Instead, he led a very active social life. He used his scooter to go out and have lunch with friends, do his family's shopping at the supermarket, go to Starbuck's for a Frappuccino, go to movies by himself, etc. Moreover, he acted as a rich and powerful speaker in conversation. Indeed, my mother complained that her own voice got lost because everyone became so interested in working out what Chil was saying.

How was it possible for someone with almost no vocabulary or syntax to act as a powerful speaker? Providing an answer to this question requires that we expand our analytic focus beyond the linguistic abilities of the isolated speaker, to take into account what Linell (2009) calls languaging, the dialogic, co-operative process through which multiple parties build utterances and meaning in concert with each other. Basically, by using his limited vocabulary to make precisely placed interventions into the stream of linguistically rich talk being produced by his interlocutors, Chil got them to produce the words he needed to say (Goodwin, 2007). Consider his use of the word *No* in Figure 1.[1]

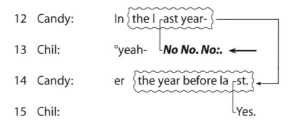

12	Candy:	In {the I ̤ast year-} ——————
13	Chil:	°yeah- └*No No. No:.* ←———
14	Candy:	er {the year before la ̤st.}
15	Chil:	└Yes.

Figure Foreword.1 Making Meaning Together

The participants have been discussing the great amount of snow that has fallen in Chil's neighborhood in recent years. In line 12 Candy starts to make a comment about how much fell "last year." Before this even comes to completion, Chil in line 13 objects with a strong "*No No. No:.*" Rather than standing alone, Chil's *No* is a prototypical example of what conversation analysts describe as second pair parts (Sacks, 1992; Sacks, Schegloff, & Jefferson, 1974). Thus, Chil's interlocutors do not treat his *No* as an isolated, self-sufficient utterance, or as stating an amorphous objection to the world in general. Instead he was heard to be objecting to precisely what had just been said. Thus, in response to Chil, Candy in line 14 changes what she just said, "last year," to "the year before last."

In a very real sense Chil is the author of what is said in line 14. Candy, the person who actually speaks the words that occur here, said something different in line 12. Though Chil quite literally does not have the ability to produce the morphemes or syntax that make the statement in line 14, he is in fact acting as a speaker who makes a subtle, complex contribution to what is being talked about. He is systematically able to get others to produce the words he requires, but cannot say himself. His ability to act as a speaker does not reside in him alone, but instead emerges through a process of co-operative action with others. Despite Chil's catastrophically impoverished lexicon, his ability to produce action that indexically incorporates structure provided by the nearby talk of others into what he is saying provides him with the resources to invoke and make use of rich semantics.

The damage that causes aphasia and related forms of language impairment does reside within the brain of the individual. However, talk and interaction with others constitute the place where that impairment emerges into the lived, natural world as something consequential that structures meaning-making and social life in profound ways. As seen in Figure 1, that same social matrix provides the resources through which the limitations of the individual can be partially overcome through co-operative social action (though strong limits on this process remain: see Auer, this volume). What is at issue, and what can be the focus of both therapy and meaningful lives, is not something lodged exclusively within the individual, but a socially organized ecology of meaning-making practices made possible through the participation of multiple actors with varied abilities. Throughout his entire career, Jack Damico (as well as the contributors to this volume) provided crucial theoretical and practical demonstrations of the power of rich social and interactive analysis, from many different perspectives, for our understanding of the varied ways in which human beings can build meaning, action and lives with each other.

The implications of this are no means restricted to either speakers whose ability to produce talk has been impacted, or to special situations such as therapy, or interactions that involve people such as Chil. Such frameworks apply as well to our understanding of how talk and action are organized among fully fluent speakers. In general, and not only for people such as Chil, an action done with *No* operates on, ties to, and indexically incorporates resources found within the talk of others it is responding to. Both speakers and utterances can have a distributed organization with actors occupying alternative positions (speaker and hearer, for example) contributing different kinds of materials to a common action. The work reported in this volume allows us to understand with greater clarity crucial, but frequently unnoticed, features of ordinary language use and interaction. These features force us to expand our theoretical horizons for investigating human language and action more generally. In reviewing a number of books about children and others with profound disabilities, Nussbaum (2001) notes that almost all Western theories about human language and social life, from Rousseau to John Rawls, use as their point of departure a fully competent individual actor, for example, someone with the abilities and social maturity required to enter into a social contract. What is being demonstrated in the work presented in this volume is the importance of replacing the individual as a point of departure for analysis with something like an interactive field within which actors with different abilities situated in alternative positions can construct meaning and action in concert with each other.[2]

This same expanded social and interactive environment for the organization of lived practice is relevant as well to how we conceptualize crucial categories, such as the "patient," in our systems for health care. My father's stroke affected the life of my mother as much as it did his. Suddenly, when she was past 60, she had to provide him with physical care on a daily basis (like many suffering from his kind of stroke, the right side of his body was left paralyzed). She also faced the ongoing task of adapting to the changed ecology, noted above, required for Chil to continue to act as a speaker. Focusing only on Chil as the patient injured by his stroke is inadequate from both a theoretical perspective (as well demonstrated by the chapters in this volume it elides the cooperative processes noted above for the construction of meaning and action in concert with others), and with respect to locating who bears the actual costs of care giving. Though occurring within the skull of an individual, damage to the brain is a profound social event that, like a stone tossed into a still pond, ripples outward to reshape in most consequential ways a network of intertwined lives.

Qualitative research that investigates the social organization of making meaning within human interaction through the many perspectives articulated so powerfully in this volume is especially important at the present moment. Many of the wounded returning from recent wars, such as our interventions in Iraq, are suffering from severe head injuries. There are a number of reasons for this, including the fact that the bottoms of Humvees can be protected much more effectively than the windows at the top, and much greater success in saving the lives of those who are severely injured. Current debates about health care, and a focus on cost-effective treatment for individuals, render invisible the profound, long-term social dimensions of what is occurring. Very young people are returned home in a state that has lifelong consequences for not only them, but also their families and others close to them, who will in fact provide much of their care while never appearing in tallies of care or the cost of war. Qualitative investigation of how lives are actually lived in such circumstances, and how meaning is accomplished through interaction with others, is essential for both developing therapies and for understanding the far reaching consequences of the injury and the dimensions of care.

In sum, this is a very important volume in a number of different ways. As a fitting tribute to the work that Jack Damico has done throughout his career, it provides a state-of-the-art survey of a range of crucial perspectives for doing qualitative analysis written by many of the top scholars in the field. In addition to its clear and most important implications of therapy, the analytic frameworks it articulates offer new and important ways for conceptualizing the social dimensions of human language, action and meaning making more generally.

Notes

1. See Goodwin (2007) for detailed analysis of this sequence.
2. The research traditions that flow from the work of Bakhtin (1981) and Vygotsky (1978) are most relevant here.

References

Bakhtin, M. M. (1981). *The dialogic imagination* (Trans. C. Emerson & M. Holquist). Austin: University of Texas Press.

Goodwin, C. (2007). Interactive footing. In E. Holt & R. Clift (Eds.), *Reporting talk: Reported speech in interaction* (pp. 16–46). Cambridge, England: Cambridge University Press.

Linell, P. (2009). *Rethinking language, mind, and world dialogically: Interactional and contextual theories of human sense-making.* Charlotte, NC: Information Age.

Nussbaum, M. (2001, January 11). Disabled lives: Who cares? *The New York Review of Books, 48*(1), 34–37.

Sacks, H. (1992). *Lectures on conversation: Volume 2* (edited by Gail Jefferson). Oxford, England: Basil Blackwell.

Sacks, H., Schegloff, E.A., & Jefferson, G. (1974). A simplest systematics for the organization of turn-taking for conversation. *Language, 50*, 696–735.

Vygotsky, L. S. (1978). *Mind in society: The development of higher psychological processes.* Cambridge, MA: Harvard University Press.

Preface

MARTIN J. BALL, NICOLE MÜLLER, AND RYAN L. NELSON

The aim of this handbook is twofold: first to provide a survey of qualitative research methods as applied to communication disorders; and second, to recognize and celebrate Jack Damico's leading role in advocating these methods and applying them in his own work. That qualitative research within the field of communication disorders is now an accepted approach to investigating communication breakdown is amply illustrated in this volume. That Jack S. Damico has been a leader in this development is also clearly shown throughout the book in the references to his work and descriptions of his contributions. Indeed, as editors, we felt this volume would not adequately reflect the current state of the art if we did not have a contribution from him. Therefore, although it might be deemed unusual, this *festschrift* contains not only discussion and description of Jack's work, but also a chapter by him.

The book is divided into three parts. In the first of these, nine different theoretical and methodological approaches that fall within the remit of the handbook are discussed in some detail, and their applications to disorders of communication explored. The second part contains 10 briefer studies of a variety of disorders (including both language and speech disorders; both acquired and developmental problems; both written and spoken interactions; and both intercultural and intra-familial communication). These chapters represent illustrations of some of the main approaches outlined in Part I, as well as the introduction of other qualitative research traditions. The final part of the book contains two retrospective chapters that, among other themes, reflect on the strengths and weaknesses of a qualitative approach, on explication in qualitative research, and on the place of qualitative research within the overall field of scientific endeavor.

We would like to thank all those involved in the production of this collection: the contributors themselves, of course, but also all those at Psychology Press who guided the book through to production. We would especially like to mention Stephanie Drew, Paul Dukes, and Lee Transue in this last regard.

Introduction
An Appreciation of Jack Damico

NANCYE ROUSSEL

It is often the case that a prophet or visionary is not recognized in his native place or by those closest to him, but the same cannot be said of Jack S. Damico. Those of us who have called him colleague and friend over the past 20 plus years here at the University of Louisiana, Lafayette have always recognized his leadership and the value of his work, both within our academic community and extending throughout the fields of communication sciences and disorders. One need only glance at the contents page of this volume, with representation from colleagues, collaborators and former students spread across the world, to begin to appreciate the scope and influence of his work. And so, in honor of his 60th year, we endeavor to express our appreciation to Jack for a lifetime of teaching and research that has been steadily focused on the traditions of qualitative discovery and investigation.

Jack's career in higher education began in 1985 with his return to his native Louisiana and acceptance of a position on the faculty of Louisiana State University (LSU). As he began his academic career, he was already recognized by many in the profession for his innovative work in qualitative assessment of language which led to the development of the Clinical Discourse Analysis (CDA) and Systematic Observation of Communicative Interaction (SOCI) which were published in 1985 and 1992 respectively. These tools grew from Jack's recognition of the limitations of the standardized tools he was expected to use as a Speech-Language Pathologist with the Albuquerque Public Schools (1976–1980). His interest in language assessment and service delivery in the schools has never waned. In the intervening years, he has collaborated with many colleagues for articles, chapters and presentations addressing such topics as ADHD, autism spectrum disorders, literacy acquisition, descriptive language assessment and assessment of language minority students. He has been featured as keynote speaker or plenary session speaker at gatherings of school-based speech-language pathologists across the nation and across the world (Australia, New Zealand, South Africa, Ghana, Egypt, and Canada). He has also given of his time and expertise as consultant to the United States Department of Education, New Zealand Department of Education, Navajo Nation, and Jicarilla Apache Boards of Education as well as numerous state departments of education and individual school districts.

In 1991, Jack was named as the first Doris B. Hawthorne Eminent Scholar in Communicative Disorders at the University of Louisiana at Lafayette, a position he has held continuously since that time. As one of only a handful of professors holding these prestigious appointments, Jack became an emissary for a university that had high aspirations and the goal of becoming a major research university. He rose to the challenge, helping to develop the Department of Communicative Disorders from a department with an established clinical tradition (Master's programs in Speech-Language Pathology and Audiology) to a department with both clinical and research foci (Masters in Speech-Language Pathology and PhD in Applied Language and Speech Sciences). Jack was instrumental in the recruitment and assembly of an expanded faculty with the clinical and research experience necessary to accomplish the objectives of the department and university. Many of these individuals were drawn to the department in part due to Jack's established reputation within the academic community and the opportunity to collaborate with him professionally. He has not disappointed and, in the ensuing years, has co-edited book projects and journals, written chapters and refereed articles, and presented at national and international meetings and conferences with many of his colleagues on the faculty of Communicative Disorders. Jack increased the visibility of the department on both the national and international scene as an active workshop and continuing education presenter and has presented invited lectures and colloquia at numerous universities both within and outside the United States. Over the years, the department has also benefitted from his vision and clinical expertise as he has worked with others on the faculty to develop innovative clinical programs in literacy and aphasia rehabilitation that serve as teaching and research laboratories for students, as well as providing services to the community. Honors have come his way. In 1991, he was given the Ruth Beckey Irwin Best Clinical Practices Award by The Ohio State University. In 2001, he was selected as a Fellow of the American Speech-Language Hearing Association, and in 2005, he was selected as a Distinguished Professor by the University of Louisiana at Lafayette Foundation. Never one to rest on his laurels, in 2012, Jack was named as Co-Director of the Hawthorne Center for Special Education and Communicative Disorders (with Martin Ball) and has plans to establish the Center as a major disseminator of qualitative research involving all aspects of communicative disorders.

Mentoring students and aspiring scholars has always been a high priority for Jack. Early in his career (1989–2001) he served the National Student Speech Language Hearing Association in a number of capacities including editor of the NSSLHA journal from 1992–1996. In 2000, he was given a Research in Higher Education Mentoring Award by ASHA. Across his career, he has directed or co-directed 14 dissertations and is working with nearly as many current students. All of the dissertations have used qualitative methods of inquiry and as such continue to expand the use of qualitative research in the field of communicative disorders. Jack's mentorship often continues beyond the dissertation stage, as evidenced by the number of former students listed as co-authors and co-presenters on his vita. Significant collaborations with former students such as Nina Simmons-Mackie and Ryan Nelson have given the profession seminal papers and chapters on the contributions of qualitative research and methods in aphasia and clinical service delivery, literacy acquisition and reading intervention, and issues of English language learners in U.S. schools.

The measure of a man is hard to sum up in a list of accomplishments. Those of us who have had the privilege to sit in Jack's classes and seminars, collaborate on research projects and papers, and discuss ideas and plans for the future know that the breadth of his influence in the field of communicative disorders can't be quantified. In one of my earliest memories of conversations we have had, Jack encouraged me, as I contemplated pursuing a PhD, by saying something to the effect that as researchers, we stand on the shoulders of the giants that came before us. While I never remembered the exact quote or the source, the sentiment and the encouragement he gave was something that I never forgot. I now know that he was quoting Sir Issac Newton, who referenced a 12th-century metaphor in saying, "If I have seen further, it is by standing on the shoulders of giants." On behalf of students and colleagues past and present, we would like to say thank you to Jack Damico for providing such strong shoulders for us to stand on.

I

Qualitative Approaches to Research

1

Case Studies and Their Frameworks
Positivist, Interpretive, and Emancipatory

JUDITH FELSON DUCHAN

Case studies have had a strong presence in the study of communication disorders throughout its history. And they continue to do so. Their historical
importance has been extraordinary, given that they often appear in the lower
rungs of researchers' status hierarchy. This form of research has typically been
regarded as less valid and less generalizable than studies that have many subjects and that are carefully controlled (Gillam & Gillam, 2006; Oxford Centre
for Evidence-Based Medicine, 2001). This set of criticisms, I will argue, arise
from unfairly levied positivistic assumptions about the nature of reality and
about the purpose of research.

In this chapter I will describe the importance of case studies as an investigative mode and will show that case studies are designed to achieve different
research goals and that these goals differ depending upon the philosophical
framework used by the researcher. The frameworks most often brought to
bear by case study researchers are positivist and interpretive. But there is a
third framework, emancipatory, that is coming into its own. I will argue that
emancipatory studies, though not often done by researchers, have the greatest
potential for achieving far-reaching benefits. Furthermore, I argue, there are
both moral and political reasons for shifting our thinking and our research
practices to become more emancipatory.

Positivist research favors multiple subject designs, especially those using
randomized controlled trials. The assumption of researchers using this framework is that truth exists in the world outside theories, interpretations, or value
judgments by the researcher. Indeed, positivist researchers go to great lengths
to eliminate subjectivity of researchers so as to allow them to discover the
truths in the objective reality. Their research involves creating controlled
experiments in which they identify and isolate independent and dependent
variables so as to prove or disprove their research hypotheses. Case studies
done within the positivist framework typically rely on quantitative analyses
and experimentally controlled conditions.

Researchers working with an interpretive framework, unlike positivists, see the world as being interpreted or socially constructed. Reality in this view is different for different people and under different conditions. The phenomena under study are regarded as complex, interdependent, and necessarily subjective. Those doing case studies in the interpretive framework prefer qualitative methods over quantitative ones and prefer working within naturally occurring conditions rather than experimentally controlled ones.

Emancipatory case studies are done to right the imbalances in power relations between the powerful and powerless in society, including the unequal relationships between researchers and those researched. The case study methods of emancipatory research are designed to give voice and social and communicative access to the powerless. The goals, in this framework, are those of participants. Participants are also involved in the choosing, design, and implementation of the research endeavor. Emancipatory case studies often use action research, participatory research, and phenomenology. Commonplace among emancipatory case studies are the personal narratives written by people with disabilities. Authors of such studies do not call what they have done a "case study" but rather regard themselves as storytellers who are portraying their personal life experiences.

Throughout this chapter I will give examples of case studies from within each of the three frameworks. I will also show the long lasting contributions of case studies in our field by pointing to some historic examples. I will argue that case study researchers need to respond to a moral imperative raised by the emancipatory framework to make our work more liberating and relevant to those we study and support. This shift would involve a different set of skills and new sensibilities. I will end with a set of suggestions for how to develop these skills and sensibilities by drawing from the life-long body of work of Jack Damico and his colleagues.

The Nature of Case Study Research

Let me begin by outlining what case study research has come to mean over the years. Case studies, like nouns, are usually studies of people (a child, an adult, someone with a communication disability); places (a classroom, nursing home, speech clinic); or things (a treatment, interaction, social service, or historical event). Case studies are most often thought of as in-depth investigations of singular instances of a phenomenon, but they also often involve comparisons across several cases.

Studying single cases can afford the researcher with a variety of insights. For positivists, case studies are used as pilot investigations or so-called fishing expeditions, as an early stage in research. For researchers working within the interpretive framework, case studies can offer an in-depth understanding of a participant or issue. And for those working within an emancipatory framework, case studies can provide a voice and redress inequities experienced by the disempowered. Besides individually focused stories, case studies designed in the emancipatory framework are sometimes aimed at institutions and sometimes conditions that result in social control and oppression.

Case studies can make use of a variety of research methods and strategies. Positivists prefer controlled experiments. Those working in the interpretive and emancipatory frames lean toward in-depth interviews, ethnographic observations, story gathering, text or artifact selection, and collaborative action research groups. The data, once acquired, can be analyzed in a variety of ways, using both quantitative and qualitative methods, micro as well as macro analyses, grounded theory and phenomenological approaches. (See other chapters in this volume for details on these various qualitative methodologies.)

Examples of Case Studies Done within Different Philosophical Frames

Positivists are inclined to use quantitative methods when analyzing case study information. Many studies done in this vein involve quantifying categories of information found in the case study data so as to track, say, the impact of a treatment on a client's performance. When doing case studies positivists are inclined to place experimental controls on the case, so as to test the impact of an independent variable.

Dodd and Bradford (2000) did such a case study with three children who had phonological disorders. In it they compared three therapy methods administered to each child, each involving 12 sessions over a 6-week period. The authors used a multiple base-line design to measure the accuracy of children's productions over time and across the different interventions.

The Dodd and Bradford (2000) study of three cases qualifies as positivist because it quantifies the data, collects it under carefully controlled conditions, and measures progress using a multiple-base line comparison. The logic of the paradigm also allows one to treat the interventions as the isolable variables that cause the changes in the post treatment measures. The authors of this three-person case study, true to their positivist inclinations, worry about generalizing from the small sample size: "The results of the study should be interpreted with caution due to the small sample size of a heterogeneous group and the cumulative effects of intervention" (p. 205).

Interpretive studies of individuals have been used to motivate new clinical categories, to refute commonly held misconceptions about our clients' inabilities, and to provide a venue for clients to speak for themselves. Studies of individual clinical cases have revealed unexpected information about particular clients, giving clinicians ways to better advocate for them and to tailor their services to fit their circumstances. Interpretive researchers tend to choose naturally occurring contexts for gathering their data. Once collected, the data is analyzed for themes and patterns, using both obvious and non-obvious (thick) descriptions.

Two fine examples of interpretive case studies can be found in this volume. Fujiki and Brinton (Chapter 17) offer us a study of the life course of a 25-year-old individual who was diagnosed with a language disorder at 4 years of age. Their aim was to "put a face" on the findings of large longitudinal studies. They argue that the child's story "illustrates the importance of adopting a holistic approach in considering the multiple factors that may be associated with LI." The authors find, unexpectedly, that the child's primary problems when he became a teenager were not identified by his family and teachers as language impairment, but rather social in nature and tied to the boy's anxiety.

The case study of Hallé and Le Dorze (Chapter 16, this volume) is of the support provided by a daughter to her mother who had severe aphasia. The study provides a counter to the commonly held assumption about the negative impact that aphasia has on family members. According to Hallé and Le Dorze, "These results appear divergent to previous studies of the impact of aphasia in families and of caregiving where positive aspects are not the norm." The interviews of the daughter, over time, shows her persistent focus on her mother's competence rather than deficits—a stance that was key to her caregiving strategies. The authors conclude, "This study of caregiving is an example of how complex social phenomena involving communication can be advantageously studied within a qualitative framework...."

In both of the above interpretive case studies the authors treat the participant in their study as part of a complex milieu. Both studies also serve to "put a face" on previous generalized findings and to make them concrete. And in both studies the face is not what would have been expected from the results of experimental research. The cases thereby serve to make specific, test, and even falsify previous research through counterexample.

Interpretative case studies have also been used to inform clinical practice directly, as exemplified by an article by Nina Simmons-Mackie and Jack Damico (2001) in which the authors provide guidance to clinicians for how to use case study research methods to determine their client's communicative status or progress. They suggest gathering information through ethnographic interviews, personal journals, and personal encounters and then show how to analyze collected data to find out about the client's lifestyles and viewpoints. Using a specific case example of a client with aphasia, the authors focused on contexts, people, and feelings associated with her communication. The aim of their example was to find out about this person's "use of communication as a social tool and her perceptions of herself as a communicator" (Simmons-Mackie & Damico, 2001, p. 27).

Emancipatory case studies of, with, and by people with communication disabilities are but a small part of the case study researcher's consciousness. That is not to say that there are no such studies. Personal and caregiver narratives, for example, have long been and continue to be an important source for helping understand the lived experiences of those with communication disabilities (Grandin & Scariano, 1996; Hussey, 2010; Johnson, 1930; Park, 1967; Robillard, 1999; Sinclair, 1992). What is also needed, I would argue, are case studies focusing on service delivery that will change the oppressive power relationships between people with disabilities and their service providers—in particular, their speech-language pathologists.

There are two recent sterling examples of such service-directed case studies. The first is by Susie Parr (2004), a speech pathologist and researcher in England. It is an ethnographic study of 20 people with severe aphasia. The aim of the study was "to chart the detail of day-to-day life, the challenges faced by people with aphasia, their families and paid carers, and the degree to which statutory health and social services and other voluntary sector and independent agencies are meeting with their support needs." The study served to give voice to those who are usually invisible and to reveal their social isolation and the corresponding failure of service providers to meet their needs.

A second study is a textual analysis of the language used to describe cases in case study research. Mitzi Waltz (2005) analyzed classic studies of people with autism. Her study revealed freak-like portrayals of people with disabilities (what she calls "enfreakment"). She also critiques the medical model of disability that objectifies people by portraying them as a medical condition (p. 422). Waltz found that the case study researchers such as those written by Leo Kanner (1943) marginalized the cases they describe. They did this by failing to represent the lived experiences of those with autism and by, instead, using medical discourse that depersonalizes and objectivizes them.

Influential Case Studies From the History of Communicative Disorders

There are a number of classic case studies, like those analyzed by Waltz (2005), that have served a foundational role in the history of communicative disorders. The studies have become classic because they have been pivotal in shifting practices or understandings and thereby have become milestones in the field. The following five are but a sampling of many case study classics. All five are best depicted from within an interpretive framework:

1. In 1802, Jean Marc Itard (1774–1838) published his account of his unsuccessful attempts to socialize a young boy, Victor, who had been found in the woods and thought to be a "feral child" raised by animals. Itard reported in detail on Victor's responses to his teaching regimens. Although Victor did not meet Itard's hopes or expectations, his case study became known

as foundational in special education (*New World Encyclopedia*, 2008), and as a historical description of a child with autism (Frith, 2003). In recent years the case entered into the popular culture and has been depicted in movies and books (e.g., Dawson, 2010; Truffaut, 1970)

2. In 1861 Paul Broca (1824–1880), a French physician and neurosurgeon, reported on the language and behavior of Monsieur Leborgne. M. Leborgne had severe aphasia. As Broca (1861) described him: "He understood all that was said to him; he even had very fine hearing; but, regardless of the question addressed to him, he always responded: *tan, tan*, in conjunction with greatly varied gestures by means of which he succeeded in expressing most of his ideas." Broca found upon autopsy that M. Leborgne had a brain lesion in the inferior frontal gyrus of the left hemisphere. Broca used his autopsy results to argue for a connection between language and a particular area of the brain, the area that has became known as Broca's area. The case study of M. Leborgne is also significant because it was an early instance of what came to be identified as the diagnostic category of aphasia (Lorch, 2011).

3. In 1936, a book called *The Origins of Intelligence* was published in French, later to be translated into English (Piaget, 1952). In it the author, Jean Piaget (1896–1980), described in detail his observations of his own three children Jacqueline, Lucienne, and Laurent. Piaget used his observations to show stages in his children's development before language and to argue that this sensori-motor knowledge, such as his children's understandings about the permanence of objects, provides the children with the conceptual underpinnings they need for later language learning. These detailed observations and theories built from his studies of his three children were path breaking for those in developmental language disorders, and led to new a new theory and field of study of genetic epistemology (Piaget, 1970), as well as to assessment instruments designed to evaluate the sensory motor abilities of preverbal children (Uzgiris & Hunt, 1989).

4. In 1943, Leo Kanner (1894–1981), an American psychiatrist, published an account of 11 of his clients, whom he diagnosed as having "Autistic Disturbances of Affective Contact" (Kanner, 1943). He presented each of his 11 cases in detail, giving a background history and description of their symptoms. The parallels between these 11 individual case studies led Kanner to identify a set of common symptoms for his proposed diagnostic category of autism. This case study offered a set of symptom categories some of which are still used to diagnose people as autistic.

5. In 1976 Jerome Bruner and Virginia Sherwood (1976) published a case study of how mothers teach their children to play peek-a-boo. The authors found that the six mothers in their study arranged their teaching so as to "scaffold" the various parts of the peek-a-boo activity. The idea of scaf-

folding took hold as a construct and led to the appreciation of the key role that events, scripts and routines play in children's early language learning (Nelson, 1986; Snyder-McLean, Solomonson, McLean, & Sack, 1984; Sonnenmeier, 1994). The study triggered what was called the pragmatics revolution (Duchan, 1983).

Evaluating Case Study Research from Different Philosophical Frameworks

The literature is full of positivist-based critiques of case studies that were done within interpretive framework sensibilities, such as those above. These critiques are drawn from positivist assumptions about science and reality that lead to researchers to focus on issues related to objectivity, generalizability, and verifiability of the case study design and results.

Flyvbjerg, a researcher favoring the interpretive framework, recounts some of these positivist criticisms in his 2011 chapter case studies. He calls the positivist criticisms "misunderstandings." Among those are the following:

> One cannot generalize on the basis of an individual case; therefore, the case study cannot contribute to scientific development.
>
> The case study contains a bias toward verification, that is, a tendency to confirm the researcher's preconceived notions. (p. 302)

I would argue that these positivist objections having to do with generalization and experimenter bias are not due just to a lack of understanding. Rather, they originate in a misframing of the research enterprise done by the interpretive or emancipatory researcher. Resolving the objections to case study research often requires a shift in thinking about the research project, not just providing additional information.

For example, generalizing from an individual case is not a problem for those working within an interpretive frame. Their interest is on the individual case, say, how individuals construct and experience their world. Nor is generalization an issue in clinical case studies. These clinically driven studies done within the interpretivist frame are designed to determine the nature and/or growth of competence in particular individuals, not groups of individuals.

Generalization from single cases is sometimes an issue for interpretive researchers. For example, some studies are done to falsify generalizations, such as the two cases from this volume presented in chapters by Fujiki and Brinton and Hallé and Le Dorze. Another use of case studies relate to a population of similar cases are those that "give a face to" a previously held generalization as was done in the study cited above by Simmons-Mackie and Damico (2001).

But, for the most part, interpretive researchers are not concerned with positivist concerns about generalization because they view the world in holistic terms. In this view reality involves complex, situated, intertwined relationships among entities, not isolated principles or truths or rules that can be extracted from one situation and generalized to another.

A second criticism from positivists has to do with experimenter bias. This worry stems from the positivist view that there exists a world outside the interpreted one that can be contaminated or distorted by the expectations or experiences of the researcher. The distortions, so the argument goes, get in the way of verifying whether the research results are real or skewed by the researcher's preconceived ideas.

But those who work within an interpretive framework presuppose a reality that is infused with meanings and inherently dependent on the point of view of the interpreter. It is the job of the researcher to take into account and study this expected bias rather than control for it. Altheide and Johnson (2011), two well-known interpretive researchers, review different versions of reality (realism) that can be found among interpretive researchers. They conclude that it is interpretive research that does the best job in uncovering and understanding this built-in bias:

> These different versions of realism share certain basic ideas: that human social life is meaningful, and that it is essential to take these meanings into account in our explanations, concepts and theories; furthermore, to grasp the importance of the values, emotions, beliefs, and other meanings of cultural members, it is imperative to embrace an interpretivist approach in our scientific and theoretical work. (p. 582)

Finally, those in the emancipatory framework bring their own critiques to case study evaluation. They point to how case study research often depicts people in ways that are depersonalizing and disempowering. They also point to elements in case studies that blame the person with the disability rather than the social conditions that marginalize them.

Of greatest concern is the depersonalized nature of the research enterprise. Waltz (2005), for example, has described some classic case studies in the field of autism as "written from a position of power, using an authoritative voice to construct an official discourse about autism in which the words and views of those described are rarely heard" (p. 421).

Most case studies done in the field of communicative disorders can be faulted for leaving the person out of the picture. The very term "case study" is depersonalizing, with people being treated as "cases" rather than as people with voices, opinions, and life histories. Many research studies, in the name of objectivity, fail to give voice to those under study (Kovarsky, 2008). This is true for most case studies, even when those studies focus on a particular individual.

In such studies, cases are often depicted as objects, with the descriptions focusing on their test scores, communication disabilities, and speech or language progress, leaving out their voices or personal views.

The raison d'etre for much emancipatory research is to counteract this problem of depersonalization (Oliver, 1997). One way this is done in emancipatory research is for the researcher to get out of the way so that those being studied have a say and a role in the research.

A second critique of case studies levied by emancipatory researchers focuses on the power differential between the researcher and the researched. These power inequities infuse many aspects of case study research. Informed consent, for example, presupposes a researcher's primacy and establishes the researcher's control over the project:

> Although the aim of informed consent is presumably to protect respondents, informing them of the possibility of harm in advance and inviting them to withdraw if they so desire, it also … gives control of the research process to the researcher. (Fine, Weis, Wessen, & Wong, 2000, p. 113)

Another powerful emancipatory-based critique comes from disability rights movement. It has become known as the problem of "blaming the victim" (Ryan, 1976). This problem occurs when lack of access is seen as arising from the disability rather than from social or physical barriers. Blaming the victim grows out of the medical model of disability in which disabilities are cast as biological rather than social in origin and nature.

> The medical model characterized disability as a personal problem for which individuals ought to seek medical intervention in the hope of cure, amelioration, or care. (Mertens, Sullivan, & Stace, 2011, p. 228)

The social model provides an alternative to the medical model (Byng & Duchan, 2005; Duchan, 2001; Simmons-Mackie, 2001). It blames barriers to access rather than the person or their impairment for their social exclusion. The New Zealand Ministry of Health's 2001 disability strategy reflects this social model sensibility:

> Disability is not something individuals have. What individuals have are impairments … Disability is the process which happens when one group of people create barriers by designing a world only for their way of living, taking no account of the impairments other people have … Our society is built in a way that assumes that we can all move quickly from one side of the road to the other; that we can all see signs, read directions, hear announcements, reach buttons, have the strength to open heavy doors and have stable moods and perceptions. (p. 1)

Michael Oliver, a leader and founder of the disability rights movement in England, has brought the sensibilities of the social model politics into the research enterprise (Oliver, 1997). He shows instances of how blaming the impairment infuses research, even extending to how specific questions in a research survey are cast. Oliver argues that questions such as "What complaint causes your difficulty in holding, gripping or turning things?" should be reframed and rephrased like the following: "What defects in design of everyday equipment like jars, bottles, and tins, cause you difficulty in holding, gripping or turning them?" (Oliver, 1992, p. 104).

I have tried to show in this section that critiques of case study research, like the research itself, reflect what has variously been called the world-view, paradigm, or framework of the one doing the critiquing. I believe these frameworks underpinning research are necessary for creating a coherent research enterprise. This necessity raises an obvious dilemma for case study research. How does one deal with critiques that are raised from outside one's framework?

In my judgment it is appropriate to ignore outside criticism in some instances but not in others. Positivist-based criticism of interpretive studies seem unfair and inappropriate, since the interpretive research was not intended to achieve positivist renderings of such things as generalizability or verifiability. Also, from the interpretive point of view, controlling the conditions of a study in order to achieve such positivist goals would interfere with the researcher's very efforts to discover naturally occurring, constructed meanings.

But the emancipatory criticisms are another matter, in my view. These criticisms are politically based and bring with them a moral imperative. The call for personalized, socially based, egalitarian research has its own inherent legitimacy and goes beyond any researcher's point of view. It is in response to this moral mandate involving the civil rights of those being researched that I move to the final section of this chapter. Here I will appeal to case study researchers using positivist and interpretive frameworks to adopt emancipatory sensibilities and methodologies.

Shifting to Emancipatory-Based Research

How might researchers go about creating the sea change needed to shift to emancipatory sensibilities and practices? I first look to the work of Jack Damico to find some possible answers.

Since his entry into the profession in the late 1980s, Jack Damico has been writing about inclusionary and egalitarian practices. His early work focused on how to provide quality clinical services in culturally sensitive ways (Hamayan & Damico, 1991).

So, from the beginning of his research career, Jack Damico's work has exemplified and promoted a reflective, ethnographic, and egalitarian stance toward clinical practice, the very ideas that are needed for developing emancipatory attitudes and for doing emancipatory case study research.

His more recent research, especially the body of discourse studies done with Nina Simmons-Mackie, has involved case studies of interactions between clinicians and their clients. Here, too, the focus has been on egalitarianism. The striking examples that Simmons-Mackie and Damico present in this work uncover the ways clinicians' discourse serves to disempower their clients.

Damico and his colleagues not only point to the disempowering aspects of social exchange, they also go on to offer clinicians specific alternative and more emancipatory discourses for interacting with their clients (Damico & Armstrong, 1990–1991; Damico & Damico, 1997; Damico, Simmons-Mackie, & Hawley, 2005; Simmons-Mackie & Damico, 1999, 2008). For example, in their study of the discourse of corrections that take place in interactions between different aphasia therapists and their clients, Simmons-Mackie and Damico (2008) found that corrections by clinicians were of two types: exposed and embedded. Exposed corrections focused on the error and often served to derail the conversation (Clinician: Tell me what you do with that? Client: Needle and tread. Clinician: What do you DO with it? Client: Needle and tread. Clinician: Sew. You Sew with a needle and thread …) (Simmons-Mackie & Damico, 2008, p. 10). Embedded corrections, on the other hand, were tucked into the conversation, moving it along (Client: They only there for one, two year because they got malargah. Clinician: Oh no. Even the physicians got malaria. Wow.) (p. 11).

The results of this 2008 study revealed that the exposed corrections occurred in discourse that focused on correcting errors and eventually the impairment. The conversationally embedded corrections were part of a different kind of therapy, one that emphasized social participation. The authors conclude: "… the impairment-focused sessions were characterized by power differentials and expectations consistent with an authoritarian style of interaction" (Simmons-Mackie & Damico, 2008, p. 13). They continue: "Exposed corrections often silence the voice of the speaker and highlight lapses in competence that could impugn the image of the error maker" (p. 14).

Damico and Armstrong (1990–1991), in an article on empowerment, offer a set of ways that clinicians can go about countering the dominating style and how to go about moving toward more emancipatory practices. They recommend that clinicians should:

- Value and respect individuality and diversity in the clients and the client families.
- Develop collaborative and trusting relationships with clients, families, and colleagues.
- Function as an advocate for clients.

- Focus on functional and naturalistic skills and activities during service delivery.

The final strategy that Damico and Armstrong (1990–1991) offer has particular pertinence for clients and clinical researchers moving toward emancipatory practice:

- Empower yourself to step forward as a change agent.

Just like for clinicians in the Damico case studies, researchers typically are the ones holding the power in case studies. They choose the topic, select participants and methods, and write up of the results for themselves and their fellow researchers. These processes treat the client as passive, failing to give them voice or power in the process. Emancipatory sensibility calls for the same kind of shift that Jack Damico and his colleagues have outlined in their articles for clinicians. We should first empower ourselves as researchers to step away from tradition so as to empower our clients to take a role in the research process. In so doing we will become change agents for their and our own emancipation.

References

Altheide, D., & Johnson, J. (2011). Reflections on interpretive adequacy in qualitative research. In N. Denzin & Y. Lincoln (Eds.), *Sage handbook of qualitative research* (4th ed., pp. 581–594). Thousand Oaks, CA: Sage.

Broca, P. (1861). Remarks on the seat of the faculty of articulated language, following an observation of aphemia (loss of speech). *Bulletin de la Société Anatomique de Paris, 36*, 330–357. Retrieved from http://psychclassics.asu.edu/Broca/aphemie-e.htm

Bruner, J. S., & Sherwood, V. (1976). Early rule structure: The case of peekaboo. In R. Harre (Ed.), *Life sentences: Aspects of the social role of language* (pp. 55–62). New York, NY: John Wiley.

Byng, S., & Duchan, J. (2005). Social model philosophies and principles: Their applications to therapies for aphasia. *Aphasiology, 19*, 906–922.

Damico, J., & Armstrong, M. (1990–1991). Empowerment in the clinical context: The SLP as advocate. *The NSSLHA Journal, 18*, 34–44.

Damico, J., & Damico, S. (1997). The establishment of a dominant interpretive framework in language intervention. *Language, Speech and Hearing Services in Schools, 28*, 288–296.

Damico, J. S., Simmons-Mackie, N. N., & Hawley, H. (2005). Power and language from a clinical perspective. In M. Ball (Ed.), *Clinical sociolinguistics* (pp. 63–73). London, England: Blackwell.

Dawson, J. (2010). *Wild boy.* New York, NY: Sceptre.

Dodd, B., & Bradford, A. (2000). A comparison of three therapy methods for children with different types of developmental phonological disorder. *International Journal of Language and Communication Disorders, 35*(2), 189–209.

Duchan, J. (1983). Recent advances in language assessment: The pragmatics revolution. In R. Naremore (Ed.), *Recent advances in language sciences* (pp. 147–180). San Diego, CA: College Hill Press.

Duchan, J. (2001). Impairment and social views of speech-language pathology: Clinical practices re-examined. *Advances in Speech-Language Pathology, 3*(1), 37–45.

Fine, M., Weis, L., Wessen, S., & Wong, L. (2000). For whom? Qualitative research, representations, and social responsibilities. In N. Denzin & Y. Lincoln (Eds.), *Handbook of qualitative research* (2nd ed., pp. 567–605). Thousand Oaks, CA: Sage.

Flyvbjerg, B. (2011). *Case study.* In N. Denzin & Y. Lincoln (Eds.), *The Sage handbook of qualitative research* (4th ed., pp. 301–316). Thousand Oaks, CA: Sage.

Frith, U. (2003). *Autism: Explaining the enigma.* London, England: Blackwell.

Gillam, S., & Gillam, R. (2006). Making evidence-based decisions about child language intervention in schools. *Language, Speech and Hearing Services in Schools, 37,* 304–315.

Grandin, T., & Scariano, M. (1996). *Emergence: Labeled autistic.* New York, NY: Warner Books.

Hamayan, E., & Damico, J. (Eds.). (1991). *Limiting bias in the assessment of bilingual students.* Austin, TX: PRO-ED.

Hussey, M. (2010). I am no longer silent. *Topics in Stroke Rehabilitation, 17*(1), 6–9.

Itard, J. M. G. (1802). *An historical account of the discovery and education of a savage man: Or, the first developments, physical and moral, of the young savage caught in the woods near Aveyron in the year 1798.* Retrieved from http://books.google.com/books?id=E63cRcnV2hIC&source=gbs_summary_s&cad=0

Johnson, W. (1930). *Because I stutter.* Retrieved from http://www.uiowa.edu/~cyberlaw/wj/bis/wjbis.html

Kanner, L. (1943). Autistic disturbances of affective contact. *Nervous Child, 2,* 217–50. Retrieved from http://www.garfield.library.upenn.edu/classics1979/A1979HZ31800001.pdf

Kovarsky, D. (2008). Representing voices from the life world in evidence-based practice. *International Journal of Language and Communication Disorders, 1,* 47–57.

Lorch, M. (2011). Re-examining Paul Broca's initial presentation of M. Leborgne: Understanding the impetus for brain and language research. *Cortex, 47,* 1228–1235.

Mertens, D., Sullivan, M., & Stace, H. (2011). Disability communities: Transformative research for social justice. In N. Denzin & Y. Lincoln (Eds.), *The Sage handbook of qualitative research* (4th ed., pp. 227–241). Thousand Oaks, CA: Sage.

Nelson, K. (1986). *Event knowledge: Structure and function in development.* Hillside, NJ: Erlbaum.

New World Encyclopedia. (2008). Jean Marc Gaspard Itard. Retrieved from http://www.newworldencyclopedia.org/entry/Jean_Marc_Gaspard_Itard

New Zealand Ministry of Health. (2001). New Zealand disability strategy. Wellington, NZ: Author. Retrieved from www.odi.govt.nz/documents/publications/nz-disability-strategy.pdf

Oliver M. (1992). Changing the social relations of research production? *Disability, Handicap and Society, 7*(2), 101–114.

Oliver, M. (1997). Emancipatory research: Realistic goal or impossible dream? In C. Barnes & G. Mercer (Eds.), *Doing disability research* (pp. 15–31). Leeds, England: The Disability Press.

Oxford Centre for Evidence-Based Medicine. (2001). Levels of evidence. Retrieved from http://www.cebm.net/index.aspx?o=5653

Park, C. (1967). *The siege: the first eight years of an autistic child.* Boston, MA, Little, Brown.

Parr, S. (2004). *The social exclusion of people with marked communication impairment following stroke.* London, England: Joseph Rowntree Foundation. Retrieved from http://www.jrf.org.uk/publications/social-exclusion-people-with-marked-communication-impairment-following-stroke

Piaget, J. (1952). *The origins of intelligence in children.* New York, NY: International University Press.

Piaget, J. (1970). *Genetic epistemology.* New York, NY: W.W. Norton.

Robillard, A. (1999). *The meaning of a disability: The lived experience of paralysis.* Philadelphia, PA: Temple University Press.

Ryan, W. (1976). (2nd ed.). *Blaming the victim.* New York, NY: Vintage.

Simmons-Mackie, N. (2001). Social approaches in clinical practice: Examining clinical assumptions. *Advances in Speech-Language Pathology, 3*(3), 47–50.

Simmons-Mackie, N., & Damico, J. S. (1999). Social role negotiation in aphasia therapy: Competence, incompetence and conflict. In D. Kovarsky, J. Duchan, & M. Maxwell (Eds.),

Constructing (in)competence: Disabling evaluations in clinical and social interaction (pp. 313–341). Mahwah, NJ: Erlbaum.

Simmons-Mackie, N., & Damico, J. (2001). Intervention outcomes: Clinical applications of qualitative methods. *Topics in Language Disorders, 21*(4), 21–36.

Simmons-Mackie, N., & Damico, J. (2008). Exposed and embedded corrections in aphasia therapy: Issues of voice and identity. *International Journal of Language and Communication Disorders, 43*, S1, 5–17.

Sinclair, J. (1992). Bridging the gaps: An inside-out view of autism. In E. Schopler & G. Mesibov (Eds.), *High functioning individuals with autism*. New York, NY: Plenum Press. Retrieved from http://pubpages.unh.edu/~jds/Autism.htm

Snyder-McLean, L., Solomonson, B., McLean, J., & Sack, S. (1984). Structuring joint action routines: A strategy for facilitating communication and language development in the classroom. *Seminars in Speech and Language, 5*(3), 213–228.

Sonnenmeier, R. (1994). Script-based language intervention: Learning to participate in life events. In J. Duchan, L. Hewitt, & R. Sonnenmeier (Eds.), *Pragmatics: From theory to practice* (pp. 134–148). Englewood Cliffs, NJ: Prentice Hall.

Truffaut, F. (1970). *The wild child*. Retrieved from http://en.wikipedia.org/wiki/The_Wild_Child.

Uzgiris, I. & Hunt, J. (1989). *Assessment in infancy: Ordinal scales of psychological development*. Urbana: University of Illinois Press.

Waltz, M. (2005). Reading case studies of people with autistic spectrum disorders: A cultural studies approach to issues of disability representation. *Disability & Society, 20*(4), 421–435.

2

Micro and Macro Traditions in Qualitative Research

NINA SIMMONS-MACKIE

Jack S. Damico has a distinguished career aimed at improving the lives of and services for people with communication disorders. In large part, he has accomplished this by asking questions about the services offered to our clients: What happens in therapy for aphasia? How do clinicians promote literacy? How do speech-language pathologists assess students from diverse cultures? Indeed, his interests have been varied: second language acquisition, diversity and multiculturalism, language disabilities in children, literacy, classroom interaction, and therapy for adults with aphasia. However, a thread that is woven through his work is the need to question, to explore, and to expose, rather than blithely accept the status quo. In this process Jack (and his many students) learned that qualitative research traditions fulfill this need to go beyond hypothesis testing and into the domain of discovery—to ask what's going on? with the expressed intent of reinforcing or improving our clinical goings on. As his student, friend, and colleague, I have been honored to join Jack on his journey to explore aspects of our field using various qualitative research methods.

Qualitative research constitutes a variety of traditions that employ systematic methods to help us understand social action and experience (e.g., Creswell, 1998; Damico & Simmons-Mackie, 2003; Lincoln & Guba, 1985). These traditions are uniquely suited to discovering and understanding the complexities of communication and communication disorders as socially embedded phenomena. Choice of a particular qualitative tradition is typically driven by the research question of interest. However, the reverse also holds: "ways of seeing, and of framing questions, are strongly influenced by the methods we have at our disposal, because the way we see shapes what we can see, and what we think we can ask" (Mason, 2006, p. 113). In other words, researchers often frame questions that fit into their conceptions about doing research. It, therefore, seems important to explore qualitative research as a science from a variety of perspectives. This chapter will explore micro and macro perspectives. It should be noted that micro and macro perspectives are being presented contrastively as dual positions; in reality, the conduct of qualitative research, like the social phenomena that are investigated, is complex and multidimensional and conforms poorly to rigid accounts. The student of qualitative research can be quickly overwhelmed by the wide variety of philosophical foundations and the vast array of methodologies. In addition, the inherent flexibility and nonlinearity of design often confounds those who are unfamiliar with specific qualitative traditions. In fact, one of the motivations for offering this chapter is to offer one way of simplifying and conceptualizing qualitative research.

Contrasting Micro and Macro Perspectives

The study of communication involves an interesting paradox: How does one study communication since it is both a local and global phenomenon? (Erickson, 1992, 2004). That is, communication is a product of the immediate local context and participants, and a global phenomenon responsive to external cultural and social constraints, history, and experience. Consequently, communication can be studied at the local level as it emerges within a moment-to-moment social interaction and is co-created by participants using resources available within the immediate context; communication can also be studied as a manifestation of the broader influence of culture and society since talk is shaped by social norms, conventions, and beliefs. Qualitative research traditions tend to reflect these complementary orientations to the study of communication from either a micro perspective or from a broad macro perspective. Moreover, both micro and macro perspectives have contributed significantly to knowledge in the field of communication disorders and provide one orientating framework for understanding the array of qualitative research approaches. This chapter will explore micro-analytic and macro-analytic perspectives in qualitative research using examples from studies of services offered to individuals with communication disorders.

The macro perspective in qualitative research involves a focus on the social, cultural, political, or historical contexts and meanings of a particular event, group, or phenomenon. Macro-analytic traditions tend to investigate broad perspectives associated with communicative events, "uncovering attitudes and patterns of communication, and understanding macro-functions such as the 'establishment or reinforcement of group identity'" (Saville-Troike, 1989, p. 14). Macro-level research addresses attitudes, knowledge, values, goals, or patterns of communication associated with groups or communities in order to gain a description or understanding of social or cultural issues. That is, the macro-level of analysis helps us to understand the world in which something of interest occurs. Examples of qualitative traditions within a macro-analytic perspective are ethnography and grounded theory research. For example, ethnographic research is often concerned with painting a cultural picture that describes a group of people or a system (Agar, 1986; Creswell, 1998; Wolcott, 1994). Grounded theory researchers investigate complex social phenomena in an effort to offer *theories* relevant to the phenomena, group, or events (Chenitz & Swanson, 1986; Corbin & Strauss, 2008; Glaser, 1992).

The micro perspective involves a detailed and focused study of a particular circumscribed event, such as a particular conversation, text, or interaction. In fact, "research focusing on language and communication often involves microanalysis, discourse analysis or textual analysis, through which speech events, including text, and subtle interactions are recorded (often on videotape) and analyzed" (Marshall & Rossman, 2011, p. 93). Various approaches to discourse analysis such as conversation analysis (Sacks, 1992; Sacks, Schegloff, & Jefferson, 1974) or sociolinguistic interactional analysis (Schiffrin, 1994; Tannen, 1984) fit within a micro perspective. For example, conversation analysis is an analytic tradition that employs systematic methods of analyzing the moment-to-moment management of talk-in-interaction with a particular focus on specific turns at talk (Heritage, 1984; Heritage & Atkinson, 1984; Psathas, 1995; Sacks et al., 1974). The aim of conversation analysis is to identify how people structure and organize talk in order to achieve social actions. Such an analysis of detailed local phenomena can provide insight into the broader social organization. That is, how people manage simple day-to-day events, such as conversation, tells us something about how society at large functions.

Having made some general distinctions between macro and micro perspectives, the remainder of this chapter will demonstrate applications of these analytic perspectives to the study of speech-language therapy and the importance of these qualitative orientations for discovering aspects of practice that should be further researched, reinforced, or changed. In describing the usefulness of qualitative discovery in health related fields, Nichols (2009) states, "if we are to practice ethically and call ourselves professionals, we should step back occasionally from our long-held beliefs, and look critically on the principles held most dear" (p. 526). Qualitative research offers new ways of "understanding the complexity of health care, new tools for collecting and analysing data, and new vocabulary to make arguments about the quality of the care we offer" (Nichols, 2009, p. 527).

Macro and Micro Perspectives on Speech-Language Therapy

Speech-language therapy has been described as "a complex, goal-directed activity undertaken to improve an individual's communication" (Simmons-Mackie & Damico, 1999b, p. 313). Like communication, the conduct of therapy is both a locally operated phenomenon that depends on what is going on in the moment and a product of the history, culture, and experiences of the participants. The topic of speech-language therapy is particularly relevant since our honoree, Jack S. Damico, has made significant contributions to this area of investigation. Micro and macro research will be contrasted by addressing a variety of questions such as: What are considered problems of interest in each perspective? How is context defined? What counts as evidence? How are the data analyzed? What are the types of results?

What Types of Questions or Problems Are Suitable?

Macro Questions.   Research questions of interest from a macro perspective are typically those that focus on relatively broad topics or issues related to social communities, groups, or events. Speech-language therapy is an *event* offered by a specific *group* (speech-language pathologists) that is designed to improve the communication of another *group* (people with communication disorders). Thus, a number of qualitative studies have focused on understanding speech-language therapy as a particular social or cultural phenomenon associated with particular groups of people. Typically, open-ended questions launch the research, such as: What are the historical origins of speech-language pathology? (Duchan, 2001–2011); How are speech-language pathology practices shaped by institutional constraints and organizational policy? (Kovarsky, 2008); What happens in speech-language therapy? (Simmons-Mackie & Damico, 1999a); How is speech-language therapy terminated? (Hersh, 2003, 2009). While these questions might seem overly broad or simplistic, in fact, the everyday conduct of therapy is a remarkably complex activity that is grounded in the prevailing social order, norms, or culture of participants. In other words, macro-study of speech-language therapy has the potential to help us understand why we do what we do and in the process help to improve services. A variety of qualitative research traditions has been employed in macro studies of speech-language therapy.

Duchan (2001–2011) has taken a macro-analytic stance towards the study of the origins of speech-language therapy in an application of historical research. Historical research is a qualitative tradition that relies on studying artifacts, literature, historical records, or interviews to describe, analyze, and explain past events, groups, or systems (Barzun & Graff, 1985; Damico & Simmons-Mackie, 2003). By interviewing relevant individuals, visiting historical sites, and studying written documents and historical objects, Duchan traced the development of the profession of speech-language pathology. She notes that

> A reflective historical stance attained through historical studies provides a way to evaluate today's practices. Working from a historical and outside perspective can offer clinicians new angles from which

to view their taken-for-granted ideas and practices. A reflective historical stance also provides a source of courage for critically analyzing and changing those current practices that need changing. (Duchan, 2001–2011)

Based on her historical research, Duchan suggests that current practices in speech-language pathology have been greatly influenced by a movement towards professionalism that occurred during the middle of the 20th century in an effort to improve the standing and reputation of the profession. For example, the medical model became the preferred paradigm for assessing and treating communication disorders. Thus, early speech therapists sought to adhere to characteristics of medical practice such as maintaining professional distance from patients, seeking cause-and-effect relationships, and making informed decisions based on data. In fact, "This wholesale adoption [of the medical model] is evidenced in the effort of the profession to standardize the diagnostic terminology and to use Latinized forms borrowed from medicine" (Duchan, 2001–2011) and in the reliance on objective tests and measurements as the accepted methods of assessing speech and language. In addition, the profession embraced science as a way to improve standards and upgrade the status of the profession. In other words, in order to gain professional stature the field of speech-language therapy oriented towards a positivist definition of scientific method consisting of hypothesis testing, objective measurement, and experimentation. This influence continues as evident in Finn, Bothe, and Bramlett's (2005) statement in an article contrasting science and pseudoscience: "there is a consistent theme across the discipline: the application of the scientific method to the nature and treatment of communication disorders" (p. 172). Through a macro-level qualitative analysis of historical data Duchan demonstrated key influences on the *institution* of speech-language pathology and showed how these influences have shaped the profession.

In another macro-level study of speech-language pathology researchers demonstrated that these early influences on the culture of speech-language pathology have created potentially negative consequences. In a study of evidence-based practice (EBP) in speech-language pathology, Kovarsky (2008) and Kovarsky and Curran (2007) exposed potential problems associated with professional culture and historical origins. These researchers noted the growing prominence of EBP in the speech-language pathology literature and the pressure for clinicians to adhere to EBP guidelines for clinical practice. Given the practical implications of clinical practices that are driven by available evidence, the researchers considered that the topic held significant importance. The investigators analyzed written materials such as professional position statements (e.g., American Speech-Language-Hearing Association documents), technical reports, and other professional sources of information. They also drew from the personal experience narratives of clients and their significant others regarding speech-language assessment and intervention. The professional documents defined EBP as the clinical application of research evidence along with considerations of clinician expertise and client values and preferences. However, beyond this basic definition, professional documents and policies stressed the virtues and importance of high quality scientific research while minimizing the importance or validity of subjective experiences of clients and family members. Based on study findings, Kovarsky (2008) argued that

> Current quality of evidence hierarchies in EBP are based on an epistemology of logical positivism and privilege cause–effect explanations grounded in objective, empirically testable variables that exist external to the self. Unfortunately, the dismissal of subjective, phenomenologically oriented information has functioned to marginalize and silence voices from the life-worlds of clients when constituting proof of effectiveness. When these voices are excluded, our understanding of the social significance, magnitude and ecological validity of evidence is compromised. (p. 55)

In other words, Kovarsky traced a bias in professional conceptions of EBP to the historical preference for the scientific method and positivistic orientations to science. By showing preference to the voice of scientific evidence and essentially ignoring the subjective voice of clients, the profession failed to adhere to conceptions of person-centered medicine (e.g., DiLollo & Favreau, 2010; Stewart et al., 2003; Worrall, 2006). Application of macro-level findings such as these can improve current practices by uncovering hidden influences and customs.

In another macro-analysis, Hersh (2001, 2003, 2009) employed principles of grounded theory to study discharge from aphasia therapy. Her study touched on issues similar to those described above: the issue of whose voice influences intervention for communication disorders. She conducted interviews with people with aphasia, family members, and speech-language pathologists and examined clinical records. Her findings demonstrated that speech-language pathologists tended to manipulate and control the discharge process. In other words, the voice or authority of the clinician tended to drive the discharge process (often as a response to external demands on time and resources). She suggested that observed client acquiescence to imposed discharge might be similar to Goffman's (1959) "veneer of consensus," a phenomenon that, in fact, signals professional control and gate keeping, rather than a true reflection of client agreement (Hersh, 2003, p. 1026). Again, Hersh's discoveries, like those of Kovarsky, suggest habituated and acculturated ways of acting that should be examined as they relate to current conceptions of person-centered practices in health care (e.g., DiLollo & Favreau, 2010; Worrall, 2006).

These examples of macro level perspectives to qualitative research demonstrate the potential to study aspects of communication disorders and/or speech-language pathology as a social and cultural phenomenon with a history, norms, and beliefs that influence what we do on a daily basis.

Micro Questions. Questions of interest in micro-analytic studies in communication disorders tend to focus on particular aspects of discourse or social interaction with the aim of displaying the complexity and technical components of communication, describing and understanding a particular aspect of discourse such as repair of errors or turn taking, or exposing a potentially important feature of communication disability or practice. For example, questions related to describing the complexity of social action and defining the mechanics of therapy discourse have been addressed such as: How do people with aphasia negotiate unintelligibility in clinical dyads in the face of linguistic deficits? (Damico, Simmons-Mackie, & Wilson, 2006); How do people with aphasia and their clinicians manage repair? (Lindsay & Wilkinson, 1999); How do clients and therapists achieve rapport in therapy? (Walsh, 2007); What are the functions of feedback in therapy for aphasia? (Simmons-Mackie, Damico, & Damico, 1999). Micro-analyses also seek to demonstrate how institutional and cultural ways of acting manifest within the moment to moment conduct of therapy. For example, the literature has addressed participants' clinical roles and expectancies (e.g., Kovarsky & Maxwell, 1992; Simmons-Mackie & Damico, 1999b), manifestations of power and dominance within therapy interactions (Damico & Damico, 1997; Leahy, 2004; Walsh, 2008), or construction of identity in therapy (Horton, 2007; Simmons-Mackie & Elman, 2011). O'Malley (2011) studied how students learn to be professional using a discourse analysis of interactions between student clinicians and clients. She focused on discovering how clinicians learned to balance socio-relational aspects of therapy (e.g., maintaining rapport) versus their own therapy agendas. Others have studied the structural organization of speech-language therapy. For example, Ferguson and Armstrong (2004) summarized findings from studies that analyzed discourse patterns in therapy interactions. In their review, the authors provided an interpretation of their metastudy of the research and highlighted the mismatch between person-centered practice and what actually goes on in many therapy interactions. They suggested that the professional rhetoric that espouses collaborative or person-centered practice in speech-language pathology does not necessarily match what is actually done in face-to-face clinical work, and they suggested, the "need to evaluate critically the processes and nature of acculturation that occurs during the first stages of professional development as a student speech-language therapist through to the ongoing development of professional practice" (p. 469). Thus, the authors used micro-level findings from discourse analyses to infer macro-level implications. Simmons-Mackie and Damico (2011) expanded on these findings in a discussion comparing client or relationship-centered practice to the traditional therapist-centered practice of speech-language pathology. In other words, a review of micro-studies of speech-language therapy provided information relevant to training clinicians and improving practices of existing clinicians. Furthermore, researchers have demonstrated findings at a micro-level that complement broad macro results relative to entrenched patterns of clinical practice. Thus, macro and micro level analyses provide different perspectives and triangulated evidence. The broad findings help to expose the social norms, beliefs, or biases that prevail, while the micro-level analyses inform us about the behavioral realization of social orientations within day-to-day interactions. Such details regarding the manifestations of institutional or cultural ways of acting help us pinpoint and describe specific areas for professional change.

What Is Context?

Traditional linguistic analyses typically have approached the study of language as an encapsulated phenomenon that can be examined independent of society and culture. Qualitative researchers, however, tend to draw from anthropological and sociological foundations that view language and communication as a key locus of social life and an observable instantiation of culture and social organization (Goodwin & Duranti, 1992). In other words, communication can only be appreciated in relationship to context. The concept of what makes a context is critical in considering choices among qualitative traditions. As Goodwin and Duranti (1992) discussed in the seminal text, *Rethinking Context,* the notion of context "means quite different things within alternative research paradigms" (p. 2). In describing context the authors adopted Goffman's (1974) concept of framing: "The notion of context involves a fundamental juxtaposition of two entities: (1) a focal event; and (2) a field of action within which that event is embedded" (i.e., the frame), and the two entities cannot be separated (Goodwin & Duranti, 1992, p. 3). The question, of course, is how one defines the boundaries of the frame for a given research study or particular research tradition. Cicourel (1992) delineated local versus broad definitions of context, and this conception helps orient us to relevant context in micro versus macro perspectives.

Macro Context. Relevant context from a macro perspective is typically defined broadly as that which is present and observable during an event (e.g., an actual therapy session), the knowledge and experience of participants (e.g., what participants say in interviews, diaries, artifact review, literature review) and related data that inform understanding of the event or participants (e.g., documents, interviews of other people, institutional policies, objects). Thus, researchers access the big picture to understand the broad perspective including analysis of elements present in therapy sessions, as well as extra-situational context such as social norms or institutional policies (Goodwin & Duranti, 1992). Many elements are considered relevant to the macro context. For example, in a study of aphasia therapy, Simmons-Mackie and Damico (1999a) considered participants' talk, manner of dress, and ways of acting as well as setting characteristics, written materials, institutional policies, and available inservice education to be part of the clinical context that represented therapy and served as potential clues to the culture and social organization of the system. Thus, the context for macro-level research on speech-language therapy is widely encompassing, including internal and external features associated with therapy interactions.

Micro Context.   Context from a micro perspective tends to be more restrained, although perspectives on context vary somewhat across mico approaches. However, Hammersley (2003) points out that, unlike many approaches to analysis of social phenomena, micro-analyses (such as conversation analysis and discourse analysis) typically eschew analytic leaps that attribute motivation or general attributes to participants or events.

> First they [conversation analysts and discourse analysts] reject the attribution of substantive and distinctive psychosocial features to particular categories of actor as a means of explaining human behaviour. Second, they reject use of what the people they study say *about* the world as a source of information that can ever be relied on for analytic purposes. (p. 251)

For example, conversation analysts consider that crucial context involves that which the participants make relevant in their talk. In discussing how context is made relevant during interaction, Goodwin and Duranti (1992, p. 4) suggest that "What analysts seek to describe is not what they consider context (...), but rather how the subject himself attends to and organizes his perception of the events and situations that he is navigating through." For example, conversation analysts view context as locally produced and dynamic or "transformable from moment to moment" (Drew & Heritage, 1992, p. 21). Thus, Heritage (1984) notes: "A speaker's action is context-shaped in that its contribution to an on-going sequence of actions cannot adequately be understood except by reference to the context—including, especially, the immediately preceding configuration of actions—in which it participates" (p. 242). In the following segment of aphasia therapy, interaction the participants are orienting to their shared roles as parents who need a reliable baby sitter. Neither party has invoked therapy as a key element of the interaction in this segment of unpublished data.

SLP: So how's Neil?
Client: Problem ... uh problem wi ... uh wi:: baby sitter.
SLP: Oh no! I hate that.
        I finally got someone reliable, but I live in fear that she will leave.
Client: Yea ... big big prob-em.
        Needing baby sitter.... always.
SLP: Yea, I know what you mean.

The speakers orient to the topic of baby sitters, and the speakers' roles as parents frame the talk, rather than their roles as therapist–client. This does not mean that the sequence is not relevant to the overall analysis of the interaction as therapy, but rather that the researcher is not free to interpret this segment as representing some particular therapeutic action simply by virtue of its occurrence within the larger context and under the institutional purview of speech-language therapy. Thus, parties involved in an interaction invoke and orient to differing contextual frames in a dynamic manner and qualitative micro-analysis requires a careful examination of what context is oriented to by participants, how the participants negotiate roles and identities from moment to moment and what resources they use.

While on the whole micro approaches to discourse analysis do not fit into broad macro-analytic conceptions of context, discourse analysis comprises a heterogenous group of analytic practices with a range of perspectives on how context is defined. Conversation analysis represents perhaps the most restrictive definition of context, while other approaches allow the investigator to consider additional aspects of context. For example, some discourse analysts layer what participants "say" about segments of discourse onto the analysis of the actual discourse itself (Schiffrin, 1994; Tannen, 1984) expanding the context from what is visible within the interaction to the internal context of participant knowledge or intuitions.

What Data Are Allowable?

Closely related to considerations of context is determination of what counts as evidence in a particular investigation. Again, we find a contrast between macro and micro approaches.

Macro Data.   Corbin and Strauss (2008) describe macro approaches as the "wide angle lens" of qualitative research. In an effort to capture the big picture, a wide range of data sources are allowable as evidence. Speech, gestures, actions, images, furniture, settings, documents, writing, time, spatial organization, sounds, objects, or historical reports might help elucidate a social or cultural phenomenon or group of interest. Data might be generated in a variety of ways such as observation, interview, recording, document or artifact review, or historical searches. The particular data sources used depend in part on the qualitative tradition employed (e.g., historical research, ethnography, phenomenology) and on the topic of interest.

An example of a macro approach to data collection is found in a study of traditional aphasia therapy conducted by Simmons-Mackie and Damico (portions presented in Simmons, 1993; Simmons-Mackie & Damico, 1999a; Simmons-Mackie et al., 1999). The investigators were interested in addressing the broad question what goes on in aphasia therapy? with the ultimate aim of understanding why certain things are done (or not done). They used a range of data sources including interviews of relevant informants, participant observation of therapy sessions, review of artifacts (i.e., medical records, notes, client homework), analysis of video-recorded therapy sessions, and focus group discussion of recorded sessions. In order to describe and understand aphasia therapy as a particular social event, the researchers avoided filtering the data early in the research process; rather, they documented many aspects of therapy sessions such as therapy routines, tasks and language used to manage tasks, non-task related behaviors of participants, the physical setting of therapy, characteristics of participants (e.g., education, ethnicity, age, manner of dress), materials and objects present before, during, and after therapy sessions (e.g., paper, score sheets, picture cards), emotional tone of the interaction, and written documents such as medical charts and therapist notes. For example, the physical setting of an observed session was described in unpublished field notes as follows:

> Treatment was conducted in a quiet room that looked like an office, with participants seated across a table from each other. A desk with office materials, files and books was next to the table. On the wall were framed certificates and diplomas of the speech-language pathologist. The arrangement of furnishings and materials conveyed the impression that this was a place for "work" not "fun."

Layered upon the observations of the physical setting were observations about the participants. For example, the speech-language pathologists tended to dictate seating arrangements, introduce the activities, control materials, manage time, and keep track of client behavior. Speech-language pathologists in the study tended to wear business clothes (e.g., suits, dresses) or white coats over their clothing, while clients tended to wear casual clothes (e.g., warm-up suits). Interviews with speech-language pathologists provided further data on how they viewed their roles and responsibilities, what they considered important, and perspectives on why they behaved in certain ways. From a macro perspective, these diverse sources of evidence accumulated to create a detailed picture of aphasia therapy and serve as potential clues to the beliefs and knowledge that drive the conduct of therapy. The big picture converged to suggest that speech-language pathologists in the studied settings constituted a cultural group who presented themselves as professionals and experts and were distinguishable and separate from their patients—the people who needed help.

Micro Data.   Micro-analysis has been likened to the use of a "high powered microscope to examine each piece of data up close" (Corbin & Strauss, 2008, p. 59). The data for most micro-analyses in communication disorders typically consist of video or audio recorded discourse, transcripts of discourse, or segments of written text. In conversation analysis, the allowable data are largely restricted to the local context, i.e., that which is available within the interaction and noticeable to the participants and analyst. Other micro traditions tend to allow additional data that relate directly to analysis of the discourse. For example, Simmons-Mackie and Elman (2011) conducted a sociolinguistic interactional analysis of a group aphasia therapy session. The data included in the analysis were the video recording and transcript of the session as well as an interview with the speech-language pathologist who conducted the therapy session. The interview data were used to understand the goals and experiences of the clinician regarding the session under study.

How Are Data Analyzed?

Corbin and Strauss (2008) have discussed micro-analysis and macro-analysis as they relate to different forms of coding in qualitative research, with micro referring to highly detailed coding that attempts to crack open meanings or mechanisms, and macro referring to less detailed coding that aims to capture the broader essence of an event or phenomenon.

Macro Analysis.   There are many approaches to analyzing macro-level data and these typically depend on the particular research tradition employed and the type of data to be analyzed. Perhaps the most wide-spread strategy for analyzing macro-level data involves identifying categories of meaning across the data (e.g., Spradley, 1980). "A *category* is a collection of similar data sorted into the same place, and this arrangement enables the researchers to identify and describe the characteristics of the category" (Morse, 2008, p. 727). Members of a category are often coded using descriptors or labels. For example, in the Simmons-Mackie and Damico (1999a) study of aphasia therapy, the researchers identified several categories that defined sessions such as therapy setting, routines, goals, tasks, materials, feelings, therapist characteristics, and client characteristics. They then subdivided the categories; for example, the category of therapy routines could be subdivided into openings, task introductions, doing tasks and closings. In some cases, dividing the data into categories allows the researcher to develop a taxonomy that helps describe the event or phenomenon of interest. For example, after interviewing 50 people with aphasia, Worrall and colleagues (2011) categorized the stated post-stroke goals of interview participants. Once categories of goals were identified, they were further analyzed according to the International Classification of Functioning, Disability and Health (ICF; WHO, 2001) in order to sort the results in a manner consistent with familiar therapy frameworks. The resulting categorization or classification of therapy goals provides an orderly system to help speech-language therapists understand what people with aphasia want out of therapy.

While some qualitative research focuses on developing taxonomies or categorical descriptions of a phenomenon, much macro-analysis proceeds to an interpretive level in which a unifying theme, theory, or insight (or multiple themes, explanations, or insights) is identified. In fact, interpretation is one of the unique and defining characteristics of qualitative research, allowing the researcher to blend categorical findings, insights from the literature, and introspection into a cohesive whole that explains the phenomenon or some aspect of the phenomenon under investigation. Morse (2008) distinguishes qualitative themes from categories: "*A theme* (…) is a meaningful 'essence' that runs through the data. Just as a theme in opera occurs over and over again, sometimes in the foreground, sometimes in the background, and sometimes co-occurring with other tunes, so does the theme in our research. It is the basic topic that the narrative is about overall" (p. 727). For example, a theme of several of the macro-analyses described above relates to habituated practices and biases within the practice of speech-language therapy and the need to explore and eliminate enculturated biases where appropriate (Duchan, 2001–2011; Kovarsky, 2008).

Micro Analysis. Micro-analytic studies in communication disorders typically involve detailed analysis of discourse or text. Elements of discourse such as syntactic structure, semantic content, speech fragments, timing, pronunciation, body movement, gesture, fluency, and intonation have all been the foci of analyses. Such data have been collected through observation, audio, video, and/or written transcripts. However, the actual approach to data analysis is highly varied depending on the qualitative orientation of the researcher. For example, conversation analysts attend to minute details within a sequence of turns such as identifying patterns of gaze or variations in body position occurring in fractions of seconds. The placement of actions in the sequence of talk is pinpointed, and the discovery of what happens next provides insight into the resources and strategies employed to manage discourse goals or the functional underpinnings of the segment. Simmons-Mackie and Damico (2009) conducted a detailed analysis of interactions of participants in two group therapy sessions. By analyzing the sequential patterns of talk, the researchers were able to demonstrate the importance of mirrored action and gesture as resources for managing and monitoring engagement and participation of clients in therapy interactions. The authors argued that mutual engagement between therapist and client was a key element of the therapy relationship. The following segment demonstrates mirrored action between two of the session participants; the segment occurred after Clinician 1 began describing her pet parrot to the group (Simmons-Mackie & Damico, 2009, p. 23).

Joe: He has a big uh cage uh? ((holds hands wide apart))
Clinician 1: He has a big cage outside ((holds hands wide apart))
but when he comes in I put him in a little cage. ((moves hands closer))
He likes that cage … it's a big one. ((hands wide apart))
Joe: It's a big one, yeah, yeah.

The mirroring of wording and gesture constituted a visible sign to each other and to observers that these two group members were mutually engaged. The authors contrasted such examples of engagement with moments of disengagement in group therapy. The authors concluded that the microanalysis of "these group therapy sessions provides insight into discourse behaviors that promote substantive conversational engagement of people with aphasia in a group setting" (Simmons-Mackie & Damico, 2009, p. 23). Thus, a focus on details of the interaction (e.g., gestures) through micro-analysis of small segments of discourse occurring within two therapy sessions helped to isolate patterns that inform us about the mechanics of doing therapy.

Other approaches adopt somewhat different analytic approaches. In an example of a micro-analytic approach to analyzing speech-language therapy, Merrills (2009) applied Clark's (1996) joint action theory as the framework for analyzing how participants in child language therapy talk about talking. The analysis identified the different instances of talking about talking and found layers of interaction within the therapy segments analyzed. Merrills' description of the layering of joint action alerts clinicians to the need to consider the complexity of the therapy interaction and attend to layers of therapy activities during sessions (including metalinguistic talk) in order to improve children's language. In another example of discourse analysis, Ferguson and colleagues (2010) employed an adaptation of systemic functional analysis (Young & Harrison, 2004) to study how people with aphasia, their family members, and their speech-language pathologists talked about therapy goals. The researchers coded lexico-grammatical features such as the use of 1st versus 3rd person pronouns, negatives, and modal auxiliaries (e.g., can, would, must) in spoken goal descriptions of participants. One finding was that clients tended to infer therapy goals, rather than state these explicitly. The results led Ferguson and colleagues to suggest that clinicians listen for implicit messages of clients during goal setting discussions.

What Are the Types of Results or Claims?

Macro Results. Results of macro-level studies typically include a detailed description along with presentation of taxonomies, theories, insights, or explanations (depending on the particular goals of the investigation). For example, Parr (2007) conducted an ethnographic investigation of life with severe aphasia after rehabilitation ends. Although the study did not directly address speech-language therapy, the implications for service delivery were significant. After analyzing 60 sets of field notes, Parr identified social exclusion as a *key theme* that permeated the experience of life with severe aphasia. Using excerpts from her field notes and analyses, Parr *described* three levels of social exclusion including exclusion at the infrastructural level (e.g., limited access to work, lack of services, poor access to media), the interpersonal level (e.g., limited association with groups, reduced access to social places), and the personal level (e.g., feelings of dependence, low self-esteem, anger). The concept of social exclusion was elaborated as it related to failure of social systems and rehabilitation. Parr contrasted the theme of social exclusion derived from most of the participants with a few examples of social inclusion and engagement and used the contrast to suggest methods of modifying services to foster social inclusion. She concluded that "People with severe aphasia can have access to choice, opportunity, engagement, and enjoyment. The challenge to service providers lies in creating the conditions for this to happen" (p. 120). Thus a detailed description and macro-analysis of the lives of 20 people with chronic severe aphasia provides important insights on the theme of social exclusion and highlights service delivery gaps and needs for this group.

Micro Results. The results of micro-analysis depends on the problem studied and the aims of the investigation. As noted previously, some micro-level studies of speech-language therapy aim to display and describe technical components of therapy interactions such as strategies, resources, actions, or timing. For example, the study of engagement in group therapy (described above) illustrated interactive resources that clinicians used (or might use) to effectively engage clients in a clinical interaction (Simmons-Mackie & Damico,

2009). Thus, the results expand our understanding of clinical interaction and inform therapy practice.

Micro-analytic approaches have also been used to depict manifestations of larger social or cultural norms, beliefs, or influences within moment-to-moment interactions. Such studies offer insights into issues of concern related to speech-language therapy practices or management of communication disabilities and attempt to relate findings to larger social issues. For example, a number of studies of speech-language therapy analyze the moment-to-moment conduct of therapy to expose concerns about control and power asymmetries, disempowerment of individuals with disability, or institutional constraints on social action (e.g., Damico & Damico, 1997; Ferguson & Armstrong, 2004; Horton, 2004, 2007; Simmons-Mackie & Damico, 1999b). In a micro-analytic study of error correction in aphasia therapy investigators identified discourse behaviors that could promote disempowerment (Simmons-Mackie & Damico, 2008). In this study the investigators contrasted two types of correction occurring in therapy interactions: exposed and embedded corrections. Based on a detailed analysis of discourse including client responses to corrections, the authors suggested that the practice of "exposing corrections" during certain therapy interactions might "reinforce a sense of 'helplessness' and disempowerment" in people with communication disabilities (Simmons-Mackie & Damico, 2008, p. 5). Such findings demonstrate the potential for macro level issues to be viewed through the lens of micro-analysis.

Concerns about the Micro and Macro Duality

The preceding discussion has contrasted micro and macro traditions in qualitative research. However, social and communicative lives are "lived, experienced and enacted simultaneously on macro and micro scales" (Mason, 2006, p. 12). Therefore, it is important to consider that we are forcing the study of such complicated and multi-dimensional phenomena into a dualistic framework only for clarity of purpose and convenience. While simplifying conceptions of qualitative research in this manner helps us understand several key characteristics, we should do so with the clear understanding that qualitative research "in action" is not so easily compartmentalized. In fact, characterization of qualitative research using a relatively rigid and artificial dichotomy might be troubling to many. Creating a dualism oversimplifies the complex, embedded social phenomena that are typically the subject of qualitative research and inadvertently might encourage researchers to limit themselves to one or the other, thereby hindering the creative pursuit of social explanation or theory (Mason, 2006).

An alternative to conceptions of micro and macro perspectives as a duality is to consider a continuum from a relatively narrow focus at one end to a relatively open-ended focus at the other end. Along this continuum we might find many applications of qualitative research. In fact, within each contrast question addressed above in this chapter (e.g., what is context? What types of data are allowed?), we might visualize a continuum from a micro to macro approach with variations in the microness or macroness occurring across the questions for a particular study. For example, existing studies of identity negotiation in speech-language therapy represent different points along a micro–macro continuum. At the micro end, a study by Horton (2007) employed conversation analysis to detail the process of topic generation in speech-language therapy sessions. The precise mechanics of topic control were described across multiple samples. The results demonstrated not only the mechanics of topic control, but also revealed how topic control by therapists restricted the display of clients' inherent competence and hampered negotiation of positive identity. Moving towards the macro end of the continuum is a study of identity negotiation in group therapy with individuals with traumatic brain injury by Kovarsky, Shaw, and Adingono-Smith (2007). In this study the researchers transcribed and analyzed videotaped therapy sessions in order to describe instances associated with identity construction—a micro approach. The discourse analysis performed by Kovarsky and colleagues, like that of Horton (2007), resulted in findings of significant therapist control of sessions with a strong focus on the problems and impairments of the clients. However, in the Kovarsky study the instances of identity construction were not reported to demonstrate a specific discourse structure or device. Rather, the discourse examples represented a conceptual category that fit into a broader notion of spoiled identity. Thus, a detailed analysis of therapy discourse was the primary focus of the study, but the authors used a macro approach to interpret the behaviors (categorizing related behaviors), and also conducted an in-depth interview with the speech-language pathologist, explored the institutional setting of the therapy sessions, studied relevant literature related to the conduct of speech-language therapy and drew on introspection related to their own experiences to build an argument regarding the institutional creation of spoiled identity and the social management of clients as "damaged goods" (as per Goffman, 1963).

Another approach to avoiding the dualism inherent in orienting to qualitative research as either micro or macro is to envision the array of qualitative research methodologies more creatively. This is reflected to some degree in the growing tendency of clinical researchers to adopt a pragmatic approach to qualitative research involving the application of qualitative methods without a specific philosophical orientation (Smith, Bekker, & Cheater, 2011). For example, researchers might use qualitative interviews to explore a research question or topic independent of a framing philosophy (e.g., phenomenology). This pragmatic approach to separating methods from their philosophical origins can, on the one hand, fulfill pragmatic needs of clinical researchers, but, on the other hand, result in loss of scientific rigor and creation of a hodgepodge of results. So, while we avoid pigeon holing types of research, we run the risk of creating superficial and undisciplined investigations.

Perhaps a more informed approach would be to adopt a multidimensional frame in addressing research questions. In other words, researchers might adopt a creative stance involving layering of qualitative research traditions that address the multidimensional nature of certain research questions and allow for a program of research that collectively informs clinical practice. While researchers are constrained to some degree by the philosophical foundations of each qualitative tradition(s) adopted, the potential to combine or layer studies or approaches is appealing. For example, one might conduct a micro-analysis of therapy discourse within a conversation analytic tradition to identify certain mechanics of clinical interaction (e.g., correction, repair), and piggyback the analysis onto a phenomenological investigation exploring the perspectives and experiences of the speech-language pathologists and clients who participated in the therapy interactions (via in-depth qualitative interviews). When exploring such options, several issues arise. First it is possible that uninformed layering of traditions such as conversation analysis and phenomenology complicates the research process and creates a confusing hybrid. In other words, approaching the study from two different philosophical traditions could create a tension between beliefs that negatively impacts the research. Alternatively, such a layered approach that allows study of a topic from different qualitative perspectives might create complementary findings, triangulated results, and enriched understanding. In fact, Mason (2006) suggests that "Mixing methods helps us to think creatively and 'outside the box', to theorize beyond the micro-macro divide, and to enhance and extend the logic of qualitative explanation," and she argues for "development of 'multi-nodal' dialogic explanations that allow the distinctiveness of different methods and approaches to be held in creative tension" (p. 9). While her discussion focuses largely on mixing quantitative and qualitative research, the arguments hold true for mixing approaches within the qualitative traditions when it would clearly serve the purposes of an investigation. Perhaps this discussion reflects Erickson's suggestion that any research should connect large social issues and small local occurrences: "When considering the evidentiary warrant for assertions, my rule of evidence is that for any assertion of a high level of abstraction we must be able to show clear linkages across a chain of lower order research questions and answers, down to the lowest possible levels of inference in observation and interpretation of visible and audible human action" (Erickson, 1984, p. 61).

Conclusion

Qualitative research encompasses a variety of traditions that are "multimethod in focus, involving an interpretive, naturalistic approach to its subject matter" (Denzin & Lincoln, 1994, p. 2). Qualitative research traditions are varied, yet when appropriately employed qualitative methods constitute a rigorous and systematic means of discovering and understanding features of our social and cultural world. Qualitative research traditions are increasingly contributing to the knowledge base in speech-language pathology (Damico & Simmons-Mackie, 2003; Simmons-Mackie & Damico, 2003). This chapter is offered as one way of conceiving of and clarifying options in qualitative research. While contrasting micro or macro orientations helps to flesh out characteristics of qualitative traditions and approaches, this imposed organization should be considered just that—an orderly description imposed onto multidimensional and dynamic philosophies and methodologies for purposes of clarification.

In action, the pursuit of qualitative research can be complicated, circular, time-consuming, fascinating, frustrating, engaging, and imminently rewarding. In our joint pursuit to expand our knowledge of qualitative research, Jack Damico and I have not only experienced extremes of frustration and satisfaction, and discovered much about communication and clinical practices, but also we have discovered the meaning of collaboration, collegiality, and friendship. What better way to end the chapter than with Jack Damico's own words regarding qualitative research:

> We have had a long and beneficial history of using experimental and quasi-experimental paradigms and traditions of inquiry to understand human communication sciences and disorders. As we recognize the pervasiveness, utility, and potential of the qualitative paradigm, we can advance our knowledge and research potential even further— when we view clinical speech-language pathology as a cultural institution that must readily address our needs and continue to work in the best interests of our clients and our society, we can ask for no better goal. (Damico &Simmons-Mackie, 2003, p. 140)

References

Agar, M. (1986). *Speaking of ethnography*. Newbury Park, CA: Sage.

Barzun, J., & Graff, H. F. (1985). *The modern researcher, 4th ed*. San Diego, CA: Harcourt Brace Jovanovich.

Chenitz, W., & Swanson, J. (1986). *From practice to grounded theory: Qualitative research in nursing*. Menlo Park, CA: Addison-Wesley.

Cicourel, A. (1992). The interpenetration of communicative contexts: examples from medical encounters. In A. Duranti & C. Goodwin (Eds.), *Rethinking context: Language as an interactive phenomenon* (pp. 291–310). Cambridge, England: Cambridge University Press.

Clark, H. H. (1996). *Using language*. Cambridge, England: Cambridge University Press.

Corbin, J., & Strauss, A. (2008). *Basics of qualitative research, 3rd ed.* Thousand Oaks, CA: Sage.

Creswell, J. (1998). *Qualitative inquiry and research design: Choosing among five traditions.* Thousand Oaks, CA: Sage.

Damico, J. S., & Damico, S. (1997). The establishment of a dominant interpretive framework in language intervention. *Language, Speech, and Hearing Services in Schools, 28,* 288–296.

Damico, J. S., & Simmons-Mackie, N. (2003). Qualitative research and speech-language pathology: Impact and promise in the clinical realm. *American Journal of Speech-Language Pathology, 12,* 131–143.

Damico, J. S., Simmons-Mackie, N., & Wilson, B. (2006). The negotiation of intelligibility in an aphasic dyad. *Clinical Linguistics & Phonetics, 20,* 599–605.

Denzin, N., & Lincoln, Y. (1994). *Handbook of qualitative research.* Thousand Oaks, CA: Sage.

DiLollo, A., & Favreau, C. (2010). Person-centered care and speech and language therapy. *Seminars in Speech & Language, 31,* 90–97.

Drew, P., & Heritage, J. (1992). *Talk at work.* Cambridge, England: Cambridge University Press.

Duchan, J. (2001–2011). *The history of speech-language pathology.* Retrieved September 15, 2011 from http://www.acsu.buffalo.edu/~duchan/new_history/overview.html

Erickson, F. (1984). What makes school ethnography 'ethnographic'? *Anthropology and Education Quarterly, 15,* 51–66.

Erickson, F. (1992). Ethnographic microanalysis of interaction. In M. LeCompte, W. Millroy, & J. Preissle (Eds.), *The handbook of qualitative research in education* (pp. 201–225). New York, NY: Academic Press.

Erickson, F. (2004). *Talk and social theory.* Cambridge, England: Polity Press.

Ferguson, A., & Armstrong, E. (2004). Reflections on speech-language therapists' talk: Implications for clinical practice and education. *International Journal of Language and Communication Disorders, 39,* 469–507.

Ferguson, A., Worrall, L., Davidson, B., Hersh, D., Howe, T., & Sherratt, S. (2010). Talk about goals for aphasia therapy: A systemic functional analysis. *Journal of Interactional Research in Communication Disorders, 1,* 95–118.

Finn, P., Bothe, A., & Bramlett, R. (2005). Science and pseudoscience in communication disorders: Criteria and applications. *American Journal of Speech-Language Pathology, 14,* 172–186.

Glaser, B. (1992). *Basics of grounded theory analysis.* Mill Valley, CA: Sociology Press.

Goffman, E. (1959). *The presentation of self in everyday life.* New York, NY: Anchor Books.

Goffman, E. (1963). *Notes on the management of spoiled identity.* New York, NY: Simon & Schuster.

Goffman, E. (1974). *Frame analysis: An essay of the organization of experience.* New York, NY: Harper Colophon.

Goodwin, C., & Duranti, A. (1992). Rethinking context: An introduction. In A. Duranti & C. Goodwin (Eds.), *Rethinking context: Language as an interactive phenomenon* (pp. 1–42). Cambridge, England: Cambridge University Press.

Hammersley, M. (2003). Conversation analysis and discourse analysis: methods or paradigms? *Discourse and Society, 14,* 751–781.

Heritage, J. (1984). Conversation analysis. In J. Heritage (Ed.), *Garfinkel and ethnomethodology* (pp. 233–292). Cambridge, England: Polity Press.

Heritage, J., & Atkinson, J. M. (1984). Introduction. In J. Atkinson & J. Heritage (Eds.), *Structures of social action: Studies in conversation analysis* (pp. 1–27). Cambridge, England: Cambridge University Press.

Hersh, D. (2001). Experiences of ending aphasia therapy. *International Journal of Language and Communication Disorders, 36,* 80–85.

Hersh, D. (2003). "Weaning" clients from aphasia therapy: Speech pathologists' strategies for discharge. *Aphasiology, 17,* 1007–1029.

Hersh, D. (2009). How do people with aphasia view their discharge from aphasia therapy? *Aphasiology, 23*, 331–350.

Horton, S. (2004). Critical reflection in speech and language therapy: Research and practice. *International Journal of Language and Communication Disorders, 39*, 486–490.

Horton, S. (2007). Topic generation in aphasia language therapy sessions: Issues of identity. *Aphasiology, 21*, 283–298.

Kovarsky, D. (2008). Representing voices from the life-world in evidence-based practice. *International Journal of Language and Communication Disorders, 43*, 47–57.

Kovarsky, D., & Curran, M. (2007). A missing voice in the discourse of evidence-based practice. *Topics in Language Disorders, 27*, 50–61.

Kovarsky, D., & Maxwell, M. (1992). Ethnography and the clinical setting: Communicative expectancies in clinical discourse. *Topics in Language Disorders, 12*, 76–84.

Kovarsky, D., Shaw, A., & Adingono-Smith, M. (2007). The construction of identity during group therapy among adults with traumatic brain injury. *Communication and Medicine, 4*, 53–66.

Leahy, M. (2004). Therapy talk: Analyzing therapeutic discourse. *Language, Speech and Hearing Services in Schools, 35*, 70–81.

Lincoln, Y. S., & Guba, E. G. (1985). *Naturalistic inquiry*. Beverly Hills, CA: Sage.

Lindsay, J., & Wilkinson, R. (1999). Repair sequences in aphasia talk: a comparison of aphasic-speech and language therapist and aphasic-spouse conversations. *Aphasiology, 13*, 305–325.

Marshall, C., & Rossman, G. (2011). *Designing qualitative research, 5th ed*. Thousand Oaks, CA: Sage.

Mason, J. (2006). Mixing methods in a qualitatively driven way. *Qualitative Research, 6*, 9–25.

Merrills, D. (2009). Staying on the same wavelength: Talking about talking in paediatric speech and language therapy sessions. *Clinical Linguistics & Phonetics, 23*, 70–91.

Morse, J. (2008). Confusing categories and themes. *Qualitative Health Research, 18*, 727–728.

Nichols, D. (2009). Qualitative research: Part one, philosophies. *International Journal of Therapy Rehabilitation, 16*, 526–533.

O'Malley, M. P. (2011). Exploring gender and power in clinical interactions. In R. Fourie (Ed.), *Therapeutic processes for communication disorders* (pp. 93–104). East Sussex, England: Psychology Press.

Parr, S. (2007). Living with severe aphasia: Tracking social exclusion. *Aphasiology, 21*, 98–123.

Psathas, G. (1995). *Conversation analysis*. Thousand Oaks, CA: Sage.

Sacks, H. (1992). *Lectures on conversation, Volumes 1 & 2* (G. Jefferson. Ed.) Oxford, England: Blackwell.

Sacks, H., Schegloff, E., & Jefferson, G. (1974). A simplest systematics for the organization of turn-taking in conversation. *Language, 50*, 696–735.

Saville-Troike, M. (1989). *The ethnography of communication: An introduction, 2nd ed*. New York, NY: Blackwell.

Schiffrin, D. (1994). *Approaches to discourse*. Oxford, England: Blackwell.

Simmons-Mackie, N., & Damico, J. S. (1999a). Qualitative methods in aphasia research: Ethnography. *Aphasiology, 13*, 681–687.

Simmons-Mackie, N., & Damico, J. S. (1999b). Social role negotiation in aphasia therapy: Competence, incompetence and conflict. In D. Kovarsky, J. Duchan, & M. Maxwell (Eds.), *Constructing (in)competence: Disabling evaluations in clinical and social interaction* (pp. 313–341). Mahwah, NJ: Erlbaum.

Simmons-Mackie, N., & Damico, J. S. (2003). Contributions of qualitative research to the knowledge base of normal communication. *American Journal of Speech-Language Pathology, 12*, 144–154.

Simmons-Mackie, N., & Damico, J.S. (2008). Exposed and embedded corrections in aphasia therapy: issues of voice and identity. *International Journal of Language & Communication Disorders, 43*, 5–17.

Simmons-Mackie, N., & Damico, J. S. (2009). Engagement in group therapy for aphasia. *Seminars in Speech and Language, 30*, 18–26.

Simmons-Mackie, N., & Damico, J. S. (2011). Exploring clincial interaction in speech-language therapy: narrative, discourse and relationships. In R. Fourie (Ed.), *Therapeutic processes for communication disorders* (pp. 35–52). Sussex, England: Psychology Press.

Simmons-Mackie, N., Damico, J., & Damico, H. (1999). A qualitative study of feedback in aphasia therapy. *American Journal of Speech-Language Pathology, 8*, 218–230.

Simmons-Mackie, N., & Elman, R. J. (2011). Negotiation of identity in group therapy for aphasia: The Aphasia Cafe. *International Journal of Language & Communication Disorders, 46*, 312–323.

Simmons, N. (1993). *An ethnographic investigation of compensatory strategies in aphasia* (Unpublished doctoral dissertation). Louisiana State University, Baton Rouge.

Smith, J., Bekker, H., & Cheater, F. (2011). Theoretical versus pragmatic design in qualitative research. *Nurse Researcher, 18*, 39–51.

Spradley, J. P. (1980). *Participant observation.*, New York, NY: Holt, Rinehart & Winston.

Stewart, M., Brown, J., Westin, W., McWhinney, I., McWilliam, C., & Freeman, T. (2003). *Patient-centered medicine: Transforming the clinical method.* Oxon, England: Radcliffe Medical Press.

Tannen, D. (1984). *Conversational style: Analyzing talk among friends.* Norwood, NJ: Ablex.

Walsh, I. (2007). Small talk is "big talk" in clinical discourse: Appreciating the value of conversation in clinical discourse. *Topics in Language Disorders, 27*, 24–36.

Walsh, I. (2008). Whose voice is it anyway? Hushing and hearing 'voices' in speech and language therapy interactions with people with chronic schizophrenia. *International Journal of Language & Communication Disorders, 43*, 81–95.

Wolcott, H. (1994). *Transforming qualitative data: Description, analysis and interpretation.* Thousand Oaks, CA: Sage.

Worrall, L. (2006). Professionalism and functional outcomes.. *Journal of Communication Disorders, 39*, 320–327.

Worrall, L., Sherratt, S., Rogers, P., Howe, T., Hersh, D., Ferguson, A., & Davidson, B. (2011). What people with aphasia want: Their goals according to the ICF. *Aphasiology, 25*, 309–322.

Young, L., & Harrison, C. (2004). *Systemic functional linguistics and critical discourse analysis.* London, England: Continuum.

3
Ethnography

RYAN L. NELSON, KATHLEEN ABENDROTH, AND KAREN LYNCH

In an open letter to the *Journal of Interactional Research in Communication Disorders*, published in the inaugural issue, Duchan (2010) describes some of the advancements regarding communicative disorders as a complex social action over the last 30 years. Duchan lauds these advancements but states more is needed. Similarly, a recent letter from the editor of the *American Journal of Speech-Language Pathology* (Hammer, 2011) lamented speech-language pathologists' misunderstanding and misrepresentation of qualitative research along with clinical implications these traditions hold. Hammer acknowledged the value of qualitative investigation and welcomed submission to the journal of studies employing such methods. Both of these advocacy pleas referenced the work of Jack S. Damico and his scholarly insistence for nearly three decades on moving inquiry in the discipline towards methods that would embrace the complexity of human interaction (see, for example, Damico, 1985, 1988; Damico & Hamayan, 1992; Damico & Simmons-Mackie, 2003; Damico, Simmons-Mackie, Oelschlaeger, Elman, & Armstrong, 1999).

As the chapters in this handbook describe, there is great clinical potential for systematic observation, rich description, and thick interpretation of the lived world from the perspective of those who live it. Damico in our discipline and others in the social sciences (e.g., Geertz, 1973) have made this abundantly clear. However, recognition of this potential has been slow. Perhaps integration of qualitative methods in our clinical discipline has only been reluctantly accepted because the field of communication disorders often too closely resembled the "other social and cultural specialists ... with far too much fashionable theory and intellectual faddism and insufficient attention to the realities of everyday life" described by Atkinson, Coffey, Delamont, Lofland, and Lofland (2001, p. 5). This chapter aims to assist in providing more explicit application by briefly describing ethnography and how specific principles associated with this tradition can be used to embrace the complexities of human interaction. This will be accomplished by discussing how ethnography may be utilized when investigators are interested in revealing cultural and social aspects of human life. The chapter unfolds by first presenting a cursory account of the history of ethnography, describing the elements of data collection and analysis we believe are most relevant to communicative sciences and disorders, and concludes with some limitations and caveats. Along the way, illustrations of how principles of ethnography have been applied in clinical settings will be presented with discussion of where we believe opportunity for further inquiry resides.

Origins of Ethnography

Stated concisely, "[e]thnography is the work of describing a culture" and life from the "the native point of view" (Spradley, 1979, p. 3). Ethnography has grown out of the fields of anthropology and sociology; these disciplines are oriented to a belief that social and cultural phenomena are different from those typically investigated in the physical sciences. Consequently, researchers in these areas needed methods well suited for empirical investigation of the variables that made up these differences (Atkinson & Hammersley, 1994). While no clear, distinct boundaries exist between ethnography and several other interpretive methods, most qualitative researchers cite the Chicago School of sociology as one of the major ontological influences on the development and advancement of this tradition of inquiry (Atkinson et al., 2001; Hammersley & Atkinson, 2007). Deegan (2001) describes the impact of this group as systematically creating a focus on the social worlds experienced in the face-to-face functioning of everyday life. Through the use of life histories, interviews, and personal interaction combined with statistical data, researchers associated with the Chicago School explored the nature of social phenomena with an aim of interpreting the structures, meanings, and functions of everyday life for those in the context of investigation (Deegan, 1988). From this institution's core ethnographies an anchor was established that fixed on the social nature of self and how a person becomes human through interactional processes. Of specific interest to the field of communicative sciences and disorders, the construction of patterns of shared language and meanings within communities or social groups was implicitly represented in these core early ethnographies.

The early field of anthropology also contributed substantially to ethnography as we know it. Anthropologists such as Boas, Malinowski, and Radcliffe-Brown influenced the development of methods and application of ethnography through a focus on making sense of social and cultural characteristics of existing so-called primitive societies (Geertz, 1973, 1983; Atkinson et al., 2001). These early attempts took the form of monographs containing first-hand accounts of long-term participant observations about a particular group of people (MacDonald, 2001). Development of ethnography in sociology and anthropology occurred more in parallel rather than consecutively; however, both were driven by a need to embrace the complexity of the human condition and a rejection of the growing use of decontextualized, experimental methods associated with positivism, which was gaining momentum through much of the early twentieth century (Hammersley & Atkinson, 2007).

Over the years, ethnography has found its way into many disciplines and fields of study concerned with understanding contextually sensitive, complex phenomena that require adequate interpretation in an empirically defensible manner (Atkinson et al., 2001). While there remains vigorous debate associated with the extent and consequences of the rejection of positivism in various aspects of ethnography (e.g., Atkinson et al., 2001; Atkinson, Coffey, & Delamont, 2003), we are most concerned with the implications of the evolution of ethnography as it relates to clinical populations and how this method repudiates tenets of logical positivism that continue to create challenges for researchers in the field of communicative sciences and disorders.

Reactions to Positivism

Logical positivism of the 1930s and 1940s gave rise to the priority of scientific theories associated with social research methods gathering definitions based largely upon what is (a) directly observable, (b) able to be operationalized so that the behaviors may be controlled and manipulated through experimentation, and (c) capable of generalizability of findings to populations that have been statistically represented through utilization of careful sampling procedures (Hammersley & Atkinson, 2007). Implications and applications of these tenets in clinical settings have revealed the limitations of logical positivism that have been described by researchers in the field of communicative sciences and disorders. That is, researchers with a clinical focus have described how the application of the principles of logical positivism limit or prevent understanding of how authentic sociocultural phenomena can be interpreted so that authentic and meaningful assessment, instruction, and growth can occur (Damico & Ball, 2010; Damico & Nelson, 2010; Damico et al., 1999; Ericks-Brophy & Crago, 1993; Kovarsky & Crago, 1991; Kovarsky & Maxwell, 1992; Muma & Cloud, 2010; Nelson & Damico, 2006; Simmons-Mackie & Damico, 1999, 2003). Methods such as ethnography have been used and are ideal for overcoming some of these limitations.

Early advocates of ethnography recognized that research embracing tenets of logical positivism contradicted principles of naturalism, suggesting that the artificiality required for experimentation lacked fidelity to the phenomena of focus. Furthermore, concentration solely on observable behaviors ignored the unique ways in which persons interpreted their experiences. Mehan (1974) demonstrated this in the following example.

> A question from [a] language development test instructs the child to choose "the animal that can fly" from a bird, an elephant, and a dog. The correct answer (obviously) is bird. Many first grade children, though, chose the elephant along with the bird as a response to that question. When I later asked them why they chose that answer they replied: "That's Dumbo." Dumbo of course is Walt Disney's flying elephant, well known to children who watch television and read children's books as an animal that flies. (p. 249)

The role of individual interpretation based upon experience in this example reveals one potential limitation among many in standardized methods. As Mehan (1974) argued, in order to understand social interpretations, methods must be embraced that give access to the meanings that guide the individual or group's behaviors. With this perspective, the aim of investigation shifted from generalizability to description of behaviors in the form of detailed accounts of the concrete lived experiences of those within a particular culture. This shift in focus allowed for an interpretation of how the beliefs and social rules function and are negotiated within the day-to-day workings of life.

An application of how rich interpretation of the beliefs and meanings of daily life in persons with communicative disorders can be accounted for was reflected in a recent ethnography. Parr (2007) described the day-to-day impact on persons with aphasia as they negotiate the consequences of stroke once rehabilitative therapy ends. Her ethnography represents principles of the well suitedness of ethnography for the field as outlined by other researchers in the communicative sciences and disorders (e.g., Damico & Simmons-Mackie, 2003; Simmons-Mackie & Damico, 1999). Namely, ethnography is ideal for study of the mundane realities of specific individuals in the natural settings in which they abide, while maintaining the methodological flexibility to account for variables revealed as the process of interaction unfolds (Damico et al., 1999; Nelson & Damico, 2006). The end result in Parr's study was a deep description and an in-depth understanding of social exclusion in persons with aphasia. By "watching people in their own territory and interacting with them in their own language, on their own terms" (Kirk & Miller, 1986, p. 9, cited in Simmons-Mackie & Damico, 1999), Parr's work is illustrative of the promise and clinical value of ethnography for seeing the world through the eyes of those associated with communication sciences and disorders.

Implementing Ethnography

Determining a Focus

People's identities evolve and are locally intertwined within the context in which they act (Goffman, 1959, 1963). Consequently, the processes that govern structures and acts of significance to these individuals may not be easily revealed to a researcher with whom they are unfamiliar, nor may they be understood by those unfamiliar with the subjects and context. In order to discover these meanings and gain the desired understanding of how the social action under focus is accomplished, *ethnographers must be able to immerse themselves in the given context.* Rock (2001) suggests that the intimacy needed to gain understanding is more easily achieved if the researcher, at least at some level, respects their informants and that this feeling is, in some way, reciprocated. Wilcox and Corwin (1990) suggest that the goal of ethnography in communication sciences and disorders should be to learn from people who have, for a variety of reasons, experienced the world in a different way. This was demonstrated through their focus on understanding deafness from a cultural perspective as seen through the world of a young deaf child, BoMee. Their ethnography revealed complexities of a multicultural society in the day-to-day negotiations of the child and her efforts to construct social competency. The intricacies of these negotiations were only revealed through careful and rigorous reflection upon the rich descriptions the researchers gained from the vantage point of high familiarity with the subject. Similarly, Damico (1990) approached speech-language pathologists as a cultural group in order to understand the motivating mechanisms of practitioners in public school settings. In order to reveal the underlying complexity of motivation in practice, the clinicians had to accept the researcher into their world and he, for his part, had to immerse himself into their lived experience over the course of the 14-month ethnography.

As is typical of the initiation of ethnography, Wilcox and Corwin (1990) and Damico (1990) approached the study with loosely identified areas of inquiry. Their primary motivation was to determine what was going on or how the interactions of those they were interested in were being accomplished. This approach to inquiry stands in stark contrast to experimental methods where specific hypotheses are carefully formulated so that they can be systematically tested in a fairly linear, start-to-finish manner (Creswell, 1998).

For the ethnographic researcher, *the issue of access becomes important* because of the type of data and familiarity with the data that is required. Access involves more than just being granted permission of physical presence or legal and ethical authorization to collect artifacts. James (2001) illustrates the complexity of access in her study of childhood. She notes the intent of ethnography to describe the world through the lens of those who experience it as they go about doing what they normally do. James describes particular challenges in accomplishing this with populations where clear differences exist between researcher and subject. She notes that in studies of childhood, power relationships often result in children–researcher interactions that would not typically occur in child-child or child-caregiver interactions. For example, while investigating how preschoolers interact, King (1984) found that only through hiding in an unoccupied playhouse was he able to gain access to the natural interactions of the children he was researching and still be sufficiently immersed in the environment enough to carefully observe.

Undergirding ethnography is a philosophy that *the research design be flexible*. Flexibility is required so that the social actions emerging from access to the focused group can be described and analyzed in sufficient detail and from the necessary perspectives so that adequacy of interpretation can be achieved. It is from this philosophically open stance that the ethnographer identifies a focus of inquiry and begins the process of data collection and analysis. Because of the depth of focus and density of the data, ethnographies typically consider a small number of individuals or contexts in a cyclical manner of increasingly narrow concentration (Agar, 1986). This is accomplished through use of several sources and principles of data collection and analysis traditionally associated with ethnography. While data collection and analysis are cyclically intertwined, they are described below separately for ease of presentation and description.

Data Collection

The cultural inferences arrived at through ethnography grow from interpretation of three primary sources: what people say, what people do, and the artifacts that they make and use (Spradley, 1979). Regardless of the data collection techniques, ethnographies must be tied to the settings in which the social action occurs. When field notes, interviews, and collected artifacts are separated from the social context in which they are produced, the defining character of ethnography is lost. This suggests that setting, which must include both the physical context as well as the interactional context, must be captured and represented with its meanings thickly described. Qualitative researchers in the field of communication sciences and disorders typically use sources and data collection strategies long associated with ethnography. How the data are used to reveal the dynamics of social institutions and organizational structures is what we believe is of the greatest import in the context of this chapter.

Participant Observation

Participant observation is one of the primary data collection tools of ethnographic research. The nature of this method of collection is ideal for many of the settings in which researchers and practitioners in this field find themselves. Yet, learning to be an effective participant observer may be challenging. This arises from the dual purpose that is created as one plays both the role of interactive participant and of observer. Spradley (1980) states that once someone learns the cultural rules, those rules become implicit. As researchers enter the context, they must operate from both an insider and an outsider perspective. They must act appropriately for the situation while still maintaining the disciplined subjectivity necessary to function as a researcher. As explained by Atkinson and colleagues (2001):

> Participant observation alone would normally result in strange and unnatural behaviour were the observer not to talk with her or his hosts, so turning them into informants or "co-researchers". Hence, conversations and interviews are often indistinguishable from other forms of interaction and dialogue in field research settings. (p. 5)

Ethnographers using participant observation must perceive through a broad lens the action going on around them because it is here that many of the most important variables of the social action are discovered (Spradley, 1980). This requires the participant observer to reflect upon how he or she is reacting in certain situations. This balancing act is typically assisted by methods of documentation as the researcher may make initial notes and jottings that are later expanded upon into field notes in a more narrative form (Spradley, 1980). In addition to objective observations, expanded notes will often contain subjective reactions and impressions. The position the researcher holds as one who must balance the insider/outsider experience is crucial in helping explicate the meanings underlying mundane realities of the culture being studied. From these notes, analysis can be conducted to identify trends and areas of foci relevant to the investigation.

Semi-Structured Interviews

Many disciplines have utilized ethnographic interview techniques, in the form of semi-structured interviews, as primary and secondary data sources. The aim of the interviewing process is to collect data that reveal the culture of the person being interviewed. Specifically, insights into their perceptions and worldviews are obtained through strategic use of questioning techniques designed to elicit the informant's "story" (Spradley, 1979). Westby (1990) describes the process as one where rapport is established so that the appropriate questions can be asked of the right people in a way that encourages the individual to talk about the social situations in their daily lives.

In clinical settings, overt efforts must be made to minimize the power differential that usually exists between researcher and client (Spradley, 1979; Westby, 1990). Augustine (1995) and James (2001) describe related strategies for interviewing children. Similar to Spradley's (1979) concern for minimizing power differentials, these researchers recognize that the skill of the interviewer in providing supports necessary for the interviewee to convey their story is something that must be negotiated within the context of the interview. Predetermined questions may serve as a starting point, but responsiveness and reflexivity to that which is shared within the context of the interview are what ultimately yields data appropriate for understanding the culture of the informant. Consequently, a defining attribute of a semi-structured interview is the discovery of relevant questions. Consistent with the entire ethnographic endeavor, the ability to allow questions to emerge is more easily accomplished when the interviewer sees him/herself as a student of the interviewee's. The actions of the interviewer must convey interest in gaining understanding of the interviewee's lived experience. In these contexts, both the interviewer and interviewee wear the cloak of responder and questioner. Semi-structured interviews are characterized by carefully worded, open-ended, descriptive questions, asked with the intent of allowing the interviewee to convey what is of greatest importance.

During the interview, the researcher tries to remain empathetic and non-judgmental of the world as it is described to them. What makes these interviews unique and an important part of ethnography is how the researcher, through his or her questions and responses, attempts to maintain the assumption that the interviewee is the expert of the world in which he or she lives. Ethnographers realize that the complexities of the culture of those interviewed are directly tied to the interviewees' unique interpretations of experience.

Data obtained from interviews are typically recorded electronically and transcribed or captured through processes similar to that of field notes used in participant observations. These accounts of information obtained through the interview are analyzed to determine patterns of interest to the research focus.

Behavioral Recordings

Due to the nature of clinical interactions, ethnographers in the field of communicative sciences and disorders often have access to video or audio recordings of interactions of particular interest. Simmons-Mackie (Chapter 2, this volume) and others in this handbook have demonstrated how qualitative researchers, including ethnographers, can utilize behavioral video and audio recordings. Nelson (2004), for example, collected over 25 hours of video from the clinical interactions of children with language impairment engaged in shared reading in order to describe how they constructed proficient literacy skills over time. The advantages of these types of electronically recorded data are that they can be analyzed multiple times. This can allow the ethnographer to describe and interpret the complex systematicity that underlies mundane day-to-day interactions. Abendroth (2008) relied heavily upon video analysis when she investigated the subtle and systematic ways in which typically developing siblings of children with autism provided mediation during play activities. However, Hammersley and Atkinson (2007) cautioned that, as with all data collection, these interpretations from recordings must be carefully supported. They note that often the angle of the camera lens or sensitivity of microphones may miss important variables from the interaction that are critical to understanding the interaction under investigation.

Artifact Analysis

The three data sources described to this point have consisted primarily of what informants say and do (Geertz, 1973). Artifact analysis allows a focus upon what persons make and use as they participate in the institutions of interest to ethnographers. Hammersley and Atkinson (2007) suggest that much of the mundane activity influential in the creation of social worlds involves manipulation of objects for the creation of material goods and the constructed meanings derived out of interpersonal relationships associated with and in the pursuit of these objects. Within the field of communication sciences and disorders, artifacts of interest frequently include products written by clients, significant others, clinicians, teachers, doctors, and other service providers. Additionally, individuals use objects to structure their environment and support their identities. For instance, Lynch (2010), in her investigation of the impact of aphasia on the literate lives of individuals, described how one person with aphasia, in spite of substantial literacy difficulties, carried a book around throughout his daily activities. In order to understand the day-to-day impact of aphasia on this person's literate life, how books assisted in accomplishing affiliation and identity had to be considered. The object of "book" as an artifact reflective of the cultural world for this person was important for coherence. Similarly, objects are often strategically positioned in clinical settings to facilitate specific types of interactions. The consideration of artifacts that make up the physical world is often necessary as a data collection source in ethnography if we want to make sense of social worlds. Furthermore, in our digital age, textual artifacts are becoming more frequently associated with social networking; fieldwork focusing on these virtual realities will need to be included more often as data sources. Ethnography is ideally situated to embrace the complexities associated with new mediums that contribute to the fabric of social life.

Triangulation

With the cyclical nature of data collection and analysis, a critical means of ensuring authenticity of data collection is triangulation. Agar (1986) wrote that in order to carefully define a social event from the standpoint of an ethnographic research design, the technique of triangulation should always be employed. That is, a systematic process of comparing and contrasting data from different data collection procedures, contexts, and time frames to assist in achieving a high degree of authenticity should be used. Triangulation is typically achieved through collection of data from multiple meaning-making activities in multiple contexts and documented through multiple data collection procedures. This allows the researcher to test his or her interpretations of the meanings derived from collected data and determine the inquiry direction and type of additional data that may be needed. Simmons-Mackie and Damico (1999) describe this process as a means of "auditing" the authenticity of the data and the levels of understanding the researcher has of it.

Lamination

Lamination is a strategy of verification used in ethnography (Agar, 1986). This strategy includes eliciting and documenting informants' reactions to the researcher's interpretations. Once data are collected and analyzed by the researcher and some initial conclusions are drawn, the ethnographer may ask the informants what they believe is occurring in, and what the significance of, the same data source is. This layer of understanding can function as an additional means of establishing a thickness of data interpretation and can be quite valuable in leading the researcher to the desired coherence.

Data Analysis

There is no distinct stage of data analysis in ethnography (Hammersley & Atkinson, 2007). Instead, analysis begins as the researcher formulates and develops the research question and begins the data collection process. For the purposes of communication sciences and disorders, the end result of analysis is coherence of understanding and interpretation. This is often achieved when the researcher understands how meanings of events or reactions to specific authentic social interactions were able to unfold (Simmons-Mackie & Damico, 1999). In ethnography, "what we call our data are really our own constructions of other people's constructions of what they and their compatriots are up to" (Geertz, 1973, p. 9). This representational act requires analysis even at the most basic levels. In the same text, Geertz suggested that ethnographers attempt to identify and interpret through analysis how an individual's actions are impacted by "structures of signification" (Geertz, 1973, pp. 9-10). This point by Geertz is consistent with Agar's (1986) position that data analysis should reveal what was most relevant in documenting the social worlds and organizational structures of interest to the researcher. Predetermined categories, criteria, or themes of interest strike at the heart of the emergent, flexible intent of the methodology and should be avoided. Instead, cyclical analysis leading towards coherence should direct the variation, amount, and type of data collected. As data are collected and analyzed, the interpretations should be verified as the ethnographer moves to an increasingly more narrow, yet deeper, understanding of the themes that underlie the social phenomenon. The iterative process of analytic interaction with the data is captured in the following:

> Anthropologists, for instance, reflect upon fieldnotes: how they are constructed, used and managed. We come to understand that field-notes are not a closed, completed, final text: rather, they are indeterminate, subject to reading, rereading, coding recording, interpreting, reinterpreting. (Atkinson et al., 2001, p. 3)

Creswell (1998) describes the analytic process as organizing data so that the cyclical review explained by Atkinson can occur, and codes and taxonomies, qualitative as well as quantitative descriptions, can be generated and repeatedly refined and analyzed until coherent patterned regularities and themes emerge.

This process of analysis demands disciplined subjectivity from the ethnographer as he or she attempts to maintain a position of neutrality amidst the emergence of themes. Rigorous circumspection is required to ensure that data collection and analysis does not simply follow the path of least resistance, but leads to interpretations of social meanings that (a) are more plausible and credible, (b) connect the specific phenomenon with a larger understanding of the focus, and (c) clarify and enlighten to the point of an "a-ha moment" from the perspective of the researcher (Agar, 1986; Simmons-Mackie & Damico, 1999).

Agar (1986) describes the role of analysis in ethnography and ways in which the researcher can arrive at thick interpretation necessary for the level of acceptability. As data are collected, the ethnographer is oriented towards understanding how the day-to-day workings of the individuals or groups are accomplished and towards the meanings that underlie their social worlds. While analyzing collected data, the researcher may look for or experience instances of breakdown. These *occasioned* or *mandated* breakdowns in understanding between the researcher's expectations and the meanings, actions, and reactions of those focused on, create the opportunities for the resolution that leads to the expanded understanding of coherence. Resolutions are initiated and achieved through a conscious testing of the researcher's understanding of bounded strips of a phenomenon. Agar explains this process as a systematic way to determine if the practical interpretation of a specific schema can eliminate the occurrence of breakdown. In order to arrive at coherence, one must consider *anticoherence* as a possibility. That is, when the ethnographer begins to have an understanding of what is going on, he or she tries to challenge that understanding by collecting or analyzing data that will expose breakdowns in those interpretations.

Presentation of Ethnographic Findings

Ethnography does not claim to be an objective, detailed accounting of an individual or group of individuals. It does not aim towards replicability or intend to predict future events. Rather, ethnography involves the process of mediating for the audience, a representation of frames of meaning constructed from interpretations of the researcher's experience with the studied individuals or groups (Agar, 1986). As researchers within the field of communication sciences and disorders prepare to present their ethnography, they typically frame the data and interpretation within the structure provided by their discipline. That is, the interpretation and the representation of the patterns of meaning are couched within both the culture and terminology of the field. This can be complicated since the concept of disability and disorder is socially constructed, yet mechanistically defined (Damico, Müller, & Ball, 2010) and the social lives of individuals from the cultures of inquiry typically do not fit neatly into decontextualized categories (Damico & Augustine, 1995). Published ethnographic and related qualitative research traditions allow for the complexity of the human existence within the contexts of interest to be more richly represented and understood. For example, Nelson's (2004) investigation into the acquisition of literacy in children classified with common language impairment and reading disability categories, showed that they progressed along uniquely different trajectories while exhibiting vastly different strategic reactions to literacy instruction. Similarly, Simmons-Mackie, Damico, and Damico (1999) found that the structure and role of feedback in aphasia therapy significantly influenced the affective context of the treatment.

For the researcher, presentation of ethnography creates the challenge of representing to the reader the lived experience in a manner that allows interpretation of the situation from the perspective of those who actually live it. Themes of interpretations are often presented through detailed description from the authentic, and often daily, events of those under investigation. In this way, the reader should be able to clearly recognize evidence supporting the interpretation.

Misconceptions and Directions

Ethnography is not merely the process of describing in fine detail the minutia of daily living. As Hanson (1965) has famously indicated, observation, description, and interpretation are inherently theory laden. Many of the attempts to apply ethnographic methods to communicative disorders have fallen prey to shallow descriptions of behavioral responses based largely on a priori assumptions because the researcher—unfamiliar with crucial principles of ethnographic research—struggles to force the phenomenon under investigation into artificial themes. These thin descriptions have resulted in criticism of ethnographic methods as lacking rigor or serving only exploratory purposes.

While it has not been widely used in communication sciences and disorders, ethnography has a rich history that certainly holds clinical relevance. The editors referenced at the beginning of this chapter, and indeed the thrust of Jack S. Damico's career as a clinical researcher, have recognized a missing element within the discipline when it comes to our understanding of the realities and clinical considerations associated with the lives of those we strive to serve within the field. Too often clinical research does not adequately resemble the realities of clients, families, and clinicians. The complexities of human communication are fragmented and ignored (Damico, 1988). The qualitative research tradition of ethnography can reveal meanings of authentic behaviors and expand our understanding of communication sciences and associated disorders.

References

Abendroth, K. (2008). *The use of systematic meditational strategies by siblings of children with autism spectrum disorder.* Ann Arbor, MI: UMI Dissertation Services.

Agar, M. (1986). *Speaking of ethnography.* Newbury Park, CA: Sage.

Atkinson, P., Coffey, A., & Delamont, S. (2003). *Key themes in qualitative research: Continuities and change.* Walnut Creek, CA: Alta Mira Press.

Atkinson, P., Coffey, A., Delamont, S., Lofland, J., & Lofland, L. (Eds.). (2001). *Handbook of ethnography.* London, England: Sage.

Atkinson, P., & Hammersley, M. (1994). Ethnography and participant observation. In N. K. Denzin & Y .S. Lincoln (Eds.), *Handbook of qualitative research* (pp. 248–261). Thousand Oaks, CA: Sage.

Augustine, L. (1995). Strategies for effective child interviewing. *National Student Speech-Language Hearing Association Journal, 22,* 14–23.

Creswell, J. (1998). *Qualitative inquiry and research design: Choosing among five traditions.* Thousand Oaks, CA: Sage.

Damico, J. S. (1985). Clinical discourse analysis: A functional approach to language assessment. In C. S. Simon (Ed.), *Communication skills and classroom success: Assessment of language-learning disabled students* (pp. 165–204). San Diego, CA: College-Hill Press.

Damico, J. S. (1988). The lack of efficacy in language therapy: A case study. *Language, Speech and Hearing Services in Schools, 19,* 51–67.

Damico, J. S. (1990). Prescriptionism as a motivating mechanism: An ethnographic study in the public schools. *Journal of Childhood Communication Disorders, 13,* 85–92.

Damico, J. S., & Augustine, L. E. (1995). Social considerations in the labeling of students as attention deficit hyperactivity disordered. *Seminars in Speech and Language, 16,* 259–274.

Damico, J. S., & Ball, M. J. (2010). Prolegomenon: Addressing the tyranny of old ideas. *Journal of Interactional Research in Communicative Disorders, 1,* 1–30.

Damico, J. S., & Hamayan, E. V. (1992). *Multicultural language intervention: Addressing culturally and linguistically diverse issues.* Chicago, IL: Riverside.

Damico, J. S., Müller, N., & Ball, M. J. (2010). Social and practical considerations in labeling. In

J. S. Damico, N. Müller, & M. J. Ball, (Eds.), *The handbook of language and speech disorders* (pp. 11–37). Oxford, England: Blackwell.

Damico, J. S., & Nelson, R. (2010). Reading and reading impairments. In J. S. Damico, N. Müller, & M. J. Ball (Eds.), *The handbook of language and speech disorders* (pp. 267–295). Oxford, England: Blackwell.

Damico, J. S., & Simmons-Mackie, N. (2003). Qualitative research and speech-language pathology: A tutorial for the clinical realm. *American Journal of Speech-Language Pathology, 12,* 131–143.

Damico, J. S., Simmons-Mackie, N. N., Oelschlaeger, M., Elman, R., & Armstrong, E. (1999). Qualitative methods in aphasia research: Basic issues. *Aphasiology, 13,* 651–666.

Deegan, M. J. (1988). *Jane Addams and the men of the Chicago School, 1892–1920.* New Brunswick, NJ: Transaction Books.

Deegan, M. J. (2001). The Chicago School of ethnography. In P. Atkinson, S. Coffey, J. Delamont, J. Lofland, & L. Lofland (Eds.), *Handbook of ethnography* (pp. 11–25). London, England: Sage.

Denzin, N., & Lincoln, Y. (Eds.). (1994). *Handbook of qualitative research.* Thousand Oaks, CA: Sage.

Duchan, J. (2010). JIRCD: An open letter to the journal. *Journal of Interactional Research in Communication Disorders, 1,* 157–164.

Ericks-Brophy, A., & Crago, M. B. (1993). Inuit efforts to maintain face: Elements from classroom discourse with Inuit children. In D. Kovarsky, M. Maxwell, & J. Damico (Eds.), *Language interaction in clinical and educational settings. ASHA Monographs, 30,* 10–16.

Geertz, C. (1973). *The interpretation of cultures.* New York, NY: Basic Books.

Geertz, C. (1983). *Local knowledge: Further essays in interpretive anthropology.* New York, NY: Basic Books.

Goffman, E. (1959). On face-work: An analysis of ritual elements in social interaction, *Psychiatry, 18,* 213–231.

Goffman, E. (1963). *Behavior in Public Places.* Glencloe, IL: Free Press.

Hanson, N. R. (1965). *Patterns of discovery.* Cambridge, England: Cambridge University Press.

Hammer, C. S. (2011). Expanding our knowledge base through qualitative research methods. *American Journal of Speech-Language Pathology, 20,* 1–2.

Hammersley, M., & Atkinson, P. (2007). *Ethnography: Principles in practice* (3rd ed.). New York, NY: Routledge.

James, A. (2001). Ethnography in the study of children and childhood. In P. Atkinson, A. Coffey, S. Delamont, J. Lofland, & L. Lofland (Eds.), *Handbook of ethnography* (pp. 246–257). London, England: Sage.

King, R. A. (1984). The man in the Wendy House: Researching infants' schools. In R. G. Burgess (Ed.), *The research process in educational settings: Ten case studies* (pp. 117–139). Lewes, England: Falmer Press.

Lynch, K. (2010). *An investigation of the impact of aphasia on the reading behaviors of individuals with dyslexia secondary to a cerebral vascular accident.* Ann Arbor, MI: UMI Dissertation Services.

Kovarsky, D., & Crago, M. (1991). Toward the ethnography of communication disorders. *National Student Speech Language Hearing Association Journal, 18,* 44–55.

Kovarsky, D., & Maxwell, M. (1992) Ethnography and the clinical setting: Communicative expectancies in clinical discourse. *Topics in Language Disorders, 12,* 76–84.

MacDonald, S. (2001). British social anthropology. In P. Atkinson, A. Coffey, S. Delamont, J. Lofland, & L. Lofland (Eds.), *Handbook of ethnography* (pp. 60–79). London, England: Sage.

Mehan, H. (1974). Assessing children's school performance. In H. P. Dreitzel (Ed.), *Recent Sociology,* no. 5, *Childhood and Socialization.* London, England: Collier Macmillan.

Muma, J., & Cloud, S. (2010). Autism spectrum disorders: The state of the art. In J. S. Damico,

N. Müller, & M. J. Ball (Eds.), *The handbook of language and speech disorders* (pp. 153–177). Oxford, England: Blackwell.

Nelson, R. (2004). Investigation of the process of improved literacy construction in individuals with poor reading abilities and an identification of language impairment. *Dissertation Abstracts International, 65*(11), 5674B. (UMI No. 3153731)

Nelson, R., & Damico, J. S. (2006). Qualitative research in literacy acquisition: A framework for investigating reading in children with language impairment. *Clinical Linguistics and Phonetics, 20*, 631–639.

Parr, S. (2007). Living with severe aphasia: Tracking social exclusion. *Aphasiology, 21*, 98–123.

Rock, P. (2001) Symbolic interactionism and ethnography. In P. Atkinson, A. Coffey, S. Delamont, J. Lofland, & L. Lofland (Eds.), *Handbook of ethnography* (pp. 26–38). London, England: Sage.

Simmons-Mackie, N., & Damico, J. S. (1999). Qualitative methods in aphasia research: Ethnography. *Aphasiology, 13*, 681–687.

Simmons-Mackie, N., & Damico, J. S. (2003). Contributions of qualitative research to the knowledge base of normal communication. *American Journal of Speech-Language Pathology, 12*, 144–154.

Simmons-Mackie, N. N., Damico, J. S., & Damico, H. L. (1999). A qualitative study of feedback in aphasia treatment. *American Journal of Speech-Language Pathology, 8*, 218–230.

Spradley, J. P. (1979). *The ethnographic interview.* New York, NY: Holt, Rhinehart & Winston.

Spradley, J. P. (1980). *Participant observation.* New York, NY: Holt, Rhinehart & Winston.

Westby, C. E. (1990). Ethnographic interviewing: Asking the right questions to the right people in the right ways. *Journal of Childhood Communication Disorders, 13*, 101–111.

Wilcox, S., & Corwin, J. (1990). The enculturation of BoMee: Looking at the world through deaf eyes. *Journal of Childhood Communication Disorders, 13*, 63-73.

4

The Ethnography of Communication Disorders Revisited

DANA KOVARSKY

Introduction

My first job as a practicing speech-language pathologist was in Albuquerque, New Mexico, in 1980. As part of my duties, I was required to attend a number of in-service activities. I remember listening to a mind numbing presentation about how practitioners could use pieces of Styrofoam shaped like peanuts to teach children how to read through a series of stimulus-response-reinforcement chains. Although never stated explicitly, language was represented as discrete objective bits of behavior that simply had to be chained together and memorized. Consistent with a conduit metaphor of communication (Duchan, 1993; Kovarsky & Walsh, 2011a; Reddy, 1979), meaning could then be transmitted along a pipeline, via writing or speaking, to a relatively passive receiver.

Based on this experience, it was with no small amount of trepidation that I attended a second in-service. This time, however, Jack Damico was the presenter and he discussed how Grice's Conversational Maxims could be applied to assess the oral language abilities of school-aged children. Instead of narrowly fixating on pieces of grammatical form, language and language disorders were squarely situated in terms of certain properties of communication. It was this reframing of language as communication, also a part of the pragmatics movement in speech-language pathology (Duchan, Hewitt, & Sonnenmeier, 1994), that helped lay the groundwork for the ethnography of communication disorders (ECD). In fact, Jack Damico was also part of a seminar presented at an annual convention of the American Speech-Language-Hearing Association when ECD was launched as a named field of inquiry within communication disorders (Kovarsky et al., 1988).

In what follows, the conceptual underpinnings of the ethnography of communication and ECD are discussed. Next, some of the contributions the latter has made to the study of communication disorders are considered. Finally, some brief comments are offered regarding future directions.

The Ethnography of Communication

The ethnography of communication was intended to help bridge the gap between the study of language and culture by providing detailed "description[s] in cultural terms (ethnography) of the patterned uses of language and speech (speaking)" (Sherzer, 1977, pp. 4–5). From its inception in the early 1960s, this field has been an interdisciplinary endeavor characterized by hybridity. In their first reader addressing the ethnography of communication, John Gumperz and Dell Hymes included contributions from ethnomethodologists (conversation analysts included), sociologists, and anthropologists (Gumperz & Hymes, 1972).

The field was launched, in part, because of a concern for the scholarly predilections from the fields of linguistics and anthropology. Hymes (1987) criticized linguistics for its overly narrow focus on the structural properties of language without accounting for those aspects of social life that made language relevant. At the same time, he disapproved of anthropology because it did not fully address the role of language in constructing culture. One major way that Hymes sought to resolve this conceptual blind spot between linguistics and anthropology was through the study of speech events.

Framed by a SPEAKING mnemonic (Hymes, 1964), the speech event was intended to be a unit of analysis as basic to the field as the sentence was to structural linguistics:

> The speech event is to the analysis of verbal interaction what the sentence is to grammar. When compared with the sentence, it represents an extension in size of the basic analytical unit from single utterances to stretches of utterances, as well as a shift in focus from emphasis on text to emphasis on interaction. (Gumperz, 1972, p. 17)

In fact, Hymes' conception of a speech event paved the way for his later formulation of communicative competence; a notion that served as a rebuttal to Chomsky's (1965) claim regarding the primacy of linguistic competence in understanding child language acquisition. While Chomsky focused on the underlying abstract rules of grammar divorced from their use in interaction, Hymes elevated the idea of language as communication.

> Within the developmental matrix in which knowledge of the sentences of language is acquired, children also acquire knowledge of a set of ways in which sentences are used ... We have to account for the fact that a normal child acquires knowledge of sentences, not only as grammatical, but also as appropriate. He or she acquires [communicative] competence as to when to speak, when not, and what to talk about with whom, when, where, [and] in what manner. In short a child becomes able to accomplish a repertoire of speech acts, to take part in *speech*

events, and to evaluate their accomplishment by others. (emphasis added; Hymes, 1972b, pp. 277, 286)

As "activities or aspects of activities that are directly governed by rules or norms for the use of speech [or communication]" (Hymes, 1972a, p. 56), speech events referred to those occasions that members of a culture recognized as distinct wholes. In contrast to interactions where communication played a more subordinate role, in speech events, it was speech that constituted the event. These events were separate from other types of discourse and characterized by distinct rules for communicative behavior with recognizable temporal boundaries (Gumperz, 1972). For example, Ochs (1973) examined *Kabary*, a kind of ceremonial speech found on the plateau area of Madagascar. Used during events like circumcisions, marriages, deaths, and bone turnings, it entailed a kind of "winding speech" characterized by *ohatra* (examples and comparisons), *ohabolana* (proverbs appropriate to specific topics), and *hainteny* (passages of extended metaphor focused on the habits of plants and animals in the local environment) (Ochs, 1973, p. 225).

In fact, when ECD was called into existence, it was clear that speech-language therapy was ripe for analysis as a speech event (Damico & Damico, 1997; Kovarsky, 1990). These analyses, as will be discussed later, illuminated a number of interactional asymmetries that worked together to help achieve an event dominated by the interpretive perspective of the speech-language pathologist.

Although the analysis of speech events is extremely useful, it does not address situations where speech plays a more minor, yet important, role in constituting culture (Duranti, 1997, p. 289). For instance, an examination of exchanges that take place during service encounters, like interactions in a restaurant (Merritt, 1980) or a beauty shop (Walsh, 2007), also have the potential to illuminate relations between language and culture. Toward this end, Sherzer (1987) proposed a broader, discourse-centered approach for ethnographers of communication to follow. As a unit of analysis that includes spoken, written, and manual modes of communication, "it can be brief like a greeting ..., or lengthy like a novel or a narration of personal experience" and evaluated "in textual, sociocultural [or] social-interactional terms" (Sherzer, 1987, pp. 296–297). Through a range of discursive activities, the shared rules for the production and interpretation of cultural behavior are actualized. Since discourse is a way of both constructing and inhabiting culture, the study of culture must include "the actual forms of discourse produced and performed by societies and individuals" (Sherzer, p. 306). This perspective takes the study of language and culture beyond the analysis of speech events and into a variety other routine, and not so routine, social activities.

It was against this backdrop of the speech event and, more broadly, discursive analysis that a call was raised for the ethnography of communication disorders.

The Ethnography of Communication Disorders

Recognizing the mutually constitutive relationship between language and culture, the purpose of ECD is to study communicative incompetence and disorder as they emerge in a variety of discursive activities (Kovarsky & Crago, 1990). Since its inception, there have been at least three major contributions that ECD has made to the field of communication disorders. First, a more nuanced understanding of communication disorder has emerged. Second, ECD has illuminated the nature of our clinical discourse practices. Finally, "communicative participation" is emerging, perhaps more implicitly than explicitly, as a unit of analysis for examining the construction of communicative competence, incompetence, and disorder. In what follows, each of these contributions is discussed.

Understanding the Nature of Communication Disorders

Damico (1988) presented a poignant, retrospective case study about a young language-disordered child fictitiously named Debbie. Although previously dismissed from therapy, she had reappeared on his caseload at 12 years of age with significant language difficulties that manifested themselves in social and academic contexts. One important factor that contributed to this therapeutic failure had to do with what was termed a *fragmentation fallacy* regarding the nature of language and, in turn, language assessment.

The fragmentation fallacy promotes a view of language as a series of separate modules with heavy emphasis placed on discrete components of language form (syntax, morphology, phonology) because they are easier to objectify. If a clinician can facilitate a client's ability to correctly process and/or produce these problematic fragments of psycholinguistic behavior, then the goals of therapy are met and the disorder either no longer exists, or its consequences are significantly enough reduced to be of little concern. In Debbie's case, discrete point tests, focused on evaluating separate components of language form, were used to qualify her for therapy, plan intervention, and justify her original dismissal from treatment (Damico, 1988, p. 57). Because both assessment and intervention failed to account for the synergistic relationships between language form, content, and use, significant problems with discourse were overlooked. In particular, since isolated constituents of grammar were judged to be adequate structurally, there was no additional analysis to determine if they were being used appropriately in different contexts.

Building upon Damico's plea (1993) for a more synergistic and pragmatically situated understanding of language in context, an epistemology of social constructionism has been used to argue against traditional conceptions of language and communication disorders that locate impairments squarely inside the psycholinguistic heads of afflicted individuals. Instead of claiming that there is an objective human reality that exists independent of social processes, constructionism holds that reality (conceptions of competence and incompetence included) is something that is realized through the give and take of interaction (Gergen, 1994; Jorgensen Winkler, 1999). Instead of metaphorically viewing individuals with communication disorders as half-empty, or improperly filled, psycholinguistic containers (Duchan, Maxwell, & Kovarsky, 1999), the constructionist view of disorder contextualizes communicative incompetence as something that emerges (or not) from an interactional substrate in which meanings are construed and individuals are held accountable for their performances based upon particular interactional expectancies and communicative values (Kovarsky & Walsh, 2011a). This is not to say that internal differences in language ability fail to exist. Rather, it is the interpretation of these abilities in interaction that problematizes people (Kovarsky, Shaw, & Adingono-Smith, 2007; Simmons-Mackie & Damico, 1999).

Put another way, communication disorders, as well as our helping practices, are cultural constructions. In her investigation of childhood language socialization among the Inuit of Ungava Bay in Arctic Quebec, Crago (1990) illuminated cultural differences in how talkativeness was evaluated with respect to children's abilities. One youngster stood out because he was verbally precocious, something that, in her view, revealed advanced abilities.

> One of the boys was particularly intriguing even from the beginning of taping. His language seemed advanced for his age and he talked frequently. His tapes had more entries per minute than any other child's tapes. From my perspective he was a very bright and very verbal little boy. (p. 80)

Because his verbal abilities appeared to distinguish him from the other children, one of the native Inuk teachers was asked for her perspective. After listening to a description of how much this boy talked, the teacher replied:

> Do you think that he might have a learning problem? Some of these children who do not have such high intelligence have trouble stopping themselves. They don't know when to stop talking. (p. 80)

In reaction to the teacher's reply Crago wrote, "I was amazed by her response. It was as if my perspective had been stood on its head" (1990, p. 80). In this community, children are socialized into learning by looking and listening. Not only are interactions in the home between older mothers and children often characterized by verbal silence, nonverbal modeling by more competent cultural members is a prominent teaching style (Crago & Eriks-Brophy, 1994, pp. 46–50). As a sign of competence and intelligence, silence, not verbosity, is more highly valued.

In other words, characteristics of communication that are highly prized in one community may be disvalued in another and viewed as signs of incompetence. Communication disorders do not exist independent of the cultural contexts in which they are constituted. Ironically, analyses of clinical discourse reveal that some of our own professional practices designed to support those with communication problems may, in fact, help construct a version of the client as incompetent.

The Analysis of Clinical Discourse in Communication Disorders

Within ECD, a fair amount of analysis has been devoted to the kinds of discursive worlds created and inhabited through assessment and intervention. One of the most consistent findings has to do with the interactional asymmetries present in traditional therapy. Speech-language pathologists (SLPs) select and control the pace of activities, develop and implement goals that are deemed appropriate for intervention, regulate access to the interactional floor, highlight those aspects of communication that are worthy of therapeutic work, and, in general, manage the distribution, flow, and evaluation of information (Kovarsky, 1990; Kovarsky & Duchan, 1997; Panagos, 1996). It is the interpretive framework of the clinician that dominates (Damico & Damico, 1997). Errors in client performance are exposed through 3-part quiz question sequences (SLP request for known information-client response-SLP evaluation of response) and then, if necessary, subjected to repair work until a reply is provided that the clinician judges to be appropriate. For example, in the following extract, a crystal garden has been constructed from a set of written instructions and the therapist (T) asks the child (C) what the next therapy activity will be:

Example 1

1. *T:*   What do you get to do next?
2. *C:*   Um: (T looks at C and smiles) clean up.
3. *T:*   Okay ((pause))
4. *T:*   Before we clean up I'm going to get you to: (T holds up two sheets of paper while smiling)
5. *C:*   Oh: write a report about it.
6. *T:*   (T smiling) Heh heh heh heh.
7. *T:*   (speaking in a teasing tone) Is that excitement in your voice? (C and T smile)
8. *T:*   We'll do it quickly. (Kovarsky, 1990, p. 36)

The extract begins with a quiz question. When the child does not provide the desired response, a negative evaluation is provided through the use of "okay" and a verbal pause. Then, the clinician initiates repair work with a hint (holding up paper) and C provides the desired response in turn 5 as is evidenced by the laughter and good natured teasing that follow. Since laughter and humor can function communicatively to promote positive engagement in interaction among those with communication disorders (Kovarsky, Curran, & Zobel Nichols, 2009; Simmons-Mackie & Damico, 2009), they may be used to lubricate the therapy process and gain client compliance with the therapeutic agenda (Simmons-Mackie & Shultz, 2003; Walsh, Leahy, & Litt, 2009).

Because intervention hinges on identifiable errors in communicative performance that can be subjected to repair work (van Kleeck & Richardson, 1986; Kovarsky & Maxwell, 1992), therapeutic contexts are constructed to bring mistakes to the surface so they can be corrected. This reveals an inherent paradox built into the fabric of traditional methods of therapy: "The goal of therapy is to build communicative competence, yet the assumptions required for treatment demand that the client be incompetent" (Simmons-Mackie & Damico, 1999, p. 313). As the following snippet from an interview with a child in therapy reveals, it is not only the therapist that adopts an error-maker expectancy.

Example 2

Ripich: What do you usually do in therapy?
Child: Well, I'm supposed to make the bad *r* sounds, and Mrs. Smith is supposed to make the good *r* sounds.
Ripich: Don't you ever make the good *r* sounds?
Child: No! I'm supposed to make the bad *rs*. (Ripich & Panagos, 1985, p. 343)

From this child's perspective, irrespective of the success of any clinician-initiated repair work, she is the one responsible for producing errors during therapy. Although the beneficiaries of intervention generally tend to acquiesce and assume the role of error-maker, there are rare uncomfortable moments that can occur during therapy precisely because clients are challenging this presupposition of incompetence (Kovarsky & Walsh, 2011b). Simmons-Mackie and Damico (1999) describe a therapy session that ends abruptly with a client walking out early because her complaints about the quality of therapy are not taken at face value and only treated as further evidence of her own communication disorder. Instead of supporting her efforts to communicate and express an alternate point of view, the therapeutic context was constructed in such a way as to treat her voiced criticisms of intervention as evidence of her incompetence. The interactional substrate of therapy helped minimize her voice as a competent consumer of therapy services.

Given that therapy is supposed to foster communicative competence, there is a concern that traditional therapy has the potential to promote a client's sense of self-as-damaged-goods (Kovarsky et al., 2007). In the following example, SLP1 and SLP2 are conducting group therapy among adults with traumatic brain injury. The clients had just finished a game requiring them to guess what objects their peers were drawing without any verbal clues. SLP1 asked the clients to explain why it was difficult to ascertain what someone else sketched. In response, the clients provided a number of plausible answers like "[it's] bad art" or "the angle you were looking at [made it difficult]." SLP1 rejected these explanations and began searching for an alternate reason by recycling her original request.

Example 3

1. *SLP1:* How come some one person can look at something and see one thing and somebody else looks at it and sees something else?
2. *J:* They like it.
3. *S:* It's just an idea they're thinking (touches forehead).
4. *B:* Heh heh.
5. *S:* Their thoughts. Their thoughts.
6. *SLP1:* Yeah or their interpretations. And it goes along with not only drawings but words too. And sometimes after a head injury it's difficult to interpret things or you may interpret things one way and be stuck on that way and not be able to see another person's view.
7. *J:* Might even be thinking about something else anyway.
8. *SLP1:* Pardon me?
9. *J:* Might have somethin' else on our mind.
10. *SLP1:* You might have yeah and that can get in the way. But sometimes it's just difficult to be flexible and see more than one viewpoint. And that happens to people even who don't have head injuries. That you just kind of get stuck on one thought.
11. *J:* Yup.
12. *SLP1:* But interpretation of words pictures ideas is uh sometimes difficult too following an injury xx.
13. *J:* Might be tired. (Kovarsky et al., 2007, p. 59)

As the interaction progressed, SLP1 made it clear that even though normal people could have trouble properly identifying the pictures and viewpoints of others, this group was experiencing difficulties because of their brain injuries (turns #6, #10 and #12). J continued to suggest alternate explanations that were quite reasonable—individuals might misidentify artwork because they were distracted by other thoughts (turns 7 and 9), or they were simply tired (turn 13). However, it was SLP1's interpretive perspective that dominated. Throughout this session, the process of "helping" patients involved evaluating their responses to quiz questions as inadequate even when their answers were plausible, often with the explanation that their "difficulties" were due to brain injury.

In this way, the interactional substrate of therapy supported the construction of therapy participants as damaged goods. This is not a simple matter because people, in fact, do suffer from brain injuries that impair cognitive-communicative abilities and, subsequently, damage identity. However, therapeutic practices that have the potential to threaten a positive sense of self even further as a way of helping people are themselves problematic. SLPs face a daunting challenge: They must construct discourse environments to manage spoiled identities in ways that lead to a more positive sense of self. In fact, findings like these have led to the development more socially sensitive models of intervention that do more to support discourse equality and rely less on exposed repair sequences designed to highlight client incompetence (Simmons-Mackie, Elman, Holland, & Damico, 2007).

The discursive construction of disorder has not only been documented in face-to-face therapy interaction (Kovarsky & Walsh, 2011b), it has also been revealed in specific cultural practices for problematizing people through the construction of a diagnosis of disability (Foster-Galasso, 2005; Mastergeorge, 1999; Polich, 2005). Duchan (1999) compared evaluation reports focused on diagnosing disorder with progress reports directed toward detailing the successes and failures of therapy. She found that evaluation reports were far more likely to describe individuals by using negatively valenced terminology. On the other hand, progress reports cast clients in a much more positive light.

> Evaluation reports, intended to demonstrate the need for services, are thereby designed to bring out negative aspects of the client's performance. Progress reports, on the other hand, are intended to convey that an intervention program has been successful and thus needs to be continued. (Duchan, 1999, pp. 238–239)

In other words, the different clinical agendas associated with these two types of reports influenced the extent to which client performance was interpreted as a sign of competence versus incompetence. Whether in face-to-face interaction, or in professional written reports one-step removed from face-to-face encounters, communicative disorders do not exist independent of the cultural contexts in which they are constituted.

From this constructivist, discursively saturated view of ability and disability, *communicative participation* has begun to emerge as a unit of analysis for examining the relations between language, culture and communication disorder. Although this construct is not necessarily explicitly recognized by all those who have critically examined our clinical discourse practices, it does reflect their concern for the often unrecognized relationship between communicative incompetence and the discursive context in which it emerges.

Communicative Participation

Broadly defined, communicative participation refers to how individuals participate in a range of discourse activities in contextually situated ways that, in turn, reflect on the manner of their involvement in culture. Such participation may be characterized according to a series of five, interdependent aspects of communicative activity that include lifeworld participation, participant structure, participant role, participant accommodation, and participant resources (Kovarsky, Culatta, Franklin, & Theodore, 2001).

Lifeworld Participation

Humans do not only exist in the physical world in the way that an apple is housed in its skin (Buber, 1965). Instead, we build the lifeworlds we inhabit through language by imbuing events, activities, relationships, and even geographical spaces with social and cultural meaning (Basso, 1996; Stewart, 1995). Lifeworld participation reflects moments of cultural focus that reveal the importance of communication in experiences of value and disvalue. Among other things, these experiences have the potential to include or exclude in ways that impact on identity and relationships, and on an individual's sense of place, involvement or belonging in the social world.

Maxwell, Poeppelmeyer, and Polich (1999) describe hard of hearing individuals who are members and nonmembers of the Deaf community—the capital letter "D" in "Deaf" reflects cultural, as opposed to simply audiological, status. Some, though not all, nonmembers reveal feelings of having nowhere to belong in either Hearing or Deaf communities.

> *Carly:* I feel like I am caught between two different worlds and I don't fit into either one of them completely because I'm not deaf. With my hearing aids I know what it's like to be hearing. Without them, I know what it's like to be deaf. So I can be sympathetic. I know what the problems are facing deaf people, but at the same time, I'm a hearing person with my hearing aid, and so I know all the benefits or whatever that go with that … I just don't fit in with either one.

> *Casey:* I am deaf but not Deaf, Hearing but not hearing.

> *Unnamed individual:* Actually, I have never felt completely comfortable with either hearing or deaf; I always seem to be somewhere in the middle, sort of like a man without a country. (p. 133)

In contrast, there are hard of hearing who, through the use of American Sign Language in Deaf communities, are able to construct a positive sense of belonging and selfhood.

Jan: It wasn't until I went to Gallaudet that I met signing people. To me, it was like coming home. For the first time in my life, I felt like I really belonged. When I found the deaf, I found me. (p. 144)

In a different investigation, Simmons-Mackie and Damico (2001) recounted a post-treatment lifeworld transformation of Karen, a woman diagnosed with moderate Broca's aphasia and mild apraxia of speech. Reflecting on her life as a school teacher before having a stroke, Karen said "uh … uh … always, always … uh … busy, busy, busy. Teachin … teachin … always. I love it … it's me." According to her sister, "she [Karen] used to be a real fireball. I mean she never stopped, ya know … at school, at home and there were always projects, special projects at school and all."

After her stroke but before therapy began, Karen described her life and her sense of self in the following ways.

(shrugs) nothing … here (points to television) … sleep … eat … eat … eat … EAT (laughs) … Eat … and (points to newspaper) and shows (points to television) … Phone (holds hand to ear as in talking on the phone) … "uh … yes … um … uh…bye"… and eat (Karen and clinician laugh)

Useless … no money, no work … bad for (husband's name).

Me … nothing … nothing … Before a teacher … now, I don know what. What? (Simmons-Mackie & Damico, 2001, pp. 28–31)

Comments such as these and additional observations all revealed that Karen was marginalized from the social world compared to her previous level of involvement based almost exclusively on changes in her ability to communicate. Not only was her sense of place threatened, she also expressed deep concern for her identity: "Before a teacher … now, I don't know what. What?"

Intervention focused on reducing barriers to communicative engagement in a range of social activities that included volunteering in a preschool, attending a club, walking with a friend, and hosting family potluck dinners. As therapy progressed, the comments of Karen and her family revealed a qualitative shift in her involvement in the social world and her sense of self:

Karen: I work … no money (laughs) … Wonderful … babies just wonderful. Me! (pointing to self) I did it! I did it! (smiling) … Busy … maybe too busy now (laughs). Maybe teacher now, yea? (gets an old picture; points to picture) Fat … not now! Walk walk walk (smiling).

Husband: She's a different person now. She laughs a lot and I don't feel so put upon—oh, that sounds selfish but I mean, she has a life!

She's not so afraid to do things. (Simmons-Mackie & Damico, 2001, pp. 31–32)

Lifeworld expressions of value and disvalue are not only revealed in personal experience narrative vignettes like those just presented, they are also reflected in the ways that discourse participation is structured in different situations.

Participant Structure

The term "participant structure" was coined by Philips (1972) in order to expose different, culturally embedded values for when and how individuals were expected to take part in classroom interaction. Her work focused on explaining the cultural reasons why Native American children from the Warm Springs Reservation in Oregon refrained from engaging in certain classroom activities that were communicatively organized or structured for participation in particular ways; ways that called upon these students to have their individual emerging competencies evaluated publicly by a teacher in front of their peers. It was discovered that in this native community, a preference was placed on learning through silent observation, with competency to be publicly displayed only after a skill had been mastered. In other words, a primary participation structure for educating children in the classroom stood in stark contrast to how learning was organized at home. Noting similar preferences for learning among the Inuit, Eriks-Brophy and Crago (1993) observed that native Inuit teachers tended to shift classroom participation structures away from evaluating individual students and toward assessing peer groups as a whole.

The concept of participation structure also reveals itself in different kinds of clinical activities. Maxwell (1993) investigated conflict talk that occurred in a university clinic setting during a multidisciplinary team meeting staffed by faculty and by students earning their Master's degrees in speech-language pathology, audiology, and education of the deaf. The purpose of the team was to provide assessments and recommendations for children with hearing impairments. In the following exchange, the participants included a senior staff person (SSP), an educational psychologist who was a permanent clinic staff member (PS), an audiologist who served as the team's director (T1), the team speech-language pathologist (T2), and a graduate student involved in the team as part of a clinical practicum assignment (PT2). T1 was recommending that an FM hearing system be used at home with a particular child during different activities; this included dinnertime when a microphone would be passed around the table so that family members could speak into it. SSP asked T1 to indicate what situations would be appropriate for FM system use "like homework assignments, one-on-one situations, as opposed to dinner table round robin conversations." The extract begins with T1's response.

Example 4

1. *T1:*   … she she would hear better in any situation dinner table included if it were if the FM system were used (nods head)
   (T2 hand on back of neck, looking down)
2. *SSP:*   You mean pass the microphone around::nd (.) wo::::w (mimics passing around mic)
   (SSP nods, eyes roll, smiles, looks around table, puts palms to cheeks, looks down and shakes head [side to side] repeatedly with right hand on cheek)
3. *T1:*   Microphone passed around exactly
4. *PS:*   No family's going to sit for that (spoken quietly while looking at SSP)
5. *T1:*   NO family is a pretty steep po:leemic against that when you consider [a deaf man recently visiting the team] does that routinely with all of us when we go out to dinner so I don't know (volume gradually rising and talking faster) that no family's the answer cuz I can list fifteen families that do that at [two other geographical areas] so it's not impossible
   (SSP holding cheek, stares forward, signs while T1 is speaking, looks down and back at T1)
6. *PT2:*   That's out of the norm though
   (SSP swings head away from T1 toward speaking student, rictus smile)
7. *T1:*   It's not easy either
8. *PS:*   Wouldn't you agree that's out of the norm though
9. *PT2:*   (leans forward nodding rapidly)
10. *T1:*   YES! But if you want to include her in the in conversations (Maxwell, 1993, pp. 80–81)

T1 (a professional audiologist) argued that based upon his own experiences (turn 5), an FM system should be used at dinnertime even if it meant that participants had to adapt by handing a microphone around a table when they wanted to speak. SSP, PS, and PT2 all argued that the change in communicative organization precipitated by the use of an FM system went against cultural norms for how conversation should be organized at dinnertime: "you mean pass the microphone around wow," "no family's gonna sit for that," and "that's out of the norm though."

In other words, team members were disagreeing over the extent to which the participant structuring of interaction during mealtime should be altered. They seemed particularly concerned that the communicative accommodations participants were being asked to make at home would force changes in the structure of an everyday event when their goal was to include this hearing impaired child in culturally normal activities without altering them. Beyond the unstated fact that practices within a culture are not homogeneous and they are subject to change, T1 replied that if their intent was "to include her in conversation," something that would potentially enhance lifeworld participation, then an FM system was warranted. Even if an alteration in the structure of interaction was required, the FM system would allow her to take a more active role as both a speaker and a listener. As is discussed subsequently, the realization of these communicative roles can be complex.

Participant Roles

Goffman (1981) described some of the complexities associated with speaker and hearer roles for those within perceptual range of an encounter. Of course, the terms "speaker" and "hearer" are not restricted solely to spoken communication. Instead, these terms are intended to include sender and receiver roles across different modes (spoken, written, sign) of communication. Speakers can be described in terms of the positions they occupy as authors, animators and principals of the messages being conveyed. The author is responsible for the selection of the ideas being expressed, the animator is the entity that actually produces the message, and the principal is the one held to account for the position being presented. Those in the role of hearer can be described in terms of whether or not they are primary or secondary recipients of a message, or they are merely bystanders.

Simmons-Mackie, Kingston, and Schultz (2004) analyzed instances when a non-aphasic individual would speak for (or animate) a message when the actual author was a person with aphasia. In the following example, Paul (a man with aphasia) and Gail (his wife) are ordering food at a restaurant. The waitress gazes at Paul as she waits for him to place his order.

Example 5

1. *Paul:* Uh uh uh the uh hab [uh ((gazing at waitress))
2. *Gail:* [He'll have a hamburger
3. *Paul:* ((Paul shifts his gaze to Gail with a surprised look, then frowns)) (Simmons-Mackie et al., 2004, p. 116)

When Paul struggled to present his food order over the course of a conversational turn, Gail became an interpreter and produced a message that she presumed he wished to convey. Her move to animate his message constituted a "face" (or public self-image) threat because it presumed that he did not have the competence to complete his own utterance. In response, Paul interpreted Gail's effort to speak for him as "unwelcomed butting in" that only served to highlight difficulties he was seeking to overcome (Simmons-Mackie et al., 2004, p. 115).

Ascriptions of competence are, among other things, based upon the abilities of individuals to coordinate animator and author roles simultaneously. Troubles managing these roles are also evidenced in the problems faced by those with physical disabilities who rely on augmentative technologies to communicate. Although individuals with severe motor speech difficulties may have the ability to author messages, they can have tremendous difficulty animating them quickly enough to meet the socially driven time constraints associated with face-to-face interaction (Higginbotham & Wilkins, 1999). Robillard, a sociologist with amyotrophic lateral sclerosis who became paralyzed, wrote that the time consuming process of animating messages through the use of an alphabet board during a hospital stay "generated frustrations, resentments, and attributions about my intelligence [and] my motivations" (Robillard, 1994, p. 386).

In addition, even though, perceptually speaking, Robillard's hearing was not a problem, his ability to fully occupy the role of hearer (either as a primary or a secondary recipient) was compromised. He described how he was placed in the role of a bystander at his own birthday party by a well-intentioned nurse who was assigned to care for him.

> Part of my objection to having a nurse on the occasion of the party and in similar settings is that by having a nurse standing by me, caring for me, a person who cannot read my lips, I feel separated from the people in my immediate surround. The nurse is a buffer, which most people will not penetrate. I find on social occasions that having a nurse is equivalent to being assigned the role of a permanent side participant, *an overhearer*, and an uninvolved visual witness. (emphasis added; 1994, p. 103)

For Robillard, as well as others, the manner in which speaker and hearer roles are realized becomes visible as participants seek to accommodate to one another's communicative needs during interaction.

Participant Accommodation

Known as listener adaptation (Glucksberg, Krauss, & Higgins, 1975) or recipient design (Schegloff, 1979), participant accommodation refers to how messages are designed to meet the needs of listeners. It is here that the field of Conversation Analysis, with its analytic focus on the sequential relations between turns at talk (Atkinson & Heritage, 1984; Jefferson, 1995), has made a significant contribution to how meaning is constructed in interaction. Goodwin (1995) described a man with aphasia, Rob, who would only speak three words ("yes," "no," and "and"). He was able to affect communicative meaning by participating in question-answer adjacency pair sequences that operated like a guessing game.

Example 6

1. *Nurse:* English muffin?
2.   (3.4 seconds of verbal silence)
3. *Rob:*   Ye:s
4.   (.4)
5. *Nurse:* A:[nd what would you like on it.
6. *Wife:*   [Just one.
7. *Nurse:* Jelly?
8.   (1.0)
9. *Rob:*   No:
10.   (.8)
11. *Wife:* Butt[er?
12. *Nurse:*   [Butter?
13.   (0.3)
14. *Rob:*   Yes.
15.   (0.6)
16. *Nurse:* Okay. (Goodwin, 1995, p. 237)

Even though Rob was severely constrained in his use of linguistic resources (grammar and lexicon), participants were able to accommodate to this problem interactionally through a particular type of adjacency pair structuring. The first pair parts consisted of requests for information that narrowed potential response options (turns 1, 3, 11, and 12) in order to capitalize upon the few words he could produce as second pair parts (turns 3, 9, and 14). That is, questions were tailored to account for his limited verbal output in ways that took advantage of the abilities Rob did possess—like his capacity to use three words according to the pragmatic rules for turn-taking in interaction.

As this example reveals, internal linguistic faculties are not a simple, direct predictor of communicative competence because competence is something that is achieved through the give and take of situated encounters as participants accommodate to one another in order to construct meaning. It was not only the interactional work done by all parties that allowed Rob to engage in this kind of mundane, everyday lifeworld activity, but also the communicative resources brought to bear by all the participants.

Participant Resources

Individuals draw upon a variety of communicative means in order to participate in discourse. This includes spoken, written, signed, gestural (the kinetics of entire bodies in movement included), temporal, and spatial resources that function to affect communicative meaning. The following extract was taken from a meeting of the Gateway Café, a social support group for adults with traumatic brain injury. One of the participants, Dave, was diagnosed with expressive aphasia, ataxia, and flaccid dysarthria. His speech was slow and labored, and his utterances ranged from 1 to 4 words in length. Dave was preparing to play a game of Scrabble with staff members (staff1 and staff2) and was trying to establish the order for taking game turns among those players seated around a table.

Example 7

1. *Staff1:* Let's see (moving the Scrabble board) is it facing the right way? Yeah it is.
2. *Dave:* (points to Scrabble board and holds up index finger to represent the number 1, then holds up additional finger to represent the number 2)
   Twelve.
   (points to Staff2)
3. *Staff2:* Twelve?
4. *Dave:* Clockwise.
   (moves right hand clockwise in a circle to represent the directional movement of a clock)
5. *Staff2:* Oh it starts at twelve (pointing to herself with right hand).
   [That's all right.
6. *Staff1:* [You're saying like twelve and it will go around?
7. *Staff2:* We'll just start (.) it's easier.
   (Staff2 points right hand at Dave and then moves it in a clockwise direction, establishing Dave as the twelve o'clock position that will take the first turn in the Scrabble game)
8. *Staff 1:* We can do it clockwise this way.
9. *Staff2:* Yeah. (Papino, McCarthy, & Kovarsky, 2008)

In an effort to accommodate to an audience that might have difficulty understanding his speech, Dave held up one and then two fingers (turn 2) immediately prior to saying the number 12, after which he pointed to Staff2 (turn 3). When Staff2 checked her comprehension by repeating the number 12 (turn 4), he followed by saying "clockwise" while producing a gesture that was both iconic (it represented the face of a clock) and directional (referencing a clockwise direction). In a series of next turns, both staff members achieved an understanding of Dave's suggestion; that Staff2 should be the first person to take a game turn (noon on the clock) with successive game turns being assigned by rotating in a clockwise direction. Through his use of words, gestures, timing (the temporal placement of his words and gestures in interaction), and space (referencing people's positions around the table in terms of an imaginary clock), understanding was built incrementally over a series of conversational turns as all parties collaborated to construct meaning.

Although tempting to assume from a clinical point of view, positive experiences in the lifeworld are not necessarily predicated on an increased number of communicative resources being available to an individual. In another meeting of the Gateway Café, a different male participant with TBI (MP3) was coaxed by female (FS1, FS2, and FS3) and male (MS1) college student staff into telling jokes that he had presented earlier at a local nightclub. Based on previous observations when MP3 had attended the Café, he was well liked, thought to be a skillful communicator, and often treated as "the life of the party." After telling one, poorly received, off-color joke that played upon the use of "pussy" as a homonym, he then embedded another joke into an ongoing activity. The group was preparing to play a board game that required them to choose between different colored boxes.

Example 8

1. *FS3:* What color should we pick from what color box (pointing to a board game and making a circle around the board with her hand)=
2. *MP3:* =I don't care as long as it's wet and squishy it's a cool box to me. (FS3 lifts eyes, blinks, and smiles while looking at FS1) (FS1 then leans in, clenches hands into fists and hunches her back) (a female participant looks at FS1 and pulls hood of sweatshirt over her head all the way to cover her mouth as if to hide her embarrassment)
3. *FS2:* (rapidly moves eye gaze from side to side while FS1 picks up sandwich and gazes at it) [Do you want the blue?
4. *FS1:*   [Rel:::x. (leaning back in chair and gazing at MP3) (male participant with TBI smiles) ((palpable silence))
5. *MP3:* OKAY I'm sorry. (smiles)
6. *FS1:* Heh heh heh.
7. *MS1:* (smiles and opens sandwich) [Heh heh heh.
8. *FS2:* [Heh heh. (smiling) (Kovarsky, Schiemer, & Murray, 2011, p. 329)

Once again, the joke revolved around the use homonymy, except this time the word was "box." Together, the nonverbal reactions of the audience (lifting the eyes, blinking, smiling, pulling a sweatshirt over the head, rapid gaze shifts from side-to-side), FS2's attempt ignore the joke by continuing to distribute game pieces (turn 3), and FS1's aggravated command that he "relax" (turn 4) all revealed that MP3's attempted humor created offense. In fact, MP3 realized that his joke had gone awry and apologized (turn 5). For the moment, the staff appeared to accept his apology by laughing at his gaffe in turns 6, 7, and 8.

As the meeting progressed, however, MP3 continued to use sexually explicit humor even though he had been directly warned against this by FS1. Eventually, the breach in etiquette occasioned by his jokes resulted in the staff working together to turn off a running video camera and to withdraw from their interaction with him. In terms of communicative resources displayed, MP3 had strong linguistic skills, a subtle understanding of the referential meanings of words (homonomy included), and an ability to deliver material in a way that, culturally speaking, could be recognized as a joke. However, even with all this, his performance could be characterized as problematic. Although MP3's comedic routine might have been appropriate in the nightclub where it was previously used, his jokes were evaluated negatively in the Café as the staff sought to disengage and end the encounter. A few weeks later, he returned to the Café and apologized saying that "got a little out of line" and "carried away," and that he was "having too much fun" at the expense of the feelings of others.

Comparing examples 7 and 8, it was not simply the amount of resources available to each of these different participants (Dave and MP3) that led to a sense of positive lifeworld involvement. Dave, the individual who struggled to make his speech intelligible, had a more affirming communicative experience than MP3 whose engagement with others was characterized by contentiousness even though he was more facile linguistically. In other words, lifeworld experiences of value and disvalue are achieved through the use of communicative resources in particularistic encounters that come with their own expectancies for interactional etiquette.

As a whole then, communicative participation is perhaps best understood according to the complex and mutually constitutive relations that exist between the 5 layers just described—lifeworld participation, participant structure, participant roles, participant accommodation, and participant resources. For example, Robillard, the sociologist with amyotrophic lateral sclerosis, had difficulty accessing the temporal resources needed to participate in face-to-face interaction (*participant resources*). Because of this, it was hard for him and many of those he interacted with to design messages to meet their respective communicative needs (*participant accommodation*). The troubles interlocutors experienced in accommodating to one another served to highlight the problems he had occupying a number of different *participant roles*; both as a speaker capable of animating his own messages in conversational time, and as a hearer who wanted to be treated as more than a mere bystander in interactions that concerned him.

It was the temporal dimension of *participant structure* in face-to-face encounters that created the most difficulty. Robillard struggled, often unsuccessfully, to make himself known as a speaker or a listener quickly enough within the durational boundaries associated with being a ratified participant in conversation. In contrast, as revealed in his book (1994), he was more successful at engaging others through email because the organization of time for social participation was different. More specifically, there was a far greater tolerance for longer durations of silence between interactional turns at communicating during email exchanges. In many other circumstances, however, cultural expectations for the structuring of participation led to a variety of negative experiences when he sought to involve himself in the lifeworld (*lifeworld participation*). As one nurse put it when he tried to engage her in conversation through the use of an alphabet board in an intensive care unit, "I am the nurse from hell and do not try any of that communication shit with me" (Robillard, 1994, p. 338).

Concluding Remarks

Explorations into ECD have allowed us to hold an evaluative mirror up to our disciplinary face with respect to how we characterize and approach communication disorders. Incompetencies with language and communication do not exist in a social vacuum as aberrant psycholinguistic processes located primarily within the individual. Instead, incompetence is an interactional accomplishment that is made real through a variety of discursive activities. Communication disorders are actualized as culturally constituted problems with communicative participation. In fact, our helping practices themselves are cultural constructions that are steeped in evaluative judgments about how to define and diagnose ability and disability, about who shall receive services (and what sorts of interventions are appropriate), and about how to determine the success of our clinical efforts.

Recognition of the symbiotic relationship between disorders of communication, culture, and professional practice has resulted in some interesting new lines of research. Irene Walsh has been exploring how the interactional practices of speech-language pathologists can applied or adapted to working with adults with mental health problems whose difficulties are characterized by problematic communication.

> People with mental health disorders are complex in their clinical presentation and demeanor, potentially the result of long or protracted histories of "interpersonal scarring" (Watkins, 2001). While clinicians [from the field of communication disorders] may find such complexity overwhelming, we examined how engagement, self-disclosure, presencing via silence, and humor and playfulness as manifest in talk, can all function to foster positive relationships in clinical contexts. (Walsh & Kovarsky, 2011, p. 136)

Beyond potential discursive transformations wrought by working with populations traditionally the province of other professions, there is also a need to examine how the Internet may (or may not) be changing the discourse of assessment and intervention through activities like Telepractice, or even through access to Youtube.

Finally, although some discursively oriented scholarship has turned a critical eye toward current conceptions of Evidenced-Based Practice (EBP; Kovarsky, 2008), more is needed. EBP is rooted in a philosophy of logical positivism that, however well-intentioned, has only served to exacerbate the fragmentation fallacy that Damico argued against years ago. Evidence of treatment effectiveness typically rests on the selection of decontextualized fragments of communicative behavior intentionally chosen because they can be quantified for the purpose of demonstrating causality. This narrow focus on discrete bits of psycholinguistic behavior frustrates "our attempts to address the complex phenomenon of communicative discourse [by replacing it] with a superficial and modular approach to description, assessment, and remediation [that] is naïve and insufficient" (Damico, 1993, p. 93).

Grounded in an epistemology of social constructionism where language and social reality (communication disorders included) cannot be divorced from one another, concepts from ECD may help lessen the risk of aggravating the fragmentation fallacy. In particular, additional research is needed to determine if *communicative participation*, because of its analytical focus on the mutually constitutive relationship between language, culture, and communication disorder, may offer a more nuanced, contextually sensitive construct for representing the outcomes of intervention.

One thing is clear when looking across all the work that has been accomplished or envisioned since its inception: The goal of ECD is **not** to generate new knowledge that pathologizes people by characterizing them as bundles of deficits (an ominous and cynical reading of what it means to be a "speech–language pathologist"). Rather, the purpose of ECD is to illuminate how communication disorders are constructed, made relevant and managed through the culturally situated, communicative activities that bring them to life in the first place.

References

Atkinson, J. M., & Heritage, J. (1984). *Structures of social action: Studies in conversation analysis*. Cambridge, England: Cambridge University Press.

Basso, K. H. (1996). *Wisdom sits in places*. Albuquerque: University of New Mexico Press.

Buber, M. (1965). *The knowledge of man*. In M. Friedman (Ed.), M. Friedman & R. Gregor Smith (Trans.). New York, NY: Harper & Row.

Chomksy, N. (1965). *Aspects of the theory of syntax*. Cambridge, MA: M.I.T. Press.

Crago, M. B. (1990). The development of communicative competence in Inuit children: Implications for speech-language pathology. *Journal of Childhood Communication Disorders*, 13(1), 73–84.

Crago, M. B., & Eriks-Brophy, A. (1994). Cultural, conversation, and interaction: Implications for intervention. In J. F. Duchan, L. E. Hewitt, & R. M. Sonnenmeier (Eds.), *Pragmatics: From theory to practice* (pp. 43–58). Englewood Cliffs, NJ: Prentice Hall.

Damico, J. S. (1988). The lack of efficacy in language therapy: A case study. *Language, Speech, & Hearing Services in Schools, 19,* 51–66.

Damico, J. S. (1993). Establishing expertise in communicative disorders: Implications for the speech-language pathologist. *ASHA Monographs, 30,* 92–98.

Damico, J. S., & Damico, S. K. (1997). The establishment of a dominant interpretive framework in language intervention. *Language, Speech, & Hearing Services in Schools, 28*(3), 288–296.

Duchan, J. F. (1993). Issues raised by facilitated communication for theorizing and research on autism. *Journal of Speech & Hearing Research, 36,* 1108–1119.

Duchan, J. F. (1999). Reports written by speech-language pathologists: The role of agenda in constructing client competence. In D. Kovarsky, J. Duchan, & M. Maxwell (Eds.), *Constructing (in)comptence: Disabling evaluations in clinical and social interaction* (pp. 223–244). Mahwah, NJ: Erlbaum.

Duchan, J. F., Hewitt, L. E., & Sonnenmeier, R. M. (1994). *Pragmatics: From theory to practice.* Englewood Cliffs, NJ: Prentice Hall.

Duchan, J. F., Maxwell, M., & Kovarsky, D. (1999). Evaluating competence in the course of everyday interaction. In D. Kovarsky, J. Duchan, & M. Maxwell (Eds.), *Constructing (in) competence: Disabling evaluations in clinical and social interaction* (pp. 3–28). Mahwah, NJ: Erlbaum.

Duranti, A. (1997). *Linguistic anthropology.* Cambridge, England: Cambridge University Press.

Eriks-Brophy, A., & Crago, M. B. (1993). Inuit efforts to maintain face: Elements from classroom discourse with Inuit children. *ASHA Mongraphs, 30,* 10–16.

Foster-Galasso, M. (2005). Diagnosis as an aid and a curse in dealing with others. In J. Felson Duchan & D. Kovarsky (Eds.), *Diagnosis as cultural practice* (pp. 17–32). Berlin, Germany: Mouton de Gruyter.

Gergen, K. (1994). *Realities and relationships: Soundings in social construction.* Cambridge, MA: Harvard University Press.

Glucksberg, S., Krauss, R., & Higgens, E. T. (1975). The development of referential communication skills. In F. Horowitz (Ed.), *Review of child development research, Vol. 4* (pp. 305–345). Chicago, IL: Chicago University Press.

Goffman, E. (1981). *Forms of talk.* Philadelphia: University of Pennsylvania Press.

Goodwin, C. (1995). Co-constructing meaning in conversations with an aphasic man. *Research on Language & Social Interaction, 28*(3), 233–260.

Gumperz, J. J. (1972). Introduction. In J. J. Gumperz & D. Hymes, *Directions in sociolinguistics: The ethnography of communication* (pp. 1–25). New York, NY: Holt, Rinehart & Winston.

Gumperz, J. J., & Hymes, D. (1972). *Directions in sociolinguistics: The ethnography of communication.* New York, NY: Holt, Rinehart & Winston.

Higginbotham, J., & Wilkins, D. P. (1999). Slipping through the timestream: Social issues of time and timing in augmented interactions. In D. Kovarsky, J. Duchan, & M. Maxwell (Eds.), *Constructing (incompetence): Disabling evaluations in clinical and social interaction* (pp. 49–82). Mahwah, NJ: Erlbaum.

Hymes, D. (1964). Toward ethnographies of communication: The analysis of communicative events. *American Anthropologist, 66*(6), 1–34.

Hymes, D. (1972a). Models of interaction in language and social life. In J. J. Gumperz & D. Hymes (Eds.), *Directions in sociolinguistics: The ethnography of communication* (pp. 35–71). New York, NY: Holt, Rinehart & Winston.

Hymes, D. (1972b). On communicative competence. In J. Pride & J. Holmes (Eds.), *Socioinguistics* (pp. 269–293). Baltimore, MD: Penguin.

Hymes, D. (1987). Tonkawa poetics: John Rush Buffalo's "Coyote and Eagle's Daughter." In J. Sherzer & A. Woodbury (Eds.), *Native American discourse: Poetics and rhetoric.* Cambridge, England: Cambridge University Press.

Jefferson, G. (Ed.). (1995). *Lectures on conversation: Harvey Sacks*. Oxford, England: Blackwell.

Jorgenson Winkler, C. (1999). How opposing perceptions of communication competence were constructed by Taiwanese graduate students. In D. Kovarsky, J. Duchan, & M. Maxwell (Eds.), *Constructing (in)competence: Disabling evaluations in clinical and social interaction* (pp. 83–110). Mahwah, NJ: Erlbaum.

Kovarsky, D. (1990). Discourse markers in adult-controlled therapy. *Journal of Childhood Communication Disorders, 13*(1), 29–42.

Kovarsky, D. (2008). Representing voices from the life-world in evidence-based practice. *International Journal of Language & Communication Disorders, 43*(S1), 47–57.

Kovarsky, D., & Crago, M. (1990). Toward the ethnography of communication disorders. *National Student Speech Language Hearing Association Journal, 18*, 44–55.

Kovarsky, D., Culatta, B., Franklin, A., & Theodore, G. (2001). "Communicative participation" as a way of facilitating and ascertaining communicative outcomes. *Topics in Language Disorders, 22*(1), 1–20.

Kovarsky, D., Curran, M., & Zobel Nichols, N. (2009). Laughter and communicative engagement in interaction. *Seminars in Speech & Language, 30*(1), 27–36.

Kovarsky, D., Damico, J. S., Maxwell, M., Panagos, J., Prelock, P., & Keyser, H. (1988, November). The ethnography of communication and its contribution to the study of communication disorders. Seminar presented at the American Speech-Language-Hearing Association Convention. Boston, MA.

Kovarsky, D., & Duchan, J. (1997). The interactional dimensions of language therapy. *Language, Speech, & Hearing Services in Schools, 28*(3), 297–307.

Kovarsky, D., & Maxwell, M. (1992). Ethnography and the clinical setting. *Topics in Language Disorders, 12*(3), 76–84.

Kovarsky, D., Schiemer, C., & Murray, A. (2011). Humor, rapport and uncomfortable moments in interactions with adults with traumatic brain injury. *Topics in Language Disorders, 31*(4), 325–335.

Kovarsky, D., Shaw, A., & Adingono-Smith, M. (2007). The construction of identity during group therapy among adults with traumatic brain injury. *Communication & Medicine, 4*(1), 53–66.

Kovarsky, D., & Walsh, I. P. (2011a). The discursive construction of language disorders. In C. N. Candlin & J. Crichton (Eds.), *Discourses of deficit* (pp. 195–214). New York, NY: Palgrave MacMillan.

Kovarsky, D., & Walsh, I.P. (2011b). Uncomfortable moments in speech-language therapy discourse. In C. N. Candlin & S. Sarangi (Eds.), *Handbook of communication in organisations and professions* (pp. 193–214). Berlin, Germany: De Gruyter Mouton.

Mastergeorge, A. M. (1999). Revelations of family perceptions of diagnosis and disorder through metaphor. In D. Kovarsky, J. Duchan, & M. Maxwell (Eds.), *Constructing (in)competence: Disabling evaluations in clinical and social interaction* (pp. 245–256). Mahwah, NJ: Erlbaum.

Maxwell, M. (1993). Conflict talk in a professional meeting. *ASHA Monographs, 30*, 68–91.

Maxwell, M., Poeppelmeyer, D., & Polich, L. (1999). Deaf members and nonmembers: The creation of culture through communication practices. In D. Kovarsky, J. Duchan, & M. Maxwell (Eds.), *Constructing (in)competence: Disabling evaluations in clinical and social interactions* (pp. 125–148). Mahwah, NJ: Erlbaum.

Merritt, M. (1980). On the use of OK in service encounters. In R. W. Shuy & A. Shunkal (Eds.), *Language use and the uses of language* (pp. 162–172). Washington, DC: Georgetown University Press.

Ochs, E. (1973). A sliding sense of obligatoriness: The poly-structure of Malagasy oratory. *Language in Society, 2*, 225–243.

Panagos, J. M. (1996). Speech therapy discourse: The input to learning. In M. D. Smith & J. S. Damico (Eds.), *Childhood language disorders* (pp. 41–63). New York, NY: Thieme Medical Publishers.

Papino, S., McCarthy, M., & Kovarsky, D. (2008, November). *The narrative of generalization and moments of dialogic interaction in the Gateway Café*. Paper presented at the American Speech-Language-Hearing Association Convention. Chicago, IL.

Philips, S. (1972). Participant structures and communicative competence: Warm Springs children in community and classroom. In C. B. Cazden, V. P. John, & D. Hymes (Eds.), *Functions of language in the classroom* (pp. 370–394). New York, NY: Teachers College Press.

Polich, L. (2005). The diagnosis of deafness in Nicaragua. In J. Felson Duchan & D. Kovarsky (Eds.), *Diagnosis as cultural practice* (pp. 223–240). Berlin, Germany: Mouton de Gruyter.

Reddy, M. J. (1979). The conduit metaphor—a case of frame conflict in our language about language. In A. Ortony (Ed.), *Metaphor and thought* (pp. 284–297). Cambridge, England: Cambridge University Press.

Ripich, D. N., & Panagos, J. M. (1985). Accessing children's knowledge of the sociolinguistic rules for speech therapy lessons. *Journal of Speech & Hearing Disorders, 50*, 335–346.

Robillard, A. B. (1994). *Meaning of a disability: The lived experience of paralysis*. Philadelphia, PA: Temple University Press.

Schegloff, E. A. (1979). Identification and recognition in telephone conversation openings. In G. Psathas (Ed.), *Everyday language: Studies in ethnomethodology* (pp. 23–78). New York, NY: Irvington.

Sherzer, J. (1977). The ethnography of speaking: A critical appraisal. In M. Saville-Troike (Ed.), Linguistics and anthropology. *Georgetown University roundtable on languages and linguistics* (pp. 43–57). Washington, DC: Georgetown University Press.

Sherzer, J. (1987). A discourse-centered approach to language and culture. *American Anthropologist, 89*, 295–309.

Simmons-Mackie, N., & Damico, J. S. (1999). Social role negotiation in aphasia therapy: Competence, incompetence, and conflict. In D. Kovarsky, J. F. Duchan, & M. Maxwell (Eds.), *Constructing (in)competence: Disabling evaluations in clinical and social interaction* (pp. 313–342). Mahwah, NJ: Erlbaum.

Simmons-Mackie, N., & Damico, J. S. (2001). Intervention outcomes: A clinical application of qualitative methods. *Topics in Language Disorders, 22*(1), 21–36.

Simmons-Mackie, N., & Damico, J. S. (2009). Engagement in group therapy for aphasia. *Seminars in Speech & Language, 30*(1), 18–26.

Simmons-Mackie, N., Elman, R. J., Holland, A. L., & Damico, J. S. (2007). Management of discourse in group therapy for aphasia. *Topics in Language Disorders, 27*(19), 5–23.

Simmons-Mackie, N., Kingston, D., & Schultz, M. (2004). "Speaking for another": The management of participant frames in aphasia. *American Journal of Speech-Language Pathology, 13*, 114–127.

Simmons-Mackie, N., & Shultz, M. (2003). The role of humor in aphasia therapy. *Aphasia, 17*(8), 751–766.

Stewart, J. (1995). *Language as articulate contact*. Albany: State University of New York Press.

Van Kleeck, A., & Richardson, A. (1986). What's in an error? Using children's responses as language teaching opportunities. *Journal of the National Student Speech-Language-Hearing Association, 14*, 25–50.

Walsh, I. P. (2007). Small talk as "big talk" in clinical discourse: Appreciating the value of conversation in SLP clinical interactions. *Topics in Language Disorders, 27*(1), 24–36.

Walsh, I. P., & Kovarsky, D. (2011). Establishing relationships in speech-langauge therapy when working alongside people with mental health disorders. In R. J. Fourie (Ed.), *Therapeutic processes for communication disorders* (pp. 123–138). New York, NY: Psychology Press.

Walsh, I. P., Leahy, M., & Litt, M. (2009). "Cajoling" as a means of engagement in the dysphagia clinic. *Seminars in Speech & Language, 30*(1), 37–47.

Watkins, P. (2001). *Mental health nursing: The art of compassionate care*. Oxford, England: Butterworth Heinemann.

5
Conversation Analysis

RAY WILKINSON

Introduction

There is now a large, and rapidly growing, body of work which uses Conversation Analysis (CA) to examine a range of communication disorders and difficulties. Collections of papers can be found, for example, in Goodwin (2003) on aphasia, Mates, Mikesell, and Smith (2010) on fronto-temporal dementia, and Egbert and Depperman (2012) on hearing impairments. Conversation Analysis has been used not only as a research method for analyzing communication disorders; in the field of acquired disorders, in particular aphasiology, it has also been central to the development of novel forms of planning, implementing and evaluating intervention which aims to improve conversations involving a person with a communication disorder (PWCD) (see Wilkinson & Wielaert (2012) for an overview of such work within aphasiology). Clinical resource packs such as Supporting Partners of People with Aphasia in Relationships and Conversation (SPPARC; Lock, Wilkinson, & Bryan, 2001) have also facilitated the use of this approach by clinicians in the assessment and treatment of PWCDs in everyday health care settings.

One of the reasons that CA has proven to be an attractive method for researchers and clinicians within the field of communication disorders is that its use has allowed analysis (and intervention) to be focused directly on naturally occurring conversations between PWCDs and their significant others within everyday life. Conversation is the main site of spoken language use and interpersonal communication in daily life and, ipso facto, it will be important to know how a communication disorder presents there. Conversation is also the place where the impairments associated with particular communication disorders are likely to be most pervasively evident and disruptive (Goodwin, 1995) and where the amelioration of those impairments and their functional consequences should ultimately be evident if treatment is to be judged as functionally efficacious (Wilkinson, 2010).

CA is primarily a qualitative approach. Overviews of the field of CA with a focus on what has been found about particular communication disorders using this approach can be found in Wilkinson (2008) and Antaki and Wilkinson (2013). In this chapter, the focus will be on the qualitative methodology of CA and the application of this methodology within communication disorder research.

What Is Conversation Analysis?

Conversation Analysis is an approach used to investigate the organization of social interaction, particularly those forms of social interaction which involve talk (Schegloff, 2007). These investigations can focus on various forms of talk-in-interaction, not only the type of informal talk between friends, family members or colleagues which constitutes conversation, but, in principle, any form of interaction between two or more people that involves some form of verbal component. This can include forms of institutional interaction (Heritage, 2004) where one or more of the participants can be seen to be acting to accomplish a work-related activity. In the realm of communication disorders, for example, investigations have drawn on CA to analyze the nature of the social interactions between clinicians and their clients, including the doing of therapy (e.g., Simmons-Mackie, Damico, & Damico, 1999) and the carrying out of assessment activities, such as picture naming testing (Muskett, Body, & Perkins, 2012). On the whole, however, there has been more of a focus on using CA to investigate how communication disorders impact on everyday conversations between the PWCD and his or her everyday conversation partners (such as family members or friends), how the participants within the conversation can be seen to deal with the limitations imposed by the communication disorder, and how intervention can improve the nature of the conversations involving the PWCD.

Background to CA and Its Application within the Field of Communication Disorders

The influences on the field of CA are manifold (see Schegloff, 1992) but are predominantly rooted within sociology and in the work of two sociologists in particular, Erving Goffman and Harold Garfinkel. Among other things, Goffman influenced CA in terms of the notion that social interaction constitutes a distinct Interaction Order (Goffman, 1983), a domain that can be studied in its own right and not simply as a site where other psychological, linguistic or sociological phenomena become available for analysis. From Garfinkel, and his work in the form of sociology he termed "ethnomethodology" (Garfinkel, 1967), CA developed the notion that the appropriate target of investigation was the participants' own practices and procedures—their "ethnomethods"—through which they produce and recognize social actions and build up intelligible courses of meaningful action and activity (Heritage, 2004).

These influences are evident in the application of CA to communication disorder research and practice. For example, within this field, CA can be seen to constitute a distinct, interaction-focused approach (Wilkinson, 2010) which, with its focus on aspects of talk-in-interaction such as turns, sequences, topic and repair, differs from other approaches, such as those focused on, for example, impairment, communication or psychosocial aspects of the communication disorder. While social interaction can constitute a site, and a form of data, where aspects of impairment, communication and psychosocial functioning (and the inter-relationships between them) can be observed and analyzed, a CA analysis can capture distinct interactional features of how the communication disorder impacts on everyday functioning and how it is dealt with.

Another way in which such influences are evident is in the fact that CA investigations of communication disorders focus primarily on the participants' own behaviors and how they respond to each other's behavior, rather than on the researcher's/analyst's judgments of that behavior. Such a stance constitutes a radical break from traditional approaches within the field of communication disorders, where it is the clinician/researcher (often through the use of published assessment tools) who is in the position of making judgments as to whether a certain communicative performance is adequate, intelligible, appropriate, and so forth. For example, a CA approach to the investigation of whether a communication disorder is creating difficulties within conversations typically focuses on the participants' own treatment of some aspect of the talk as troublesome, often through the analysis of their repair activity. The analysis of repair within typical conversation (e.g., Schegloff, Jefferson, & Sacks, 1977; Schegloff, 2000) has highlighted the practices through which participants in conversation treat something as a trouble source (i.e., the proximate cause and target of the repair) by initiating repair on it. It was noted in those analyses that trouble sources often doubly dissociate from errors: when errors occur they may not be treated as trouble sources (in other words, they do not have repair initiated on them) and many trouble sources turn out not to be errors in the usual, normative, sense of that term, but rather might be, for example, reformulations of the utterance underway. Similarly, in conversations involving a PWCD, it is the trouble sources that are particularly of interest from a conversation analytic perspective since these highlight what the participants themselves are treating as problematic and are attempting to resolve. While there may be many speech or language errors in the PWCD's talk, many of these may not be treated as trouble sources. On the other hand, what may be treated as a trouble source may not be an error. An example of the latter phenomenon, examined by Bloch and Wilkinson (2004), is the production of electronic speech produced by augmentative and alternative communication (AAC) devices such as Voice Output Communication Aids (VOCAs) used by people with dysarthria. While this electronic speech is regularly intelligible and correctly produced (in terms of, for example, pro-nunciation and grammar), it is regularly a trouble source for recipients, in that they can be seen to initiate repair on it in the form of other-initiation of repair (Schegloff, 2000) such as "pardon?" or a guess at what has been produced. One reason for this regular lack of understandability of VOCA-produced speech, despite the intelligibility of the individual words, is that the delay in produc-ing it may mean that the recipient cannot understand which preceding utter-ances the VOCA-produced utterance was meant to be heard as being linked to or responding to (Bloch & Wilkinson, 2004).

As such, the issue of the understandability of an utterance within interac-tion becomes for the analyst, such as the clinician or researcher, an issue not so much of external judgment (by the analyst him/herself or through the use of raters) but of empirical investigation of the participants' behavior to see what *they* treat as understandable or not. Such a shift has a number of posi-tive features. One is that there is strong ecological validity in taking seriously the participants' own lifeworld and examining a phenomenon such as under-standability, or communicative adequacy, from the participants' own per-spective as an issue which has to be addressed and dealt with in interaction. A second positive feature, linked to the first, is that such an approach side-steps the potential subjectivity of an analyst external to the interaction decid-ing what he or she finds difficult to understand within that interaction and then extrapolating that as a general feature of that PWCD's communicative adequacy. Third, this approach, with its focus on the empirical data-driven examination of participants' behavior, facilitates new discoveries, including those which the analyst might not have been expecting or have chosen to investigate. The Bloch and Wilkinson (2004) findings about VOCA-produced speech regularly being intelligible but not understandable perhaps constitute an example of this.

The practice of examining participants' own treatment of an utterance as problematic extends beyond the issue of understandability to that of appro-priacy. While the notion of appropriacy is perhaps most focused on in the case of communication disorders which have a cognitive element, such as dementia, traumatic brain injury (TBI) or autism, it can be used within the analysis of a range of communication disorders (see e.g., Penn, 1985). There is, however, a considerable risk of subjectivity in an external analyst's judg-ing what constitutes appropriate verbal or non-verbal behavior within others' interactions (Lesser & Milroy, 1993). As with issues of understandability, CA investigations focus on participants' own treatment of something as inappro-priate, and this can bypass the issue of analyst subjectivity. For example, in Denman and Wilkinson's (2011) study of a man with TBI touching his female carer, it was evident that on occasion the carer treated the touching as inap-propriate. This was seen through her responses to the touching in the form of verbal reminders of codes of appropriate behavior, as well as her non-verbal behaviors such as tapping his touching hand or withdrawing her own hand when it was being touched.

This focus on participants' own behavior as a means of examining difficulties in interaction is not the only approach which might be useful to examine these phenomena, and it does have its limitations. For example, participants may for a number of reasons choose not to treat something as problematic for them even when it is, and, as such, their external behavior cannot be assumed to be an accurate reflection of internal thoughts or feelings in these interactions. However, for reasons such as those outlined above, this CA focus on participant behavior can be an extremely useful methodological resource in examining the impact of a communication disorder within interaction. It can also be useful in planning intervention, where patterns of repair or displays of negative emotions (such as anger, embarrassment or frustration) can provide the clinician with indications of what behaviors are being treated as problematic and of where further investigations may be useful as a precursor to possible intervention targeting these behaviors (Lock et al., 2001).

The Methodology of Conversation Analysis and Its Application within the Field of Communication Disorders

CA's methodology can be broken down into three stages. These stages—data collection, data transcription, and data analysis—will be presented here in order.

Data Collection

In conversation analytic work generally, including that applied to speakers with a communication disorder, there is a focus on naturally occurring interactional data, that is, on working on social interactions which would have been occurring even if the analyst was not recording them. The aim here is to be able to base analysis on the type of behaviors that the participants would be displaying in daily life generally, rather than on behaviors which may be being elicited or displayed (either consciously or unconsciously) for the recording. While it is recognized that participants will be aware of the recording process, and that this may influence them to some degree (e,g., in avoiding some personal or delicate topics), there are ways of minimizing this influence. These include the recorder informing the participants that what is of interest is the participants' natural behavior, and not, for instance, the non-communication disordered participant eliciting talk in various ways in order to highlight to the analyst what the PWCD can or cannot do. It also includes getting the participants used to the recording process, for example, by recording them over a period of time, and perhaps by training them to use the recording equipment and leaving it with them—often for a week or two—for them to record themselves.

Social interactions can be either audio-recorded or video-recorded. Typically in CA work, the aim is to have available for analysis the resources that were drawn on by the participants in producing the recorded interaction. In other words, audio-recording is sufficient for telephone calls, since in this form of interaction, it is the participants' talk alone, and not their non-vocal resources such as eye gaze or gesture, which is the resource used by each to produce and understand the interaction. In face-to-face interactions, on the other hand, video-recording is typically used, since it allows the relevant non-vocal behavior to be captured and analyzed. Most CA work applied to communication disorder interactions has made use of video-recordings. First, this is because most of the recordings made have been of co-present interactions rather than phone calls (although there are exceptions, such as Rendle-Short's (2002/3) analysis of a girl with Asperger's syndrome making a phone call to her friend). Second, it is often the case that the non-vocal resources, such as gesture, writing, and the use of augmentative and alternative communication (AAC) devices, take on an added salience in the interactions of PWCDs, where they can be used to compensate in some manner for limitations in verbal communication. The use of video-recordings allows for the capture and subsequent analysis of these resources in terms of how they are used within interaction.

The CA approach to collecting data involving a PWCD can be viewed as a form of observational data collection (where the participants are observed engaging in their everyday interactions) and contrasted to testing and report forms of data collection. Testing includes naming tasks (usually eliciting nouns or verbs by presenting pictures of objects or actions), picture description tasks (to elicit one or more sentences), and narrative tasks (where a story, procedure—such as how to make a cup of tea—or personal narrative—such as how the person became ill—is elicited). Data can also be elicited by asking the PWCD to read aloud, repeat after the tester, or to engage in role play where he or she is requested to communicate as they would in a particular, imagined situation. Report data can be collected by means of formal or informal interviews or questionnaires through which aspects of the PWCD's life (such as their communication abilities and difficulties) can be reported to the data collector, either by the PWCD, or by someone in the PWCD's environment.

Each of these forms of data collection will have consequences for the data that are collected and what can be reasonably inferred from those data. Each also has limitations. In observational studies of recorded interaction such as those used within CA, for instance, there is always the possibility that certain aspects of the way in which that communication disorder impacts on daily life will happen not to be captured on the particular recording or recordings analyzed. Such possibilities can, however, be lessened through, for example, recording a reasonable sample of interaction, perhaps on different days and with different conversation partners. A strength of testing approaches is that, unlike observational approaches, they provide a high level of control over what aspects of communication are collected (for instance, particular nouns, speech sounds, sentence structures, speech acts etc.). There are, however, serious questions concerning whether the data elicited provides a reasonable representation of how the PWCD presents in naturally occurring interactions outside of the testing situation. The tasks through which data is elicited, such as naming tests, are themselves forms of talk-in-interaction (Muskett et al., 2012), albeit ones which differ from conversation in significant and systematic ways (Heeschen & Schegloff, 2003). As such, it is perhaps not surprising that certain speakers with aphasia, for example, have been shown to present with systematically different features of grammatical structure when compared (a) in testing and (b) talking interactively with another speaker (Beeke, Wilkinson, & Maxim, 2003; Wilkinson, 1995). Report methods too have their limitations, in particular when the aim is to find out about participants' conduct at the level of particular aspects of everyday interactional behavior. Much of this behavior, in the form of repairs, overlaps, silences and many other interactional phenomena occurring second-to-second within conversation, cannot be reported upon by the participants themselves since it is not available to conscious awareness and constitutes too much detail to be monitored, remembered and reported on by an informant (cf. Heritage, 1984).

As such, in order to investigate interactional functioning at any meaningful level of detail, it is necessary to observe naturally occurring interactional data itself. For this purpose, neither test data nor reports about everyday interactions will act as adequate substitutes. Recordings of naturally occurring interactions also have the advantage of being able to be replayed numerous times in order to closely examine particular phenomena, and provide for the possibility of new phenomena which would never have occurred to the analyst to test for or search for.

It is also the case that if it is the PWCD's conversations with family, friends or other everyday conversation partners that are of interest, it cannot be assumed that how the PWCD presents in institutional interaction (e.g., talking to a speech and language pathologist) will necessarily provide a valid representation of those everyday conversations. There are a number of reasons for this, including the fact that institutional interactions typically differ in systematic ways from non-institutional conversation (Heritage, 2004), and that the particular style of the everyday conversation partners (e.g., spouse, best friend etc.), based on their relationship and shared history with the PWCD, is likely to have a significant impact on the conversation in ways which will differ from that of the institutional participant, however "informal" or "friendly" that participant attempts to be.

Finally, it can be noted that different approaches to data collection can be used in combination. For example, certain CA-influenced assessment tools such as the Conversation Analysis Profile for People with Cognitive Impairments (CAPPCI; Whitworth, Perkins, & Lesser, 1997) allow the analyst to use naturally occurring interactions of the PWCD and his or her conversation partners, and to interview one or more of the participants about their conversational behavior. Combinations such as this may provide complementary information, with the recording capturing the participants' interactional behaviors and the interview capturing more general ethnographic knowledge about the participants, and in particular about the PWCD. This can include, for instance, how the PWCD's conversational behaviors and style compare to before the onset of the disorder (in the case of acquired disorders), who the PWCD talks to on a regular basis and what types of topics are discussed, or what the participants feel are the main problems for them. Such information can obviously be of use when planning and evaluating intervention.

Data Transcription

Conversation analytic studies focus not only on what people say but how they say it. They also focus on the relationship between one speaker's talk and the talk of the other speaker(s) in the interaction. In addition, despite the terms "conversation analysis" and "talk-in-interaction," which might suggest an exclusive focus on verbal talk, CA is deeply interested in non-vocal aspects of interaction, such as eye gaze, gesture and body movement, as well as how people engage with the material world around them. This is a huge area of activities, which can range from doctors writing a prescription while talking to a patient, to airline pilots dealing with the control panel in the cockpit while talking to air traffic controllers (for a selection of such work see, e.g., Streeck, Goodwin, & LeBaron, 2011).

The CA transcription system and set of symbols, originally developed by Gail Jefferson, has evolved over time to capture what are seen to be the most relevant features of the phenomena on the recordings which CA practitioners make. All transcription systems are to some extent selective, focusing in on the issues which are of particular relevance for the analyst of that particular discipline. The CA system aims for relatively easy readability while attempting to capture the details of interactional behaviors which are relevant to the analysis. It does not, on the whole, focus on how something was said to the degree that can be captured by a close phonetic analysis. At the same time, however, CA transcription can incorporate elements of phonetic transcription (see e.g., Couper-Kuhlen, & Selting, 1996), and International Phonetic Alphabet (IPA) symbols can be used within CA transcriptions of communication disorder data as relevant.

For the reader approaching a CA transcript for the first time, or for someone attempting to produce one for the first time, one notable feature is the fact that CA transcripts aim to represent all the verbal output of speakers. So features of talk which are likely to be left out of most other transcription systems (including transcription systems in communication disorder research), such as repetitions, self-repairs, and hesitation markers such as "uhm," are included. This practice is linked to the CA notion that in principle any feature of talk may be being produced to achieve an interactional function, even those aspects of talk which do not appear intuitively obvious candidates for such a role. Almost 50 years of CA research has shown such a methodological stance to be amply justified, since many such features have been shown to be not simply performance errors or psycholinguistic detritus but rather, practices which are produced in systematic ways and understood by recipients to be doing specific interactional work. One such example is Goodwin's (1980) work on the use of self-repairs in the form of restarts of sentences (where a sentence is started, aborted before completion and another is then produced). Such restarts, while from a psycholinguistic perspective could be judged simply as an error or false start, are shown by Goodwin to be performing a particular interactional function, which is to solicit gaze from a recipient who has not been gazing at the speaker as the first attempt at a sentence was produced. That recipients indeed hear them this way is evident in the fact that in response to these sentence restarts they systematically bring their gaze to the speaker (Goodwin, 1980). Such a phenomenon is unlikely to have been discovered if these restarts were judged a priori as irrelevant and the transcription of that data tidied up by leaving them out. Goodwin's finding is also a good example of a phenomenon which all competent members of a culture orient to or, in other words, are aware of at some level and do themselves both as speakers and hearers, but are probably not consciously aware that they do. Such practices, which occur below the level of conscious awareness, are manifold in interaction; transcribing all aspects of verbal behavior allows such practices to be discovered and systematically analyzed.

CA work has highlighted the importance of sequential and temporal features of talk-in-interaction. Participants in interaction are highly sensitive to where some element of talk is placed in relation to what has preceded it, and consider talk in terms of "why that now?" (Schegloff & Sacks, 1973) to make sense of what that element of talk may be doing by being produced at that particular point within the interaction. For example, following a question, what is produced next by another speaker will be examined in the first instance as a potential answer to that question, since the question has made an answer sequentially relevant and expected (Schegloff, 2007). The timing of when elements of talk are produced is also closed monitored by participants. Gaps and overlaps between turns-at-talk tend to be minimized in conversation (Sacks, Schegloff, & Jefferson, 1974) and pauses of more than a second within turns are relatively rare and are noticeable to participants (Jefferson, 1989). The CA transcription system is designed to capture many of these sequential/ temporal features. Silences within and between turns are closely timed to a tenth of a second, and the beginning and end of the overlap of speakers' talk, as well as the co-occurrence of talk and non-vocal activity, are represented.

This close focus on sequential and temporal features of interaction has proven useful in communication disorder research for uncovering some of the ways in which the disorder impacts on everyday interactions. Two brief examples will be mentioned here. Long silences within turns have been shown to lead to people with aphasia losing their turns (Perkins, 1995). Second, in the case of Parkinson's Disease, it has been shown how these speakers are particularly vulnerable to being overlapped by others, as well as what the negative consequences of these overlaps can be for these speakers' participation within conversation (Griffiths, Barnes, Britten, & Wilkinson, 2012). In general, CA transcription has provided a means of capturing and representing how interactional contributions are produced by PWCD in real time, including how long such a contribution might take (with silences, for example, included) and what the temporal links are between the talk of the PWCD and the other participant(s) in the interaction.

In CA work, the analysis is typically carried out by making use of both the recording and the transcript together. In other words, the transcript does not substitute for the recording or remove the need to return to the recording. Rather, by using the transcript alongside the recording, it is expected that the analyst will notice more of the features present in the data, and perhaps particularly *patterns* of features present in the data, than would be possible by only listening to/viewing the recording alone. One reason for this is that since there can be so much happening in even a brief section of recording, it can be difficult for the analyst to notice or remember the interactional phenomena present without the aid of a transcription.

In communication disorder research and (perhaps particularly) clinical practice, the time involved in transcription can be perceived as a negative feature of this approach. If time is limited there can still be ways to bypass doing the type of full and detailed transcription which is used in CA research papers. Clinical resource packs such as SPPARC (Lock et al., 2001), for instance, provide a set of categories of relevant interactional behaviors which can be used by the clinician when examining recordings of aphasic conversation in order to plan intervention or evaluate that intervention. The use of these categories allows the clinician to notice within the recording relevant behaviors and patterns of behaviors without doing an in-depth transcription of the data. At the same time, however, it would appear to be the case that producing a transcription of reasonable standard of some of the data will provide the opportunity for noticing more of the relevant features of the data, and this in turn is likely to feed into a more useful and valid analysis and/or intervention plan.

Data Analysis

Much CA work is focused on explicating the practices that participants use as part of producing meaningful and coherent actions and sequences of action within talk-in-interaction. Actions include, for example, requesting, offering, complaining, informing, giving advice, and many others. Many of these actions typically function as part of sequences of action (Schegloff, 2007). Requests and offers, for example, each make relevant from another participant either an acceptance or a declining of the request or offer. The practices used by participants in talk-in-interaction are often grouped together within CA work into organizations of practice (Schegloff, 2007). These include turn organization and turn-taking organization (involving how turns-at-talk are constructed element-by-element and how these turns are allocated), sequence organization (involving how a turn is formed to be heard as coherently linked to a prior turn), repair organization (involving how trouble in speaking, hearing or understanding is highlighted and dealt with) and overall structural organization (involving how placement of an utterance at a particular place in the interaction informs how that utterance is constructed and understood).

These findings concerning how typical interaction is constructed and understood by participants can be drawn upon through comparative analysis to uncover the impact a particular communication disorder has on speakers. The results of these investigations can be built up speaker by speaker to start to uncover what effects a particular communication disorder, say aphasia or stammering, tends to have generally on affected speakers (and, as a knock-on effect, on their recipients) in interaction. One difference from other forms of communication disorder research and practice is that CA analysis tends to focus on all participants. While the PWCD may be of focal interest, the way in which other participants may talk—for example, by adapting the way they talk—is also focused upon.

Different communication disorders will have different recurring features which give the conversations involving people with this particular form of communication disorder a particular fingerprint (cf. Drew & Heritage, 1992). Some findings, for example, have highlighted the types of actions which are produced in these conversations and how they are distinctive in particular ways compared to typical (non-communication disordered) conversation. In aphasic conversation, for example, it has been shown that some conversation partners of people with aphasia regularly produce pedagogic behavior. This can take forms such as producing known-answer questions (Schegloff, 2007) to the person with aphasia, where the conversation partner asks questions to which she or he already knows the answer. These pedagogic behaviors are distinctive in that they are not commonly used in typical conversation, but rather are more commonly found in contexts such as testing or teaching environments (Schegloff, 2007). This type of action can be deployed for a number of reasons, including, for instance, because the conversation partner may feel that part of their role is to educate the PWCD or give them practice at producing a particular word or other verbal element (such as a speech sound or grammatical structure). In interactions involving speakers with dysarthria, a distinctive feature is the regular production of other-initiations of repair by the conversation partner. In these interactions, this action is regularly used to display that the conversation partner is having some difficulty in understanding the person with dysarthria (Bloch & Wilkinson, 2004, 2009).

While CA is primarily a qualitative approach, the judicious use of quantification may be employed for comparative purposes (Heritage, 2004), such as comparing conversations pre- and post-intervention. It is in the field of aphasia where intervention based on CA analyses has been developed and primarily carried out and where methods of evaluating possible change in conversation post-intervention have been deployed. Some of these studies have used quantification as well as qualitative analyses to evaluate change (e.g., Booth & Perkins, 1999; Wilkinson, Bryan, Lock, & Sage, 2010). The use of quantification for comparative purposes is likely to continue to be developed, both in CA more generally (Heritage, 2004), and in CA-inspired work in the field of communication disorders.

Conclusion

In this chapter, the application of Conversation Analysis within the field of communication disorders has been discussed, with a particular focus on its qualitative methodology in terms of data collection, data transcription and data analysis. The use of CA within this field is (with a few exceptions) relatively recent, with work starting to be systematically carried out by a number of researchers from around the mid-1990s. Aphasia was one of the earliest communication disorders to be investigated in this way and is still a focus of much analytic work. In recent years, however, a number of other areas have also started to be the focus of a significant amount of work using this approach, including dementia, autism, dysarthria, and hearing impairment. Intervention informed by CA has so far been linked primarily with aphasia (Wilkinson & Wielaert, 2012), but there would appear to be no reason why other communication disorders could not also be targeted using a similar type of interaction-focused intervention.

References

Antaki, C., & Wilkinson, R. (2013). Conversation analysis and the study of atypical populations. In J. Sidnell & T. Stivers (Eds.), *Handbook of conversation analysis* (pp. 533–550). Oxford, England: Blackwell-Wiley.

Beeke, S., Wilkinson, R., & Maxim, J. (2003). Exploring aphasic grammar 2: Do language testing and conversation tell a similar story? *Clinical Linguistics and Phonetics, 17*(2), 109–134.

Bloch, S., & Wilkinson, R. (2004). The understandability of AAC: A conversation analysis study of acquired dysarthria. *Augmentative and Alternative Communication, 20*(4), 272–282.

Bloch, S., & Wilkinson, R. (2009). Acquired dysarthria in conversation: Identifying sources of understanding problems. *International Journal of Language and Communication Disorders, 44*(5), 769–783.

Booth, S., & Perkins, L. (1999). The use of conversation analysis to guide individualised advice to carers and evaluate change in aphasia: A case study. *Aphasiology, 13*(4–5), 283–304

Couper-Kuhlen, E., & Selting, M. (Eds.). (1996). *Prosody in conversation: Interactional studies.* Cambridge, England: Cambridge University Press.

Denman, A., & Wilkinson, R. (2011). Applying conversation analysis to traumatic brain injury: Investigating touching another person in everyday social interaction. *Disability and Rehabilitation, 33*(3), 243–252.

Drew, P., & Heritage, J. (1992). Analyzing talk at work: an introduction. In P. Drew & J. Heritage (Eds.), *Talk at work: Interaction in institutional settings* (pp. 3–65). Cambridge, England: Cambridge University Press.

Egbert, M., & Depperman, A. (Eds.). (2012). *Hearing aids communication.* Mannheim, Germany: Verlag für Gesprächsforschung.

Garfinkel, H. (1967). *Studies in ethnomethodology.* Englewood Cliffs, NJ: Prentice Hall.

Goffman, E. (1983). The interaction order. *American Sociological Review, 48*, 1–17.

Goodwin, C. (1980). Restarts, pauses, and the achievement of a state of mutual gaze at turn-beginning. *Sociological Inquiry, 50*(3–4), 272–302.

Goodwin, C. (1995). Co-constructing meaning in conversations with an aphasic man. *Research on Language and Social Interaction, 28*, 233–260.

Goodwin, C. (Ed.). (2003). *Conversation and brain damage.* New York, NY: Oxford University Press.

Griffiths, S., Barnes, R., Britten, N., & Wilkinson, R. (2012). Potential causes and consequences of overlap in talk between speakers with Parkinson's disease and their familiar conversation partners. *Seminars in Speech and Language, 33*(1), 27–43.

Heeschen, C., & Schegloff, E. A. (2003). Aphasic agrammatism as interactional artifact and achievement. In C. Goodwin (Ed.), *Conversation and brain damage* (pp. 231–282). New York, NY: Oxford University Press.

Heritage, J. (1984). *Garfinkel and ethnomethodology.* Cambridge, England: Polity Press.

Heritage, J. (2004). Conversation analysis and institutional talk: Analyzing data. In D. Silverman (Ed.), *Qualitative research: Theory, method and practice* (pp. 222–245). London, England: Sage.

Jefferson, G. (1989). Preliminary notes on a possible metric which provides for a 'standard maximum' silence of approximately one second in conversation. In D. Roger & P. Bull (Eds.), *Conversation: An interdisciplinary perspective* (pp. 166–196). Clevedon, England: Multilingual Matters.

Lesser, R., & Milroy, L. (1993). *Linguistics and aphasia: Psycholinguistic and pragmatic aspects of intervention.* London, England: Longman.

Lock, S., Wilkinson, R., & Bryan, K. (2001). *Supporting Partners of People with Aphasia in Relationships and Conversation (SPPARC).* Bicester, England: Speechmark Press.

Mates, A., Mikesell, L., & Smith, M. S. (Eds.). (2010). *Language, interaction and frontotemporal dementia: Reverse engineering the social mind.* Sheffield, England: Equinox.

Muskett, T., Body, R., & Perkins, M. (2012). Uncovering the dynamic in static assessment interaction. *Child Language Teaching and Therapy, 28*(1), 87–99.

Penn, C. (1985). A profile of communicative appropriateness: a clinical tool for the assessment of pragmatics. *The South African Journal of Communication Disorders, 32*, 18–23.

Perkins, L. (1995). Applying conversation analysis to aphasia: clinical implications and analytic issues. *European Journal of Disorders of Communication, 30*(3), 372–383.

Rendle-Short, J. (2002/3). Managing interaction: A conversation analysis approach to the management of interaction by an 8-year old girl with Asperger's syndrome. *Issues in Applied Linguistics, 13*(2), 161–186.

Sacks, H., Schegloff, E. A., & Jefferson, G. (1974). A simplest systematics for the organization of turn-taking in conversation. *Language, 50*(4), 696–735.

Schegloff, E. A. (1992). Introduction. In H. Sacks, *Lectures on conversation* (2 vols.), edited by G. Jefferson (pp. ix–lxii). Oxford, England: Blackwell.

Schegloff, E. A. (2000). When 'others' initiate repair. *Applied Linguistics, 21*, 205–243.

Schegloff, E. A. (2007). *Sequence organization in interaction.* Cambridge, England: Cambridge University Press.

Schegloff, E. A., Jefferson, G., & Sacks, H. (1977). The preference for self-correction in the organization of repair for conversation. *Language, 53*, 361–382.

Schegloff, E. A., & Sacks, H. (1973). Opening up closings. *Semiotica, 8*, 289–327.

Simmons-Mackie, N., Damico, J., & Damico, H. L. (1999). A qualitative study of feedback in aphasia treatment. *American Journal of Speech-Language Pathology, 8*, 218–230.

Streeck, J., Goodwin, C., & LeBaron, C. (Eds.). (2011). *Embodied interaction: Language and body in the material world.* Cambridge, England: Cambridge University Press.

Whitworth, A., Perkins, L., & Lesser, R. (1997). *The Conversation Analysis Profile for People with Aphasia (CAPPCI).* London, England: Whurr.

Wilkinson, R. (1995). Aphasia: conversation analysis of a non-fluent aphasic person. In M. Perkins & S. Howard (Eds.), *Case studies in clinical linguistics* (pp. 271–292). London, England: Whurr.

Wilkinson, R. (2008). Conversation analysis and communication disorders. In M. J. Ball, M. Perkins, N. Müller, & S. Howard (Eds.), *The handbook of clinical linguistics* (pp. 92–106). Oxford, England: Blackwell.

Wilkinson, R. (2010). Interaction-focused intervention: A conversation analytic approach to aphasia therapy. *Journal of Interactional Research in Communication Disorders, 1*(1), 45–68.

Wilkinson, R., Bryan, K., Lock, S., & Sage, K. (2010). Implementing and evaluating aphasia therapy targeted at couples' conversations: A single case study. *Aphasiology, 24*(6), 869–886.

Wilkinson, R., & Wielaert, S. (2012). Rehabilitation for aphasic conversation: Can we change the everyday talk of people with aphasia and their significant others? *Archives of Physical Medicine and Rehabilitation, 93*(Supplement 1), 70–76.

6
Phenomenology

JACQUELINE J. HINCKLEY

If I set out on a trip to a country I've never been to before, I have two different ways to plan my trip. I can select a pre-determined itinerary including the sights I expect to see and when I expect to visit them. In this case, I use information about locations, distances, hotels, and restaurants that has already been reported by previous visitors. This leads me to have certain expectations about what I am going to do and see during my trip. Upon my return, much of my report about my trip will be a description of my originally planned itinerary and whether things went according to the plan.

Another way to plan my trip is to know only the most basic information about where I am going, and discover where to go and what to do after I've arrived. Every mundane activity, like figuring out where to eat and knowing where to sleep, becomes an opportunity to consider differences between my way of doing these things and the way they are done in this new place. When I return home from this kind of trip, I will tell adventurous stories of new experiences, peppered with my emotional reactions to them.

This latter style of traveling could be considered *phenomenological*, in that it emphasizes the sensory and perceptual experiences of routine activities in a way that allows me to consider my preexisting biases or expectations. In speech-language pathology, we might be interested in the experiences of living with a communication disorder, or the experiences of conducting clinical activities. Phenomenology is concerned with the process of critical distancing in order to appreciate meaning in the mundane. "For what concerns such a philosophy is … the methodical exploring and probing, in the setting of and through reflective wonder, of this 'new land': that 'world' in so far as it is experienced by us, and ourselves in so far as we experience it" (Zaner, 1970, p. 50). The purpose of this chapter is to introduce the philosophical principles of phenomenology, describe the research methods that are most closely associated with these principles, and provide examples of phenomenological research in communication sciences and disorders.

Phenomenology is most efficiently described as an approach to inquiry that is based on philosophical assumptions about humans and the world, and provides principles that guide the selection of research methods and procedures (Waksler, 2001, p. 67). A phenomenological philosophy embraces all sensory and perceptual human experiences and intends to take these experiences as primary. A process of disengagement from those experiences and reflection upon them is undertaken in order to understand the meaning of these experiences to human consciousness.

Humans are necessarily engaged in the ongoing experience of everyday life. In order to make explicit the meaning of this experience, disengagement or "distancing" must occur. Phenomenology has often been described as primarily a reflective enterprise (Toombs, 2001, p. 1) and a process of writing, during which meaningful reflection occurs (van Manen, 2001). This view of phenomenology is summed up as "engaging in the radical reflection of everyday experience" (Toombs, 2001, p. 2). The intention is to make explicit assumptions about aspects of everyday life that are typically taken for granted, and to focus on the conscious experience of the everyday.

Philosophical Roots and Assumptions

Two important ideas stemming from studies in psychology and logic led to the development of phenomenology as a discipline in the first few decades of the 20th century. An important contributor to the study of mental activities and processes at that time was William James. James (1904) defined consciousness as "awareness of content," knowledge of the experience of things in the world. An important aspect of James' definition was the separation between the experience of the knower and the object to be known. The implication of this separation is that there are objects or experiences that can be outside of someone's consciousness.

Studies in logic that preceded and began in the 1900s were also a force in the development of phenomenology. Logic studies advanced the idea that propositions were elements that could be combined or manipulated in various ways, and this was further reinforced by the dominant work of mathematicians in logic (King & Shapiro, 1995, pp. 496–500). The overwhelming contribution of the study of logic was to assert that interpretations and meanings, as represented in propositions, were real, objective elements. Logic processes and products came to form the basis of much of traditional science inquiry. Phenomenologists point out that propositions are not truly perceptual observations, but rather interpretations based on observations. These propositions have become something "objective," and internal perceptual experiences have become "subjective" (Gurwitsch, 1974, p. 17; Fjelland & Gjengedal, 1994, p. 7).

In the context of studies in consciousness and logic, Edmund Husserl (1963, 1964) attempted to formulate a philosophical view that addressed both the "subjective" elements of perceived experience with the "objective" interpretation and manipulation of assertions and observations. As one of the key figures in the development of phenomenology, he proposed that there could be a philosophy that overarched all of these other disciplines, in which subjective experiences are the subject of objective acts of reflection (or intentional objects). Over the last 100 years, phenomenology has become one important branch of philosophy, logic and ethics being the other branches. Logic is a branch of philosophy that studies reasoning and carries implications for how we should reason. Ethics is a branch of philosophy in which right and wrong is studied, and pertains to how we should act. Phenomenology is a branch of philosophy that studies experience, and results in understanding how we experience.

Elements of Phenomenology

There are three key elements of phenomenology. The first is the primacy of the first-person point of view in order to study consciousness. Consciousness is most validly and perhaps reliably studied when we study our own conscious experience. As Zaner (1970, p. 122) wrote: "... my own consciousness is presented to me far more clearly, fully, and directly than is that of the other person. Thus, if we want to focus on consciousness (as did Descartes, Hume, Kant, and others), and if we want the best available samples of it in order to make our descriptive judgments with the best evidence, then there is no alternative except to reflect on my own consciousness, and each of you on his own."

Another important component of phenomenology is the description of the individual's experiences in the world. This is often referred to as the "life-world." "The life-world is defined as comprising all items and objects which present themselves in pre-scientific experience and as they present themselves prior to their scientific interpretation in the specific modern sense" (Gurwitsch, 1974, p. 17). In this definition is the important separation of perceptual experience from the development or consciousness of interpretation and meaning. Another important phrase in phenomenology is the term "lived experience," which signifies the experiences that we are conscious of as we live through them.

The third defining element in phenomenology is the process and act of reflection. This is a conscious and purposeful shifting of attention from the act of experiencing the current world, to seeking meaning in world experiences and in its conscious experience. Phenomenological reflection is intended to be an active process, a "radical disengagement" from current experiences to focus on the possible meanings of past experiences (Toombs, 2001, pp. 1–2), "an attitude of reflective attentiveness" (van Manen, 2001, p. 461).

The grand theme in phenomenology is the understanding of experiences and their meanings to the individual, as they are experienced. Phenomenology does not attempt to describe psychological inner states, motivations, feelings, plans, or intentions of others; rather it is an attempt to understand the meanings that shape the inner lives of others (van Manen, 2001, p. 469). "The difference between experimental cognitive research and qualitative phenomenological inquiry is that the former looks for mechanisms and behavioral patterns while the latter focuses on lived experiences and meanings" (van Manen, 2001, p. 468).

French philosopher Merleau-Ponty extended the reach of phenomenological philosophy, developing the notion of the "lived body" (1996/1945). This advanced the concept of embodiment and resisted Cartesian notions that separate the mind and body. To Merleau-Ponty, the experience of the body or "body image" is one part of consciousness, which he defined as both perception and reasoning. His concept of "motor intentionality" refers to an essential bodily understanding of the world. Merleau-Ponty studied the phantom limb experiences of amputees as a demonstration that body perception is a part of consciousness that has developed from the sense and actions of the body. Speech was also an important aspect of embodiment in his work. As he wrote about in the *Phenomenology of Perception* (1945), speech is a way for the body to act on a thought that has become conscious, and a way for the speaker to communicate these thoughts to someone else's consciousness.

Seven types of phenomenology have been described (Embree, 1997). One of these, hermeneutical phenomenology, studies how we understand and engage things around us in our human world. This hermeneutical phenomenology applies the basic principles of phenomenology to an understanding of ourselves. Martin Heidegger (1889–1976) was an important proponent of the hermeneutical approach, in which the social and linguistic context of things, people and events in the world are critical to understanding their meaning. Rather than engaging in critical distancing to analyze the meaning of experiences, the words and actions that surround and are part of an experience are assessed to interpret meaning. Heidegger (1975) argues that we cannot help but perceive something without immediately attributing some meaning to it. For example, if we hear a door slam, or we hear a word spoken, we can only separate these acoustical events from meaning by purposefully listening in a special way. Phenomenology is an acceptance of what is, and this includes the meanings that are derived from common everyday experiences of the individual. The individual will go through his or her everyday life, cooking breakfast, driving to work, and each of these activities have meaning. Small differences in the way these routines unfold have meaning and become part of the individual's experience.

Phenomenology of Practice

In some sense, all of phenomenology is concerned with practice, because it is the study of our experiences and how we experience life (van Manen, 2007, p. 13). The specific phrase "phenomenology of practice" has been used to describe how phenomenology can address questions of how we should act in our personal and professional everyday lives, and has been particularly applied to the professions in education and health care. The work of Merleau-Ponty forms an important philosophical basis for phenomenology of practice, particularly in health care, because of his emphasis on embodiment and the relationship between subjective experience and the body (Carel, 2011). Even the placebo effect has been described as the body's understanding of the therapeutic context, separately from consciousness or expectations (Frenkel, 2008).

Many aspects of our everyday experiences are difficult to interpret or understand using typical scientific forms of inquiry. While cognitive processes and mechanisms can be subject to deductive scientific approaches, other sources of knowledge come from the embodied experience itself—the relational, social, perceptual components of an experience that may or may not be conscious. Theory "thinks" the world, but a phenomenology of practice "grasps" the world (van Manen, 2007, p. 20). A phenomenology of practice can address the experiential components of doing clinical work, or living with a communication disability. Phenomenology offers promise in the pursuit of understanding clinical expertise, and how the skilled clinician successfully embeds scientific knowledge with practical, embodied knowledge about a particular client. Theoretically driven, deductive studies of clinical practice and phenomenological studies of practice are complementary, and need to co-exist to contribute to the most well-rounded understanding of clinical practice (Leonard, 1994; van Manen, 1995). According to Dreyfus & Dreyfus (1996) "... while practice, without theory, cannot alone produce fully skilled behavior in complex coping domains such as nursing, theory without practice has even less chance of success" (p. 29).

The phenomenology of practice is well suited to the task of exploring how we actually go about doing clinical work. A theoretically driven approach begins with a theory and asks what practice would look like if the theory were applied. A phenomenological approach sets out to understand the experience of clinical practice, without regard to predictions or the search for some absolute truth. Instead, phenomenological approaches ask what the meaning of the lived experiences is.

Practice is embodied; it is dependent on our interpretation of the many physical, contextual, relational, and temporal cues that is not captured in conceptualizations and theoretical representations. Our knowledge of how a client may be feeling, whether the timing is right to begin or end a certain task or topic, many of our clinical impressions are combinations of theoretically sound concepts with experiential knowledge that comes from seeing the client, being present in the room.

There are several ways in which a phenomenology of practice is appealing to those who wish to explore the embodied, experiential aspects of practice. Phenomenology provides a link between world experiences and theoretical, scientific knowledge. For example, a phenomenological approach recognizes the differences between a scientific inquiry of disability and the experience of living with a communication disability. It can also help to explore the difference between a scientific or cognitive understanding of clinical practice and how practice is actually done or implemented. Phenomenology can help to explain these theory-to-practice gaps.

Since phenomenological approaches allow for the exploration of our own biases and interpretations, they can reveal how theoretical, social, cultural, and professional thinking traditions influence our understandings and interpretations of experienced clinical phenomena. How do cultural backgrounds affect the relationship between a client and a clinician? A phenomenological approach would not address this question with cultural inventories and outcome measures, but rather with rich descriptions of the experiences of clinicians and clients who differed in cultural background.

A defining element of the phenomenological approach is the first-person point of view; the recognition that the best source of understanding of the conscious meaning of a context or event is to begin with our own consciousness. This principle is completely consistent with a person-centered or relationship-centered approach to clinical care. Person-centeredness is an approach that helps us integrate our clients' values into all of our professional activities. Person-centeredness views the client and the clinician as complete persons. The client should not be diminished for seeking help, and the clinician should not be warranted an undue position of authority. A hallmark of person-centeredness is shared decision-making within a therapeutic partnership between the client and clinician (Ersser & Atkins, 2000; Mead & Bower, 2000). Principles of person-centeredness are consistent with phenomenology's acknowledgement that the best source for information about experience is the person to whom that experience has accrued.

A second defining characteristic of phenomenology is the exploration of the lifeworld, all of the contextual elements of a person's experience. Phenomenology provides a philosophical underpinning for context-sensitive studies of experience. Context is a critical aspect to social inclusion and accessibility (Simmons-Mackie & Damico, 2007) and contributes to our understanding of the experience of disability. The experience of illness and disability depend on a unique combination of personal traits, background, social support, interactions, education, and environment. Benner (2001, p. 364) has pointed out that even a common health care phrase like "activities of daily living" is subject to a particular lifeworld and the subjective experience of embodiment. Skills like bathing, dressing, and eating are routine tasks that can take on the experience of climbing Mt. Everest depending on the body and the context in which these skills must occur.

The lifeworld includes context in which the consciousness of the individual operates, and this consciousness includes the body and thoughts. An implication of this sense of the term "embodiment" is that "… a healthcare client only has a part of himself (or herself) examined when doctors probe the body in isolation" (Mazis, 2001, p. 204). A phenomenological stance insists upon a holistic view of the person and the unique environment in which the person is operating, and that all of this must be taken into account together to understand the meaning of that person's experience.

In addition to the primacy of the subject's perspective, another important aspect of the phenomenology of practice is the suspension of belief (Waksler, 2001, p. 68). Suspension of belief refers at least partially to the professional, non-judgmental stance that a clinician takes when forming an impression of the client, his or her needs, and abilities. This also references the critical element of reflection that is part and parcel of phenomenology, "an attitude of reflective attentiveness" (van Manen, 2001, p. 461). We withhold our own experience in terms of our own judgments, perceptions, or thoughts, and allow the client with his or her abilities and disabilities, social circle, and living situation to speak for himself or herself. As we go through the clinical process, we also must reflect back systematically to our own interpretations, reactions, and behaviors in a continual process of self-improvement. This process has often been referred to as "reflective practice" (Schon, 1983). "Professional practice needs to be, not only pragmatic and effective, but also philosophic and reflective so that one can act and interact with competence and tact, and with human understanding" (van Manen, 2001, p. 472).

We act with "human understanding" when we attend to and derive meaning from all of the simple, mundane nuances, events, and actions that occur within a clinical relationship. Noticing a glance, a change in position, a hesitation, a change in facial expression are seemingly small details that can impart a large effect on the nature and course of the therapeutic relationship, and perhaps the course of the entire intervention process. Phenomenology and the study of experience "tends to invoke a sense of wonder and questioning attentiveness about taken-for-granted aspects of life" (van Manen, 2001, p. 471), and it is perhaps these aspects of life that are exceptionally potent in the course of clinical care.

An understanding of the experiences of disability and caring for those with disabilities does not detract from our cognitive understanding of scientific knowledge that forms the basis for interventions. Infusing the scholarly and professional dialogue with information about the lived experiences of communication disability and intervention should expand our understanding in important and meaningful ways. Using phenomenological approaches to achieve this is one way to formally acknowledge and explore the realms of therapeutic interaction that cannot be addressed through traditional forms of scientific inquiry (Benner, 2001, p. 367).

Sources of Meaning and Inquiry

The principles of phenomenology and derived research methods are commonly applied across many different disciplines. "Phenomenology is, of course, essentially a philosophical discipline.... Phenomenological research in nursing, geriatric care, clinical psychology, preventative health care, counseling, pedagogy, and human ecology is increasingly pursued by a breed of scholars who tend to hold strong backgrounds in their own disciplines, who possess less grounding in philosophical thought, yet who are 'doing phenomenology'" (van Manen, 2001, p. 458).

Phenomenology as a discipline provides guiding principles in which various methods can fit. The discipline borrows methodologies from the social and human sciences (van Manen, 2001, p. 462). "The sense of phenomenological method, furthermore, is very much like that of the explorer when he turns to the task of recording where he has been and how he got there. Learning to think phenomenologically is very much like learning to read and actively use these records, the maps, guideposts, markings, and other paraphernalia of the explorer's and mapmaker's trade. The sense of phenomenological statements is very much like that of an explorer's so far as they claim to be descriptions of the 'land', they are at once epistemic (knowledge-claims concerning the land itself) and communicative (that is, invitations and guides intended to enable others to know what to look for).... There is no such thing as a 'method', as distinct from what is discovered thereby; and what is discovered is inseparable from the 'way' one got there" (Zaner, 1970, pp. 35–36).

Research methods that serve the principles of honoring the first-person, subject viewpoint, describing the detailed life-world, and active and deliberate reflection to derive the meaning of the phenomenon or experience can be applied in a phenomenological approach (Finlay, 2009). Narrative study of all forms generally fits into the principles of phenomenology (Frank, 2001; Hinckley, 2008; Shadden, Hagstrom, & Koski, 2008). "The role of storytelling is central to interpretive phenomenology because when people structure their own narrative accounts, they can tap into their more immediate experiences, and the problem of generating false generalities or ideologies is diminished" (Benner, 1994, p. 108). Narrative forms and those who use oral history are intuitively using phenomenological principles even if they do not explicitly acknowledge phenomenology as the framework for their work (Kirby, 2008). However, phenomenological approaches might differ from these other qualitative narrative techniques by gathering information about embodied experience that goes beyond verbal accounts. "Walking with" exercises, videotaping actions, and reports of sensual and perceptual experiences also fit into a toolkit for phenomenological research.

There are a number of methods from which we obtain both the first-person point of view and a detailed contextual or life-world description, and these methods will be described.

Gathering Experiential Accounts

Experiential accounts can be productively gathered in a number of ways in order to achieve phenomenological goals. Autoethnography and personal accounts rely on the experiences and reflection of the author/researcher. Narrative ethnographies combine the narrative as obtained through interview of a participant with the subjective reactions and thoughts of the researcher into a single written narrative. A number of interview types and techniques can also serve to collect experiential accounts. Finally, the researcher may engage in observation or participant-observation to generate accounts of experiences of the participant that may also include the experiences of the researcher.

Autoethnography

Autoethnography is the use of the researcher's own experience within a narrative form that portrays some aspect of lived experience (Ellis, 2004). It has been defined as "a form of self-narrative that places the self in a social context" (Reed-Danahy, 1997, p. 6). Autoethnography is more than just a retelling of life events, as in an autobiography. While important events and experiences are described, the researcher's reaction to these events is included in the narrative. Systematic introspection (Ellis, 1997) is applied to analyze and interpret the meaning of the events that are being studied. The emotional aspects of the experience are not simply described, but rather there is an attempt by the writer to evoke a similar experience in the reader through the use of literary or evocative writing techniques.

The act and process of autoethnography is completely consistent with core elements of phenomenology. "The task of phenomenology, then, is the reflective-descriptive explication, analysis, and assessment of the life of consciousness, and of man generally. Since his aim is to develop his discipline as rigorously as possible, and since that signifies that he must obtain the best possible evidence for the things to be studied, then clearly the phenomenologist must turn to his own mental life" (Zaner, 1970, p. 122).

Typically, there is some temporal distance between the lived event and the writing of the autoethnography. The passage of time allows for separation and reflection along with the ability to relive the event in order to re-construct it evocatively. The intent of the written autoethnography is to convey literary truth or lifelikeness. This is accomplished when the text reflects the meaning of the experience, rather than a chronology of events of sequence of facts.

Autoethnography can be judged on its achievement of lifelikeness and the meaningfulness of the dialogue between the writer and the reader (Behar, 1997; Ellis, 1997; Sparkes, 2000; Spry, 2001). The usefulness of autoethnography is whether the reader is led to an understanding of a similar experience as the writer through the reading of the narrative (Ellis, 1995; Sparkes, 2000).

Sampling

When research methods involve others' experiences besides those of the researcher, a number of different means of selecting participants can occur. Opportunistic or convenience sampling is most frequently used when the researcher engages in observation or participant-observation (Hatch, 2002). In this type of research, the participants are those with whom the researcher comes in contact. Another approach that is consistent with phenomenological principles is to use purposeful sampling. Extreme or deviant case examples can be selected to showcase highly unusual examples of a characteristic or phenomenon of interest. Maximum variation samples involve selecting individuals who represent extreme, contrasting views or experiences. Typical case samples or homogenous samples are cases that represent what is believed to be usual in terms of an experience. Snowball or chain samples take place when one participant recommends another person who shares an experience or characteristic and would fit into the study. In all of these forms of purposeful sampling, the goal is to gather experiential accounts rather than to select a representative sample from a population for hypothesis testing.

Narrative Ethnography

The narrative ethnography blends the viewpoint and experience of the researcher with the experience of the participant in a narrative form (Tedlock, 2003). It is a blending of two genres, the life history and the memoir. A life history narrative, which is typically focused on one aspect of a person's life, is combined with the reactions of the researcher as they learn about the participant's life history. In this case, the narrative of the researcher's reaction is really in the form of a memoir.

Interviews

Another procedure consistent with phenomenological principles is to gather others' experiences through interviews. Three basic interview formats have been described (Hatch, 2002). *Formal or structured interviews,* which include the subtype of standardized interviews, are those in which the researcher enters the interview with a set of questions and a pre-established time limit. *Semi-structured interviews* allow the researcher to pose follow-up questions or probe for additional information beyond the originally planned question script. In-depth interviews are typically included in the category of semi-structured interviews, because a set of general questions guides the in-depth interviews, but the researcher has the flexibility to pursue more information on any of the planned topics. Finally, *unstructured or informal interviews* are free-flowing conversations between a researcher and a participant that may or may not address any pre-determined set of questions or topics.

The importance of free-flowing, naturalistic conversations has been well-described by Benner (1994): "… we asked our pilot participants about their 'emotions', only to find that people don't ordinarily have 'emotions', though they feel strongly, or 'good' or 'bad' about things. By phrasing the question in foreign, academic (abstract) terms, we cut participants off from their every-day language use, thereby cutting them off from their ordinary spontaneous responses. Once we put our question in more conversational language, people could talk about or deny their feelings in their ordinary patterns" (p. 108).

A final method for gathering experiential accounts is to use already published nonfiction or even fictional accounts. A phenomenological approach recognizes that these accounts likely entail core elements of the experience and therefore may convey important meanings of the experience. Some fictional accounts, or some parts of fictional accounts, may also have important aspects of lifelikeness or literary truth, and for those reasons could help to convey the meaning of a particular experience. For example, poetry and drama are forms that often powerfully convey the meaning of an experience in evocative, creative ways. These, too, can be sources of meaning for a phenomenological inquiry.

In all of these forms of experiential accounts, the subjective first-person view is foremost along with a high level of contextual detail. Contextual detail includes all of the cultural, environmental, social, linguistic, relational, and actional aspects that surround the phenomenon of interest. The gathered accounts or narratives describe the life-world in which the experience has occurred, the lived experience of the individual going through the mundane and unusual, the grand and the minute.

Reflection and Interpretation

There are two methodological impulses in phenomenological inquiry and writing: the reductio (the reduction) and the vocatio (the vocative dimension). The bracketing or suspension of our everyday natural attitude, in order to emulate lived experience, is termed the reductio. This emulation occurs linguistically through writing in the context of the second aspect of phenomenological methodology, termed the vocatio. The intent of writing is to produce textual portrayals that resonate the kinds of meanings that we seem to recognize in prereflective experience. The vocative dimension expresses this concern with language.

Phenomenological research in practice is said to differ from other qualitative methods, because at heart it involves reflection and writing of each aspect of the experience. The "doing" of phenomenology is often described as writing—writing field notes, writing impressions, writing narratives, writing reactions and thoughts. The process of writing itself yields the fruit of meaning and interpretation. In traditional, quantitative approaches, the writing is simply a write-up, a report of how what was planned was actually completed. In a phenomenological approach, the writing is part of both the implementation of the methods, as well as the results.

In order for this to be achieved, the writing must be literary; it must evoke the same kind of embodied experience in the reader as it did in the writer. When that is achieved, then the reader has the opportunity to derive the same kind of meaning from the experience. This style of writing allows us to use descriptive language that can access the experience of disability and providing care. "This phenomenological writing constitutes a phenomenology in practice and promotes a phenomenology of and for practice" (van Manen, 2007, p. 22). Professional knowledge is not just cognitive, but depends on the sense of the body, personal presence, relational perceptiveness, thoughtful routines and practices, and tact for knowing what to say or do (van Manen, 2007). These embodied practice events are best described by a language that is not theoretical or solely cognitive, but evokes a body sense, an emotional reaction, an intuitive response in the reader. According to Kockelmans (1987), "... in human reality there are certain phenomena which reach so deeply into a man's life and the world in which he lives that poetic language is the only adequate way through which to point to and to make present a meaning which we are unable to express clearly in any other way" (p. ix).

Since reflective writing is method and result, a focus on the text itself is primary in a phenomenological approach. For each sentence or line in a phenomenological text, it can be asked what that sentence contributes to the meaning of the experience. This principle leads to another approach that fits comfortably within phenomenology—analysis of metaphors. Metaphorical thought is manifested in our language and reveals our culture (Lakoff & Johnson, 1980). Consideration of the metaphors demonstrated in our word and language choices is another way to explore experience and meaning in phenomenology.

Current and Future Applications in Communication Disorders

Phenomenology is being applied in a number of different ways in the study of communication disorders. The principles of phenomenology integrate well with tenets of person-centered care. Research into how to accomplish person-centered care, what goals and issues need to be addressed to accomplish person-centered care, whether person-centered care has been achieved by a service, an intervention, or a clinician, and what processes and relationships occur as part of person-centered care can all be addressed with phenomenology (e.g., Damico, Ball, Simmons-Mackie, & Müller, 2007; DiLollo & Favreau, 2010; O'Halloran, Hersh, Laplante-Levesque, & Worrall, 2010; Simmons-Mackie & Damico, 1999, 2001). As the viewpoint of the client is more actively integrated into practice and research, it is likely that phenomenological approaches will continue to become fruitful as one of our research tools. The more we recognize the role of the clinician, including the importance that the therapeutic relationship plays in clinical outcome, the more we find additional uses for phenomenological approaches. Examples of research questions that can be addressed using a phenomenological stance follow.

The study of the lived experience of individuals with communication disorders can help us address a number of important issues. Using purposeful sampling and in-depth interview techniques, it is possible to explore how individuals adapt and live successfully with a chronic communication disorder. These techniques have been used to study the coping strategies of those living with communication impairments due to traumatic brain injury (Fraas, 2011; Fraas & Calvert, 2009), stroke and aphasia (Greenfield, 2011; Kardosh & Damico, 2009; Simmons-Mackie & Damico, 1999), or multiple sclerosis (Yorkston, Klasner, & Swanson, 2001). Understanding the long-term perspectives of individuals with communication disorders can demonstrate otherwise unrecognized difficulties, like the long-term social and behavioral consequences of living with language impairment (Brinton, Fujiki, & Baldridge, 2010). Published accounts of individuals living with aphasia have been used as the source for experiential accounts to explore successful living with aphasia (Hinckley, 2006). In these examples, a phenomenologically motivated approach provides a richly contextualized and detailed answer to the question of what happens to our clients well beyond the provision of speech and language services.

The progressive experience of bodily recovery following lacunar stroke was investigated through clinical ethnography. Use of field notes, life histories, and interviews provided the text for understanding how individuals define recovery from stroke, how they experience their bodies, the meaning of the stroke experience, and how patients' views of recovery differ from the biomedical perspective. Thirteen stroke survivors participated, with their first interview occurring within 72 hours of the stroke and then throughout the acute and rehabilitation stages of recovery to 6 months post stroke. Grand themes demonstrated that recovery from stroke is not just recovery of bodily functions, but also recovery of the "social body"—a reconnection to social practices (Doolittle, 1994, pp. 210–211). This study not only illustrates the use of research methods that are consistent with phenomenological principles, but also captures how meaning is embodied and derives from bodily experiences.

We can even address the experience of individuals who have received a particular intervention approach, as one way of determining what contribution the intervention might have over the long term. For example, Cream, Onslow, Packman, and Llewellyn (2003) conducted in-depth interviews of 10 adults who stutter who had received prolonged speech therapy. They found that these adults use prolonged speech strategically, along with other approaches, to protect themselves from stuttering episodes.

The focus of these research questions can be broadened to include the primary caregivers or communication partners of individuals with communication impairments. In a series of interviews of 11 parents/carers of children who use augmentative/alternative communication devices, issues relevant to the child's needs, societal views and policies, and parental burden were described (Marshall & Goldbart, 2008), and this kind of approach has also been used to investigate strategies of primary communication partners of individuals with severe intellectual disabilities (Forster & Iacono, 2008). The study of the natural evolution of communication strategies and concerns over time can have implications for clinical practice and for health policy.

Principles of phenomenology have been used to develop a tool to elicit a client's preferences for rehabilitation goal priorities (Stineman, 2011). The Recovery Preference Exploration (RPE) asks the patient to imagine different recovery scenarios in order to elicit preferences in prioritizing treatment goals (Stineman et al., 2007). Different levels of independence are presented in a board-game style for each impairment type based on the Functional Independence Measure (FIM). The patient talks through the options while selecting different options on the board. The results generate clear personal preferences and priorities for individual patients (Kurcz, Saint-Louis, Burke, & Stineman, 2008).

Clinical processes like goal selection and goal setting are prime targets for incorporating the client's perspective. The client experiences routine clinical tasks that must be completed by the clinician in particular ways, even though these activities may not be obvious opportunities in which to solicit the client's perspective. Medical personnel, for example, will decide the need for and timing of a tracheostomy tube change. Yet in the phenomenological study conducted by Donnelly and Wiechula (2006), the patient's lived experience of a tracheostomy tube change shows that these are not just physical acts to the body, but affect the entire experience of the patient, requiring psychological preparation and trust. Similarly, ethnographic narrative shows the long-term effect of a clinical discharge report on a patient's experience and subsequent choices and behavior (Nakano & Hinckley, 2010).

It's not solely the client's lived experience that is at issue here; the clinical relationship and thus the lived experience of the clinician are also crucial ingredients to therapeutic success (Hinckley, 2010). Experience is seen as the changing of preconceptions or foreknowledge that are not confirmed by the actual situation (Heidegger, 1962; Gadamer, 2004). Since clinical practice is the accumulation of experiences, the development of clinical expertise is the accumulation of critical incidents or cases (Benner, 1984, pp. 8–9). Experience is also the interaction between preexisting knowledge and knowledge that comes from the actual, bodily experience of one or more cases. To become an expert in any area requires the novice to respond to the same situations as the expert does. In clinical practice, the beginning clinician is confronted with the same case history, presenting problems, and profiles of strengths and weaknesses for a given case as the expert clinician. The beginning clinician is expected to respond with a similar selection of goals and interventions as the expert clinician, and to implement them equally effectively and efficiently (Dreyfus, Dreyfus, & Benner, 1996, p. 259).

One way to investigate the development of expertise in speech-language pathology is to interview a purposeful sample of expert clinicians (Douglas & Hinckley, 2012). Autoethnography can also be employed as a tool for a clinician to engage in productive reflection of a particular clinical experience (Hinckley, 2005).

The clinician's experience in accomplishing difficult clinical tasks, like discharge from therapy, has been investigated by collecting experiential accounts from clinicians (Hersh, 2010). These narratives portray relationships and tensions between knowledge, policies, care, and ethics, and show how clinicians must navigate these complexities to accomplish typical clinical tasks. Brannigan (2001) argues that phenomenology provides an approach to ethical practice that goes beyond and is complementary to an ethical approach based on principlism (Brannigan, 2001; McCarthy, 2003). A narrative, phenomenological approach can offer a way to balance the principles of beneficence and patient autonomy by considering what is best for the patient consider that patient's world and lived experience, and a means to ensure that the patient's view and experience is part of the determination of ethical care (Greenfield & Jensen, 2010). For speech-language pathologists, this kind of approach to ethical practice can figure in to many routine clinical processes, like discharge, but may become even more relevant when considering end-of-life care and feeding decisions.

Conclusion

Phenomenology is a branch of philosophy that argues for the appropriate use of traditional scientific methods and the insertion of scientific data into an understanding of the exploration of meaningful experience. Aspects of clinical practice that are difficult to measure through traditional scientific methods can be addressed through various qualitative methods, and phenomenology has often been applied to the investigation of professional practices. Phenomenology asserts that experience is embodied and socially, environmentally, and mentally constructed. It provides a conceptual foundation for the study of person-centered practice and the meaningfulness of all aspects of service provision in communication sciences and disorders.

References

Behar, R. (1997). *The vulnerable observer: Anthropology that breaks your heart.* Boston, MA: Beacon.

Benner, P. (1984). *From novice to expert: Excellence and power in clinical nursing practice.* Menlo Park, CA: Addison-Wesley.

Benner, P. (1994). The tradition and skill of interpretive phenomenology in studying health, illness, and caring practices. In P. Benner (Ed.), *Interpretive phenomenology: Embodiment, caring and ethics in health and illness* (pp. 99–128). Thousand Oaks, CA: Sage.

Benner, P. (2001). The phenomenon of care In S. L. Toombs (Ed.), *Handbook of phenomenology and medicine* (pp. 351–369). Boston, MA: Kluwer.

Brannigan, M. C. (2001). Medical feeding: Applying Husserl and Merleau-Ponty. In S. L. Toombs (Ed.), *Handbook of phenomenology and medicine* (pp. 451–454). Boston, MA: Kluwer.

Brinton, B., Fujiki, M., & Baldridge, M. (2010). The trajectory of language impairment into adolescence: What four young women can teach us. *Seminars in Speech and Language, 31,* 122–133.

Carel, H. (2011). Phenomenology and its application to medicine. *Theoretical Medicine and Bioethics, 32,* 33–46.

Cream, A., Onslow, M., Packman, A., Llewellyn, G. (2003). Protection from harm: The experience of adults after therapy with prolonged-speech. *International Journal of Language and Communication Disorders, 38,* 379–395.

Damico, J. S., Ball, M. J., Simmons-Mackie, N. N., & Müller, N. (2007). Interactional aphasia: Principles and practice oriented to social intervention. In M. J. Ball. & J. S. Damico (Eds.), *Clinical aphasiology: Future directions, a festschrift for Chris Code* (pp. 92–103). New York, NY: Psychology Press.

Dilollo, A. & Favreau, C. (2010). Person-centered care and speech and language therapy. *Seminars in Speech and Language, 31,* 90–97.

Donnelly, F., & Wiechula, R. (2006). The lived experience of a tracheostomy tube change: a phenomenological study. *Journal of Clinical Nursing, 15,* 1115–1122.

Doolittle, N. (1994). A clinical ethnography of stroke recovery. In P. Benner (Ed.), *Interpretive phenomenology: Embodiment, caring and ethics in health and illness* (pp. 211–223). Thousand Oaks, CA: Sage.

Dreyfus, H. L. & Dreyfus, S. E. (1996). The relationship of theory and practice in the acquisition of skill. In P. Benner, C. A. Tanner, & C. A. Chesla (Eds.), *Expertise in nursing practice: Caring, clinical judgment, and ethics* (pp. 1–24). New York, NY: Springer.

Dreyfus, H. L., Dreyfus, S. E., & Benner, P. (1996). Implications of the phenomenology of expertise for teaching and learning everyday skillful ethical comportment. In P. Benner, C. A. Tanner, & C. A. Chesla (Eds.), *Expertise in nursing practice: Caring, clinical judgment, and ethics* (pp. 309–334). New York, NY: Springer.

Ellis, C. (1997). Evocative autoethnography: Writing emotionally about our lives. In W. G. Tierney & Y. S. Lincoln (Eds.), *Representation and the text.* Albany, NY: State University of New York Press.

Ellis, C. (2004). *The ethnographic I: A methodological novel about autoethnography.* Walnut Creek, CA: AltaMira Press.

Embree, L. (1997). *Encyclopedia of phenomenology.* New York, NY: Springer.

Ersser, S. J., & Atkins, S. (2000). Clinical reasoning and patient-centered care. In J. Higgs & M. Jones (Eds.), *Clinical reasoning in the health professions* (2nd ed., pp. 68–77). Oxford, England: Butterworth Heinemann.

Finlay, L. (2009). Debating phenomenological research methods. *Phenomenology & Practice, 3,* 6–25.

Fjelland, R., & Gjengedal, E. (1994). A theoretical foundation for nursing as a science. In P. Benner (Ed.), *Interpretive phenomenology: Embodiment, caring and ethics in health and illness* (pp. 3–26). Thousand Oaks, CA: Sage.

Forster, S., & Iacono, T. (2008). Disability support workers' experience of interaction with a person with profound intellectual disability. *Journal of Intellectual and Developmental Disability, 33,* 137–147.

Fraas, M. (2011). Enhancing quality of life for survivors of stroke through phenomenology. *Topics in Stroke Rehabilitation, 18,* 40–46.

Fraas, M. R. & Calvert, M. (2009). The use of narratives to identify characteristics leading to a productive life following acquired brain injury. *American Journal of Speech-Language Pathology, 18,* 315–328.

Frank, A. W. (2001). Experiencing illness through storytelling. In S. K. Toombs (Ed.), *Handbook of phenomenology and medicine* (pp. 229–245). Boston, MA: Kluwer Academic.

Frenkel, O. (2008). A phenomenology of the 'placebo effect': Taking meaning from the mind to the body. *Journal of Medicine and Philosophy, 33,* 58–79.

Gadamer, H. G. (2004). *Truth and method* (2nd ed., Trans. J. Weinsheimer & D. G. Marshall). London, England: Continuum.

Greenfield, B. H. (2011). Phenomenology as a philosophical orientation for understanding the transformative experience of disabling illness. *Topics in Stroke Rehabilitation, 18,* 35–39.

Greenfield, B. H., & Jensen, G. M. (2010). Understanding the lived experiences of patients: Application of a phenomenological approach to ethics. *Physical Therapy, 90,* 1185–1197.

Gurwitsch, A. (1974). *Phenomenology and the theory of science.* Evanston, IL: Northwestern University Press.

Hatch, J. A. (2002). *Doing qualitative research in education settings.* Albany, NY: State University of New York Press.

Heidegger, M. (1962). *Being and time* (Trans. J. Macquarrie & E. Robinson). Oxford, England: Blackwell.

Heidegger, M. (1975). *Poetry, language, and thought.* New York, NY: Harper & Row.

Hersh, D. (2010). Aphasia therapists' stories of ending the therapeutic relationship. *Topics in Stroke Rehabilitation, 17,* 30–38.

Hinckley, J. J. (2005). The piano lesson: An autoethnography about changing clinical paradigms in aphasia practice. *Aphasiology, 19*(8), 765–779.

Hinckley, J. J. (2006). Finding messages in bottles: Living successfully with stroke and aphasia. *Topics in Stroke Rehabilitation, 13*(1), 25–36.

Hinckley, J. J. (2008). *Narrative-based practice in speech-language pathology.* San Diego, CA: Plural Publishing.

Hinckley, J. J. (2010). Hope for happy endings: Stories of clinicians and clients. *Topics in Stroke Rehabilitation, 17,* 1–5.

Husserl, E. (1963). *Ideas: A general introduction to pure phenomenology* (Trans. W. R. Boyce Gibson). New York: Collier Books. From the German original of 1913, originally titled *Ideas pertaining to a Pure Phenomenology and to a Phenomenological Philosophy*, First Book. Newly translated with the full title by Fred Kersten. Dordrecht and Boston: Kluwer Academic Publishers, 1983. Known as *Ideas I.*

Husserl, E. (1964). *The Phenomenology of Internal Time-Consciousness.* Bloomington: Indiana University Press.

Husserl, E. (2001). *Logical investigations* (Trans. J. N. Findlay, 2 vols.). London, England. Original work published 1900.

Kardosh, B. M., & Damico, J. S. (2009). The contribution of language in shaping clinical culture: Palestinian aphasics and families living in Israel. *Asia Pacific Journal of Speech, Language, and Hearing, 12,* 243–252.

King, P., & Shapiro, S. (1995). *The Oxford companion to philosophy.* Oxford, England: Oxford University Press.

Kirby, R. K. (2008). Phenomenology and the problems of oral history. *The Oral History Review, 35,* 22–38.

Kockelmans, J. J. (Ed). (1987). *Phenomenological psychology: The Dutch School.* Dordrecht: Kluwer.

Kurcz, A. E., Saint-Louis, N., Burke, J. P. & Stineman, M. G. (2008). Exploring the personal reality of disability and recovery: A tool for empowering the rehabilitation process. *Qualitative Health Research, 18,* 90–105.

James, W. (1904). Does "consciousness" exist? *Journal of Philosophy, Psychology, and Scientific Methods, 1,* 477–491.

Lakoff, G., & Johnson, M. (1980). *Metaphors we live by.* Chicago, IL: The University of Chicago Press.

Leonard, V. W. (1994). A Heideggerian phenomenological perspective on the concept of person. In P. Benner (Ed.), *Interpretive phenomenology: Embodiment, caring and ethics in health and illness* (pp. 43-64). Thousand Oaks, CA: Sage.

Marshall, J., & Goldbart, J. (2008). 'Communication is everything I think': Parenting a child who needs Augmentative and Alternative Communication (AAC). *International Journal of Language and Communication Disorders, 43,* 77–98.

Mazis, G. A. (2001). Emotion and embodiment within the medical world. In S. K. Toombs (Ed.), *Handbook of phenomenology and medicine* (pp. 197–214). Boston, MA: Kluwer.

McCarthy, J. (2003). Principlism or narrative ethics: must we choose between them? *Medical Humanities, 29,* 65–71.

Mead, N., & Bower, P. (2000). Patient-centeredness: a conceptual framework and review of the empirical literature. *Social Science & Medicine, 51,* 1087–1110.

Merleau-Ponty, M. (1996). *Phenomenology of perception* (Trans. Colin Smith). London, England: Routledge.

Nakano, E. V., & Hinckley, J. J. (2010). Therapy discharge becomes part of the life story. *Topics in Stroke Rehabilitation, 17,* 39–46.

O'Halloran, R., Hersh, D., Laplante-Levesque, A., & Worrall, L. (2010). Person-centeredness, ethics, and stories of risk. *Seminars in Speech and Language, 31,* 81–89.

Schon, D. (1983). *The reflective practitioner: How professionals think in action.* New York, NY: Basic Books.

Shadden, B. B., Hagstrom, F., & Koski, P. R. (2008). *Neurogenic communication disorders: Life stories and the narrative self.* San Diego, CA: Plural Publishing.

Simmons-Mackie, N., & Damico, J. (1999). Social role negotiation in aphasia therapy: Competence, incompetence, and conflict. In D. Kovarsky, J. Duchan, & M. Maxwell (Eds.), *Constructing (in)competence: Disabling evaluations in clinical and social interaction* (pp. 313–341). Hillsdale, NJ: Erlbaum.

Simmons-Mackie, N., & Damico, J. S. (2001). Intervention outcomes: A clinical application of qualitative methods. *Topics in Language Disorders, 22*, 21–36.

Simmons-Mackie, N., & Damico, J. S. (2007). Access and social inclusion in aphasia; Interactional principles and applications. *Aphasiology, 21*, 81–97.

Sparkes, A. C. (2000). Autoethnography and narratives of self: Reflections on criteria in action. *Sociology of Sport Journal, 17*, 21–41.

Spry, T. (2001). Performing autoethnography: An embodied methodological praxis. *Qualitative Inquiry, 7*, 706–732.

Stineman, M. G. (2011). The clinician's voice of brain and heart: A biopsycho-ecological framework for merging the biomedical and holistic. *Topics in Stroke Rehabilitation, 18*, 55–59.

Stineman, M. G., Ross, R. N., Maislin, G., Marchuk, N., Hijirida, S., & Weiner, M. (2007). Recovery preference exploration. *American Journal of Physical Medicine & Rehabilitation, 86*, 272–281.

Tedlock, B. (2003). Ethnography and ethnographic representation. In N. K. Denzin & Y. S. Lincoln (Eds.), Strategies of qualitativeInquiry (2nd ed., pp. 165–213). Thousand Oaks, CA: Sage.

Toombs, S. K. (2001). Introduction: Phenomenology and medicine. In S. K. Toombs (Ed,), *Handbook of phenomenology and medicine* (pp. 1–26). Boston, MA: Kluwer.

van Manen, M. (1995). On the epistemiology of reflective practice. *Teachers and Teaching: Theory and Practice, 1*, 33–50.

van Manen, M. (2001). Professional practice and "doing phenomenology." In S. K. Toombs (Ed.), *Handbook of phenomenology and medicine* (pp. 67–86). Boston, MA: Kluwer.

van Manen, M. (2007). Phenomenology of practice. *Phenomenology & Practice, 1*, 11–30.

Waksler, F. C. (2001). Medicine and the phenomenological method. In S. K. Toombs (Ed.), *Handbook of phenomenology and medicine* (pp. 67–86). Boston, MA: Kluwer.

Yorkston, K. M., Klasner, E. R., & Swanson, K. M. (2001). Communication in context: A qualitative study of the experience of individuals with multiple sclerosis. *American Journal of Speech-Language Pathology, 10*, 126–137.

Zaner, R. M. (1970). *The way of phenomenology: Criticism as a philosophical discipline.* New York, NY: Pegasus.

7

Grounded Theory in Speech-Language Pathology

DEBORAH HERSH AND ELIZABETH ARMSTRONG

Introduction

Qualitative research approaches are increasingly being used in the study of communication disorders, as is attested to by the nature of this volume. There have been special issues devoted to the subject in the *American Journal of Speech-Language Pathology* (Damico & Simmons-Mackie, 2003), *Aphasiology* (Damico, Simmons-Mackie, Oelschlaeger, Elman, & Armstrong, 1999), and in the Australian journal *ACQuiring Knowledge in Speech Language and Hearing* (Davidson & McAllister, 2002). Professor Jack Damico has been a pioneer both in carrying out qualitative studies and in inspiring and educating others in the application of such approaches.

One of the newer qualitative methodologies to be used in this area is that of grounded theory. Currently, the most comprehensive descriptions of its application to the field are to be found in the publications of Jemma Skeat (Skeat 2010; Skeat & Perry, 2008a) in which she presents summaries of the varieties of topics which have been researched using grounded theory thus far. These include her own grounded theory study looking at the use of outcome measures by speech-language pathologists (Skeat & Perry, 2008b), parent and carer perspectives on quality of life for children with speech and language difficulties (Markham & Dean, 2006), and the strategies used by speech-language pathologists when discharging clients from aphasia therapy (Hersh, 2003a). This final study, part of a larger body of research examining experiences of aphasia treatment termination from client, family and speech-language pathologists' perspectives, will be referred to later in this chapter to illustrate a number of features of grounded theory research. Grounded theory studies continue to be published in the speech-language pathology area, for example, the exploration of children's views of communication and speech-language pathology (Merrick & Roulstone, 2011) and how people with acquired communication and swallowing disorders view their relationships with their speech-language pathologist (Fourie, 2009).

According to Bryant and Charmaz (2007), grounded theory has become the most widely used and popular research method in a whole range of fields, particularly since the late 1980s with the publication of *Qualitative Analysis for Social Scientists* (Strauss, 1987) and *The Basics of Qualitative Research* (Strauss & Corbin, 1990). They suggest that its application in practice professions has led to advances in those professions. Certainly, the literature on grounded theory is very extensive and potentially confusing; this chapter can only scrape its surface. But there are many excellent texts which can provide useful, comprehensive information for new researchers (Birks & Mills, 2011; Charmaz, 2006; Corbin & Strauss, 2008; Creswell, 2007) and those which take the reader into more depth (Bryant & Charmaz, 2007). However, we aim to outline its background and main characteristics, touch on a few of the debates within it and explore what differentiates it from other approaches. Finally, we argue that there are very strong reasons for considering grounded theory research in speech-language pathology and we illustrate this with examples.

Background

Grounded theory methods were developed by Barney Glaser and Anselm Strauss when they were working together on their studies of issues related to dying in hospitals (Glaser & Strauss, 1965). The methods that they developed were explained in their book *The Discovery of Grounded Theory* (1967). This work arrived at a time when quantitative research in the United States dominated as *the* scientific method, based on positivist, logico-deductive methods which stressed that science had to be objective, generalizable, and replicable. The researcher was assumed to collect facts in an unbiased way and use them to test hypotheses and existing theory. Glaser and Strauss challenged these methodological assumptions with systematic strategies for generating new theories about social processes directly from data. They sought to move beyond description to explanatory theory and abstract, conceptual understandings but always retaining a close fit with the data. Their book countered ideas that qualitative methods were simply descriptive and unsystematic or that such methods were only useful as a precursor to more rigorous and reliable quantitative studies.

Charmaz (2006) wrote that grounded theory "marries two contrasting—and competing—traditions in sociology as represented by each of its originators" (p. 6). Glaser's background was in positivism and he sought a logical and systematic approach in which theory emerged or was "discovered" from the data. Strauss's background, in pragmatism, instead was influenced by the idea of human agency and that people create structures through engaging in processes. Pragmatism was a philosophy which underpinned symbolic interactionism (Blumer, 1969; Mead, 1934). Symbolic interactionism refers to the construction of society and self through language (a set of symbols), communication and interaction. Meaning is not simply a mental process but is negotiated through interaction with others. It suggests that people do not simply create meaning and symbols or just react to the actions of others but rather they learn about, and read meaning into, those actions. In social interaction, the actors are always influencing and interpreting each other—the processes are dynamic. For an example of the application of Mead's ideas to speech-language pathology, see Duchan (2000).

Most texts on grounded theory acknowledge the different directions that Glaser and Strauss took in the years following their original publications. Glaser continued to emphasize a more traditional positivist position with the idea of an objective external reality discovered by a neutral observer through categories and theory emerging from the data. Strauss and Corbin focused on new technical procedures, particularly useful for new researchers. Glaser criticized them for being too structured in their approach and for forcing the data into pre-conceived categories. More recently, Charmaz (2006) introduced another view to the debate by combining "basic grounded theory guidelines with twenty-first century methodological assumptions and approaches" (p. 9) to come up with a constructivist grounded theory. She emphasized the role of researchers interacting with participants and bringing their own interpretations to all phases of the process to construct the grounded theory rather than just discovering it. A further development in the application of grounded theory is found in Clarke's (2005) work on "situational analysis." She suggested that social "situations" should be the key focus and grounded theory could help map these social worlds. Clarke acknowledged Strauss's attention to multiple perspectives on reality and that reality is contextually situated but argued that her addition of situational analysis highlighted that knowledge is inherently complex, partial, and unstable. Research requires more awareness of its political nature, the need for reflexivity by the researcher, the role of power relationships in discourse and the need for a more context-driven analysis which does not only involve the voices of the actors (research participants) but the many layers of context in which they are situated (Clarke & Friese, 2007). In this approach, Clarke drew heavily on Foucault's postmodern, poststructural work. Birks and Mills (2011) note the trend in the literature to describe Glaser and Strauss as the "first generation of grounded theorists" (p. 2) and researchers such as Charmaz (2006) and Clarke (2005) as second generation grounded theorists. Variations in the modes of grounded theory are reflections of changing ontological and epistemological standpoints of the time (Hallberg, 2006). Birks and Mills encourage researchers to examine their own assumptions about knowledge "to draw the best from a variety of thinkers about how grounded theory methods can be used in individual research designs" (p. 5).

What Are the Characteristics of Grounded Theory?

Researchers using grounded theory enter a field of inquiry without firm, pre-conceived ideas about what they will find in order to allow new theoretical insights to emerge. Grounded theory is particularly useful for researching topics about which little is known, where the focus is "hypothesis generating rather than testing" (Corbin & Strauss, 2008, p. 25). Nevertheless, the approach should be systematic. The main characteristics of this approach are described below.

Simultaneous Data Collection and Analysis: In many other approaches, researchers plan the phase of data collection and once this is complete, then start their analysis. But when using grounded theory, this process is iterative with the analysis of data informing the next round of data collection. Charmaz (2006, p. 24) talked about "moving back and forth between data and analysis" and stressed the continuing influence of the researcher in interpreting and framing that data. Birks and Mills (2011) make a similar point by distinguishing between data collection and data generation. They argue that the researcher has a relationship with the data and directly engages with participants to produce material for analysis as well as writing field notes or memos as sources. The data sources themselves are commonly interviews, because of the emphasis in grounded theory on understanding people's perspectives, but can include many other forms such as other documents, diaries, newspaper sources, published literature, autobiographies, videos and pictures. (Note that Glaser, 1999, reminds us that, although grounded theory is now linked to qualitative research, it was originally developed as also useful for quantitative data.) Such sources may be used in combination in a study to help triangulate and strengthen data. Corbin and Strauss (2008), for example, recommend combining observation and interview because it is a useful way of verifying interpretations with participants. Such a flexible view allows the researcher to move between data collection and analysis in a logical and dynamic way, incorporating new ideas and giving breadth to emerging conceptual developments by constant comparison (see below).

Theoretical Sampling: This refers to sampling on the basis of conceptual findings from previously analyzed data. The researcher does not decide in advance exactly who to investigate or what questions to ask but instead follows the leads of the developing concepts and emerging theory to guide who next to approach, the settings to explore and what issues to raise with participants. The developing focus for questioning is sometimes referred to as "theoretical interviewing." The process of continuous checking between data and analysis helps to guide subsequent data collection through theoretical sampling such that the emerging concepts become increasingly abstract and theoretical. Obviously, a study has to start somewhere so the initial interview(s) or data collection may be purposive or selective and then initial analysis leads the researcher to engage with, and question, the data in order to develop a move to theoretical sampling. Some researchers have discussed their difficulty knowing when to move from selective sampling to theoretical sampling and have argued that there is little guidance on doing theoretical sampling in practice, especially when it is hard to control or anticipate recruitment of participants (Draucker, Martsolf, Ross, & Rusk, 2007). Birks and Mills (2011) suggest using theoretical sampling as soon as possible "as concepts will begin to take shape even from these earliest stages of analysis" (p. 70) whereas Charmaz (2006) believes that it is more valuable only once coding categories have been developed.

Theoretical Saturation: This is a point where no new theoretical concepts are found to emerge with ongoing data collection. Corbin and Strauss (2008) define it as a point in the analysis where all categories are well developed in terms of their properties (components), or dimensions (variations of these components along a range). Saturation may not necessarily be reached at the point where repetition of stories or events in the data is evident. It is more about saturation of conceptual categories, regardless of sample size. Indeed, the issue of how many participants one might need in order to reach saturation is a complex one, dependent on many factors including the scope, aims and nature of the study, the quality of the data and amount of useful information from each participant or source (Morse, 2000).

Theoretical Sensitivity: This is difficult to define but essentially is the ability of the researcher to be perceptive and to think conceptually. It is a notion which includes reflexivity and understanding the role of the self in the research, but also recognizing all the experience and knowledge that one brings to the research process. Theoretical sensitivity is an essential part of being able to construct theory. This is explained well by Charmaz (2006, p. 135):

> Theorizing means stopping, pondering, and rethinking anew. We stop the flow of studied experience and take it apart. To gain theoretical sensitivity, we look at studied life from multiple vantage points, make comparisons, follow leads and build ideas.

Constant Comparison: This is the comparing of all levels of data or analysis with each other along the journey of the study, comparing incident with incident, with code and with category for similarities and differences. This process is really dependent on iterative data collection and analysis and it is through such successive comparative analyses that the properties of codes and categories can be refined and that theory building occurs.

Codes and Categories: Coding is a process of identifying patterns in the data and it is the beginning of theory development in the research. Regardless of the mode of grounded theory, the first step is open coding in which the data are broken up into parts in order to categorize them. With interview data, this first step may be line by line coding. The researcher needs to be open minded, to be open to seeing patterns in the data in order to label them. These labels may be in vivo codes which are based directly on the language of the participant or the label may be taken from constructs from the field. Along with ongoing theoretical sampling, and constant comparison, these labeled or coded incidents, events or situations are then related to each other along their properties and dimensions, and grouped together in order to start developing categories. Categories are higher level conceptual groupings, sometimes also called themes (although see Morse, 2008, for the argument that categories and themes are different). Strauss and Corbin (1990, 1998) introduced the idea of a second layer of coding to start this process of putting data back together again after breaking it up—axial coding. This is a way of making links between categories and subcategories and demands greater levels of abstraction than in open coding. Following axial coding, the categories become more refined and it is possible to begin to draw down to a smaller number and seemingly more important categories, ultimately to work towards a core category or overarching theme. This phase is called selective coding. In reality, open, axial and selective coding is not always a linear progression, and coding at these levels may even occur concurrently as new data is collected or generated through theoretical sampling. The researcher may dip back into earlier views of the data as part of the process of constant comparison. However, the interplay of analysis aims for a coherent sense of an overriding theme or theoretical development. Corbin and Strauss (2008) suggest that a core category should be well integrated with other categories around it, should appear frequently in the data, be consistent with the data (without being forced to fit), be sufficiently abstract to be useful towards building more general theory and finally should be strengthened by its relationship with related categories and have the greatest explanatory power. In Glaserian grounded theory, open and selective coding phases are known together as substantive coding, which is then followed by a theoretical coding phase. Theoretical coding works on building more abstract theory from the substantive codes and developing theoretical coding families which show how a theory links together. The somewhat different coding emphases in Straussian and Glaserian grounded theory can be a source of confusion (Heath & Cowley, 2004; Tan, 2010) but ultimately, being aware of them can assist making "informed and knowledgeable choices" about one's research (Walker & Myrick, 2006, p. 558).

Memos and Diagrams: Memos are tools for capturing ideas and theoretical insights throughout the research process. Birks and Mills (2011, p. 40) describe memos as "the cornerstone of quality"; "the lubricant of a grounded theory machine." These notes are about the properties and dimensions of categories, how the researcher is relating and interpreting data, and about the process and running of the project. It is an opportunity to explore ideas without feeling self-conscious. Memos reflect the transition from substantive coding to greater conceptual abstraction and reintegration of concepts within theoretical coding. They are part of the audit trail and historical record of analytical and theoretical developments. Diagrams are also useful to visualize the relationship between categories and are helpful ways of summarizing complex material. Again, keeping a record of changes to diagrams is part of having a research audit trail.

A Grounded Theory: Corbin and Strauss (2008, p. 55) define theory as "a set of well-developed categories (themes, concepts) that are systematically interrelated through statements of relationship to form a theoretical framework that explains some phenomenon." They suggest that theory development in qualitative research is sometimes seen as secondary to description but that theories are useful. Theories can be substantive (confined to a particular area), middle-range (with broader application), or formal (more abstract, general concepts applicable across several substantive areas). Substantive theories are more usual products of grounded theory studies than formal theory although this is argued as limited (Glaser, 2007).

Quality of the Research: This is a big topic, but a key point is that the research has credibility if measures are taken to ensure quality through the entire process. Birks and Mills (2011) suggest that quality grounded theory is dependent on researcher expertise (including knowledge and self-awareness), methodological congruence (fit between one's philosophical position, study aims and chosen approach) and procedural precision (rigor with maintaining an audit trail, managing data and resources and working logically).

Debates within Grounded Theory

Grounded theory is a methodology which seeks to build theory from data, i.e., from the *ground up*. The term "grounded theory" therefore can describe both the methodology and the product of the research—a theory grounded in data. Bryant and Charmaz (2007) use the term "Grounded Theory Method" or GTM to distinguish the method from "Grounded Theory," a theory developed using GTM. Another potential source of confusion here is that Corbin and Strauss (2008) define grounded theory as a "specific methodology" (p. 1), noting that a methodology is "a way of thinking about and studying social phenomena" whereas methods are the actual "techniques and procedures for gathering and analysing data." There are, then, variations in the way that grounded theory is presented and defined.

Another issue debated within grounded theory is the role of the literature review and whether the traditional position of reviewing current knowledge in depth prior to starting a study is incompatible with the open mindedness needed to see new concepts and develop new theoretical ideas. Glaser has suggested that an early literature review should be related to, but outside, the main topic of interest or that it should be delayed and that any existing published theories are simply used as another source of data in the research. Despite this, there is recognition that most researchers do come to a study with some level of knowledge of the relevant literature and there is a general expectation from supervisors, funding bodies, and ethics committees that researchers will present a literature review. However, the key idea is that the literature review should not be stifling or restricting. The researcher should not fall into the trap of simply testing already existing theories rather than engaging with the data to develop new theoretical insights. In grounded theory studies, the researcher does not know what will emerge in advance of the study and therefore should not feel impelled to review and know everything beforehand. Corbin and Strauss (2008) warn that: "It is not unusual for students to become so enamored with a previous study or theory, either before or during their own investigation, that they become literally paralyzed" (p. 36). However, they do point out that the literature can provide questions early on and during the analysis, can suggest areas for theoretical sampling and can enhance sensitivity. Birks and Mills (2011) suggest doing enough of an early literature review to satisfy the needs of the research proposal and funding requirements and also to take advantage of reading about and considering how other researchers may have used grounded theory in similar studies.

Differentiating Grounded Theory from Other Approaches

It can be difficult for new researchers to decide which qualitative methodologies might best answer a research question, particularly when several approaches commonly use the same methods, such as semi-structured in-depth interviewing. For example, both phenomenology and grounded theory sample for people with experience of a particular phenomenon and commonly use interviews in order seek out their perceptions and stories. They both use analytic methods which code, sort and identify concepts, relationships and themes. Both decontextualize these bits of data and then recontextualize them in order to see the relationships between them. While phenomenology seeks the essence of the lived experience under examination, and grounded theory aims to understand the relationship of categories to a core category, both approaches search a central core of knowledge and meaning. Practitioners and clinicians will be interested in both forms of research. It is this degree of overlap which can confuse how to proceed. Starks and Trinidad (2007) provide an excellent explanation of the similarities and differences between grounded theory, phenomenology and discourse analysis and illustrate how the same data might be addressed by each of the approaches. They show how the different approaches influence how a researcher might frame their question, sample, attend to the data, analyze and draw conclusions. In order to use a particular approach, the researcher needs to understand the history, philosophical underpinnings, goals and potential products of their choice. The reader is also directed to Creswell (2007) for a clear overview of similarities and differences in qualitative research approaches. Finally, it is not uncommon to see published studies claiming to use grounded theory but presenting no evidence of moving beyond a descriptive level of coding. Birks and Mills (2011) wrote that the application of selected grounded theory methods, without moving on to theory development, may be inherently useful and effective but is better viewed as descriptive exploratory research. Sandelowski (2000) defends such "qualitative descriptive" studies as valuable in their own right, allowing the researcher to describe phenomena without having to delve into layers of interpretation. She claims that qualitative descriptive studies may "have hues, tones and textures" (p. 337) from a range of other methodologies such as grounded theory but that does not mean that they *are* grounded theory. These influences should be recorded, but qualitative descriptive studies should not have to claim to *be* anything that they are not. A good example of a study with "hues" of grounded theory but which explicitly stated that it was not claiming to *be* grounded theory is that of Markham, van Laar, Gibbard, and Dean (2009). They ran focus groups with children and young people with speech, language and communication needs in order to explore their perception of their quality of life experiences. Their aim was to describe participants' perceptions rather than develop a theory of their quality of life but they incorporated analytic induction, iterative data collection and analysis and constant comparison. They complemented these grounded theory influences with the use of another approach, Framework analysis (Ritchie & Lewis, 2005). The methods employed in this study are well described and this paper is a good example of how researchers work flexibly in practice.

So Why Should We Use Grounded Theory in Speech-Language Pathology?

While Skeat and Perry (2008a) warn that grounded theory is not quick and easy, they provide good reasons for its application to the field of speech-language pathology, particularly for studies focusing on social processes or in areas where theoretical frameworks are scarce. However, this approach is still relatively new. Their search of major databases (CINAHL, MEDLINE, EMBASE, ERIC, PUBMED) revealed only eight grounded theory studies in speech-language pathology and only two of those developed a theory product (Hersh, 2003a; Trulsson & Klingberg, 2003). The others used techniques from grounded theory but did not seek to develop a theoretical model. Skeat and Perry (2008a) also say that this tendency in speech-language pathology may reflect the time-consuming nature of such research. Nevertheless, Skeat (2010) pointed out that, despite the different modes and approaches in grounded theory, it remains a flexible method:

> As health professionals, social processes of action and interaction define much of what we do, particularly in diagnosis and therapy. Therefore grounded theory has the potential to help us understand the actions and interactions that take place in the clinical setting. Additionally, processes of professional practice ... could also be explored using grounded theory. (p. 109)

We also suggest that grounded theory offers a useful approach within speech-language pathology for a number of reasons. First, it is a profession ultimately concerned with communication, interaction and social processes—even if more traditional research has tended to focus on the language components and skills underpinning these processes. The symbolic interactionist perspective, more prominent in Straussian grounded theory, is attentive to the power of language and communication in influencing social processes and the implication for when this communication breaks down.

A second reason is that grounded theory is useful for opening up new areas about which little is known. There are many areas in speech-language pathology where further in-depth investigation would be useful. This is not just in relation to understanding clients' experiences and how they live with a range of communication and swallowing disorders, but could also have the potential to shed light on interactions and processes within therapy, within professional or teaching environments. The latter areas of focus have been approached to date from a variety of discourse and Conversation Analysis perspectives in the work of, for example, Ferguson (2008), Ferguson and Armstrong (2004), Horton (2008) and Simmons-Mackie and Damico (2008); however a grounded theory approach would provide a different perspective and the potential for further theoretical development. There is a lack of middle-range theories in speech-language pathology. The profession is not always in a position of looking to test theories which are already out there but needs to build from the ground up and to develop professionally-relevant theoretical frameworks and conceptual understandings.

Third, constructivist grounded theory is very focused on the role of the researcher as a reflexive agent in the process, co-constructing the process with the participant as well as bringing clinical experience to the analysis (and making this explicit in the analysis). This reflexivity and sensitivity is well recognized and encouraged in clinical practice (Fourie, 2011) and therefore speech-language pathologists may already have a range of skills to prepare them for sensitive research. They are already skilled interviewers—speech-language pathologists bring particular skills in being able to analyze data which is incomplete (such as in interviews with people with aphasia) and understand how to triangulate verbal output in interviews with the non-verbal messages which participants may employ. There are already papers on interviewing people with communication difficulties (Lloyd, Gatherer, & Kalsy, 2006; Luck & Rose, 2007), and it is no longer excusable to exclude such individuals from research as has happened in the past (Carlsson, Paterson, Scott-Findlay, Ehnfors, & Ehrenberg, 2007; Dalemans, Wade, D., van den Heuvel, & de Witte, 2009).

Fourth, there are parallels between the systematic exploratory methods of grounded theory and those of clinical inquiry, assessment, intervention and review. The methods of constant comparison, of iterative data collection and analysis are intuitively close to clinical practice. Speech-language pathologists make use of dynamic assessment and their assessments and treatments are often iterative processes. They draw on data and build up from there. They collect data systematically. They use elements of constant comparison when building up clinical experience with many clients over time—how is this person different or similar to other people I have treated? What can I learn about this person to help him or her in this situation? They ask questions, they keep records, they explore, they review. They build clinical schema. These parallels, if made explicit, may at least show that there are shared skills between research and clinical investigation, and the flexibility of being able to learn a little more with each clinical encounter. As clinicians and researchers become more familiar with qualitative research in the field of speech-language pathology, grounded theory will be one of the options on offer.

Finally, speech-language pathologists are recognizing that their role is not just in dealing with the impairment but in addressing the social consequences of communication and swallowing disorders. Their role has expanded, along with the ICF framework (World Health Organization, 2001) and the prevalence of social approaches for intervention (Simmons-Mackie, 2000) to influence clients' participation in society more generally. From this perspective, research with a broad social focus, and research which seeks to explore social consequences fits well with grounded theory.

Example of a Snapshot of Grounded Theory Research: The Use of Initial Coding and Memos

This example is taken from Hersh's (2003b) research on client and professional experiences of aphasia treatment termination. It demonstrates how she used memos to draw out ideas from raw interview data. The interview was with a speech pathologist, Patricia (pseudonym) who worked in private practice. This interview was carried out midway into data collection once it became evident that it was important to contrast the experiences of therapists in the public and private sectors. Patricia had agreed to talk about her experiences of discharging people with aphasia from therapy but had not agreed to refer any of her previously discharged clients to the study. This clip is the opening exchange in the interview. The numbers down the left hand side are the text unit (in this case, interview turn) reference numbers:

Raw Interview Data

3 DH: Perhaps just to start off to kind of link up the context, can you think of any case where, for you, the discharge point for a patient with aphasia was in some way tricky, or stuck in your mind or just raised issues for you as a therapist?

4 P: I think in private practice, the major issue … is having them accept discharge. I think I can remember with at least five cases I've seen where they drag on and drag on and they just won't let you go. They don't want to give up hope, they don't want to have to face the fact that they're …they've slowed right down in improvement and contrary to the literature when I was studying, people do keep improving for years and years and years if you've got the time and the patience and there's the money available. But the two that I really made no gains in a year, you were … you ask yourself what are they actually paying for? Are they paying for company? Are they paying for undivided attention? Or are they paying for some sort of rapport? They always talk better with us than with anybody else, don't they? So they're paying for something. But I just felt it was an impossible situation in both of them, in two in particular, and they're both very angry. In one the family are very angry but the patient is relieved. She didn't want to keep going because she knew she couldn't do it and she'd had enough and she'd got family pressure to do some work every day and there was nothing that … so they were very angry with me. So you couldn't interview them.

5 DH: That's OK.

6 P: And the other one, the man did what I always like to do, he discharged me but he discharged me with anger. And anger was his most favorite occupation

in life in any case, probably before the stroke as well, so you couldn't interview him. And so we have those and then the other ones are where they reluctantly accept, you know, how you go from weekly to fortnightly to monthly to 3 month to … and wean them off, and I think they grieve all over again and they have to actually come to terms with accepting that we believe it's not worth paying for. I mean they … because they're paying, they think well, I'm paying you so …

7 DH: Keep coming.

8 P: Keep coming. And yes you can do that if there's even some gains but ethically you just argue with yourself if there's nothing and if you see after 6 months they actually can now do something they couldn't do before … I've got one I've been seeing about five years. And now she can name things around the room and respond to questions and 50% of the time, it's the right word whereas 6 months ago, the right word came second try, the first thing that came into her head came out of her mouth first and then she'd say no and correct it. So that's a gain. That's a real life, every day, "Mum's happy" sort of gain. But if they're not … yes. So they've gone through the grief and they have to really lose the person, lose us, face where they are and that they're always going to stay like that, that there's very little hope, otherwise we wouldn't stop, and I think once they've worked through that, and come to terms with that and said, "OK, bye bye, here's a box of chocolates" or "here's a card," or "here's a….," you know, someone will write us a letter saying "thank you very much," you know, "Dad is very happy," bla bla, they don't want to talk about it. So that's why I think here, we didn't … [name of a colleague] and I spoke at length about it right at the very beginning and they were the two reasons: (a) they're either very angry with us for leaving them in the lurch or (b) they've worked through it, come to a decision, made that decision, why would we want them to have to go through that all again?

9 DH: Why talk about it and have to re-live it?

10 P: That's right.

Document Memo for this Section
Text unit 4 is wonderfully dense, full of coding and information. I didn't realize it immediately at the time, but what Patricia was doing was justifying to me why she hadn't linked me with any clients. She chose too to illustrate her reasoning, one with an angry carer, the other grieving (see text unit 8). Note her comment "so you couldn't interview them" perhaps meaning "I don't want you to hear them talk badly of me"? (I possibly could have spoken to them and they might have been happy to find a channel to discuss their feelings.)

What Is the Role of the Issue of Paying for Improvement?

Text unit 6: Patricia's [SP] ideal is that patients discharge her, that they take the responsibility for themselves. But in the case she describes here, the man discharges her with anger. She again repeats that I couldn't interview this man because he was angry, an example of my sample being vetted by the therapists. Note the phrase "reluctant acceptance" which I have coded under (1441) SP perceptions of patient emotions about discharge. Note also how she says "You know how you go from weekly to fortnightly ..." which is interesting because it documents how it is assumed that everyone does this (and I am finding that they do), that it is common practice but not really documented as a specific practice. Patricia implies that, for some, discharge involves them grieving all over again, and "accepting that we believe it's not worth paying for." This is a great reference to the discharge point as being significant for adjustment and for the loss of the therapist and the hope that being in therapy entails. Within the private system she suggests that in some way people are buying hope. They expect that if they can continue to keep paying for something then it should be able to continue. It is like going into a shop and being told that you can't buy something because you can't really benefit from it and someone else should have it.

Text unit 8: Also dense and continues to explain why she didn't refer patients for my study.

At this point, the analysis of the interview was through open coding but also placing sections of text into already existing "boxes" developed from coding previous interviews. Hersh used the software package available at the time (NUD.IST) to help manage and organize the data. Sections of the text units were coded multiple times.

Example of the Coding

Text unit 4: Speech pathologists/professional identity ("They always talk better with us than with anybody else, don't they?"); therapy/setting/private practice; SP beliefs about recovery and timelines ("people do keep improving for years and years and years if you've got the time and the patience and there's the money available"); SP beliefs about patient adjustment ("They don't want to give up hope, they don't want to have to face the fact that they're ... they've slowed right down in improvement"); therapeutic relationships/dependence and reliance; clinical factors/patient and family wishes; speech pathologists/discharge/emotions about ... /by patients and carers.

Text unit 6: speech pathologists/therapy/setting/private practice; discharge/strategies/weaning/spacing sessions; speech pathologists/discharge/emotions about … /by patients and carers; speech pathologists/discharge/outcomes/SP outcomes ("the man did what I always like to do, he discharged me …").

Text unit 8: speech pathologists/professional ethics ("but ethically you just argue with yourself if there's nothing"); beliefs about patient adjustment ("they have to really lose the person, lose us"); clinical factors/therapy benefit.

Overall, this example shows how the process of coding and writing memos drew out different points from this section of interview. The gatekeeping of potential participants for the study was an interesting issue later discussed in the methodology section of the thesis. Patricia's assumption that spacing sessions was common practice was also echoed by other participants despite the lack of any reference to it in the literature at the time. It appeared to be an example of practice knowledge. It eventually was discussed in the thesis as one of the "separation" strategies in the discussion on "weaning" (Hersh, 2003a). Weaning was an issue that emerged from the data; initially, Hersh was looking at *why* speech-language pathologists discharged clients, but from the interviews, it emerged that *how* they did this was important. The coding of this section helped to break up or unpack the many strands held within a rich text unit but the memo was important in capturing overriding ideas at the time around relationship, dependence, adjustment, family involvement, and so on. The ethical issue, particularly for clinicians in private practice, of not wanting to continue to treat someone who was not improving (despite their wish to continue coming) was raised in this section. The analogy of going into a shop to buy something that is refused was helpful at the time in making sense of experiences with private therapy.

Conclusion

There are many good reasons why grounded theory is a useful addition to the collection of qualitative research approaches in speech-language pathology. This chapter has briefly summarized the background to this approach, its characteristics, and its relationship to other qualitative approaches. Since Skeat and Perry's useful paper in 2008, there have been more published studies by speech-language pathologists using grounded theory (e.g., Attrill & Gunn, 2010; Fourie, 2009; Hersh; 2009; Merrick & Roulstone, 2011) as well as grounded theory studies by other professionals of relevance to our field (e.g., Chetpakdeechit, Hallberg, Hagberg, & Mohlin, 2009; Folke, Paulsson, Fridlund, & Söderfeldt, 2009). With grounded theory now such a prominent research methodology in health and the social sciences, speech-language pathology is set to join the tide and reap the benefits of this approach.

References

Attrill, S., & Gunn, S. (2010). Clients becoming teachers: Speech-language pathology students' understanding of rehabilitation following clinical practicum in a rehabilitation setting. *International Journal of Speech-Language Pathology, 12*(2), 142–151.

Birks, M., & Mills, J. (2011). *Grounded theory: A practical guide.* London, England: Sage.

Blumer, H. (1969). *Symbolic Interactionism: Perspective and method.* Englewood Cliffs, NJ: Prentice Hall.

Bryant, A., & Charmaz, K. (Eds.). (2007). *The Sage handbook of grounded theory.* London, England: Sage.

Carlsson, E., Paterson, B. L., Scott-Findlay, S., Ehnfors, M., & Ehrenberg, A. (2007). Methodological issues in interviews involving people with communication impairments after acquired brain damage. *Qualitative Health Research, 17*(10), 1361–1371.

Charmaz, K. (2006). *Constructing grounded theory: A practical guide through qualitative analysis.* London, England: Sage.

Chetpakdeechit, W., Hallberg, U., Hagberg, C., & Mohlin, B. (2009). Social life aspects of young adults with cleft lip and palate: Grounded theory approach. *Acta Odontologica Scandinavica, 67,* 122–128.

Clarke, A. E. (2005). *Situational analysis: Grounded theory after the postmodern turn.* Thousand Oaks, CA: Sage.

Clarke, A. E., & Friese, C. (2007). Grounded theorizing using situational analysis. In A. Bryant & K. Charmaz (Eds.), *The Sage handbook of grounded theory* (pp. 363–397). London, England: Sage.

Corbin, J., & Strauss, A. (2008). *Basics of qualitative research: Techniques and procedures for developing grounded theory* (3rd ed.) Thousand Oaks, CA: Sage.

Creswell, J. W. (2007). *Qualitative inquiry and research design: Choosing among five approaches* (2nd ed.). Thousand Oaks, CA: Sage.

Dalemans, R., Wade, D., van den Heuvel, W., & de Witte, L. P. (2009). Facilitating the participation of people with aphasia in research: a description of strategies. *Clinical Rehabilitation, 23,* 948–959.

Damico, J. S., Simmons-Mackie, N. N., Oelschlaeger, M., Elman, R., & Armstrong, E. (1999). Qualitative methods in aphasia research: Basic issues. *Aphasiology, 13,* 651–665.

Damico, J. S., & Simmons-Mackie, N. N. (2003). Qualitative research and speech-language pathology: A tutorial for the clinical realm. *American Journal of Speech-Language Pathology, 12*(2), 131–143.

Davidson, B., & McAllister, L., (2002). An introduction to qualitative research approaches. *ACQuiring Knowledge in Speech, Language and Hearing, 4,* 28–31.

Draucker, C. B., Martsolf, D. S., Ross, R., & Rusk, T. B. (2007). Theoretical sampling and category development in grounded theory. *Qualitative Health Research, 17*(8), 1137–1148.

Duchan, J. (2000). Assessing socially situated participation: A way of integrating communication and social assessment approaches. *Seminars in Speech and Language, 21*(3), 205–213.

Ferguson, A. (2008). *Expert practice: A critical discourse.* San Diego, CA: Plural Publishers.

Ferguson, A. J., & Armstrong, E. (2004). Reflections on speech-language therapists' talk: Implications for clinical practice and education. *International Journal of Language and Communication Disorders, 39*(4), 469–507.

Folke, S., Paulsson, G., Fridlund, B., & Söderfeldt, B. (2009). The subjective meaning of xerostomia – an aggravating misery. *International Journal of Qualitative Studies on Health and Well-being, 4,* 245–255.

Fourie, R. (2009). A qualitative study of the therapeutic relationship in speech-language therapy: Perspectives of adults with acquired communication and swallowing disorders. *International Journal of Language and Communication Disorders, 44*(6), 979–999.

Fourie, R. J. (2011). *Therapeutic processes for communication disorders.* Hove, Engand: Psychology Press.

Glaser, B. (1999). The future of grounded theory. *Qualitative Health Research, 9*(6), 836–845.

Glaser, B. (2007). Doing formal theory. In A. Bryant & K. Charmaz (Eds.), *The Sage handbook of grounded theory* (pp. 97–113). London, England: Sage.

Glaser, B. G., & Strauss, A. L. (1965). *Awareness of dying.* New York, NY: Aldine.

Glaser, B. G., & Strauss, A. L. (1967). *The discovery of grounded theory: Strategies for qualitative research.* New York, NY: Aldine.

Hallberg, L. (2006). The "core category" of grounded theory: Making constant comparisons. *International Journal of Qualitative Studies of Health and Well-Being, 1,* 141–148.

Heath, H., & Cowley, S. (2004). Developing a grounded theory approach: A comparison of Glaser and Strauss. *International Journal of Nursing Studies, 41,* 141–150.

Hersh, D. (2003a). "Weaning" clients from aphasia therapy: Speech pathologists' strategies for discharge. *Aphasiology, 17*(11), 1007–1029.

Hersh, D. (2003b). *Experiences of treatment termination in chronic aphasia* (Unpublished doctoral dissertation). Flinders University, Adelaide, Australia.

Hersh, D. (2009). How do people with aphasia view their discharge from therapy? *Aphasiology, 23*(3), 331–350.

Horton, S. (2008). Learning-in-interaction: Resourceful work by people with aphasia and therapists in the course of language impairment therapy. *Aphasiology, 22*(9), 985–1014.

Lloyd, V., Gatherer, A., & Kalsy, S. (2006). Conducting qualitative interview research with people with expressive language difficulties. *Qualitative Health Research, 16*(10), 1386–1404.

Luck, A. M., & Rose, M. L. (2007). Interviewing people with aphasia: Insights into method adjustments from a pilot study. *Aphasiology, 21*(2), 208–224.

Markham, C., & Dean, T. (2006). Parents' and professionals' perceptions of quality of life in children with speech and language difficulty. *International Journal of Language and Communication Disorders, 41,* 189–212.

Markham, C., van Laar, D., Gibbard, D., & Dean, T. (2009). Children with speech, language and communication needs: their perceptions of their quality of life. *International Journal of Language and Communication Disorders, 44*(5), 748–768.

Mead, G. H. (1934). *Mind, self and society.* Chicago, IL: University of Chicago Press.

Merrick, R., & Roulstone, S. (2011). Children's views of communication and speech-language pathology. *International Journal of Speech-Language Pathology, 13*(4), 281–290.

Morse, J. (2000). Determining sample size. *Qualitative Health Research, 10*(1), 3–5.

Morse, J. (2008). Confusing categories and themes. *Qualitative Health Research, 18*(6), 727–728.

Ritchie, J., & Lewis, J. (2005). *Qualitative research practice: A guide for social science students and researchers.* London, England: Sage.

Sandelowski, M. (2000). Whatever happened to qualitative description? *Research in Nursing and Health, 23,* 334–340.

Simmons-Mackie, N., & Damico, J. (2008). Exposed and embedded corrections in aphasia therapy: Issues of voice and identity. *International Journal of Language and Communication Disorders, 43*(S1), 5–17.

Skeat, J. (2010). Using grounded theory in health research. In P. Liamputtong (Ed.), *Research methods in health: Foundations for evidence-based practice* (pp. 106–122). Victoria, Australia: Oxford University Press.

Skeat, J., & Perry, A. (2008a). Grounded theory as a method of research in speech and language therapy. *International Journal of Language and Communication Disorders, 43*(2), 95–109.

Skeat, J., & Perry, A. (2008b). Exploring the implementation and use of outcomes measurement in practice: a qualitative study. *International Journal of Language and Communication Disorders, 43*(2), 110–125.

Simmons-Mackie, N. N. (2000). Social approaches to the management of aphasia. In L. E. Worrall & C. M. Frattali (Eds.), *Neurogenic communication disorders: A functional approach* (pp. 162–187). New York, NY: Thieme.

Starks, H., & Trinidad, S. B. (2007). Choose your method: A comparison of phenomenology, discourse analysis and grounded theory. *Qualitative Health Research, 17*(10), 1372–1380.

Strauss, A. (1987). *Qualitative analysis for social scientists*. New York, NY: Cambridge University Press.

Strauss, A., & Corbin, J. (1990). *Basics of qualitative research: Grounded theory procedures and techniques*. Newbury Park, CA: Sage.

Strauss, A., & Corbin, J. (1998). *Basics of qualitative research: Grounded theory procedures and techniques* (2nd ed.). Newbury Park, CA: Sage.

Tan, J. (2010). Grounded theory in practice: Issues and discussion for new qualitative researchers. *Journal of Documentation, 66*(1), 93–112.

Trulsson, U., & Klingberg, G. (2003). Living with a child with a severe orofacial handicap: Experience from the perspectives of parents. *European Journal of Oral Science, 111*, 19–25.

Walker, D., & Myrick, F. (2006). Grounded theory: An exploration of process and procedure. *Qualitative Health Research, 16*(4), 547–559.

World Health Organization (2001). *International classification of functioning, disability and health (ICF)*. Geneva, Switzerland: Author.

8
Pragmatics as Interaction

MICHAEL R. PERKINS

Introduction

In this chapter I will provide an assessment and critique of the way in which mainstream conceptualization of pragmatic impairment has been implicitly determined by the use of taxonomies derived from linguistic theory and cognitive neuropsychology, which happen to be particularly suited to quantitative research paradigms, and will argue instead for the advantages of a data-driven qualitative approach.

Pragmatics—the branch of linguistics that examines language use—has been applied extensively in the study, assessment and remediation of communication disorders. As a focus of study rather than a research method, clinical pragmatics is neither inherently qualitative nor quantitative, and indeed a great deal of the research carried out in this area has used quantitative analysis. In this chapter, however, I will argue that the subject matter of clinical pragmatics is best understood in all its richness when approached qualitatively. I consider both the strengths and limitations of the major theoretical and methodological assumptions in pragmatic research and their implications for how we characterize pragmatic impairment. I also consider the wide range of conditions that are commonly described as instances of pragmatic impairment, and argue that the coverage of the term is too broad and disparate for it to be useful as a diagnostic category. Instead, I describe an alternative approach which views pragmatic impairment as the result of complex interactions at many levels—including the sociocultural and that of moment-by-moment social action between individuals, as well as the neurological, cognitive and linguistic—rather than as the direct manifestation of a specific underlying deficit within an individual.

Pragmatics and Pragmatic Impairment

A cartoon by Danny Shanahan, published in the *New Yorker* in 1989, shows a man who has fallen into a river shouting to his dog: "Lassie! Get help!!" In the next frame we see Lassie on a psychoanalyst's couch. This is a classic example of pragmatic misunderstanding which would typically be described as a failure on Lassie's part to accurately relate the speaker's utterance to the situational context and thus to recognize his communicative intent. Such misunderstandings are not restricted to fictitious canines but are also common in individuals with conditions such as autism and right hemisphere brain damage (RHD) (who also, incidentally, would often struggle to get the joke in the Lassie cartoon). For example, a research assistant of mine once presented an 11-year-old autistic child with a piece of paper divided into seven rectangles and asked him to write the days of the week in each rectangle. He responded by writing "the" in the first rectangle, "days" in the second, and so on (Perkins, 2007, p. 20). Pragmatics involves more than just comprehension, though, and is equally evident in the way we express ourselves. As speakers, whatever we say needs to be properly designed and fitted to its communicative purpose, taking into account factors such as what our addressee is likely to already know, what they can see and hear, and what has already been said so far by both parties. People with autism and RHD are often not very good at this either. In Extract 1, from Bishop and Adams (1989), a child with autism spectrum disorder (ASD) is relating an event to an adult he doesn't know very well.

Extract 1
1. *Child:* my brother was feeling sick on Monday
2. *Adult:* right
3. *Child:* . and I took my trouser off
4. *Adult:* uhuh . why did you take your trousers off?
5. *Child:* he was sick on my trouser

The adult's response in line 4 shows she is unable to make sense of the child's utterance "and I took my trouser off" as it stands, and is moved to elicit further background information. This suggests that the child may have either overestimated what the adult already knows, or been unable to design his utterance to incorporate sufficient information for the adult to make sense of it.

At the heart of pragmatics, then, lies the relationship between language use (both comprehension and production), context and inference. However, any analysis of pragmatic behavior in real life settings (as opposed to the invented scenarios commonly used as illustrations in many pragmatics textbooks and theoretical articles) invariably leads to consideration of a wide range of other linked factors. For example, the ability to design an utterance that is fit for purpose clearly requires competence in syntax, semantics, phonology, phonetics and prosody, and a deficiency in any of these areas will therefore have pragmatic consequences. People with aphasia, for instance, are often unable to encode enough detail in their sentences because of problems with lexical retrieval and grammatical formulation, leaving their interlocutors with very little to go on when trying to infer the intended meaning. Similarly, children with developmental speech problems and adults with severe dysarthria can be difficult to understand because the realization of a series of phonologically contrastive sounds such as /t, s, ʃ/ as a single sound such as [t] or [x] means that any distinction between word sets such as *tip*, *sip* and *ship* is lost and can only be retrieved through inference from context. In addition to language, paralinguistic features such as gesture, eye gaze, facial expression and body posture provide further resources for encoding meaning which, together with language, constitute an integrated communicative signaling system (Clark, 1996; Goldin-Meadow, 2000,) and all of these can also contribute to the pragmatic enterprise—or detract from it, should they be compromised in any way. Finally, the inferential process itself relies on input from a range of cognitive activities such as paying attention, remembering, abstracting and problem solving, and also perceptual activities such as auditory and visual processing (e.g., failure to detect sarcasm from facial expression by the visually impaired). Another way of looking at pragmatics, then, is to see it as getting the balance right between what is encoded (e.g., using syntax, phonology and gesture) and what is left to be inferred. Anything that interferes with this balancing act— whether it be problems with lexical retrieval, auditory discrimination or inferential processing—has direct pragmatic consequences. When viewed in this way, there are very few, if any, aspects of interpersonal communication which do not contribute at least indirectly to pragmatic performance.

Given the wide range of disparate factors involved in pragmatics, it is hardly surprising that a similarly wide and disparate range of manifestations of pragmatic impairment have been described. Thus, in addition to what might be regarded as more core pragmatic difficulties such as a failure to accurately process indirect requests, detect irony and stay on topic, the following are just a few of the many behaviors to have been described as symptomatic of pragmatic impairment: inappropriate body posture, physical proximity, eye gaze, vocal intensity, tense use, lexical choice, pausing, initiation, repetition, volubility, range of speech acts and conversational rapport (Bishop, 2003; Penn, 1985; Prutting & Kirchner, 1983). The quantity and variety of putative symptoms is at least matched by the number of instruments available for assessing pragmatic impairment, and these can sometimes bear very little resemblance to one another in terms of their criteria and focus (Perkins, 2007, 2010). This can lead to a situation where an individual assessed as pragmatically impaired using one protocol would not be so described using a different one. Clearly pragmatic impairment is such a many-headed hydra that its diagnostic value as a single undifferentiated label can be minimal—even counter-productive. Whenever it is used in clinical and research contexts, it is essential to specify what analytical measure has been used and which particular features have been targeted. However, even the analytical criteria used and the status of the categories on which they are based can also be called into question, which is where we now turn our attention.

Explaining Pragmatic Impairment

An essential step in most research studies (but particularly those using quantitative methodologies) is to organize and structure one's primary data into categories. In pragmatics—and clinical pragmatics in particular—this approach has largely defined the field. We are thus used to seeing assessment and treatment of so-called pragmatic impairments based on the identification of discrete—and countable—phenomena such as speech acts, clarification requests, cohesive ties, topic shifts and repetitions. But how do we arrive at such categories in the first place, and how does a particular phenomenon, condition or set of behaviors come to be termed "pragmatic"?

Pragmatic Theory

When clinicians first moved beyond language structure in their attempts to pin down the functional properties of communicative behavior in the 1970s (Gallagher & Prutting, 1983), they naturally turned to what pragmatic theory had to offer. Speech act theory (Austin, 1962) furnished categories such as speech act, which could be further subdivided according to the speaker's communicative purpose and state of mind, and whether it aimed to effect change or draw attention to some state of affairs (Searle, 1976). Grice's (1975) theory of conversational implicature proposed four maxims (quality, quantity, relevance and clarity) to account for how we are able to work out what others mean from what they say. Relevance theory (Sperber & Wilson, 1986) addressed the same issue using a single principle of relevance which offset communicative gain against processing cost. Theories of discourse provided accounts of how strings of utterances could be sequenced coherently and made cohesive through the use of devices such as anaphora and discourse particles (Halliday & Hasan, 1976). Clinical pragmatic assessments, profiles and checklists have made abundant use of such theory-derived categories to quantify type and degree of pragmatic impairment using constructs such as the relative frequency of particular types of speech act, cohesive ties or breaking of conversational maxims. Even the avowedly qualitative approach of conversation analysis has described phenomena such as turn construction unit, overlap and repair, which have proved amenable to quantification for research purposes (see chapter 5, this volume, and also Perkins, 2011a, for an extensive summary of clinical pragmatic research studies which have drawn on the theoretical approaches above).

One cause for concern about adopting categories from pragmatic theory for clinical research is that these theories were devised to account for typical rather than atypical communication, and their proponents have shown little interest in, or even awareness of, pragmatic impairment. Even in the rare cases where clinical behavior has been examined by theoreticians, it has almost invariably been used solely as evidence for or against a particular theory (e.g., Wearing, 2010). Furthermore, the focus of pragmatic theorists has typically been narrow, with little interest shown in accounting for the full range of phenomena which have been regarded as pragmatic, and thereby at risk of impairment. For example, the restricted range of a recent handbook article on pragmatics was justified solely on the grounds that this particular focus had "been of interest to linguists and philosophers of language in the past thirty years or so" (Sperber & Wilson, 2005, p. 468). Clinical pragmaticians, on the other hand, have to contend with conditions which are not directly addressed by pragmatic theory (e.g., the role played by non-linguistic systems such as gesture, facial expression and sensorimotor processing in conveying and inferring communicative intent; Perkins, 2007).

A further limitation of pragmatic theory is that although its terminology may be useful for describing atypical pragmatic behavior, it often has little to say about what may have caused it—something which can be crucial for differential diagnosis and treatment programs. This can be an issue when the same pragmatic difficulties are observed in very different clinical populations—for example, failing to infer a speaker's communicative intent by individuals with autism (a developmental disorder) and RHD (an acquired neurological disorder). This has given rise over the last two decades or so to a complementary strand of clinical pragmatic research—sometimes called "neuropragmatics" (Stemmer, 2008)—which focuses on the underlying neurological and cognitive conditions which appear to be linked to pragmatic impairment.

Neurological and Cognitive Explanations of Pragmatics

It is well known that damage to various regions of the brain—particularly prefrontal cortex, orbitofrontal cortex and the left, right and ventromedial frontal lobes—can lead to behavior that many would describe as pragmatically impaired (Stemmer, 2008). The effects are usually couched in cognitive terms, such as problems with Theory of Mind (ToM) (the attribution of mental states to oneself and others), executive function (planning, controlling, inhibiting, decision making and multi-tasking), memory and the processing of emotions. Affected individuals are commonly described as having a deficit in such areas, and there are many tests available for quantifying the degree of deficit. It is also common to find these systems/capacities/processing sites described in modular terms, i.e., as discrete, self-contained mental entities. Indeed, Wilson (2005) goes as far as to regard pragmatics itself as a specific component of a

ToM module (although though it should be noted that her view of pragmatics is a comparatively circumscribed one).

The move to account for pragmatic impairment in terms of underlying cognitive causes may be seen as positive in the sense that it extends the symptomatology of conditions seen as having a pragmatic dimension and shows how similar sets of behavioral symptoms may have quite distinct cognitive origins in different individuals. For example, seemingly bizarre topic shifts have been linked to problems with memory and attention in TBI (Perkins, Body, & Parker, 1995) whereas in autism they have been attributed to obsessive interests (Baron-Cohen and Wheelwright, 1999). However, such reductionist modes of explanation can also have the effect of constraining our understanding of pragmatics within an over-rigid framework whereby clinical conditions are seen as pragmatic only by virtue of their etiology, and independently of their behavioral manifestation.

The Pursuit of the Essence of Pragmatic Impairment

In a recent review article, Stainton (2011, p. 86) examines "what makes something a *genuine* pragmatic impairment" (my emphasis). In a careful and cogently argued account (Stainton is a philosopher), he provides examples of what would commonly be regarded as instances of pragmatic impairment and then proceeds to examine different ways of pinning down the essential property that they all share. I have drawn attention to the terms "genuine" and "essential" because they point to a common assumption in much current thinking in clinical pragmatics which in my view is open to question— namely, that all pragmatic impairments share a single underlying property or essence. I have already alluded above to why this might be considered illusory, i.e., since the term "pragmatic impairment" is applied to such a varied range of conditions there couldn't possibly be a single etiology. A common way of trying to circumvent this issue is to restrict the range of clinical conditions to which the term can genuinely apply. For example, Stainton regards an inability to process sarcasm or indirect requests as genuinely pragmatic if there is an identifiable underlying neurological cause and difficulty with non-literal language by people with autism as genuinely pragmatic because autism is a medical condition. Implicit in such a position is what Crystal (1980) defined as the "medical model" of clinical linguistics, whereby communication difficulties could only be seen as a genuine disorder if some underlying cause could be specified in anatomical, physiological or neurological terms, as opposed to the "behavioral model" whereby a condition can be regarded as an impairment purely by virtue of its behavioral characteristics, whether or not any underlying cause is known. The behavioral model is now widely accepted. In fact, autism, which Stainton regards as a cause of pragmatic impairment because it constitutes a medical condition, is actually diagnosed purely on behavioral grounds because there is no universally accepted underlying neurological cause (and even if there were, it is unlikely that professionals such as psychiatrists would make use of it for diagnostic purposes, as neurological conditions do not figure in their diagnostic practices). Indeed, some studies have shown that certain supposed underlying cognitive deficits which are definitive of autism, such as inflexibility of thought, may be explicable purely in terms of the way in which interactions between autistic and non-autistic individuals unfold (Muskett, Perkins, Clegg, & Body, 2010). In short, on the back of some rather dubious reasoning and despite a great deal of evidence to the contrary, the assumption that pragmatic impairment *must* be a unitary condition with a single underlying cause is so strong and overriding in some quarters that it is often not even questioned.

A further illustration of this mindset is an extensive treatment of pragmatic impairment by Cummings (2009) who defines pragmatics in terms of a small set of features, including implicature, presupposition, deixis, coherence and narrative structure, which she claims are directly derived from a pragmatic mental module. Despite providing no overt rationale or justification—beyond her own stipulation—for her selection of this specific set of features (Stainton, 2010), she is nevertheless strongly critical of others who seek to define pragmatic impairment in any other terms (Perkins, 2011b).

Cummings' take on pragmatic impairment is an extreme variant of the cognitivist view, mentioned above and widely held by cognitive neuropsychologists and many linguistic theorists, which accounts for communicative behavior in terms of a set of underlying cognitive and linguistic systems, capacities or competences, frequently regarded as modular. Communicative impairments are seen as a direct result of underlying damage in one or more of these systems. There is no space here for even a modest evaluation of cognitivism (see Edwards, 1997, for a critique from the perspective of discursive psychology, and Perkins, 2007, for an assessment specifically focused on clinical pragmatics), so I will restrict myself to a few brief points with a specific bearing on pragmatic impairment and research methodology.

Most studies of pragmatic impairment adopt an experimental methodology whereby one or more individuals perform tasks in controlled conditions in accordance with a particular protocol. Performance is evaluated using strict criteria, and ranked against a set of independently established norms. To illustrate this, a capacity widely seen as canonical in the assessment of pragmatics is the possession of a theory of mind (ToM), sometimes referred to as mind-reading ability. This is typically assessed by asking participants to comment on a story or role-play which requires insight into others' mental states such as being able to evaluate something as true or false. Performance can be graded as representing first-order or second-order ToM ability (Happé, 1993). Failure to perform within the normal range is commonly described as having a ToM deficit, and, by implication, also a pragmatic deficit (Martin & McDonald, 2003). A central issue here is that there is no means of accessing the putative cognitive entity ToM other than indirectly through performance on a particular task. Even fMRI studies which purport to locate ToM in a particular region of the brain (Gallagher et al., 2000) are simply showing neural activity due to task performance. ToM is, in fact, nothing more (nor less) than a theoretical construct proposed to account for such task performance. However, in some kind of mental reversal it has somehow come to be widely regarded as an a priori cognitive entity which exists independently of any means of accessing it and is amenable to discovery. Although cognitive neuroscientists may deny this view when pressed, the a priori assumption is nonetheless implicit in the way ToM is almost universally referred to in research publications (e.g., "Impairments in a theory of mind lead to a highly restricted use of language" [Tager-Flusberg, 1997, p. 155], to cite just one example). ToM is by no means unique in this regard: the reification of what are essentially methodological artifacts is standard practice in cognitive neuropsychology and other experimentally based disciplines. However, it is rarely questioned within the disciplines themselves.

To cite one further example within the field of clinical pragmatics, the same types of behaviors attributed to a ToM deficit have sometimes been attributed to a deficit in executive function (EF), with some arguing that EF is a necessary prerequisite for ToM (Ozonoff, Pennington, & Rogers, 1991) while others argue the exact opposite (Fine, Lumsden, & Blair, 2001). Although such disagreements come down to factors such as the specific tests used, the features or subtypes of ToM and EF targeted and whether the focus is on comprehension, production or a combination of both, the treatment of ToM and EF as two distinct, pre-existing entities which are only indirectly accessible through a range of experimental tasks lends a certain spuriousness to the whole argument.

The Influence of Methodology on Mainstream Accounts of Pragmatic Impairment

What I have argued above is that the predominant view of pragmatic impairment and how it is characterized is both theoretically and methodologically driven. The experimental method requires the organization of primary data into discrete categories, and the most readily available and accessible sources of discrete categories have so far proved to be pragmatic theory and cognitive neuropsychology. Both these disciplines, to a large extent, happen to share a common ideology of realism (accepting the reality of things we are unable to observe directly) and essentialism (phenomena have a set of inherent characteristics that constitute their essence). They are also reductionist in that they aim to account for pragmatic behavior in terms of underlying neuropsychological causes. The essential properties of pragmatic impairment are those which are deemed so by current mainstream theories of pragmatics.

In the remainder of this chapter, I will explore the consequences of approaching clinical pragmatics instead from a data-driven qualitative research perspective.

Emergentist Pragmatics

The need for discrete, countable categories in quantitative research on clinical pragmatics outlined above has led to the research agenda described above which might be summarized as follows:

Agenda 1: Let's postulate something called "pragmatic impairment" which arises when a deficit occurs in those abilities/behaviors/modules seen by theorists as instantiating the core properties of pragmatics. Then let's come up with a theoretically derived set of criteria on the basis of which we can stipulate what counts or doesn't count as a pragmatic impairment.

In other words it is top-down, stipulative, ecologically neutral and theory driven.

In contrast, qualitative research generally aims to be data-driven, ecologically sensitive, heuristic and bottom-up. Applied to clinical pragmatics, it might be summarized as:

Agenda 2: A wide range of behaviors are evident in communication breakdown, some of which have been labeled as "pragmatic." Let's examine how these are manifested in ordinary social interaction and see what grounds there are—if any—for distinguishing the pragmatic ones from the non-pragmatic.

I shall now outline an approach to clinical pragmatics which reflects this qualitative agenda. The perspective known as emergentist pragmatics (EP)[1] sees pragmatics not as some a priori phenomenon waiting to be discovered, but rather as an epiphenomenal consequence of interactions across a wide variety of domains (Perkins, 1998). If, instead of stipulating in advance what can or cannot count as pragmatic, we examine the many clinical behaviors that have been referred to in pragmatic terms, it soon becomes apparent that most, if not all, of them may be regarded as either inherently pragmatic, or at least as having pragmatic consequences, to the extent that they are concerned with how communicative acts are designed with the recipient in mind

(Perkins, 2007). The feature which pragmatic theorists happen to have paid most attention to so far is inference; for example, how you design your utterance based on what you infer I already know, and how I infer your intended meaning based on how you've designed your utterance. However, as noted earlier, to be able to do this requires concomitant ability in all other aspects of the communicative process from encoding meaning via syntax, phonology and gesture to decoding it via auditory and visual perception. Inference is not inherently pragmatic on its own, nor is syntax, memory or facial expression. Each of these *becomes* pragmatic when it is drawn on during a communicative act. Pragmatics can therefore be seen as an *emergent consequence* of interactions between any processes involved in interpersonal communication. To put it another way, "[p]ragmatics is what you get when entities such as language, social cognition, memory, intention and inferential reasoning collide in socio-culturally situated human interaction, rather than its being instantiated or uniquely grounded in any single one of these" (Perkins, 2007, p. 50). With regard to the nature of the entities themselves, EP is deliberately agnostic as to their ontological status as cognitive modules, processing systems or anything else since, as argued above, these are ultimately best-guess theoretical and methodological constructs which cannot be known independently of such frameworks. However, EP still makes use of terms such as syntax, attention, memory etc. for purely heuristic purposes when it is descriptively convenient to do so, as we shall see below.

A further central feature is a focus on association and interaction between the various strands of communicative processing, as opposed to the focus on the dissociation between discrete components and their distinctive properties and functions which is a by-product of the experimental approach. So, for example, a problem with syntactic production may be partially offset—or compensated for—by more extensive use of gesture, redistributing the encoding of meaning across modalities. Such trade-offs have become an important strand of clinical linguistic research since an influential article by Crystal (1987), but within EP the crucial feature is that compensatory adaptation be motivated by the requirements of interpersonal communication. For example, if the encoding of meaning using gesture rather than syntax is in response to an interlocutor's poor hearing, it is inherently pragmatically driven. Interaction—whether it be between different linguistic levels and cognitive domains, between different input and output modalities or between communicating individuals—is therefore at the heart of EP. Pragmatics is the emergent outcome of all of these.

An important corollary is that instead of the common assumption made in experimental research that atypical behavior is the direct consequence of a specific underlying deficit, in EP it is assumed to be a consequence of the way complex interactions between linguistic, cognitive and sensorimotor activity play out between participants during communication on a moment by moment timescale. At every point in a conversation, multiple and simultaneous choices are made which determine what is said, who it's said to, why it's said, why this is said and not that, and why it's said this way and not that way. These choices are influenced by factors such as (a) what all conversational participants know, think, remember and want, and (b) what encoding and decoding resources are available. Because all of these are so closely intertwined, a limitation anywhere, for example in the deployment of resources such as memory, syntax or hearing, will have ramifications across the entire system.

A clear consequence of such a holistic and interactional approach is that in the study of pragmatic impairment there is in principle nothing one can afford to ignore.

The Methodological Implications of Emergentist Pragmatics

Emergentist pragmatics is not a research method. Indeed, some of its key aspects, such as trade-offs across processing domains, are amenable to study via experimental and quantitative means (e.g., Bock, 1982: Campbell & Shriberg, 1982; Fey et al., 1994). However, in such studies interacting elements such as syntax and phonology are typically operationalized as performance on a particular test in laboratory conditions, which, despite focusing on a single feature such as mean number of morphemes/phonemes per utterance, is often taken as representing syntactic/phonological performance in every aspect. If instead one's primary focus is on naturally occurring interaction between individuals on unique occasions, and one aims to avoid recourse to cognitivist entities such as syntax modules and ToM, then a qualitative approach is inevitable.

In the remainder of this chapter I will provide two illustrations of research studies of individuals with what may be broadly described as pragmatic difficulties whose focus is primarily on interactions, rather than on entities, and where the interactional domain extends from the linguistic and cognitive activity of individuals to social action between individuals. Clearly, in any discussion of interaction there has to be some specification of the entities which are interacting. However, as will be seen, the entities investigated are nothing more than aspects of behavior which are amenable to description, and no assumptions are made regarding their status as manifestations of any underlying system, modular or otherwise. There is no prior specification of what analytical methods should be used. In fact, the specific methods used are those which are deemed to provide the best fit with the behaviors being investigated. What each study has in common is the focus on individuals communicating spontaneously in relatively uncontrived situations. They also both illustrate that behaviors commonly identified as evidence of pragmatic impairment represent an interactional solution to competing demands on compromised communicative resources.

Case Study 1

Perkins (2007) presents a case study of Peter, a 9-year-old child with subtle and complex communication difficulties. According to assessments and checklists based on categories from pragmatic theory, he could clearly be labeled as pragmatically impaired. For example, by virtue of being unclear, saying sometimes too little and sometimes too much, and being irrelevant he contravened each of Grice's four maxims of conversation. He could also on occasion be described as incoherent, repetitive, poor at topic introduction and maintenance, and unable to make clear who and what he was referring to (referential inadequacy). However, his level of communicative performance varied considerably from one occasion to another which suggested that a simple label of pragmatic impairment was neither discerning enough nor diagnostically helpful. Detailed analysis of an hour-long video-recording of his interaction with an adult revealed a complex and subtle interplay of many factors. For example, his problems with reference and topic maintenance were linked to excessive use of opaque pronominal forms, which in turn appeared linked to poor lexical retrieval. On other occasions, however, he proved quite proficient at producing whole strings of very specific lexical items. Similarly, his sentence production could vary from haltingly delivered, discontinuous sentence fragments to quite complex structures spoken fluently. Interestingly, there appeared to be a trade-off between his lexical and syntactic performance in that his more lexically rich utterances tended to have simpler syntax whereas his more syntactically complex utterances tended to use either more nonspecific pronominal forms or words repeated from an immediately prior utterance. However, to see these trade-offs only in terms of single utterances produced by Peter is only part of the story. He would frequently design his utterances in such a way that, with input from his interlocutor, he was effectively able to distribute his syntactic production across two or more conversational turns. For example, Extract 2 illustrates a frequent pattern whereby Peter produces a noun phrase in the formulaic *you know* __ frame, waits for an acknowledgement from his interlocutor, then follows up with a sentence in which the noun phrase is substituted by an anaphoric pronoun (in this case, *they*).

Extract 2
   Peter: you know the tickets?
   Adult: yeah
   Peter: they tell you where to go

An alternative to the arguably more complex single sentence *The tickets tell you where to go* is thereby effectively jointly constructed incrementally by both parties across three turns.

What I have described here is only one part of a complex of multimodal interactions involving not just language but also gesture and eye gaze. A further possibly relevant factor is that Peter performed poorly on tests of auditory verbal memory (e.g., remembering what has already been said) and selective attention (e.g., processing language against background noise), and it may well be that this played some part in the idiosyncratic communicative strategies shown here. Thus what may be superficially labeled as a pragmatic impairment is merely an indirect consequence of many interacting factors. Indeed, Peter could also be said to have demonstrated considerable pragmatic skill in engaging the communicative resources of his interlocutor, thus presenting further evidence for why the single term "pragmatic impairment" is so inadequate.

Case Study 2

A similar picture of complex interactions is shown by Howard, Perkins, and Sowden (2012) in a study of Lucy, a 4-year-old child with a developmental speech and language disorder. Lucy's conversation was frequently accompanied by an idiosyncratic rhythmic gesture (RG) consisting of a series of finger, hand or arm movements synchronized with her speech rhythm and falling on stressed syllables. Unlike so-called beat gestures, which are used by older children and adults to add emphasis to their speech, Lucy's RGs displayed no evidence of emphasis or emotional expression. The gesture itself was puzzling as it seemed to have no obvious communicative role. It was only when it was examined in considerable detail as part of her overall conversational performance together with that of her interlocutor that an explanation began to emerge.

In an hour of video-recorded conversation with an adult, more than half of her utterances were accompanied by RG. As well as co-occurring with her speech, it also on occasion accompanied or merged with other gestures. Initially it was hypothesized that Lucy's RG might be acting as some kind of scaffold to facilitate the temporal organization of her speech production. It turned out, however, that quite to the contrary not only did her rhythmically more mature utterances not occur with RG, but when RG was used Lucy invariably reverted to prosodic patterns more typical of immature or atypical syllable-timed speech. Its effect, then, seemed to be more inhibitory than facilitative. In contrast, however, it did appear to have a positive interaction with her sentence production. When Lucy's utterances were accompanied by RGs, her sentences tended to contain more words. Also, although the onset of a RG sometimes occurred part way through an utterance, once it did start it would invariably continue until the final word, suggesting that the RG was helping in some way to bring the utterance to completion. Furthermore, Lucy was more likely to use RG when her interlocutor's prior utterance consisted of an open elicitation that required more than just a single word or phrase in response (e.g., *What's happening there?*), but less likely when she was able to make use of linguistic material in either her interlocutor's or her own immediately prior utterances. What this suggests is a three-way trade-off between RG, speech rhythm and syntax such that when under pressure (particularly from her interlocutor) to produce a full sentence, Lucy was somehow able to co-opt RG to help her to achieve this but only at the expense of simplifying her speech rhythm.

Looked at in isolation, Lucy's RG is inexplicable. It is only by taking account of its simultaneous interaction with syntax, rhythm, stress, word juncture, prior linguistic material, and processing demands generated both internally and by her interlocutor as their conversation moves forward moment by moment that it becomes amenable to explanation. Indeed, the only satisfactory way to characterize it was as a partial by-product of such interactions. Although Lucy's communication difficulties would not be described as pragmatic, using a narrow definition of the term, they are certainly pragmatic in the wider sense of addressing the requirement of designing one's conversational turn to fit both one's own communicative agenda as well as the communicative needs of one's interlocutor. Lucy's rhythmic gesture constitutes a (probably) transient—though admittedly only partly effective—strategy for doing precisely this, against a background of compromised linguistic resources.

Conclusion

An initial reaction to the two case studies briefly described above might well be that they are unusually complex and atypical. However, in my experience, they are by no means exceptional—quite the opposite, in fact. Experimental research methodologies with their cognitivist assumptions have led us to see communication difficulties as discrete disorders which derive directly from a deficit in some underlying neurological, cognitive or linguistic system or process. They predispose us to focus on only a narrow set of variables which happen to be amenable to control, thereby deflecting our attention from the virtually infinite range of phenomena—many of which we may not yet be aware—which could also be playing a role in what we are investigating. We can't know until we look.

In the case of so-called pragmatic impairment, which has been my focus here, the dominant quantitative research paradigm in conjunction with mainstream pragmatic theory has led to the widespread assumption that pragmatic ability is a unitary phenomenon deriving from a specific underlying cognitive capacity which, when damaged, gives rise to the condition known as pragmatic impairment. What I have argued here is that when examined instead from a qualitative data-driven perspective, the various behaviors which have been described as instances or symptoms of pragmatic impairment are so disparate that the term has little descriptive or diagnostic value. Instead, they are better seen as the emergent consequence of trying to resolve competing demands on compromised communicative resources when faced with the task of designing one's conversational turn to meet the particular contingences of the situation at hand. But then again, so are all communication disorders.

Although certain key processes, such as inferring, could lay some claim to being an essential feature of pragmatics, they are so inextricably integrated with so many other processes that to consider them as discrete and unitary is not only illusory but also counterproductive for research. I have tried to make the case that a focus on interaction instead of isolation, and on association instead of dissociation, provides a far more complex and messy, but ultimately more realistic, account of what can be loosely described as pragmatic ability and disability, and that the only way to operationalize this for research purposes is through a data-driven qualitative approach.

Note

1. There is only space here to sketch out a few key principles of emergentist pragmatics. For a book-length treatment see Perkins (2007), and for concise summaries with different emphases see Perkins (2005, 2008, 2010). For evaluations of emergentist pragmatics and its clinical and theoretical implications in both developmental and acquired communication disorders, see Adams (2010), Ferguson (2010), and Weed (2011).

References

Adams, C. (2010). Review of Perkins (2007). *Pragmatic Impairment. Journal of Child Language, 37*, 1141–1145.

Austin, J. L. (1962). *How to do things with words*. Oxford, England: Clarendon Press.

Baron-Cohen, S., & Wheelwright, S. (1999). 'Obsessions' in children with autism or Asperger Syndrome: A content analysis in terms of core domains of cognition. *British Journal of Psychiatry, 175*, 484–490.

Bishop, D. V. M. (2003). *The children's communication checklist, version 2 (CCC-2)*. London, England: Psychological Corporation.

Bishop, D. V. M., & Adams, C. (1989). Conversational characteristics of children with semantic-pragmatic disorder. II: What features lead to a judgement of inappropriacy? *British Journal of Disorders of Communication, 24*, 241–263.

Bock, J. K. (1982). Toward a cognitive psychology of syntax: Information processing contributions to sentence formulation. *Psychological Review, 89*, 1–47.

Campbell, T. F., & Shriberg, L. D. (1982). Associations among pragmatic functions, linguistic stress and natural phonological processes in speech-delayed children. *Journal of Speech and Hearing Research, 25,* 547–553.

Clark, H. H. (1996). *Using language.* Cambridge, England: Cambridge University Press.

Crystal, D. (1980). *Introduction to language pathology.* London, England: Edward Arnold.

Crystal, D. (1987). Towards a 'bucket' theory of language disability: Taking account of interaction between linguistic levels. *Clinical Linguistics and Phonetics, 1,* 7–22.

Cummings, L. (2009). *Clinical pragmatics.* Cambridge, England: Cambridge University Press.

Edwards, D. (1997). *Discourse and cognition.* London, England: Sage.

Ferguson, A. (2010). Review of Perkins (2007). *Pragmatic Impairment. Aphasiology, 24,* 1296–1298.

Fey, M. E., Cleave, P. L., Ravida, A. I., Long, S. H., Dejmal, A. E., & Easton, D. L. (1994). Effects of grammar facilitation on the phonological performance of children with speech and language impairments. *Journal of Speech and Hearing Research, 37,* 594–607.

Fine, C., Lumsden, J., & Blair, R. J. R. (2001). Dissociation between 'theory of mind' and executive functions in a patient with early left amygdala damage. *Brain, 124,* 287–298.

Gallagher, H. L., Happé, F., Brunswick, N., Fletcher, P. C., Frith, U., & Frith, C. D. (2000). Reading the mind in cartoons and stories: An fMRI study of 'theory of mind' in verbal and nonverbal tasks. *Neuropsychologia, 38,* 11–21.

Gallagher, T., & Prutting, C. A. (Eds.). (1983). *Pragmatic Assessment and Intervention Issues in language.* San Diego, CA: College Hill Press.

Goldin-Meadow, S. (2000). Beyond words: The importance of gesture to researchers and learners. *Child Development, 71,* 231–239.

Grice, H. P. (1975). Logic and conversation. In F. Cole & J. L. Morgan (Eds.), *Syntax and semantics 3: Speech acts* (pp. 41–58). New York, NY: Academic Press.

Halliday, M. A. K., & Hasan, R. (1976). *Cohesion in English,* London, England: Longman.

Happé, F. G. E. (1993). Communicative competence and theory of mind in autism: A test of relevance theory. *Cognition, 48,* 101–119.

Howard, S., Perkins, M. R., & Sowden, H. (2012). Idiosyncratic gesture use in atypical language development, and its interaction with speech rhythm, word juncture, syntax, pragmatics and discourse: A case study. *Clinical Linguistics and Phonetics, 26*(10), 882–907.

Martin, I., & McDonald, S. (2003). Weak coherence, no theory of mind, or executive dysfunction? Solving the puzzle of pragmatic language disorders. *Brain and Language, 85,* 451–466.

Muskett, T., Perkins, M. R., Clegg, J., & Body, R. (2010). Inflexibility as an interactional phenomenon: Using conversation analysis to re-examine a symptom of autism. *Clinical Linguistics and Phonetics, 24,* 1–16.

Ozonoff, S., Pennington, B. F., & Rogers, S. J. (1991). Executive function deficits in high functioning autistic individuals: Relationship to theory of mind. *Journal of Child Psychology and Psychiatry, 32,* 1081–1106.

Penn, C. (1985). The profile of communicative appropriateness. *The South African Journal of Communication Disorders, 32,* 18–23.

Perkins, M. R. (1998). Is pragmatics epiphenomenal?: Evidence from communication disorders. *Journal of Pragmatics, 29,* 291–311.

Perkins, M. R. (Ed.). (2005). *Clinical pragmatics: An emergentist perspective* [Special Issue]. *Clinical Linguistics and Phonetics, 19*(5).

Perkins, M. R. (2007). *Pragmatic impairment.* Cambridge, England: Cambridge University Press.

Perkins, M. R. (2008). Pragmatic impairment as an emergent phenomenon. In M. J. Ball, M. R. Perkins, N. Müller, & S. Howard (Eds.), *Handbook of clinical linguistics* (pp. 42–58). Oxford, England: Blackwell.

Perkins, M. R. (2010). Pragmatic impairment. In J. S. Damico, N. Müller, & M. J. Ball (Eds.), *The handbook of language and speech disorders* (pp. 227–246). Chichester, England: Wiley-Blackwell.

Perkins, M. R. (2011a). Clinical pragmatics. In J.-O. Östman & J. Verschueren (Eds.), *Pragmatics in practice* (pp. 66–92). Amsterdam, The Netherlands: John Benjamins.

Perkins, M. R. (2011b). Review of Cummings, L. (2009) *Clinical pragmatics. Aphasiology, 25,* 976–980.

Perkins, M. R., Body, R., & Parker, M. (1995). Closed head injury: assessment and remediation of topic bias and repetitiveness. In M. R. Perkins & S. L. Howard (Eds.), *Case studies in clinical linguistics* (pp. 293–320). London, England: Whurr.

Prutting, C. A., & Kirchner, D. M. (1983). Applied pragmatics. In T. M. Gallagher & C. A. Prutting (Eds.), *Pragmatic assessment and intervention issues in language.* San Diego, CA: College Hill Press.

Searle, J. R. (1976). A classification of illocutionary acts. *Language in Society, 5,* 1–23.

Sperber, D., & Wilson, D. (1986). *Relevance: Communication and cognition,* Oxford, England: Blackwell.

Sperber, D., & Wilson, D. (2005). Pragmatics. In F. Jackson & M. Smith (Eds.), *Oxford handbook of contemporary analytic philosophy* (pp. 468–501). Oxford, England: Oxford University Press.

Stainton, R. J. (2010). Review of Cummings, L. (2009). *Clinical pragmatics. Journal of Linguistics, 46,* 499–502.

Stainton, R. J. (2011). Pragmatic impairments. *International Review of Pragmatics, 3,* 85–97.

Stemmer, B. (2008). Neuropragmatics. In M. J. Ball, M. R. Perkins, N. Müller, & S. Howard (Eds.), *Handbook of clinical linguistics* (pp. 113–129). Oxford, England: Blackwell.

Tager-Flusberg, H. (1997). Language acquisition and theory of mind: Contributions from the study of autism. In L. B. Adamson & M. A. Romski (Eds.), *Communication and language acquisition: Discoveries from atypical development* (pp. 135–160). Baltimore. MD: Paul H. Brookes.

Wearing, C. (2010). Autism, metaphor and relevance theory. *Mind & Language, 25,* 196–216.

Weed, E. (2011). What's left to learn about right hemisphere damage and pragmatic impairment? *Aphasiology, 25,* 872–889.

Wilson, D. 2005. New directions for research on pragmatics and modularity. *Lingua, 115,* 1129–1146.

9

Systemic Functional Linguistics and Qualitative Research in Clinical Applied Linguistics

NICOLE MÜLLER, ZANETA MOK, AND LOUISE KEEGAN

Basics of SFL

Systemic Functional Linguistics (SFL) has been part of the linguistics landscape for more than half a century (a seminal paper being Halliday, 1961), and has been applied in numerous subdisciplines of linguistics and communication studies, such as, among others, child language development, computational linguistics and natural language processing, language education and second language teaching, multimodal communication and visual arts, and clinical linguistics. The bibliographies and links to resources available on the website "Information on Systemic Functional Linguistics" (www.isfla.org), maintained by Mick O'Donnell, provide a useful starting point for exploring the world of SFL. Book-length introductions to SFL are Halliday and Matthiessen (2004), and, somewhat more user-friendly for the beginner, Eggins (2004). A chapter-length overview, with specific reference to clinical linguistics, is provided by Ferguson and Thomson (2008). In this section, we present some basics of SFL. This discussion is of necessity selective, and specifically relates to the overall theme of this volume, namely qualitative methods in and approaches to disordered communication. This will be followed by examples of the use of specific tools from the SFL arsenal, applied to conversations with people with dementia.

As a theory of language use, SFL is inherently neither qualitative nor quantitative. However, we find that SFL provides us with a theoretically grounded approach and a well-defined set of tools with which to tackle questions asked in qualitative applied clinical linguistics. As far as details of approach and execution or scope of application are concerned, qualitative research means different things to different people (see e.g., Damico & Simmons-Mackie, 2003; Packer, 2010). However, a key characteristic of the qualitative enterprise is that "qualitative researchers study things in their natural settings, attempting to make sense of, or interpret, phenomena in terms of the meanings people bring to them" (Denzin & Lincoln, 2011, p. 3). An overall orientation to questions regarding meaning-construction in everyday, real life situations of language users resonates well with a theoretical approach to language that uses as a point of departure that "[l]anguage evolved, in the human species, in two complementary functions: construing experience, and enacting social processes" (Halliday & Matthiessen, 1999, p. x). Eggins (2004, p. 2) summarizes the main theoretical claims that systemic functional linguists make about language as follows: "1. that language use is functional; 2. that its function is to make meanings; 3. that these meanings are influenced by the social and cultural context in which they are exchanged; 4. that the process of using language is a *semiotic* process, a process of making meanings by choosing."

Text and Context

The quest for a functional description of language, that is, the answer to questions such as how people use language (to achieve a variety of goals), requires the analysis of *texts*. Halliday and Matthiessen (2004, p. 3) define text as "any instance of language, in any medium, that makes sense to someone who knows the language." Thus a text may be a brief exchange between two speakers, or a lengthy dissertation on how people use language, or any other constellation of language use. A text may involve a single language user (a person writing a journal for her or his own use), or many (a discussion in a support group for people who stutter), and may use the media of speech, or writing, or a combination of both (plus non-verbal communicative means, such as gestures and facial expressions), or a sign language, for example.

In terms of analysis, the question what a text means may be approached by treating a text as an object, or *artifact* in its own right, or as a *specimen* of the system of the language in which it was produced. These two approaches complement each other, in that, as Halliday and Matthiessen (2004, p. 3) point out, it is impossible to explain the meanings of the artifact, its various readings and how it is valued, without relating it to the linguistic system that produced it; at the same time, we cannot use a text as representative of the language in which it was produced without investigating its meanings in its own right. In SFL theory, a text is regarded as *instantiating* the meaning-creating resources represented by a language, and a text (and any subcomponent of a text, such as a clause) arises out of systemic choices made by a speaker.

This mutually complementary approach to and understanding of texts is important in the clinical enterprise: A narrative produced by a person with aphasia may be viewed as representative of that person's language abilities and difficulties. Thus, we use texts, for instance in the process of diagnosis, as windows on a person's language system. However, the same narrative may also be examined with regard to how its creator uses it to communicate, for instance, the experience of recovering from a stroke.

A text, of course, does not emerge in a vacuum, but rather language is used in what might best be described as a set of nested contexts. Eggins (2004) elaborates on the concepts of *context of situation* and *context of culture*. Context of situation refers to, not surprisingly, the situated event of language use. Systemic functional linguists, drawing on work by Bronislaw Malinowski and John Rupert Firth have explored the question which aspects of situational contexts are linguistically significant in that they impact how people use language (see Eggins, 2004, for further discussion and references). In SFL, these aspects of context of situation have been captured in terms of the three variables (often referred to as *register variables*) of *field, tenor,* and *mode. Mode* can be defined as the role played by language in any given interaction. Martin (1984) uses the notion of two continua describing two different types of distance: the *spatial / interpersonal distance* continuum captures the presence or absence of visual, aural, and immediate feedback. A face-to-face conversation, with maximal potential for feedback is situated at one end of this continuum, whereas a document written to be read by others at a (temporal and spatial) distance, such as a cookbook or a novel, is at the other end. The second continuum relates to what Martin (1984) labels *experiential distance,* and the distance involved is that between language and the social process taking place in any given situation. At one end of this continuum, we find situations where language accompanies an activity that interactants are carrying out. Eggins (2004) uses the example of playing a game of bridge as an illustration: as well as verbal actions (e.g., making bids, naming cards to be played) there are other actions not involving language (e.g., dealing and playing the cards). At the other and of this continuum are situations where language creates and constitutes the social process, as in, for instance, the composing of a poem or a piece of non-fiction.

Tenor refers to the relationship between the interactants, in terms of their social roles within the situational context. Three continua have been proposed that make up the register variable of tenor, namely power (equal or reciprocal, versus unequal), contact (frequent versus occasional), and affective involvement (high to low) (see Eggins, 2004; Poynton, 1985).

Field has been defined as what is being talked about, that is, it is "the situational variable that has to do with the focus of the activity in which we are engaged" (Eggins 2004, p. 67). As Eggins points out, equating *field* simply with the topic of a conversation, misses an important dimension of this variable, namely that of technicality; in other words "situations may be either technical or everyday in their construction of an activity focus" (p. 107).

Context of culture is closely related to the notion of *genre,* defined by Martin (1985, p. 248) as "how things get done, when language is used to accomplish them." That is, every culture recognizes certain types of social activities that are accomplished (largely) through language. Such activities are staged, or structured in certain ways, and members of a culture have expectations as to the adherence to these structures. If we ask the question, what does this text mean?, we need to make reference to both context of situation (field, tenor, mode), and to the context of culture in which it was produced.

Meanings and Language

As mentioned above, a fundamental assumption in SFL is that language has evolved to create meanings. It follows that language exhibits certain characteristics that permit processes of meaning creation. In this section, we shall briefly discuss several critical dimensions of language as a semiotic system (see Halliday & Matthiessen, 2004, for more detail).

System and Structure, and System Networks. The notions of system and structure have, of course, widespread currency in the field of clinical linguistics, and are, for instance, routinely used in clinical phonology to refer to the inventory of contrastive units in a person's phonology (*system*) at any given position in *structure*, that is, in the possible configurations of syllables (see e.g., Ball, Müller, & Rutter, 2010, pp. 4–12). *Structure* refers to the syntagmatic patterns in language of "what goes with what" (Halliday & Matthiessen, 2004, p. 22). SFL uses the notion of *rank*, or compositional hierarchies or layers. Thus the grammar of spoken language has the compositional hierarchy, from highest to lowest of: clause ~ phrase or group ~ word ~ morpheme, such that each higher ranked unit consists of a whole number of units of the next-lower ranking unit (some units can also form "iterative sequences" or complexes; Halliday & Matthiessen, 2004, p. 21). The paradigmatic patterns of "what could go instead of what" is referred to as *system* in SFL; a system is further defined as "[a]ny set of alternatives, together with its condition of entry" (Halliday & Matthiessen, 2004, p. 22). Eggins (2004) offers the analogy of traffic lights as an illustration of a simple semiotic system. The entry condition is represented by a vehicle approaching an intersection managed by a set of lights, and there is a finite and discrete set of oppositions, or choices: the lights may be in only one state at any given time, and the possibilities are limited to green, orange (or amber), or red. Drivers behave differently upon encountering different colors in the traffic light system, and those differences are systematic; in other words, the different colors represent different meanings.

While the ordering principle of structure is B is a part of A (for instance, a group is a part of a clause), the ordering principle of systems is that C and B are a kind of A, and while the compositional hierarchy in structure are captured by the notion of *rank*, SFL uses the term *delicacy* to refer to paradigmatic distinctions at different levels of refinement (in terms of categorical distinctions). Systemic theory (hence the name) represents grammar as *system networks*, that is, language is conceptualized as "a resource for making meaning by choosing" (Halliday, 1985, p. xxvii); any branching point in the network represents an entry condition, and presents a set of choices, one of which will be made. Thus systemic theory foregrounds the paradigmatic aspects of linguistic meaning making, while structure (the syntagmatic aspects) is considered as the output of a system network, that is, the results of choices made. Note that while systemic theorists tend to use the term *choice*, this does not imply that language use, that is, the creation of texts, is considered a consciously reflected activity: While some aspects of language use are open to reflection and introspection, and some choices made can be highly conscious and deliberate (such as a carefully crafted characterization of a person in which adjectives are deliberately chosen to damn with faint praise), whereas other levels of choice are essentially intrinsic to the language system (such as phonological systems available at any one position in syllable structure) (see Tench, 1992, for further discussion).

Systemic theory makes extensive use of system network diagrams, which for the beginner can at times be somewhat intimidating. Figure 9.1 (adapted from Halliday & Matthiessen, 2004, p. 23) diagrams the system network for MOOD in English (that is, the configuration of subject and finite, or finite verbal operator; see Halliday & Matthiessen, 2004, pp. 111–122; Eggins, 2004, pp. 151–154). A clause (the entry condition) can be classified either as major or minor, if the former, it has a Predicator (defined by Eggins, 2004, p. 155, as the "lexical or content part of the verbal group"). Major clauses are either indicative or imperative in MOOD type; if indicative, a major clause has a Mood element, that is, a Finite and a Subject. An indicative clause can be either declarative, in which case the Subject precedes the Finite, or interrogative. Interrogatives come as yes/no interrogatives, realized by the Finite preceding the Subject, or as wh-interrogatives, characterized by the presence of a wh-element which is followed by the finite.

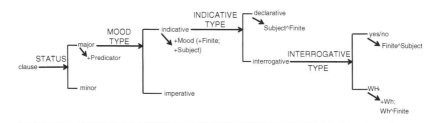

Figure 9.1 MOOD system network (based on Halliday & Matthiessen, 2004, p. 23).

Each branching of a system network represents a system, and each choice made in a system "contributes to the formation of structure" (Halliday & Matthiessen, 2004, p. 24). In other words, structure, syntagmatic order, is the realization of choices within a system: For instance, the ordering Finite^Subject is the realization of a choice within the INTERROGATIVE system, and the choice of interrogative versus declarative is, in turn, a choice within the INDICATIVE system. The analysis of structural properties (here, the sequencing of Subject and Finite) as realizations of systemic choices illustrates a further fundamental of SFL, namely that of language as a *stratified* system. The notion of *stratum* captures the relationship between content and expression. In the traffic light system mentioned above, there are only two strata: that of content (the meanings expressed by different colors of lights), and that of expression (the different colors). Natural languages, not surprisingly, are more highly stratified. SFL distinguishes between two content strata, that of (discourse) semantics, and that of lexicogrammar. The (discourse) semantic stratum is that of interpersonal and experiential meanings; the lexicogrammar stratum is that of vocabulary and grammar, that is, of wordings. Phonology (in spoken language) and phonetics are strata of expression; the former being the organization of speech sounds into system and formal structures, the latter the production and reception of speech sounds (see Halliday & Matthiessen, 2004, pp. 24–26).

Layers of Meaning and Metafunction

The basic functions of language are typically referred to as *metafunctions* by linguists working within the SFL framework. As mentioned above, SFL assumes that language has evolved to fulfill two basic functions (or metafunctions). The first of these is to construe, or make sense of, human experience, that is, to provide "a theory of human experience" (Halliday & Matthiessen, 2004, p. 29). This metafunction is labeled the *ideational* metafunction, within which SFL distinguishes two sub-components: the *experiential* and the *logical*. The *experiential* component is situated at the level of the clause as a configuration of participants in a process and any accompanying circumstances (SFL uses the term TRANSITIVITY to refer to the system of process types). This relates to the register variable of *field* mentioned above. The *logical* component is situated above the clause, and represents the construal of sequences of experiential configurations (represented by clauses) and their logical connections.

The function of construing and enacting social relationships is referred to as the *interpersonal* metafunction (relating to the register variable of *tenor*). At the same time as construing experiential configurations, clauses are used as exchange, that is, to give information, request action or information, give orders, and express the speaker's attitude towards what is said, and towards

Clause as ...	Metafunction	Analysis	**They**	**were**	**crossing**	**the street**
Representation	Experiential	Transitivity	Participant: Actor	Process: Material		Participant: Scope
Exchange	Interpersonal	Mood	Mood		Residue	
			Subject	Finite	Predicator	
Message	Textual	Theme	Theme: Topical	Rheme		

Figure 9.2 Layers of meaning in the clause.

others. At the clause level, the system of MOOD is the chief grammatical resource for interpersonal meaning.

It is important to recognize that interpersonal and experiential meaning are not alternatives, but rather two distinct kinds of meaning that happen simultaneously: When speakers use language, they talk (or write, or sign) about something, and they talk to someone. In addition, SFL recognizes a third, *textual* metafunction. This relates to the register variable of *mode*, and refers to the function of language to construct discourse, and to manage the flow of meanings in a text. The systems of THEME and INFORMATION, and of COHESION, are resources for textual meanings. Figure 9.2 illustrates the different lines of meaning in the clause, relates them to the relevant metafunctions, and exemplifies the labels used in SFL (see Ferguson & Thomson, 2008, for a similar notation).

Construing Experience: Processes and Participants

Experiential meanings are realized at the clause level via the system of transitivity, as mentioned above. This essentially means that a clause represents a configuration or *figure* of a process (for instance, an action, an event, a state of being; typically expressed by a verb group) and the entities involved in or affected by that process (an actor, a goal, a beneficiary, for example; typically expressed by a noun group), plus, optionally, circumstances (e.g., location, time, causation; typically expressed by an adverbial group, or prepositional phrase) surrounding the process-participant configuration (see Figure 9.2, experiential line). SFL classifies processes into six major types, which are illustrated in Table 9.1. Material processes are concerned with the experience of the material world and are realized as clauses of doing and happening. Mental processes reflect the experience of our consciousness, realized as clauses of sensing (see Eggins, 2004, and Halliday & Matthiessen, 2004, for further description, as well as subcategories of these processes, and the participants associated with each process).

As mentioned above, any text can be analyzed either as an artifact in its own right, within its context of use, or as a specimen of the language system that gave rise to it. Thus, an analysis or set of analyses applied to a text in

Table 9.1 Process Types (summarized from Eggins, 2004, and Halliday & Matthiessen, 2004)

Process type	Definition	Example
Material	Process of doing or happening	The girl *wrote* an e-mail. The ice *melted* in the sun.
Mental	Processes of sensing – perceiving, thinking, desiring, and feeling	He *heard* the horn. He *thought* that was a good idea. He *wants* the cake. He *loves* the rain.
Relational	Processes of characterization	Sarah *is* a girl. Jane *has* a car. The car *is* in the garage.
Verbal	Process of saying	He *said* she was sick. The teacher *told* the students to be quiet.
Existential	Process of existing	There *is* a clock on the stand.
Behavioural	Physiological and psychological	He *wheezed* the whole night. He *laughed* loudly.

the context of language or cognitive impairment can be used to gain insight into an individual person's language system. For example, Armstrong (2001) compared the process types used by individuals with fluent aphasia and non-communicatively impaired adults when they were asked to talk about various life experiences. Armstrong found that for some speakers with aphasia, there was a restriction in the variety of process types used. Specifically, a lack of relational and mental processes in some speakers' output restricted expression of their perceptions and characterizations of their experiences, and consequently limited those speakers' ability to project their own individual identity. Expanding on this finding, Armstrong (2005) showed that speakers with aphasia in her study were limited in their use of mental and relational verbs when expressing personal opinions and attitudes. Mortensen (1992) investigated the transitivity resources of a speaker with dementia using two different genres, procedural and recount contexts. While the speaker with dementia was able to provide simple core information, there was also frequent repetition, omission of participants (nominal groups), and a lack of qualifying information (circumstances and predominant use of unexpanded nominal groups).

Looking at language use within specific situational contexts, we can investigate how speakers negotiate experiential meanings within the flow of discourse, responding to choices made by other speakers. Example 9.1 shows how Ms. Beatrice, a lady in her seventies with a diagnosis of dementia of the Alzheimer's type (DAT), negotiates with her interlocutors (Ms. Frances, a lady in her eighties, also with DAT, and two graduate students, Mary and Rose), why she refers to Ms. Frances as "my little maman." (Note that the use of { }

merely delineates an experiential configuration detailed in the line below; participants are underlined; processes in bold.)

Example 9.1

		Process	Participant(s)
52.	M: Why do <u>you</u> **call** <u>her</u> <u>that</u>?	verbal	sayer, target, verbiage
53.a	B: Because she- <u>she's</u> **so good** to me.	relational	carrier, attribute
53.b	B: <u>That's</u> {<u>why I call her my little maman</u>}	relational	identified, identifier
53.c	{why <u>I</u> **call** <u>her</u> <u>my little maman</u>}	verbal	sayer, target, verbiage
53.d	B: <u>I</u> **think** {<u>her name is F.</u>}	mental	senser, phenomenon
53.e	{<u>her name</u> **is** <u>F</u>}	relational	identifier, identified
54.	M: Mhm.		
55.	R: Yeah.		
56.a	F: <u>That's</u> <u>right</u>.	relational	carrier, attribute
56.b	F: <u>You</u> **know** <u>my name</u>.	mental	senser, phenomenon
57.	B: Now <u>I</u> **call** <u>her</u> <u>my little maman</u>.	verbal	sayer, target, verbiage
58.	F: <u>That's</u> <u>right</u>.	relational	carrier, attribute
59.a	B: <u>She's</u> <u>the first one {that come see about me when I got in here.}</u>	relational	identifier, identified
59.b	{<u>that</u> **come see about** <u>me</u>}	material	actor, scope
59.c	{when <u>I</u> **got** in here}	material	actor
59.d	B: <u>I</u> was **crying**.	behavioral	behaver
59.e	B: <u>You</u> **know**.	mental	senser
59.f	B: <u>I</u> **felt** <u>so alone</u>.	mental	senser, phenomenon
60	R: mm.	material	actor, goal
61.a	B: <u>she</u> **come cover** <u>my feet</u>		
61.b	B: <u>Sh'</u>**say** {don't cry, don't cry}	verbal	sayer, verbiage
	{don't cry}	behavioral	
61.c	B: <u>Things</u> gonna **get** <u>better</u>.	relational	carrier, attribute
61.d	B: <u>They</u> did (ellipsis)	(relational)	carrier

In the above data extract, Ms. Beatrice echoes Mary's use of the verbal process "call," thus establishing that she uses "my little maman" as a label, a term of endearment, rather than confusing Ms. Frances with her grandmother; the reason for this use is given in 53.a by means of a relational process, whereby Ms. Beatrice attributes a quality to Ms. Frances. In using the mental process "think," Ms. Beatrice expresses a degree of uncertainty as to Ms. Frances's real name (the expression of degrees of uncertainty, or, in SFL terms, modalization of probability is a major function of mental processes such as think, suspect, believe, used with clause projections, as here; see Eggins & Slade, 2005, and Keegan, 2012). Ms. Frances, in 56.a and 56.b, removes any uncertainty from the situation by first confirming the state of affairs introduced by Ms. Beatrice as her own mental state, by choosing first a relational process, in which the carrier "that" refers back to the projected clause "her name is F," and then juxtaposing the mental process "know," in 56.b to Ms. Beatrice's choice of mental process "think." Ms. Beatrice's use of a relational clause in which she identifies Ms. Frances as "the first one (who took care of her)" foregrounds this role of

Ms. Frances as a bestower of care; it is here framed as a characteristic, whereas the act itself ("that come see about me") is downranked to a postmodifying relative clause. In 59.d and f, Ms. Beatrice describes her inner, emotional state first by using a behavioral process ("cry"), which would have been visible to others, and then adding the emotional motivation for the behavior, this time choosing the emotive mental process of "feeling alone." In 59.e, Ms. Beatrice appeals to her and her listeners' shared experiences by using the mental process "know," and casting the audience ("you") in the role of senser. In 61.a, Ms. Frances's role of caregiver is illustrated by specific acts ascribed to her, using a material process with Ms. Frances as actor, and in 61.b Ms. Beatrice gives a direct quote (by means of a projection using the verbal process "say"), and an unascribed quote in 61.c illustrating the encouragement she received from Ms. Frances by means of a modulated ("gonna") relational clause.

Detailed comments on process and participant choices may at first sight look as though they restate the obvious in more technical terms. However, a clause by clause reading of how speakers ascribe actions, behaviors, utterances or inner states (emotions, cognitive processes) to others and themselves can give valuable information about how they see others and themselves situated in the world. Thus experiential and interpersonal meaning are closely related, in that the way we talk about how we act upon the world and how others act upon us paints a picture of how we relate to others. In the example above, Ms. Beatrice uses actions, behaviors and utterances that she ascribes to Ms. Frances, and that illustrate her initial characterization of Ms. Frances ("because she's so good to me"). This is an interesting starting point for further analysis. For instance, given the context of dementia (recall that both Ms. Frances and Ms. Beatrice have a diagnosis of DAT), one could further investigate to what extent such characterizations are formulaic, or indeed to what extent they are grounded in real lived experience: As it turns out in this particular case, Ms. Frances, a wheelchair user, and too frail to propel her wheelchair herself, would have been physically unable to "come see about" Ms. Beatrice, and to "come cover her feet." However, Ms. Beatrice constructs a powerful picture, seemingly grounded in external reality, of an internal reality, namely her friendship for Ms. Frances (see Müller & Mok, 2012, for a more detailed discussion).

Speech Functions and Conversational Moves: Constructing Relations in Interaction

Dialogue, and especially casual conversation, has long been recognized as an important, perhaps the most important, setting for individuals to do "social work," that is, to develop, maintain and enact social relationships. In SFL, dialogue is conceptualized as a process of exchange. At the most basic level, two fundamental speech roles are distinguished, namely those of *giving* and *demanding*, as well as two types of commodities of exchange, *information*, and *goods and services*. These two dimensions yield four basic speech function types with which an exchange may be initiated: statement (giving information), offer (giving goods and services), question (demanding information), and command (demanding goods and services). Based on Halliday's four basic speech functions, Eggins and Slade (2005) offer a comprehensive system of speech functions that describe the choices a speaker has at various stages in negotiating an exchange. Figure 9.3 summarizes the basic distinctions of Eggins and Slade's system, but contains fewer degrees of delicacy. Speech function choices are typically referred to as *moves*. Moves are considered units of discourse, which are expressed by means of clauses. A turn, that

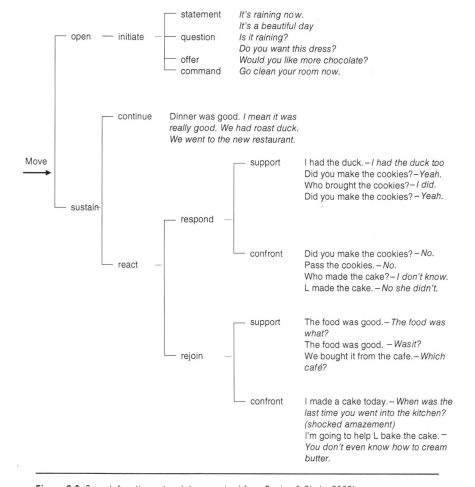

Figure 9.3 Speech function network (summarized from Eggins & Slade, 2005).

is, all the talk produced by one speaker before another speaker takes over, often realizes several moves.

An initiating opening move introduces a proposition for negotiation, by way of a speaker adopting either a giving or demanding role. Following an initiating move, a sustaining move stays with the previously introduced proposition. Sustaining moves may be contributed by the same speaker (continuing move), or by a different speaker (reacting move). Reacting moves are further categorized into responses, which move the exchange toward its close, or rejoinders, which prolong the exchange, for example through clarifications or probes. In addition, reacting moves can be either supporting (preferred or predicted options) or confronting (dispreferred options). Continuing, responding, and rejoining moves can be further classified into different subtypes, but we won't discuss these here (see Eggins & Slade, 2005). Example 9.2 illustrates a move-by-move speech function analysis, using the data extract already introduced in Example 9.1.

Example 9.2

52.	M: Why do you call her that?	Initiate: Question
53.1	B: Because she- she's so good to me.	React: Respond: Support
53.2	B: That's why I call her my little maman (1.5)	Continue
53.3	B: I think her name is F.	Continue
54.	M: [Mhm.*	React: Respond: Support
55.	R: [Yeah.*	React: Respond: Support
56.1	F: [That's* right.	React: Respond: Support
56.2	F: You know my name.	Continue (from 56.1)
57.	B: Now I call her my little maman.	Continue (from 53.3)
58.	F: That's right.	React: Respond: Support
59.1	B: She's the first one that come see about me when I got in here.	Initiate: Statement
59.2	B: I was crying. (2.0)	Continue
59.3	B: You know.	Continue (Monitor)
59.4	B: I felt so alone.	Continue
60	R: mm.	React: Respond: Support
61.1	B: she come cover my feet.	Continue
61.2	B: Sh'say don't cry, don't cry	Continue
61.3	B: Things gonna get better.	Continue
61.4	B: They did (ellipsis)	Continue

In Example 9.2, Mary initiates an exchange by asking a question ("that" in the question refers to "my little maman," an expression which Ms. B used when announcing the reason for standing in Ms. Frances's door: "I've come to visit my little maman"). Ms. Beatrice gives a supporting response; supporting in the sense that it is designed to advance the negotiation of the content offered for negotiation in the initiating move. In theory, the exchange could end here.

However, Ms. Beatrice chooses to continue by rephrasing Mary's earlier question, and thereby reinforces her message. In the absence of any reaction from her interlocutors, and after a 1.5 second pause, she adds another continuing move, in which she reinforces the messages that she *calls* Ms. Frances her "little maman" (rather than identifying her as such), even though she is aware of (though somewhat uncertain of; see ex. 9.1) Ms. Frances's given name. Now her interlocutors react, simultaneously: Mary and Rose by making minimal supporting responses, not adding any further material to the exchange. Ms. Frances, the person talked about, is most explicit in her supporting reaction and continues, confirming the accuracy of Ms. Beatrice's statement (see also the experiential analysis, Example 9.1 above). Ms. Beatrice appends a further move to the exchange, following on from her move in 53.3. Ms. Frances, in turn, again makes a supporting response, bringing the exchange to a close. Ms. Beatrice's next initiating statement relates to her earlier statement about Ms. Frances. Her interlocutors choose not to comment, and Ms. Beatrice continues. She then uses a monitoring move after a 2-second pause, followed by a series of continuing moves. Her interlocutors' only input is a minimalist reacting move from Rose, which signals acceptance. This very brief extract typifies this interaction (discussed more fully in Müller & Mok, 2012), in that the interlocutors with dementia are overall in charge of the conversation: They contribute more talk, and the larger proportion of initiating moves, thus controlling the conversational content being negotiated, and playing assertive roles. In addition, the participants with dementia were mutually supportive, evidenced by a preference for responding (as opposed to rejoining) moves. Mok's (2011) in-depth study of small-group interactions in residential care for persons with dementia demonstrated skillful use of language on the part of persons with dementia to maintain positive social relations. For instance, one woman with dementia was observed to use non-committal but still supportive responses such as registers (i.e., backchannels) when faced with incoherent and disoriented talk from her conversational partner, another woman with dementia. Thus, explicit confrontation was avoided and face for the disoriented conversational partner was maintained.

In the context of aphasia, Ferguson (1992) investigated the use of basic speech functions such as questions, statements, requests, and commands. Armstrong and Mortensen (2006) found that in a couple's interactions, the partner with aphasia was able to initiate and respond; limitations in the use of rejoinders by the person with aphasia meant a restriction in the ability to prolong the exchange and engage the conversation partner. Further, as Armstrong and Mortensen (2006) note, a speech function analysis also enables the investigation of a conversation partner's contribution, and thus the distribution of conversational responsibility.

Exchange Structure Analysis and Generic Structure Potential

Speech function analysis, especially the classification used in Eggins and Slade (2005), and studies based on their work, offers a rather elaborate system of analysis. Some studies analyzing clinical discourse use a somewhat more compact system, based on exchange structure analysis (Martin, 1992; Ventola, 1987), which categorizes moves along two dimensions: Synoptic moves, which are central to exchange completion, are distinguished from dynamic moves, which prolong the exchange, for example, through clarification or probes; moves that give information or action are distinguished from moves that request information or action. Togher and colleagues have used exchange structure analysis to investigate the conversational behaviors of interlocutors (such as police officers, or therapists) of persons with TBI. Their studies have shown that communication partners may limit giving information to and requesting information from persons with TBI compared to matched normal controls (Togher, Hand, & Code, 1996, 1997). However, Togher (2000), in a study involving group discussions with adolescent males, showed that persons with TBI were able to offer a similar amount of information compared to controls.

Move-by-move analysis can also yield information about the generic structure of an interaction. Generic structure ties in with the context of culture, in that members of a culture recognize a text as belonging to a certain genre by its crucial elements, and different genres of text are used to produce "culturally appropriate goals" (Eggins 1994, p. 25). The generic structure potential represents the inventory and sequence of stages of a genre of text (for example, a service encounter; see e.g., Hasan 1985). Generic structure potential analysis, as well as exchange structure analysis, has been employed to compare the talk of people with and without TBI in various situations such as problem solving, interviews, and service encounters (Kilov, Togher, & Grant, 2009; Togher, 2000; Togher & Hand, 1999; Togher et al., 1997). Ferguson and Elliot (2001) examined speech treatment sessions conducted by clinicians with varying levels of experience, coding each move to a generic structural element, and found that generic structure in therapy sessions with more experienced clinicians was more complex.

Structuring Messages: Themes and Rhemes

Thus far, we have illustrated two of the layers of meaning that SFL distinguishes at the clause level: clauses represent speakers' models of experience, through speakers' choices made in the constellation of processes, participants and circumstances. Clauses also function as exchanges (of goods and services); through choices made in the MOOD system, that is, constellations of Subject and Finite, speakers adopt roles of giving and taking, and simultaneously to an extent constrain the role-taking choices open to their interactants. A third line of meaning is that of the clause as message, that is, the "organization whereby it fits in with, and contributes to, the flow of discourse" (Halliday & Matthiessen, 2004, p. 64). The structuring of the clause as message is achieved through choices made in the system of THEME. The *theme* of a clause is the starting point of the message, it represents the entity that the message is about, and situates the message in its context. The *rheme*, on the other hand, is that which is not theme: it is the remainder of the message about the theme. In English, message structure is achieved through sequencing: a theme is followed by its rheme (Eggins, 2004, pp. 298–300; Halliday & Matthiessen, 2004, pp. 65–67). To illustrate, in the clause "I was so alone," "I" is the theme: Ms. Beatrice chooses to make herself the starting point of the message represented by the clause; the message is about her. In contrast, in "she come cover my feet," "she" (referring to Ms. Frances) is theme and therefore the point of the departure of the message. What Ms. Frances did ("… come cover my feet") is the rheme. In Ms. Frances's "You know my name," "you" (referring to Ms. Beatrice) is theme; the rheme "know my name" completes the message.

SFL distinguishes three types of themes. "I," "she," and "you," in the examples just mentioned, are referred to as *topical themes*. The topical theme in a clause is the first-placed constituent that plays a part in the experiential configuration: a participant, process, or circumstance. In other words, the topical theme is the element of the experiential configuration which the speaker chooses to make the point of departure of the message. The most commonly encountered, and therefore *unmarked* choice of topical theme is that which conflates actor (or other primary participant, such as the senser in mental processes, or behaver in behavioral processes) and subject, as in our examples. Every complete clause in English has one, and only one, topical theme. Topical themes may be accompanied by one or more instances of *interpersonal* or *textual* themes. Examples of interpersonal themes are vocatives, as in "<u>Beatrice</u>, you know my name," or comment adjuncts, which express how a speaker positions her- or himself vis-à-vis the message expressed in the clause: "<u>Certainly / apparently / surprisingly</u> you know my name." Textual themes signal how a clause relates to the preceding discourse. They include so-called continuatives, such as "oh," "well," or "now," and conjunctive adjuncts such as "and," "'but," "so," "meanwhile," "actually." Interpersonal and textual themes may co-occur in a clause, and multiple instances of either may be encountered in any one clause. Example 9.3 returns to the data extract already used, this time with a view towards thematic structure (themes are underlined).

Example 9.3

52.	M: <u>Why</u> do you call her that?
53.1	B: <u>Because</u> <u>she</u>- she's so good to me.
53.2	B: <u>That's</u> ...
	... <u>why</u> I call her my little maman
53.3	B: <u>I</u> think ....
	... <u>her name</u> is F
54.	M: [Mhm.*
55.	R: [Yeah.*
56.1	F: [<u>That's</u> right.*
56.2	F: <u>You</u> know my name.
57.	B: <u>Now</u> I call her my little maman.
58.	F: <u>That's</u> right.
59.1	B: <u>She's</u> the first one ....
	... <u>that</u> come see about me ...
	... <u>when</u> I got in here
59.2	B: <u>I</u> was crying.
59.3	B: <u>You</u> know.
59.4	B: <u>I</u> felt so alone.
60	R: mm.
61.1	B: <u>she</u> come cover my feet.
61.2	B: <u>Sh'</u>say ....
	... <u>don't</u> cry, don't cry
61.3	B: <u>Things</u> gonna get better.
61.4	B: <u>They</u> did (ellipsis)

There is only one textual theme in this brief extract, i.e., "because" in 53.1, which explicitly signals how this clause relates (as a response giving a cause or reason) to the preceding question. "Don't" in "don't cry" is classed as an interpersonal theme, since an element that is part of the Mood configuration (but not part of the experiential, or transitivity configuration) and occurs at the beginning of a clause is identified as an interpersonal theme. Other than this example, there are no interpersonal themes in this extract; all other themes are topical themes.[1] An absence of optional interpersonal themes (such as mood adjuncts, or vocatives) indicates that speakers choose not to exploit thematic structure to signal their position towards the message or each other—however, other systems for the expression of interpersonal meaning are of course at the speakers' disposal (see, for instance, the discussion of speaker roles and speech function moves, above). Speakers may use textual themes (such as continuity markers) to explicitly link clauses to their context; in this text, speakers choose to not use this particular tool.

A closer look at topical themes reveals how speakers anchor messages, what they make their messages about. In line 52, Mary's wh-question, with "'why" as topical theme, makes her inquiry about the reason for Ms. Beatrice's behavior. Ms. Beatrice in turn thematizes "she" (referring to Ms. Frances), and she uses (in 53.2) a construction referred to as a *thematic equative* (Halliday &

Matthiessen, pp. 69–71), with "that," coreferent with the preceding "because she's so good to me," as theme of the primary clause, and "why" as theme of the secondary clause (which restates Mary's previous question). As she continues, in line 53.3, Ms. Beatrice thematizes "I" in a projecting mental clause, thus specifying that she is expressing her own viewpoint; the message is presented from her angle. Ms. Frances thematizes "that" in line 56.1, effectively summarizing Ms. Beatrice's utterance in 53.3, and adding an evaluative rheme ("'s right"). She makes her next statement about Ms. Beatrice, choosing the unmarked subject-primary participant (senser, in this case) theme, whereas Ms. Beatrice in 57 chooses a marked theme, a circumstantial adjunct, thus highlighting what happens "now," and removing herself from the anchor position. Ms. Beatrice's theme choices in the primary clauses in the rest of the extract are all unmarked, that is, theme maps onto subject and primary participant. She alternates between "she" (using a thematic equative that highlights "'the first one" as rheme, in 59.1), "I," "'you," and back to "I" (in 59.4), effectively alternating the perspective, or camera angle between herself and Ms. Frances, and inviting her listeners' agreement by adding their perspective in 59.3.[2] For the rest of the extract, Ms. Beatrice removes herself from the picture; she first thematizes "she" (Ms. Frances), then, reporting Ms. Frances's direct speech, "things," which is taken up again by the coreferential "they" in 61.4.

Thematic structure is closely related with information structure, that is, the introduction and maintenance of new and given information in a text. These two dimensions are not identical, though, but rather represent two separate systems. An information unit is "a structure made up of two functions, the New and the Given" (Halliday & Matthiessen, 2004, p. 89). Information units may extend beyond the meanings expressed in any one clause, or a single clause may express more than one information unit. However, the default condition is that clause structure and information structure function in parallel, and that the topical theme of a clause, that is, the clause-initial constituent that is a part of the experiential configuration, represents given information, whereas the rheme represents new information.

Mantie-Kozlowski (2010; see also Müller, Kozlowski, & Doody, 2007) used theme and information unit analysis to investigate the conversational behaviors of a man with severe hypokinetic dysarthria consequent to progressive multifocal leukoencephalopathy (PML). His speech was also characterized by frequent repetitive verbal behaviors, most of them single word repetitions, and many, though not all, utterance-final. One conversational strategy found in his interactions was the production of themeless, incomplete clauses which introduced a single new item, which in turn was integrated into an unmarked Given Theme+New Rheme sequence by his conversation partner.

Text and Texture

Earlier in this chapter, we stated that any instance of language use can constitute a text. In SFL, *text* is defined somewhat more narrowly, although our original statement stands that a text can be the product of spoken, written, or signed language use, or indeed be a multimodal product (written text supported by other visual material, such as pictures or graphs, for instance). What makes a text a text, is the property of *texture,* described by Eggins (2004, p. 24, following Halliday and Hasan, 1976; emphasis in original) as involving "the interaction of two components; **coherence**, or the text's relationship to its extra-textual context (the social and cultural context of its occurrence), and **cohesion**, the way the elements within a text bint it together as a unified whole."

Coherence and Cohesion

Coherence and cohesion have, in analyses of clinical discourse, been approached from various theoretical angles. The SFL perspective discussed here largely follows Eggins's (2004) treatment. Following Halliday and Hasan (1976, p. 23), Eggins (2004, p. 29) defines coherence as the way a text relates to its context. Given the distinction between context of situation, and context of culture (see above), Eggins further distinguishes between registerial coherence, and generic coherence: a text is characterized by registerial coherence when a field, tenor and mode for all the clauses in it can be identified; that is, when the text fits into a situation. Returning to the extract we have repeatedly considered in this chapter, we can identify the field as talking about Ms. Frances, the mode as face-to-face, spoken, interactive, and the tenor as casual visitors (students) and hosts (female elders with dementia); friendly and getting to know each other. Generic coherence makes reference to the context of culture, and means that we can identify a genre of which a particular text is an example: for our extract, the genre is casual conversation.

A classic definition within the SFL framework, which is still frequently used in the SFL literature is the following from Halliday and Hasan (1976, p. 4):

> Cohesion occurs where the INTERPRETATION of some element in the discourse is dependent on that of another. The one PRESUPPOSES the other, in the sense that it cannot be effectively decoded except by recourse to it. When this happens, a relation of cohesion is set up, and the two elements, the presupposing and the presupposed, are thereby at least potentially integrated into a text.

Several subtypes of cohesion are distinguished in SFL (the details of subcategorization are treated somewhat differently in different presentations of the theory). *Reference* refers to cohesive relations established between partici-pants, how they are introduced, and how a speaker or writer keeps track of them (Eggins, 2004, p. 33). When reference is made to an entity, a speaker or writer chooses whether to treat this entity as one that is unknown (*presenting reference*), or whether it is already familiar or recoverable from the context (*presuming reference*). In the conversational extract we have been using for illustration purposes, the item "Ms. Frances," that is, reference to Ms. Fran-ces as an individual is maintained mainly by means of the pronouns "she" and "her," and the possessive "her," but also by means of the name "Frances," and the noun group "my little maman," since Ms. Beatrice has explained ear-lier in the conversation that this is her term of endearment for Ms. Frances. When the referent of a presuming referential expression can be identified from elsewhere in the text, we speak of *endophoric* reference. The most com-monly encountered subtype of this is *anaphoric reference*, where the referent has been mentioned previously in the text. This is illustrated in the chain of items referring to Ms. Frances in our conversation extract. When the referent of a referring expression can be identified from the shared environment of a text, that is, from the context of situation, this is referred to as *exophoric refer-ence*. This is illustrated in Example 9.4: "that" refers to an unnamed item in the real world, evidently identifiable to both Ms. Frances and Mary (and probably, in the situational context, identified by a gesture and gaze direction). "Yours" and "mine" are likewise contextually defined, namely by the roles of speaker and addressee.

Example 9.4

2. F   that's yours, huh?
3. M   mhm? that's mine.
4. F   coz I don't have nothin like it no more

Further discussion of subcategorization of reference can be found in Eggins (2004, pp. 33–42) and Halliday and Matthiessen (2004, pp. 549–561).

Another type of cohesive relation is *conjunction*, which refers to the cre-ation of logical relationships in a text. In expression, this is closely related to what we encountered in the form of textual themes earlier in this chapter. Example 9.4 illustrates the conjunctive relation of *enhancement*. Ms. Frances's utterance is logically tied to the preceding discourse: She provides evidence for the veracity of Mary's statement "that's mine" by explicitly establishing a causal relation (see Halliday & Matthiessen, 2004, pp. 540–549, and Eggins, 2004, pp. 47–51, for details on other conjunctive relations).

Lexical cohesion is achieved by utilizing the organization of the lexicon. Paradigmatic, or taxonomic relations are relations of classification or of com-position. Use of synonyms or of word pairs expressing contrast relations, that is, antonyms, establish the former type of lexical cohesion, as does the repetition of identical items, whereas part-whole relations (meronymy) are relations of composition. Syntagmatic lexical relations, or collocation, lie in the expectancy, based on the experience of language use that certain lexical items are more likely to co-occur in close proximity (see Halliday & Matthiessen, 2004, pp. 570–578; Eggins, pp. 42–47).

Example 9.5 illustrates both reference and lexical cohesion at work in an exchange where Mary and Ms. Frances jointly establish the referent of the lexical item "plant" introduced by Mary. Lexical cohesion is maintained at first by repetition, then through classification (a cactus is a kind of plant), while reference is established exophorically (referring to the plant in the room) and endophorically.

Example 9.5

5. M   you got a new plant. who brought you that n- that plant.
6. F   what plant?
7. M   the plant right there?
(3)
8. F   oh ye:s. what kind is that- what kind of plant is that, that is *(unintelligible, 2 syll.)*,
9. M   a cactus.

In clinical linguistics, analyses of cohesion have been applied to a variety of texts. For example, Müller and Wilson (2008) found that a man with probable dementia of the Alzheimer's type used overgeneralized pronoun and demonstrative reference (using the masculine third person pronoun for both masculine and feminine reference, and using distal "over there" for both proximal and distal locations), which led to disruptions of cohesive links, and placed a greater responsibility for disambiguation on the conversation partner. Mantie-Kozlowski (2008) investigated the collaborative use of cohesive resources in conversations between a participant with PML and a non-impaired conversation partner. A longitudinal study of (among other linguistic resources) cohesion in discourse produced by speakers with aphasia was conducted by Armstrong (1997), who found an increase in the variety and length of cohesive chains over time.

Concluding Remarks

Systemic Functional Linguistics has become an increasingly popular approach to clinical data, which lends itself well to holistic perspectives on meaning-making in context, while allowing the detailed analysis of the linguistic resources involved in the creation of meaning. The focus on language as a resource for meaning creation, the insistence on data from realistic communicative situations, and the contextualized perspective on language use are attractive to linguists who are interested in applied analyses, that is, linguistic analysis with a view towards the real communicative challenges faced by persons with a variety of communication difficulties.

Over the past few decades, there has been a trend towards the use of contextualized data collected in realistic situations in clinical linguistics and clinical communication studies, as well as towards the use of qualitative methods of analysis. Few individuals, if any, have contributed more to spreading the word about, and establishing credibility of qualitative methods in our field than Jack Damico, to whom this volume is dedicated.

Notes

1. Note that Eggins (2004, p. 279) would class "I think" as a mood adjunct, and therefore as an interpersonal theme.
2. Note that expressions such as "you know" are sometimes interpreted as mood adjuncts in SFL, depending on the nature of their delivery. We chose to interpret this instance as an independent clause, since it was produced on a separate intonation contour.

References

Armstrong, E. (1997). *A grammatical analysis of aphasic discourse: Changes in meaning-making over time* (unpublished doctoral dissertation). Macquarie University, Sydney, Australia.

Armstrong, E. (2001). Connecting lexical patterns of verb usage with discourse meaning in aphasia. *Aphasiology, 15*, 1029–1045.

Armstrong, E. (2005). Expressing opinions and feelings in aphasia: Linguistic options. *Aphasiology, 19*, 285–296.

Armstrong, E., & Mortensen, L. (2006). Everyday talk: Its role in assessment and treatment for individuals with aphasia. *Brain Impairment, 7*, 175–189.

Ball, M. J., Müller, N., & Rutter, B. (2010). *Phonology for communication disorders*. Hove, England: Psychology Press.

Damico, J. S., & Simmons-Mackie, N. (2003). Qualitative research and speech-language pathology: A tutorial for the clinical realm. *American Journal of Speech-Language Pathology, 12*, 131–143.

Denzin, N. K., & Lincoln, Y. S. (2011). Introduction: The discipline and practice of qualitative research. In N. K. Denzin & Y. S. Lincoln (Eds.), *The Sage handbook of qualitative research* (4th ed., pp. 1–20). Thousand Oaks, CA: Sage.

Eggins, S. (1994). *An introduction to systemic functional linguistics*. London, England: Pinter.

Eggins, S. (2004). *An introduction to systemic functional linguistics* (2nd ed.). London, England: Continuum.

Eggins, S., & Slade, D. (2005). *Analysing casual conversation*. London, England: Equinox.

Ferguson, A. (1992). Interpersonal aspects of aphasic conversation. *Journal of Neurolinguistics, 7*, 277–294

Ferguson, A., & Elliot, N. (2001). Analysing aphasia treatment sessions. *Clinical Linguistics and Phonetics, 15*, 229–243.

Ferguson, A., & Thomson, J. (2008). Systemic functional linguistics and communication impairment. In M. J. Ball, M. R. Perkins, N. Müller, & S. Howard (Eds.), *The handbook of clinical linguistics* (pp. 130–145). Malden, MA: Blackwell.

Halliday, M. A. K. (1961). Categories of the theory of grammar. *Word, 17*, 241–292.

Halliday, M. A. K. (1985). *An introduction to functional grammar*. London, England: Edward Arnold.

Halliday, M. A. K., & Hasan, R. (1976). *Cohesion in English*. London, England: Longman.

Halliday, M. A. K., & Matthiessen, C. M. I. M. (1999). *Construing experience through meaning: a language-based approach to cognition*. London, England: Cassell.

Halliday, M. A. K., & Matthiessen, C. M. I. M. (2004). *An introduction to functional grammar.* (3rd ed.). London, England: Arnold.

Hasan, R. (1985). *Linguistics, language and verbal art.* Geelong, Victoria, Australia: Deakin University Press.

Keegan, L. C. (2012). *An investigation of the linguistic construction of identity in individuals after traumatic brain injury* (Unpublished doctoral dissertation). University of Louisiana at Lafayette.

Kilov, A. M, Togher, L., & Grant, S. (2009). Problem solving with friends: Discourse participation and performance of individuals with and without traumatic brain injury. *Aphasiology, 23,* 584–605.

Mantie-Kozlowski, A., (2008). *Repetitive verbal behaviors in free conversation with a person with progressive multifocal leucoencephalopathy* (Unpublished doctoral dissertation). University of Louisiana at Lafayette.

Mantie-Kozlowski, A. (2010). Dysarthria in conversation: An analysis of information structure and thematic structure. *Journal of Interactional Research in Communication Disorders, 1,* 237–252.

Martin, J. R. (1984). Language, register and genre. In F. Christie (Ed.), *Children writing: Reader* (pp. 21–29). Geelong, Victoria, Australia: Deakin University Press.

Martin, J. R. (1992). *English text: System and structure.* Philadelphia, PA: John Benjamins.

Mok, Z. (2011). *The linguistic construction of interpersonal processes among people in demenita: An application of systemic functional linguistics* (unpublished doctoral dissertation). University of Louisiana at Lafayette.

Mortensen, L. (1992). A transitivity analysis of discourse in dementia of the Alzheimer's type. *Journal of Neurolinguistics, 7*(4), 309–321.

Müller, N., Kozlowski, A., & Doody, P. (2007). Repetitive verbal behaviors in PML: An exploratory study of conversation. In M. J. Ball & J. S. Damico (Eds.), *Clinical aphasiology: Future directions* (pp. 168–180). Hove, England: Psychology Press.

Müller, N., & Mok, Z. (2012). Applying Systemic Functional Linguistics to conversations with dementia: the linguistic construction of relationships between participants. *Seminars in Speech and Language, 33,* 5–15.

Müller, N., & Wilson, B. T. (2008). Collaborative role construction in a conversation with dementia: An application of Systemic Functional Linguistics. *Clinical Linguistics and Phonetics, 22,* 767–774.

Packer, M. (2010). *The science of qualitative research.* Cambridge, England: Cambridge University Press.

Poynton, C. (1985). *Language and gender: Making the difference.* Geelong, Victoria, Australia: Deakin University Press.

Tench, P. (1992). From prosodic analysis to systemic phonology. In P. Tench (Ed.), *Studies in systemic phonology* (pp. 1–18). London, England: Pinter.

Togher, L. (2000). Giving information: The importance of context on communicative opportunity for people with traumatic brain injury. *Aphasiology, 14*(4), 365–390.

Togher, L., & Hand, L. (1999). The macrostructure of the interview: Are traumatic brain injury interactions structured differently to control interactions? *Aphasiology, 9,* 709–723.

Togher, L., Hand, L., & Code, C. (1996). A new perspective on the relationship between communication impairment and disempowerment following head injury in information exchanges. *Disability & Rehabilitation, 18,* 559–566.

Togher, L., Hand, L., & Code, C. (1997). Analysing discourse in the traumatic brain injury population: Telephone interactions with different communication partners. *Brain Injury, 11,* 169–189.

Ventola, E. (1987). *The structure of social interaction.* London, England: Pinter.

II

Case Studies in Qualitative Research

10

A Critical Discourse Perspective on Understandings of the Nature of Aphasia[1]

ALISON FERGUSON

This chapter applies a critical discourse perspective to the different ways in which the communication disorder known as aphasia is currently understood. Through the use of a single case study of a woman who has acquired moderate-severe aphasia following stroke, the chapter compares a range of discourse samples that illuminate how her difficulties are identified and described. Excerpts from a written report of results of formal testing, a case history interview, a casual conversation with a clinician, and an interview for public awareness about aphasia are analyzed. These texts are also compared with an analysis of the representation of aphasia in discourse samples from websites of speech-language pathology professional associations and support groups for aphasia. Implications arising from this critical discourse perspective for the practice of speech-language pathology are discussed.

Background

Communication disorders present an important site for consideration of the relationship between language and power. For the individuals and groups affected there is a double loss: loss of communication and loss of the tool by which disorder can be addressed or mitigated (Goffman, 1968). The communication disorder that is the focus of this chapter is known as aphasia, an acquired loss or impairment of receptive and/or expressive language associated with specific brain damage, for example, from stroke (LaPointe, 2005). The reason for selecting this disorder is first that only language is affected, so that the sounds of the speech produced by these individuals are fully intelligible, while they experience marked difficulties with semantic access and retrieval (anomia or word-finding difficulty). Second, these individuals have hitherto been fully participating in their communities, and so the difficulties and disempowerment they face are solely reflective of their acquired neurological impairment, rather than associated with life-long disadvantage.

Researchers in the area of aphasia have been concerned primarily with the scientific study of the nature of the linguistic deficits of aphasia (for example, see Nickels, 2002a) with a view to developing "table-top" treatments within a clinical setting (for example, see Nickels, 2002b). However, throughout the history of aphasiology (Tesak & Code, 2008) there has been a parallel concern with the functional communication abilities of individuals with aphasia and with ways in which communication effectiveness can be maximized in the context of persisting residual difficulties (Worrall & Frattali, 2000). Over the last 10 years, this functional approach has moved toward a life participation or social participation approach in which concepts of advocacy and empowerment have attained greater prominence (Elman, 2005). However, while discourse analysis has become a well-accepted research methodology for describing the consequences of aphasia in communication interaction (Armstrong, Ferguson, Mortensen, & Togher, 2007), critical discourse analysis has yet to contribute to understandings in this area (Ferguson 2008b). The present chapter, then, represents a first look at what the methodology of critical discourse analysis can contribute to an understanding of aphasia, within a social participation framework.

This chapter looks critically at the way aphasia is constructed from two, interrelated, directions: first, through the examination of the assessment of the individual, and second, through the examination of public information about aphasia. Naturally, the assessment of the individual is fundamentally shaped by the wider social construction of aphasia, however, through pulling these interwoven threads apart for separate examination, this chapter aims to identify where and how the individual and social understandings of aphasia interrelate.

The assessment of individuals with aphasia for clinical purposes has an identified gold standard in which standardized assessment protocols dominate (Chapey & Hallowell, 2001). A standardized assessment protocol aims to control factors thought to influence language performance so that individual performance can be validly retested over time, and compared with the performance of others. For example, most standardized protocols are administered in clinical settings (to reduce noise and distractions), involve the individual in responding to predetermined eliciting questions or tasks administered by one other person (a clinician). The intrinsic limitations and caveats needed on interpretation of such protocols have long been recognized (McCauley & Swisher, 1984), and so there is an equally long-standing tradition of use of informal or individualized assessment protocols, which aim to increase the validity of observations (for example, see Holland, 1982; Prutting & Kirchner, 1987). However, despite widespread clinical use, individualized assessment remains the poor cousin of assessment methodologies, with concerns raised about test re-test reliability in particular (Perkins, Crisp, & Walshaw 1999).

This dichotomizing debate between formal and informal assessment can be seen as part of the wider social objective/subjective debate regarding the nature of knowledge, and critical discourse analysis provides a way to problematize this debate rather than perpetuate it (Skrtic, 1995). In the current chapter, written and spoken texts drawn from a standardized and an individualized assessment for M, a woman with aphasia, are critically compared.

Public perceptions and awareness of communication disorders in general, and of aphasia in particular, have become increasingly discussed in the speech-language pathology profession over recent years. Such debates center on the need for public awareness of the terms used to describe different disorders (Walsh, 2005), the need for greater recognition of the role of the profession in relation to communication disorders, and the need for greater awareness of the need to increase publicly-funded services for individuals with communication disorders. A subset of such professional discussions revolves around greater public acceptance of people with chronic communication disability, but there is little critical examination of the intrinsic paradox involved in both advocating to fix disorder and to seek acceptance for the continuing disorder (Ferguson, 2008b). The limited research into this area in aphasia has focused on the ability of members of the public to recognize terminology and communication difficulties when described (Code et al., 2001), the use of terms such as "aphasia" in the newspaper media (Elman, Ogar, & Elman, 2000), and the evaluation of the accessibility (visual, language level) of websites providing information about aphasia (Ghidella, Murray, Smart, McKenna, & Worrall, 2005). The unexamined assumption in these debates and research is that the cultural perspective of the professional is the right view, and would be beneficially disseminated and shared by members of the public and the individuals affected by aphasia.

The research presented in this chapter uses critical discourse analysis (Wodak & Meyer, 2009) to explore a set of purposively selected texts to explore the cultural construction of aphasia. A range of analytic methods are used to explore the informational and interpersonal meanings in the texts. The overarching linguistic methodology used is that of Systemic Functional Linguistics (Halliday& Matthiessen, 2004; Young & Harrison, 2004), with particular use made of aspects of transitivity analysis (Martin, Matthiessen, & Painter, 1997), exchange analysis (Berry, 1981), and the analysis of appraisal (Martin & White, 2005/2007). Detailed description of the texts and methods of analysis accompany the presentation of results of analyses in the following section.

Analyses of Texts

Constructing the Individual

The texts used for these analyses were sampled (with her permission) from the discourse of M, a 58-year-old woman who sustained a left middle cerebral artery cerebrovascular accident (stroke) 2 years prior to data collection. The residual effects of the stroke included a moderate-severe non-fluent expressive aphasia with apraxia of speech, and moderate right-sided hemiparesis. Prior to the stroke, she had been a school teacher for 30 years. At the time of data collection, she lived with her adult daughter and grandchildren, was independently mobile and able to drive a car. Her interests included painting, music, theater and she enjoys meeting friends for coffee and travelling.

Comparison of Written Texts

The following two written texts are excerpts from the written report describing the results of speech-language pathology assessment of M.

Excerpt 1: *From report on formal standardized assessment*

> Based on observation of M during an extended interview in her home, her overall communication was rated as 2 on the Aphasia Severity Rating Scale of the Boston Diagnostic Aphasia Examination (Goodglass, Kaplan, & Barresi, 2001), which is described as follows: "Conversation about familiar subjects is possible with help from the listener. There are frequent failures to convey the idea, but patient shares the burden of communication with the examiner."

Excerpt 2: *From report on informal individualized assessment*

> Description of communication: M uses speech, some writing, finger-spelling and gesture to communicate familiar ideas. She reports considerable frustration with her communication difficulty, and evidences a strong determination to communicate. Her communication attempts are most successful with partners who share some knowledge of the topic.

The focus for comparative analysis of these two texts was the experiential metafunction of language (at the lexicogrammatical level), and involved a taxonomic analysis and analysis of selected aspects of transitivity. This analysis allowed for the exploration of how the information exchanged in these texts related to the world/culture in which they arose. As summarized in Table 10.1, there was a relatively higher proportion of technical and institutional terms used in Excerpt 1 (standardized assessment—20%, individualized assessment—4.4%), while there was a relatively higher proportion of concrete and everyday words used in Excerpt 2 (standardized assessment—13%, individualized assessment—36%). The relatively higher proportion of technical and institutional terms used in the report on the standardized assessment was consistent with the scientific paradigm that informs such assessment protocols, and the relatively higher proportion of concrete and everyday words used

Table 10.1 Taxonomic Analysis of Excerpts from Reports on Standardised and Individualised Assessment

Taxonomic Category	Example 1 (report on standardised assessment) 70 words	Example 2 (report on individualised assessment) 45 words
Concrete & everyday words	9 (12.9%) e.g. home, communication, conversation, idea	16 (35.6%) e.g. communication, writing, gesture, frustration
Technical & institutional words	14 (20%) e.g. observation, Scale, patient, examiner	2 (4.4%) e.g. description, reports

in the report on the individualized assessment was consistent with the functional or life participation approach informing such assessments.

The analysis of the participants and processes in these two texts, found that in Excerpt 1 (standardized assessment) M was the object of discussion (through the use of agent-less passive constructions) rather than placed in the role of agent, compared with a more prominent role as Agent in Excerpt 2 (individualized assessment). The analysis of processes did not indicate any obvious differences, but it was notable that Excerpt 2 made use of the unusual and scientific use of evidence as a process, as in "… and (she) *evidences* a strong determination to communication." Thus, even in the context of reporting functional skills, the report conformed to the wider scientific writing conventions.

Comparison of Spoken Dialogues

The following two texts are excerpts from M's discourse in two different contexts, first within a case history interview for assessment purposes (Excerpt 3), and second within a casual conversation (Excerpt 4)—with potentially identifying details omitted.

The comparison of the texts from which these excerpts are drawn involved the analysis of the interpersonal metafunction at the discourse-semantic level, through exchange analysis (Berry, 1981). These two discourse samples elicited similar levels of language performance from M, as her mean length of utterance (in words) was 6.17 in the interview and 6.28 in the conversation, and grammatical complexity (average number of clauses per clause complex) was 1.8 in the interview and 1.2 in the conversation. However, the opportunities for M to fully participate in the available speaker roles in these two samples were different. As can be seen in Figure 10.1, in the interview context, M provided somewhat more substantive content (synoptic moves—M 84%, C 71%), while the work of repair (dynamic moves—M 16%, C 29%) was taken up by the clinician. This contrasted with the more equal distribution of interactive

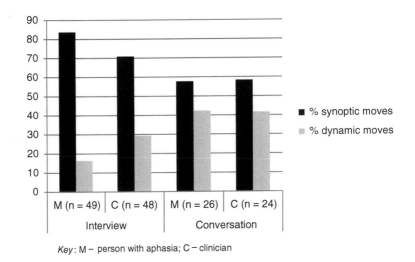

Figure 10.1 Synoptic and dynamic moves in interview and conversation.

work observed in the conversation, where both the substantive content (synoptic moves—M 58%, C 58%), and the work of repair (dynamic moves—M 42%, C 42%) were shared. Also, as can be seen in Excerpt 4, moments of word-finding difficulty in conversation were observed for the clinician as well as for M within extended repair sequences.

Excerpt 3: *From case history interview*

C	Hi I was just going to ask a few questions about your stroke.
M	Yeah, yeah, I know.
C	How long ago did it happen?
M	Two years.
C	Two years ago.
C	Oh, so what happened? What happened?
M	Is a, um, think is a, is a bicycling and head, my head.
C	You were riding?
M	Mmm Yes.
M	No, is, is a fr-, is a [country], and is a flying and is um is a two day, bang {clicked fingers} in [country]. Is holiday.
C	So it wouldn't have been a very good holiday.
M	No, no.

Excerpt 4: *From casual conversation*

M	Is you meal all right?
C	Yeah, a bit stodgy.
M	Well … German!

C	Oh yes! I was thinking, I chose the um, what's it called? I don't know what it's called. It was poached meatballs in something. And it was probably not a good choice.
M	No, no, no.
C	What did you have?
M	Is a ... sausages, keselz [DISTORTED]?
C	Kranskis?
M	Yes.
C	They were alright-ish?
M	{hand gesture for 'so-so'} Ish!
C	Certainly big serves.
M	Two nice, and is a, I can't say it. Sh-, I can't say it. Is a, sh- {finger writing an 's'}. Is a chopping {chopping gesture} {sighs}. Is a, is {M reaches for pen, C gives her writing paper} kraut.
C	Sauerkraut.
M	Yes, yeah.
C	Not good.
M	No no.
C	Would you cook anything like that?
M	No.
C	{laughs}.
M	No, well, sausages {writing} I like for, Italian sausages, and is Mexican sausages, ok.
C	Mm, a bit spicy.
M	Yes, I know {humorous tone}. That's good.

Looking more closely at the types of substantive content moves (see Figure 10.2), the interview provided opportunities for M to provide information in the role of "primary knower" (100% K1, K1f—following moves), while the clinician's moves were mainly seeking information in the role of "secondary knower" (94% K2, K2f—following moves). In contrast, during the conversation, M was also observed to be able to use her available language to seek information (20% K2, K2f), and the clinician adopted a more natural distribution of speaker roles, with the inclusion of information seeking moves (43% K1, K1f).

Standardized assessment protocols rely heavily on case history interview as the main means of observing the linguistic competence of people with aphasia. The results of the exchange analysis presented here highlight that such genres restrict the opportunities to observe the range of communicative competence of the person with aphasia, particularly in relation to their ability to participate in the range of speaker roles and in both synoptic and dynamic moves.

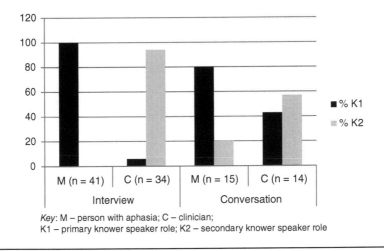

Figure 10.2 Speaker roles for moves in interview and conversation.

So, in summary, from these illustrative comparisons, it is argued that there are risks to the validity and usefulness of standardized assessment protocols as the contexts of language elicitation are restricted, obscuring the view of potential communicative strengths. Also, it can be suggested that the clear communication of the results of assessment is obscured through the adoption of the lexicogrammatical conventions of scientific writing.

Social Construction of Aphasia

In this section, the analysis turns to consider those texts that present descriptions of aphasia that are designed for the general public. The data discussed in this section were drawn from a more wide ranging study (Armstrong, Ferguson, & Mortensen, 2011) that involved the analysis of the use of the linguistic resources for appraisal (Martin, 2000; Martin & White 2005/2007) across six texts from publicly available websites from United States, Canada and Australia—three prepared by professional associations for speech-language pathologists, and three prepared by support groups for people with aphasia. Excerpts 5 and 6 provide a comparison of the ways in which the nature of aphasia is described first by the American Speech-Language-Hearing Association (ASHA—Excerpt 5), and second by an American support group, the National Aphasia Association (NAA—Excerpt 6).

Excerpt 5. *Description of aphasia from professional association website*

What is Aphasia?

Aphasia is a disorder that results from damage to the parts of the brain that contain language. Aphasia causes problems with any or all of the following, speaking, listening, reading, and writing. Damage to the left side of the brain causes aphasia for most righthanders and about half of lefthanders. Individuals who experience "damage to the right side of the brain" may have additional difficulties beyond speech and language. Individuals with aphasia may also have other problems, such as "dysarthria", "apraxia", or "swallowing problems." (ASHA, n.d)

Excerpt 6. *Description of aphasia from support group website*

What is Aphasia?

Aphasia is an acquired communication disorder that impairs a person's ability to process language, but does not affect intelligence. Aphasia impairs the ability to speak and understand others, and most people with aphasia experience difficulty reading and writing. (NAA, n.d.)

Both excerpts made use of the interrogative form for the heading ("What is aphasia?") to engage the reader, and the texts from which these excerpts were drawn attained relatively high reading grade level ratings (Flesch-Kincaid Grade Level – Microsoft Word Readability Statistics)—10.5 (ASHA) and 11 (NAA). The professional association's information focused on introducing unfamiliar terminology (each of which was hyperlinked to further information). In contrast, the support group's information focused on the difficulties experienced by people with aphasia, while attempting to mitigate anticipated stigma ("does not affect intelligence"). Across the wider data set from which these excerpts were drawn, support group information was less likely to characterize the consequences of aphasia in terms of "disorder" or "disability," but equally likely to discuss "difficulties." For both types of texts, most appraisal (i.e., linguistic expressions of appreciation of things, judgment of character, or affect/feelings) was negative for both professional association texts (19% positive to 81% negative) and support group texts (30% positive to 70% negative). When information was positively evaluated, this tended to be in relation to prospects for recovery and rehabilitation, but typically with associated caveats, for example, "If the symptoms of aphasia last longer than two or three months after a stroke, a complete recovery is unlikely. However, it is important to note that some people continue to improve over a period of years and even decades." (NAA, n.d)

The most striking finding from the analysis was the absence of the voice of people with aphasia. Across the texts, the experience of aphasia was depersonalized, with the perspective geared to engage an assumed non-aphasic reader in discussion about the person with aphasia as the other. Only one occurrence of emotive language occurred (in the Canadian support group text): "Sadly, aphasia can mask a person's intelligence and ability to communicate feelings, thoughts and emotions" (Aphasia Institute, n.d.). Even in this example, it was not the emotion of the person with aphasia that was being evoked, but rather the response of observers. People with aphasia were the objects of discussion, with their feelings described rather than expressed, for example, "(receptive aphasia) is frustrating for the person with aphasia and for the listener—can lead to communication breakdown" (ASHA, n.d.).

It is interesting then to contrast these neutralized representations of the nature of aphasia with two further excerpts from M, from a video recording she made for the purposes of raising public awareness about aphasia (for an upcoming support group conference)—see Excerpt 7 and Excerpt 8.

Excerpt 7: *Effect of aphasia—from public awareness interview*
> *Interviewer*   Tell me how that stroke has affected your communication.
> *M*   Oh is a is a terrible, terrible. Is a, I can't imagine. Is a terrible. Is a, cut off my tongue. And is a brain {points to head}. Is a, is a, terrible.

Excerpt 8: *Response to support group—from public awareness interview*
> *M*   Yeah, is a, is a, because I, is a fantastic, because I is a, is a, hope. Is a, crawl a mountain, up up up {emphatic repetition} {left hand mimes climbing}. And you is a, is a, is a … group. Is talk, is that, is a, speaker is wonderful.
> *Interviewer*   Mm.
> *M*   Aphasia group is, is, is, that is wonderful. Is hope for me.
> *Interviewer*   Yeah.
> *M*   Is climb, and climb {emphatic repetition}, is climb. Is hard. Because I rest, but I climb again.
> *Interviewer*   Yes.

In Excerpt 7, M provided an evocative expression of the impact of aphasia, making use of the powerful metaphor "cut off my tongue," and repetitive emphatic use of "terrible." In Excerpt 8, M provided a strong positive appraisal of her response to her experiences within the support group for aphasia, and again made use of a strong metaphoric expression ("climb") to describe the process of recovery and rehabilitation. The emotional expression in these excerpts contrasted sharply with neutralized website information, with both negative ("terrible, terrible") and positive ("fantastic, up up up, wonderful") evaluations providing a clear understanding of the nature and challenges of aphasia.

Through the comparison of the texts available to the public about aphasia with the texts expressing the personal impact of aphasia, it can be seen that aphasia is socially constructed as a problem of the other, and conceptualized in medical terms for professionals and in terms of social stigma for nonprofessionals. However, through considering the voice of people with aphasia, alternative ways of conceptualizing aphasia emerge that speak to others with aphasia as well as the general community.

Discussion and Conclusions

This chapter presented critical analyses of texts that present the nature of aphasia. The current analyses were, of course, limited in their scope of sampling, since the selection of texts was purposive. However, the results of analyses raise a number of directions for both current practice and for further research.

For individual assessment of aphasia, the examination of the texts revealed concerns about the validity of restricted observations (for example, through standardized assessment protocols) and highlighted the richness of conversation as a site for assessment. As discussed in the introduction to this chapter, such findings as to differences between contexts of sampling are not unique to the current study, as there has been a long-standing call for the recognition of the value of individualized assessment (Worrall &Frattali, 2000). However, the findings from the current chapter raise two further directions for consideration within the professional community. First, the commonalities revealed in the spoken discourse analysis across the texts in terms of linguistic complexity clarify the nature of assessment data that can be obtained in both contexts, and this information assists in increasing efficiency of assessment procedures. Second, the commonalities revealed in written texts reporting on assessment findings raise important questions as to the accessibility of such reports and their social function in the maintenance of professional territories. Clarifying the audience and purpose of written reporting would assist in moving such reports from their bureaucratic function to achieve a meaningful social purpose (Duchan, 1999).

The examination of texts designed to increase the public awareness of aphasia revealed the cultural underpinnings of professional understandings of aphasia (i.e., as a medical problem) and responses of other people to aphasia (i.e., concerns regarding social stigma associated with linguistic difficulties). These findings suggest that there may be a gap in the understandings of family members and people with aphasia and the understandings of the professional community. It appears that the way that professionals view aphasia is communicated to family members and volunteers in support groups, and this medical perspective sets the scene for support groups to prioritize such matters as decoding terminology, alongside their own social interactional concerns that are essentially unaddressed by professionals. It can be suggested that the objectifying perspective of professionals with regard to disability becomes a way that family members and volunteers can intellectualize the consequences of aphasia. While such distancing can be useful when emotional responses are overwhelming, it is possible that such strategies do not provide a pathway toward acceptance. For example, the social stigma issues that were apparent as important for those involved in the support group websites are dealt with through the scientific paradigm through the provision of medical labels, rather than discussed directly. In contrast, the analysis of the texts by the person with aphasia provided direct access to both the nature of the linguistic difficulties as well as the emotional responses. Endeavors to raise awareness and harness public support for people with aphasia could be assisted by further research designed to explore understandings and reactions to communication difficulty from a non-professional frame of reference, particularly in the area of media representations of speech-language pathology.

In conclusion, this chapter examined individual and social constructions of aphasia, through the critical analysis of selected spoken and written texts. The findings confirmed existing concerns regarding the need for clinical use of both standardized and individualized assessment protocols. Beyond this, findings suggested that professional representation of understandings of aphasia demand further critical examination given the differences identified in understandings of aphasia for non-professionals and people with aphasia.

Note

1. The research discussed in this chapter was originally presented at CADAAD 2008 (see Ferguson, 2008a).

References

American Speech-Language-Hearing Association. (n.d.). Aphasia. Retrieved from http://www.asha.org/public/speech/disorders/Aphasia/

Aphasia Institute. (n.d.). What is aphasia? Retrieved from http://www.aphasia.ca/about-aphasia/what-is-aphasia/

Armstrong, E., Ferguson, A., & Mortensen, L. (2011). Public and private identity: The co-construction of aphasia through discourse. In C. N. Candlin & J. Crichton (Eds.), *Discourses of deficit* (pp. 215–235). Basingstoke, England: Palgrave Macmillan.

Armstrong, E., Ferguson, A., Mortensen, L., & Togher, L. (2007). Acquired language disorders perspective. In J. Webster, R. Hasan, & C. Matthiessen (Eds.), *Continuing discourse on language: A functional perspective* (pp. 383–412). London, England: Equinox.

Berry, M. (1981). Systemic linguistics and discourse analysis: A multi-layered approach to exchange structure. In R. M. Coulthard & M. M. Montgomery (Eds.), *Studies in discourse analysis* (pp. 120–145). London, England: Routledge & Kegan Paul.

Chapey, R., & Hallowell, B. (2001). Introduction to language intervention strategies in adult aphasia. In R. Chapey (Ed.), *Language intervention strategies in aphasia and related neurogenic communication disorders* (4th ed., pp. 3–17). Baltimore, MD: Lippincott Williams & Wilkins.

Code, C., Simmons-Mackie, N., Armstrong, E., Stiegler, L., Armstrong, J., Bushby, E., ... Webber, A. (2001). The public awareness of aphasia: An international survey. *International Journal of Language & Communication Disorders, 36*(Supplement), 1–6.

Duchan, J. (1999). Reports written by speech-language pathologists: The role of agenda in constructing client competence. In D. Kovarsky, J. F. Duchan, & M. Maxwell (Eds.), *Constructing (in)competence: Disabling evaluations in clinical and social interaction* (pp. 223–224). Mahwah, NJ: Erlbaum.

Elman, R. J. (2005). Social and life participation approaches to aphasia intervention. In L. LaPointe (Ed.), *Aphasia and related neurogenic language disorders* (pp. 39–50). New York, NY: Thieme.

Elman, R. J., Ogar, J., & Elman, S. H. (2000). Aphasia: Awareness, advocacy, and activism. *Aphasiology, 14*(5/6), 455–459.

Ferguson, A. (2008a, July). *A critical discourse perspective on speech-language pathology assessment.* Paper presented at Critical Approaches to Discourse Analysis across Disciplines (CADAAD). University of Hertfordshire, Hatfield, England.

Ferguson, A. (2008b). *Expert practice: A critical discourse.* San Diego, CA: Plural Publishing.

Ghidella, C. L., Murray, S. J., Smart, M. J., McKenna, K. T., & Worrall, L. (2005). Aphasia websites: An examination of their quality and communicative accessibility. *Aphasiology, 19*(12), 1134–1146.

Goffman, E. (1968). *Stigma: Notes on the management of spoiled identity.* Harmondsworth, England: Penguin.

Goodglass, H., Kaplan, E., & Barresi, B. (2001). *Boston diagnostica Aphasia examination* (3rd ed.). Philadelphia, PA: Lea & Febiger.

Halliday, M. A. K., & Matthiessen, C. (2004). *An introduction to functional grammar* (3rd ed.), New York, NY: Arnold.

Holland, A. (1982). Observing functional communication of aphasic adults. *Journal of Speech and Hearing Disorders, 47,* 50–56.

LaPointe, L. (Ed.). (2005). *Aphasia and related neurogenic language disorders* (3rd ed.). New York, NY: Thieme.

Martin, J. R. (2000). Beyond exchange: Appraisal systems in English. In S. Hunston & G. Thompson (Eds.), *Evaluation in text* (pp. 143–175). Oxford, England: Oxford University Press.

Martin, J. R., Matthiessen, C. M. I. M., & Painter, C. (1997). *Working with functional grammar.* London, England: Arnold.

Martin, J. R., & White, P. R. R. (2005/2007). *The language of evaluation: Appraisal in English.* Houndsmills, Basingstoke, England: Palgrave Macmillan.

McCauley, R. J., & Swisher, L. (1984). Use and misuse of norm-referenced tests in clinical assessment: A hypothetical case. *Journal of Speech and Hearing Disorders, 49,* 338–348.

National Aphasia Association. (n.d.). Home page. Retrieved from http://www.aphasia.org

Nickels, L. A. (Ed.). (2002a). *Cognitive neuropsychological approaches to spoken word production in aphasia.* Hove, England: Psychology Press.

Nickels, L. A. (Ed.). (2002b). *The rehabilitation of spoken word production in Aphasia.* Hove, England: Psychology Press.

Perkins, L., Crisp, J., & Walshaw, D. (1999). Exploring conversation analysis as an assessment tool for aphasia: The issue of reliability. *Aphasiology, 13*(4–5), 259–282.

Prutting, C. A., & Kirchner, D. M. (1987). A clinical appraisal of the pragmatic aspects of language. *Journal of Speech and Hearing Disorders, 52*(2), 105–119.

Skrtic, T. M. (1995). Theory/practice and objectivism: The modern view of the professions. In T. M. Skrtic (Ed.), *Disability and democracy: Reconstructing (special) education for postmodernity* (pp. 3–23). New York, NY: Teachers College Press.

Tesak, J., & Code, C. (2008). *Milestones in the history of aphasia: Theories and protagonists.* Hove, England: Psychology Press.

Walsh, R. (2005). Meaning and purpose: A conceptual model for speech pathology terminology. *Advances in Speech-Language Pathology, 7*(2), 65–76.

Wodak, R., & Meyer, M. (Eds.). (2009). *Methods of critical discourse analysis.* London, England: Sage.

Worrall, L., & Frattali, C. M. (Eds.). (2000). *Neurogenic communication disorders: A functional approach.* New York, NY: Thieme.

Young, L., & Harrison, C. (Eds.). (2004). *Systemic functional linguistics and critical discourse Analysis.* London, England: Continuum.

11

The Limits of Collaboration— Speakership in Conversation with Persons with Aphasia

PETER AUER

Introduction

If I were asked to summarize the progress of our knowledge about verbal interaction after some 40 years of research, one aspect which would figure prominently would be the deconstruction of the notion of the speaker as it was most cogently and influentially described by Erving Goffman in his seminal "footing" paper (1979). Goffman may have been influenced by the revolutionary work of Valentin Voloshinov in the 1920s,[1] who argued that an utterance is never the result of the mental and articulatory activities of a single person—the speaker—but is embedded in a web of intertextual and dialogical links to other utterances (Voloshinov, 1929/1973). Voloshinov also pointed out that the individualistic ideology of linguistics at his time was a product of its philological orientation, which found its primary object of analysis in written texts assumed to be the product of one author-writer.[2] But while Voloshinov was primarily interested (at least in his empirical studies) in the many voices that may be embedded in one speaker's utterance, it was Goffman who showed that the notion of the "speaker," so dear to linguistics and speech act philosophers, needs to be dissected into at least three different roles: the animator or articulating human ("sounding box"), the author of a speech act (which may be articulated by others, written, etc.), and the one who is responsible for its meaning ("principal"). Coming from a different perspective and working with different methods, conversation analysis has taken this argument even further. Particularly, the work of Charles Goodwin has shown how the unfolding of an utterance in interaction is co-constructed by participants, not only through their verbal but also their non-verbal activities (Goodwin 1981).

Recent work on aphasia, and particularly on interaction with global aphasics, has provided additional evidence for abandoning the traditional model of speakership because of its monological and logocentric bias. Again, it is above all Goodwin (1995, 2003, 2004) who, in his work on a severely handicapped aphasic person whose language (in the sense of vocabulary and grammar) was extremely reduced, points out that it is possible to "construct locally relevant meaningful utterances, and indeed to function as a powerful actor in conversation" with extremely restricted linguistic competences (Goodwin, 2006, p. 119). Chil, the aphasic investigated by Goodwin, was able to function as a participant in conversation not only because he made use of multi-modal resources such as combinations of nonsense syllables, pointing, iconic gestures, and intonation, and because he placed his contributions in the appropriate and often highly pre-structured sequential positions, but above all because he "got others to produce the words he needed, with the effect that his utterances (…) were constructed through the collaborative activities of several participants" (Goodwin 2006, p. 119). In Goffmanian terms it could be said that a severely handicapped aphasic participant can still function as the principal of an utterance provided that his or her co-participants are ready and able to function as the author and animator. Of course, finding out what the intentions of the aphasic as the principal of an utterance are can require an enormous amount of additional conversational work for both the aphasic and the unimpaired partner. The deconstruction of the speaker role therefore ties in with another argument made by many researchers (such as Laakso, 2003; Laakso & Klippi, 1999; Lind, 2002; Milroy & Perkins, 1992; Oelschlaeger 1999; Oelschlaeger & Damico, 2000, 2003): aphasia shifts the burden of communication from the speaker (as the principal of the utterance) to the recipient (its author/animator).

Starting from these observations, the point I want to make in this chapter is that, although speakership may be an ideological construct of Western thinking about agency in general and agency in language behavior in particular, this very construct has an impact on the way aphasics and their partners (inter-) act. The notion of an individualistic speakership is not just a bias in the work of linguists and language philosophers; it is enmeshed in our everyday practices. Aphasic interaction is particularly interesting in this respect precisely because it is so difficult and often unlikely that the illusion of speakership can be upheld. All the evidence points to utterance-production as a joint activity. Nonetheless, as I will try to show, aphasics and their partners often hold on to this ideology and use communicative strategies which are based on it.

Contrary to much of the work on aphasia cited above, I will not only discuss verbal interaction with severely handicapped aphasics, but also include data from relatively mildly impaired aphasics with medium-severe to mild amnestic aphasias and medium-severe Wernicke aphasias. With one exception (Extract 5), all data come from the Freiburg corpus of family interaction after aphasia (cf. Bauer & Auer, 2009). I want to show that in these cases, non-collaboration in the management of aphasia can be an issue. By this I mean that either the aphasic or the spouse refuse to collaborate in dealing with a problem of formulation (often, a problem of lexical retrieval). I argue that this non-collaboration is an outcome of adherence to an ideology of single-speaker agency as the basis of verbal communication.

Collaboration

For reasons of contrast, let me start with an example of moderately successful collaboration in a couple in which the husband is suffering from a medium-severe amnestic aphasia. In the following extract, the couple and two friends are sitting at the table. The topic of this part of the conversation is the family's blacksmith business and the question of whether it should be broadened to include aluminium and stainless steel. In the course of this discussion, several technical details of working with aluminium have to be explained to the guests. In the following extract, the aphasic participant is about to explain how aluminium is coated.[3]

Extract (1): *H12rev (1468ff)*

((participants: hh (aphasic), his wife (fh), two guests/friends; Swabian dialect. Here and in the following, words or utterances which are not well-formed in adult non-impaired native German, dialectal or not, are underlined))

```
68  hh:   ENTweder du dues (–) äh (–)
          either    you do    uhm
69  fh:   elox[IEre?
          anodize
70  hh:        [des oine            isch beSCHICHte?
               the one ((alternative)) is  to-coat
72  fh:   <<affirmative> ehHE;>
73  hh:   da  machsch ebbes KUNSCHTstoff drauf,=
          there put-you some  plastic         on-it
74        [=(vorher)],
          beforehand
75  fh:   [=JA      ], (---)
           yes
76  hh:   und=es andre isch alus alusIE:[re
          and the other is   to-ano anodize⁴
77  fh:                              [Eloxiere.
                                      anodize
78  hh:   =aluxIEre.=
          anodize
79  fh:   =Eloxiere. (––)
          anodize
80  hh:   <<p>e?=
```

81	*fh:*	=E,
82		E,
83	*hh:*	Eloxie:re.
		anodize
84	*fh:*	GEnau. (--)
		exactly
85	*hh:*	und da machsch a SCHICHT druff;
		and there put-you a layer on-it

Mr. HH runs into a problem in line 68 in accessing the verb *eloxieren* ("to anodize") when he is about to explain to his guests the two ways aluminium products can be colored. Although his wife suggests the word as early as line 69, he changes the construction and first explains the second alternative (coating with plastic), a strategy I will come back to in the final section of this chapter. But since he has projected two alternative treatments by his initial *entweder* ("either") in line 68, he has to come back to anodization after having explained plastic coating. This leads to a paraphasia in line 76, i.e., *alusiere(n)*, which is marked as problematic by a pre-repair. His wife comes in immediately in order to provide the correct version. HH approximates the target word in line 77 by exchanging the paraphasic middle consonant /s/ with correct /ks/ in line 79 but fails to repeat the initial vowels correctly. FH therefore corrects him in line 79 by again repeating the correct version. HH tentatively repeats the first vowel in line 80, which is confirmed twice by his wife before he repeats the correct version, and FH closes the sequence with an affirmative *genau* ("exactly").

The collaborative character of the sequence only comes out in full when the nonverbal behavior of HH is taken into account. Although the two guests do not display their recipiency verbally, HH visibly addresses them, and only them (his wife obviously knows how to coat aluminium), by his gaze. He looks at them throughout the sequence up to line 80 when he averts his gaze from the guests and starts to look at his wife until the repair sequence is finished. At least in this phase, then, she is an invited co-speaker who, as a kind of backstage helper, provides missing parts of his utterance. In this extract, then, collaborative word-search is invited by the aphasic via his gaze on the suggested first vowel /e/ in line 80 and provided by the non-impaired family member.

Non-Collaboration

I will now turn to examples in which either the aphasic or the non-impaired partner withhold cooperation in a word-search. Two cases can be distinguished as:

- those in which the non-impaired participant refuses (or at least withholds) collaboration, and

- those in which the aphasic refuses the co-participation of the recipient in the production of his/her turn.

It should be stressed that by collaboration I mean the co-construction of propositional meaning (reference and predication). On a different level, all of the interactional dyads into which we will be looking are cooperative indeed: participants agree on how to handle the aphasia, and they agree on a common interactional (family) style (for details, see Bauer & Auer, 2009).

Non-Collaborating Partners

Stigma Management: Ignoring Aphasia

Aphasia is a stigma. While professionals and family members may not see it as such after some time, and become experts on how to deal with it, naïve partners—for instance, people who meet an aphasic for the first time—are in a different position. One of the ways for them to deal with the stigma is to ignore it (Goffman, 1963). A straightforward way of doing so is to maintain the flow of interaction at any cost without exposing the aphasic's verbal problems through repair work. This can lead to overtalk (as described in Auer, 1981) and a certain amount of vagueness since referential problems are not dealt with. The important aspect for our discussion is that ignoring aphasia also implies that full speakership is attributed to the aphasic: he or she is treated as a full-fledged, competent partner. The non-impaired partner refrains from collaboration in the construction of propositional content since this would question the aphasic's speaker role as the principal, author, and sounding box.

In the following example, Mr. HB, who suffers from a mild amnestic aphasia, is having coffee with his wife and a guest. From time to time his wife disappears and leaves him alone with the visitor. Talk is about computers; HB wants to buy one, the guest has one and gives advice on what to keep in mind when buying a new computer.

Extract (2): *BB41, 1269ffRev*

((talk about the necessity to buy a CD ROM drive; the guest, BB, has one for making backups of his photos; HB has already stated that he won't buy the drive now in order to keep the costs for the computer low. In the beginning, FB is present and clears something off the table; in line 99 she moves out of the camera angle and disengages from the conversation. Swabian dialect in HB and FB, slight Berlin accent in BB.))

```
96  bb:   weil     wenn ez   meiner FESTplatte was        passiert wär=
           because if    now to-my  hard-disc  something had happened
97         =wärn die bilder  AUCH weg.
           were  the photos  also    gone
```

> "*for if something had happened to my hard-disc my photos would be lost*"

98 fb: ja [KLAR].
      yes of-course

99 bb: [und] so::   sind se   da   auf DEM ding dann drauf.
      and like-this are they then on that thing then on
      "*and like this they are on this gimmick*"

00   ja?
      yes?

01 hb: ja.
      yes

02   <<all>und SO moin i=ez->
        and so think I now

03   <<all, stammering>(und wenn man [des   ] ha)>
          (and if   one that   ha)

04 bb: [<<p>ja>]
                 yes

05 hb: <<stammering>(wenn man=es [hat)]>
          (if   one it   has)

06 bb: [aber] das kann man nommal
             but   that can   one   again

07   SPÄter dann machen.
      later   then do
      "*but you can also do this later*"

08 hb: <<stammering> oinerseits   SO des des koschtet des
           on-the-one-hand so that that costs   that
     halt   SO   halt
     PART ADVB PART
     "*on the one hand, like it it costs like this you see*"

09   NEE, des isch mir (-) zu VIEL,
      no   that is to-me too much
      "*no, that is too much for me*"

10   da WART i nomal lieber,
      there wait I again rather
      "*I'd rather wait*"

11 bb: [undh äh   ]
      and uhm

12 hb: [(des kann i jetz] grad NED) dann (-) je nachDEM?
      (that can I now PART not) then   it-depends
      "*(right now I can't do it) then (-) it depends*"

13 bb: hm=HM

14　*hb:*　un dann– (1.0)
　　　　　and then

15　*bb:*　JA ja
　　　　　yes yes

16　*hb:*　und der kommt dann au HER, (–)
　　　　　and he comes　then also here
　　　　　"and he ((the computer seller)) also comes here"

17　　　　stellt_n UFF, (-)
　　　　　sets　it up
　　　　　"and sets it up"

18　　　　(und dued da (–) [und–)
　　　　　(and does there　and)

19　*bb:*　　　　　　　　　　[macht des ALles.
　　　　　　　　　　　　　does　that all
　　　　　　　　　　　　　"does all that"

20　　　　JAja.
　　　　　yes yes

21　*hb:*　ja::
　　　　　ye::s

I will focus on the non-impaired participant here; however, in this particular case, the aphasic also contributes to hiding his stigma via overtalk and referential vagueness. I will come back to this strategy below.

In line 02, HB starts a contribution to the ongoing conversation about computers which is a considerable challenge for him. He manages to take the turn smoothly with his *ja* (01) which confirms BB's previous point. But what he produces next—in lines 02, 03, 05—is a sequence of German words which cannot be heard as expressing a full contribution yet (the most likely interpretation "and if one has that …" is an open fragment, in which the apodosis to the if-clause still needs to be produced). It seems that HB wants to take up BB's tempo (the latter is quite a fast speaker) in order to render a rhythmically smooth transition to his own turn (cf. Auer, Couper-Kuhlen, & Müller, 1999). Nevertheless, the non-impaired partner produces a continuer (l. 04) and a comment in line 06 ("one can do this later") which is clearly sequentially misplaced; it does not orient to the aphasic's attempts to take the turn and introduce (perhaps) a new subtopic. Turn-taking is placed as an interruption of HB's ongoing attempts to formulate his contribution. Instead of waiting for the aphasic to make his point (which usually takes more time than in a non-impaired speaker), and perhaps supporting him in finding missing words (both strategies were employed by the wife in the first example), the guest employs a different strategy. He erases the aphasic's attempts to formulate a contribution by tying back to previous talk by himself. Note that HB's stammering articulations are a severe threat to the construct of the speaker-agent, who is both the principal and the author and articulator of an utterance. The remedy here is equally radical: the aphasic's contribution is sequentially deleted altogether.

In line 08 HB continues or restarts his contribution, again with a messy first part in which the verb *kosten* ("cost") alone can direct the recipient's interpretation. Lines 09/10 are relatively clear (the intended meaning is likely to be "if this is too expensive for me, I would rather wait (to buy the external drive"). The argument is continued in line 12 ("I can't do it right now") and ends in a formulaic closure ("it depends"). The continuer after *je nachDEM* invites the aphasic to produce another subtopic, which starts in lines 14/16. After the opener *un(d) dann,* a relatively long TCU-internal pause occurs. The non-impaired speaker responds to it with the continuer/agreement particle *JA ja.* Once again this appears misplaced since there is nothing to agree with at this point. Rather, the non-impaired recipient pretends or simulates that such a propositional content is available. When HB finally produces his turn, it is constructed in the format of a list of which he is able to produce the first (l. 16) and second (l. 17) component, but not the third (l. 18). The guest's way of dealing with the problem is again one which continues the flow of the interaction while it makes no attempt to recover the contents (l. 22): he adds a passe-partout list completer, *macht des alles.*

In sum, the guest cooperates with HB in maintaining the flow of the conversation, but he does not collaborate with him in co-constructing meaning. Aphasic problems abound in the sequence, but are never oriented to on the level of propositional meaning. The non-impaired participant produces next activities which are not related to those of the aphasic, and which even interrupt his ongoing, sometimes tedious production process. In addition, the non-impaired speaker easily claims the turn back in order to control the situation.

Refusing Collaboration for Language Exercises

In the previous section, I have presented a strategy which appears to be typical for co-participants neither trained in nor familiar with aphasic interaction. I now turn to a strategy which is often found in non-impaired co-participants who are well acquainted with the aphasic and who seem to care less about stigma and face-work in general, i.e., didactic sequences or language training exercises (a detailed analysis is given in Bauer & Kulke, 2004).[5] In many ways, this is the opposite strategy of the one discussed in the preceding section, since the aphasic's stigma is exposed and highlighted. In these language exercises, the non-impaired partners seem to follow (presumed or experienced) patterns of second language teaching which rest on the assumption that practice will lead to an improvement of the impairment. On another level, however, these didactic sequences and the strategy of ignoring the aphasic stigma share an orientation on the model of the monological speaker-agent.

The following example is typical of this strategy. Mr. K (HK) is a severe Wernicke aphasic. In the extract, he and his wife are having dinner.

Extract (3): *K11.1 (rev)*

((slight southwest German dialect traces in both participants))

```
01   HK:   <<chewing>(        );>
02         [<<chewing>(JETZ) emal bitte;>
                      now   PART please
03         [((points with his left hand to the plate with the ham
             while chewing, looks at plate until line 06))
04         ((puts his hand back on the table while chewing))
05         [<<chewing>(zu siesem);
                       to    this⁶
06         [((points again with left hand to the plate with ham,
             chewing, still looking at plate))
07         <<gulps>[öhm> (– ) was isch das   für    ein material  [da;
                    uhm        what is  this  kind-of a material⁷ there
                              "what kind of material is that"
08                 [((puts hand back))                            [((looks
                                                                    at FK))
09         ((slowly moves left hand to plate, almost touching it))
10         WAS isch [desch,
           what   is    this
11                  [((moves hand back))
12         ((2.0, FK looking at HK and vice versa))
13         [wAs isch DAS,
             what is this
14         [((points with left hand to plate, averts gaze from FK))
15   FK:   [überLEG  mal;
            think      PART
16         [((looks down at plate, slightly nodding))
17   HK:   ((takes back hand, makes an "I don't know"-gesture
             shortly before putting it back on the table by turning the
             palm upwards))
18   FK:   ((looks back at HK))
19         (2.0)
```

20 *HK:* ich <u>kreise</u> so   nicht (–) [(nicht <u>gebraut</u>   )]
        I   ??[8] like-that not   not   ??-ed[9]

21   [((lifts both hands and
                                   puts them back on table,
                                   slightly shrugging
                                   shoulder))

22 *FK:*   [des haben=wir doch   ]
                                   this have we PART
     aus=dem BAUernmArkt;
     from the farmers' market

23 *HK:* im   ga   ja im   ga <u>GAUtelt</u> ham=mir;
      in-the gard yes in-the gar ???   have we

24   ja,
      yes

25 *FK:* =BAUernmarkt;
      farmers' market

26   ne?
      right?

27 *HK:* JA;
      yes

28   aber du musst [mirs [(se)]
      but you must to-me-it sa
      "but you've got to t(ell?) me"

29   [(((takes his slice of bread from
                                   plate))]

30 *FK:*   [des   ] is SCHWARZwälder, (   )
                  this   is Black Forest (   )

31 *HK:* sch ach JA;
      h oh yes

32   <u>sch scho SCHOmu</u>; (–)

33 *FK:* hm=HM,

34 *HK:* <<looks at FK> [schun]<u>ger</u>; (–)>
                      ham[10]

35   [SCHIN]

36 *FK:* <<nodding>SCHINken;>
               ham

37 *HK:* <<looks away from FK> <u>sch SCHINkEr</u>;>
                           h   ham

38   << looks at his slice of bread> SCHINgert.>
                                      ham
     ((nods))

39 *FK:* SCHINken;
        ham
40   SCHWARZwälder schInken;
        Black Forest   ham
41   [genau];
        exactly
42 *HK:* [ja].
        yes
43   kannsch a bissel da   DRAUF geben?
        can-you a little there on-it   put
        'can you put a little on top here'
44   [zu dem   ],
        to^{11} this
45 *FK:* [<<bites off her slice of bread> (   )]
46   [((hands over the plate to HK))   ]

47   geb (der_s) HER
        (I) give it– (to–you)

HK is severely handicapped. He is able to bring across his intentions as long as he can use non-linguistic resources but otherwise needs other participants' collaboration. In our extract from a verbal exchange during dinner, the objects in question are available on the table, and can easily be identified by non-verbal means such as gaze and pointing gestures. HK initiates the sequence with a request (easy to recognize on the basis of the formulaic *emal bitte,* "please"). The object of this request is also easy to identify since HK points to the plate with the ham on the table in front of him. Verbal reference to what he wants is not possible for HK, however, since he cannot access the word *Schinken* ("ham"). He adds what looks like the beginning of a prepositional phrase in line 05 (*von diesem,* "of this," may have been intended) and points again to the plate. His gaze is fixed on the plate, too, leaving no doubts about the intended referent. However, his wife does not help him to find the right word, nor does she comply with his request. HK now explicitly asks her for help and that she provide the name of the desired object (l. 07). This question already foreshadows that more than referential success may be at stake. HK once again identifies the object of his request by almost touching the plate (09). In the meantime, FK has been looking at HK as well, i.e., there is eye contact for two seconds, during which FK continues to withhold her response. HK explicitly asks twice what the name of the object ("ham") is (l. 10, 13), but FK once more refuses to answer. This time, she explicitly suggests that her husband think about the right word himself. HK makes several gestures which express his inability to do so (l. 17, 21) and says something which sounds like *ich kriege es nicht gesagt* ("I don't get it said"). FK, however, further withholds help or compliance with the request. She now tries to prompt the target word, first by pointing out to HK the situation in which they bought the ham together (l. 22, 25, "farmers' market"). After HK has once more stated that she has to tell him the word (l. 28), she tries a syntagmatic prompt (l. 30, *Schwarzwälder*: the place of origin of the ham also functions as a kind of brand name, i.e., *Schwarzwälder* syntagmatically projects *Schinken*). This prompt is successful in eliciting a number of utterance fragments which could be heard as progressively improving approximations of the word *Schinken* (l. 31, 32, 34). FK shows some satisfaction with these attempts (l. 33) and provides as a final prompt the full version of the target word (l. 36) but still does not comply with the request. Although HK is not able to repeat the word correctly (l. 37, 38), his efforts are now judged sufficient by FK. In lines 43 and 44, he once more states his wish to be given the ham (without using the target word). His wife now finally complies.

In language exercises, be they part of second language teaching or part of aphasic interaction, the aim is a fully competent speaker in which principal and author coincide, i.e., a person who can say what she or he wants to say without needing another person's help. In our example, FK refuses collaboration (and even food!) as long as her husband does not live up to these expectations of a competent agent-speaker.

Non-Collaborating Aphasics

The Turn as the Domain of the Agent-Speaker: The Avoidance of Other-Repair in Aphasics

I will now turn to the aphasics themselves. As in the case of the spouses, we observed many cases in which the aphasics failed to collaborate with their partners in constructing propositional meaning. Rather, some aphasics with middle to light aphasic syndromes carefully *performed* their speakership. This implies, above all, that they insisted on the preference for (self-initiated) self-repair over other-repair (cf. Schegloff, Jefferson, & Sacks 1977). Since self-repair within one's turn is maximally sheltered from co-participants' interventions, the insistence on self-repair is arguably an effective way of performing as an agent-speaker. The following aphasic (light amnestic aphasia) is an example.

Extract (4): *HA (rev.)*

((HA, his wife FA and their baby son are sitting on the couch having breakfast. HA initiates a new topic))

```
1  HA:  [hEy weißt du [was    ] heut morgen (.)      HIER war?
        hey  know you what       today in-the-morning here was
        "hey do you know what was here this morning?"
        [(((HA looks at FA, gives her the baby))
```

2 FA: [((sighs))]

3   [bestimmt die KATze;
          surely   the cat
          [((looks at HA, sits with baby on her lap))

4 HA: [nein; (---)
          no
          [((shakes head))

5   *hab ich AUch gedacht;*
          have I also   thought
          "I thought so as well"

6 FA: was?
          what

7 HA: ein EICHhörnchen;
          a   squirrel

8 FA: ein EICHhörnchen?
          a   squirrel

9 HA: [ein EICH[hörnchen war [direkt hier am (--) [FENster,
          a squirrel   was right here at-the   window

10   [((gets up))

11   [((points with left hand to terrace door))

12   [((goes to terrace door))

13 FA: [((pats baby))

14 HA: von [(–) dem BALkon;
          of   the balcony[12]

15 FA: [((looks at HA))

16 HA: ich weiß;
          I know

17   s_ist dann (–) da   RÜber, (--)
          it is then   there over-there
          "then it went over there"

18   [zu:-
          to
          [((HA reaches terrace door, left finger points to door; he looks out
          into the garden, hand remains in pointing gesture))

19 FA: =hm=HM:::; ((looks at baby))

20 HA: =wie heißt_s? (--)
          how is-called-it
          "what's it called?"

21   <<p>[zu> (–) der– [(---)
               to   the

```
22  FA:      [mh=HM:::  ];
23           [((looking at baby, kissing him))
24  HA:  <<p,len>[WIE heißts>? (–)
                  how is-called-it
                  "what's it called"
25           [((looks out into the garden again))

26           <<p>[zu> (.) zu der <<f>TANne>;
                  to       to the      fir
27           [((lowers arm, end of pointing gesture))
28           (1.2)
             [((goes two steps backwards))
29  FA:  [((looks at HA))
```

Once more, I will somewhat artificially focus on the aphasic speaker and his strategies of disengagement here, but it will be noticed that his wife chooses complementary strategies of non-collaboration. Just as collaboration, non-collaboration is an interactional style on which both participants have to agree, i.e., it requires *cooperation*.

We focus on the search for the word *tanne* ("fir"). The problem of lexical access becomes visible when HA abandons his turn constructional unit after an elongated preposition in line 18.[13] The preposition projects a following noun. In other contexts, a hesitation format such as this may elicit a co-participant's collaboration, i.e., she or he may try to identify the referent and provide the missing word. However, in this case, the bodily constellation of the two participants makes such a form of cooperation difficult if not impossible. The aphasic speaker dissolves the face-to-face constellation with his wife starting already in line 10: he gets up and moves to the terrace door, while his wife remains seated. Since she is sitting on the sofa located on the side of the room which opens towards the garden, this means that HA moves to the periphery of her visual field: he is now standing to her left, at some distance. FA has the child on her lap and is involved with holding and patting him. Both participants are engaged in activities (walking to the door, taking and holding and taking care of the child), which make them disengage from the conversation visually and bodily (although they continue talking to each other). In this situation of endangered visual contact, the deictic components of HA's utterances are of some interest. The first pointing gesture in line 11 slightly precedes the corresponding deictic local adverbial *hier* (see Stukenbrock (in press) for the alignment of gestures and deictic verbal elements). FA turns her head and looks at him in line 15 in order to understand this deixis. At the point when HA runs into visible word-finding difficulties (l. 18), he has reached the terrace door. He is still pointing and now also looking outside at the garden. FA withdraws her gaze from him, and from that point on, neither of the two is looking at the other. FA will therefore not be able to identify the object her husband wants to refer to. (Her *hmHm* in line 19 is perhaps a continuer aligned with line 17 *s_ist dann da RÜBer,* "it went over there.") HA therefore has to identify the referent by verbal means. By dissolution of the F-formation and the aversion of gaze, HA has himself minimized the chances for FA to synchronize her verbal and nonverbal behavior with him. They have both achieved a situation in which he alone is responsible for his turn in general, and for establishing reference in particular. In this context, *wie heißt_s* ("what is it called") (l. 20, again in l. 24) is not really a question addressed to FA; at best it is a question the aphasic addresses to himself, but more likely a hesitation marker. In the second *wie heißt_s*, HA also uses prosody (reduced loudness, reduced tempo in l. 24) as well as looking away from his wife and instead at the garden as strategies to mark the ongoing word search for which he alone is responsible. In the meantime, his wife is giving her attention to the baby (l. 23). Finally, he manages to self-repair his utterance and find the missing word for the tree (l. 26). Only after the end of the word-finding sequence does FA look at HA again. In sum, HA and FA actively withdraw during the hesitation phase and give HA extra time for finding the missing word. He remains in full control of his language, as a speaker, author, *and* principal. This is the couple's established style. Only when there is absolutely no hope of accessing the word he is looking for will HA ask his wife for help.

Hiding the Problem Item

Mr. HA claims speakership, and he claims a full regiment over the turn in which this speakership finds it autonomous place. But, at the same time, he does not hesitate to expose his amnestic problems. He claims autonomy, but at the cost of making obvious that this autonomy is permanently endangered, and sometimes reaches its limits. In a way, this strategy resembles the exercise strategy discussed before. In both cases, no attempt is made to camouflage the aphasia; however, efforts are made to rescue the aphasic partner's status as a speaker-agent *despite* the impairment. But like the non-impaired partners, we also observe in the aphasics the opposite strategy to rescue speakership by hiding away their problems. As in the case of the non-impaired partners who proceed in such a way, the costs can be high: they consist of overtalk and referential/predicational vagueness.

The following example is from an interaction between a speech therapist and a fluent aphasic.[14]

Extract (5)

((narrative about how the stroke occurred, first interview in clinic))

07   und meine frAU hatte sowas   geHÖRT,
          and my   wife had something-like-that heard
          "and my wife had heard something like that"

08   .h <<len>aber wir haben nicht verMUtet;>
            but we have not suspected
            "*but we didn't suspect*"

09   .h dass es SOwas <<decr>   gewesen wäre>>; nich
            that it something-like-that been   had   you-know
            "*that it would have been something like that; you know*"

10 *T:* hm=hm
         uh=uh

11 *P:* <<all>ich bin (wiel) WEItergeschlafen;
         I have   further-slept
         "*I fell <u>(ol) on sleeping</u>*"[15]

12   =(ha')> EINgeschlafen;
            fell-asleep

13   und=eh
      and=uh

14 *T:* hm=hm
         uh=uhm

15   (1.5)

16 *P:* nich,= so IST das
      you know, it's like that

17   <<len>Etwas = eh>
           something uhm

18   sind VIEle stUnden ins   lAnd <<all>(gelungen/gejungen)->
      are many hours in-the land   <u>(wont)</u>
      "*many hours (intended: <u>went</u>[16]) by*"

19   <<len,dim>wie man wahrSCHEINlich,>
            <u>like</u> one probably
            "*(intended: <u>which</u>[17]) one would probably;*"

→20   <<dim>eh   sofOrt   (genu)>
           uhm immediately (us)
           "*uhm immediately (intended: used)*"

21   <<f>WENN> man_s gewUsst hätte.
         if   one-it known had
         "*if one had known*"

22 *T:* ja
        yes

This speaker has a recurrent strategy to make central components of his utterance prosodically disappear which contain words he has no access to. The relevant part of this extract is lines 19/20, *die man wahrSCHEINlich; eh sofOrt (genu)* ("which one would probably; uhm immediately" (use)), and line 21 *WENN mans gewUsst hätte* ("if one had known"). The problem item is the participle of the verb in the first utterance, most likely *genutzt* ("used").

The problem of lexical access occurs (at the latest) at the end of lines 19/20. Since the speaker is about to produce a subordinated (relative) clause, the verbal component will be in final position, with the participle preceding the finite verb. The position preceding the finite verb, i.e.. the participle, will also be the predictable carrier of the focal accent (*die man geNUTZT hätte*). Semantically speaking, the verb is of central importance for the interpretation of the utterance since it contains rhematic information. In short, HP has a problem of lexical access when he reaches the most important part of the utterance, in syntactic, prosodic and semantic terms. Which strategy does Mr. P make use of in order to deal with his problem? Like HA in the previous examples, he does not count on his co-participant's help to access the missing lexical item and thereby render the utterance well-formed and its propositional content clear. However, he does not try to self-repair his contribution either; instead, he leaves the problem unsolved by hiding the problem item in a prosodic diminuendo, and further camouflages it with an immediate forte restart into the following TCU. Because of this immediate restart into the next TCU and the lack of a pause between the two intonational phrases, the recipient has no chance to initiate repair. In this way, the problem item is removed from interactional repair. The recipient can only guess what is meant, but he cannot initiate a collaborative process of help and/or clarification.

Discussion

I have discussed four different ways in which collaboration in the achievement of propositional meaning can be suspended in aphasic conversation. Two of them can be said to be due to strategies used by the aphasic partner, while two of them are due to strategies used by the linguistically non-impaired partner. In all cases, however, the two parties cooperate in another sense: they accept the other party's way of dealing with the aphasic impairment, and fill the opposite role. In each case we can further distinguish a strategy which exposes the aphasic problem (language exercises on the side of the non-impaired participant, reduced speed and insistence on self-repair on the side of the impaired participant) from one which camouflages the aphasic problem (overtalk and deletion of problematic speech by non-fitting next activities on the side of the non-impaired participant, prosodic deletion and sequential inaccessibility on the side of the impaired participant). This, of course, is not meant as an exhaustive classification—no doubt, there are other ways of with-holding or avoiding the non-impaired participant's help.

All the strategies discussed in this chapter affirm the aphasic's role as the author, animator, and principal of the utterance, and they minimize the role of the recipient in producing meaningful utterances. This insistence on the role of the speaker-agent complies with, and thereby reinforces, the Western ideology of the monological speaker who is able to bring across what he or she wants to say without substantial help from the recipient. Propositional non-collaboration may expose the aphasia (in two of the four strategies), or it may camouflage it and in this case endanger the transmission of propositional content (in the two other strategies). But always, it gives control to the speaker.

Let me finally come back to our initial example (1) discussed as an exam-ple of optimal collaboration between an aphasic and his wife. If we look at the sequence again, we note that even in this example, there are phases of non-collaboration: in the beginning of the extract (ll. 70-76), the aphasic is in control of his turn-at-talk; a helpful suggestion by his wife is neglected and thereby discarded (l. 69). The difference between this and, for instance, ex. (2) is that the monological phase in this exchange is relatively short. Soon, the aphasic speaker signals that he is running into a problem, and his wife is eager to help once she realizes it. However, the aphasic has a chance to perform as a competent speaker as long as he can. The optimal exchange between an apha-sic and his partners is not achieved through maximal collaboration; rather, it means to collaborate where it is necessary but preserve the speaker's autonomy otherwise.

Notes

1. Goodwin (2006) reports that Goffman was familiar with Voloshinov's work and held it in high esteem.
2. Of course, authorship is a heavily debated issue when it comes to pre-modern texts. Equally, it goes without saying that the interweaving of voices is a constitutive feature of written texts as well as oral language.
3. Transcription follows GAT 2 (cf. Couper-Kuhlen & Barth-Weingarten, 2011).
4. This is a phonological paraphasia in which the first two vowels of the target word *eloxieren* are lowered and raised respectively, and the second intervocalic consonant cluster /ks/ is reduced. The elision of the std. German -*n* in the final unstressed syllable is dialectal.
5. They have also been reported by other researchers such as Booth and Perkins (1999, p. 289) and Kagan and Gailey (1993, p. 207).
6. Phonological paraphasia *diesem* → *siesem*, and most likely a semantic paraphasia *von* 'of' → *zu* 'to'.
7. Semantic paraphasia.
8. /kraise/ seems to contain elements of *(ich) weiß* and *kriegen* ("to get").
9. A participle, perhaps paraphasic on *gesagt* ("said").
10. Paraphasia for *Schinken*.
11. Possibly again a semantic paraphasia *von* → *zu* as above. The attempt to formulate the request using the target word (*von dem Schinken*) finally fails.
12. Semantic paraphasia: *terrace* → *balcony*.

13. Presumably HA's formulaic and in this context misplaced *ich weiß* "I know" in line 11 is a strategy to gain time to access the word even before that point.
14. This example and the speaker's strategy to adapt to his word-finding problems by camouflaging them prosodically is discussed in more detail in Auer and Rönfeldt (2004).
15. The verb *weiterschlafen* (other than *einschlafen*) requires the auxiliary *haben*, not *sein*. The speaker corrects this mistake in the following line.
16. Phonemic paraphasia.
17. Phonemic paraphasia *wie* for *die*.

References

Auer, P. (1981). Wie und warum untersucht man Konversation zwischen Aphasikern und Normalsprechern? [How and why do we analyse conversation between aphasics and non-impaired speakers?] In G. Peuser & S. Winter (Eds.), *Angewandte Sprachwissenschaft. Grundlagen - Berichte - Methoden* [Applied linguistics. Foundations - reports - methods] (pp. 480-512). Bonn, Germany: Bouvier.

Auer, P., Couper-Kuhlen, E., & Müller, F. (1999). *Language in time. The rhythm and tempo of spoken interaction.* New York, NY: Oxford University Press.

Auer, P., & Rönfeldt, B. (2004). Prolixity as adaptation: prosody and turn-taking in German 'conversation with a fluent aphasic. In E. Couper-Kuhlen & C. Ford (Eds.), *Sound patterns in interaction* (pp. 171-200). Amsterdam, The Netherlands: Benjamins.

Bauer, A., & Auer, P. (2009). *Aphasie im Alltag* [Aphasia in everyday life]. Stuttgart, Germany: Thieme.

Bauer, A., & Kulke, F. (2004). Language exercises for dinner. Aspects of aphasia management in family settings. *Aphasiology, 18,* 1135-1160.

Booth, S., & Perkins, L. (1999). The use of conversation analysis to guide individualized advice to carers and evaluate change in aphasia: a case study. *Aphasiology, 13*(4/5), 283-303.

Couper-Kuhlen, E., & Barth-Weingarten, D. (2011). A system for transcribing talk-in-interaction: GAT 2. *Gesprächsforschung, 12,* 1-51. Retrieved from http://www.gespraechsforschung-ozs.de/heft2011/px-gat2-englisch.pdf

Goffman, E. (1963). *Stigma – Notes on the management of spoiled identity.* Englewood Cliffs, NJ: Prentice-Hall.

Goffman, E. (1979). Footing. *Semiotica, 25,* 1-29.

Goodwin, C. (1981). *Conversational organization. Interaction between speakers and hearers.* New York, NY: Academic Press.

Goodwin, C. (1995). Co-constructing meaning in conversation with an aphasic man. *Research on Language and Social Interaction, 29*(3), 233-260.

Goodwin, C. (2003). Conversational frameworks for the accomplishment of meaning in aphasia. In C. Goodwin (Ed.), *Conversation and brain damage* (pp. 90-116). Oxford, England: Oxford University Press.

Goodwin, C. (2004). A competent speaker who can't speak: the social life of aphasia. *Journal of Linguistic Anthropology, 14*(2), 151-170.

Goodwin, C. (2006). Human sociality as mutual orientation in a rich interactive environment: Multimodal utterances and pointing in aphasia. In N. Enfield & S. C. Levinson (Eds.), *Roots of human sociality* (pp. 96-125). London, England: Berg Press.

Kagan, A., & Gailey, G. F. (1993). Functional is not enough: training conversation partners for aphasic adults. In A. L. Holland & M. M. Forbes (Eds.), *Aphasia treatment* (pp. 199-225). London, England: Chapman Hill.

Laakso, M. (2003). Collaborative construction of repair in aphasic conversation. In C. Goodwin (Ed.), *Conversation and brain damage* (pp. 62-188). Oxford, England: Oxford University Press.

Laakso, M., & Klippi, A. (1999). A closer look at 'hint and guess' sequences in aphasic conversation. *Aphasiology, 9*(3), 239-255.

Lind, M. (2002). *Conversational cooperation. The establishment of reference and displacement in aphasic interaction*. Oslo, Norway: Unipub.

Milroy, L., & Perkins, L. (1992). Repair strategies in aphasic discourse: towards a collaborative model. *Clinical Linguistics and Phonetics*, 6, 27–40.

Oelschlaeger, M. L. (1999). Participation of conversation partner in the word searches of a person with aphasia. *American Journal of Speech-Language Pathology*, 8, 62–71.

Oelschlaeger, M. L., & Damico, J. (2000). Partnership in conversation: a study of word search strategies. *Journal of Communication Disorders, 33*, 205–225.

Oelschlaeger, M. L., & Damico, J. (2003). Word searches in aphasia. In C. Goodwin (Ed.), *Conversation and brain damage* (pp. 211–227). Oxford, England: Oxford University Press.

Schegloff, E., Jefferson, G. , & Sacks, H. (1977). The preference for self-correction in the organization of repair in conversation. *Language, 53*, 361–382.

Stukenbrock, A. (in press) *Deixis in der face-to-face-Interaktion*. MS, U Freiburg. (To appear with: de Gruyter, Berlin.)

Voloshinov, V. N. (1973). *Marxism and the philosophy of language*. Cambridge, MA: Harvard University Press. (Original work published 1929)

12

"Life Is Hard, But I'm Trying"
Understanding the Lives of the Families Speech-Language Pathologists Serve

CAROL SCHEFFNER HAMMER

Historically, the language environments that families from low-income backgrounds provide to their children have been compared to those of middle-income families. Bernstein's *Class, Codes, and Control, Volume 1: Theoretical Studies towards a Sociology of Language* (1971) is a classic example. In his book, Bernstein presented a theory of language differences. He posited that individuals used two codes: an elaborated code and a restricted code. The elaborated code provides a speaker with an extensive range of lexical and syntactic choices that can be combined in an infinite number of ways to express his ideas. Because of the possible combinations available to the speaker, the listener is not able to predict what the speaker will say. As a result, the speaker's message can be individualized.

The restricted code, on the other hand, offers the speaker a limited number of options, which results in the speaker's message being wholly predictable to the listener. Messages are not individualized through this code. Instead, restricted messages serve to reinforce the relationship between the speaker and listener.

Bernstein (1971) asserted that the use of the codes differs by social class. Speakers of middle-socio-economic status (SES) use both codes, whereas speakers of low-SES only use the restricted code. These codes are passed on from one generation to the next. As a result, children of middle-SES parents learn both codes whereas children of low-SES parents are limited to the restricted code. Through these codes, the "genes" of a social class are transmitted from generation to generation.

Bernstein was not alone in his characterization of families of low-SES in the 1960s and 1970s. Numerous studies were conducted by researchers who also found deficits in the language environment provided by families of low-SES (cf. Bereiter & Engelmamn, 1966; Corbin & Crosby, 1965; Raph, 1965). Often the issues of race, culture, and SES were confounded in these studies (cf. Bayley, 1965; Hess & Shipman, 1965; Radin & Kamii, 1965).

In the 1970s and 1980s, researchers reacted to these deficit views of families of low-SES. It was argued that by favoring the style of the middle-SES parents over low-SES parents the strengths and capacities of children and their parents were overlooked (Adler, 1979; Farran, 1982). Additionally, researchers asserted that families of low-SES experience economic and psychological stresses that middle-class families do not (Feshbach, 1973). Gradually, the negative evaluation of low-income families seemed to subside.

In 1995, the concern over social class differences resurfaced when Hart and Risley released their book, *Meaningful Differences,* and the critique of low-income families began again. Coincidentally, the study was designed and carried out during Bernstein's time. Since the release of *Meaningful Differences,* numerous studies have showed that the vocabulary sizes of children from low-incomes are smaller than those of middle- and upper-SES families and that the language learning environments differ (cf. Hoff, 2003, 2006; Raviv, Kessenich, & Morrison, 2004). As a result of this research, the interactional behaviors of mothers from different cultures and socioeconomic groups have been judged negatively by many speech language pathologists and educators.

Undoubtedly, cultural and linguistic variations play a key role in these differences (which should not be viewed as deficiencies); however, the circumstances of living in poverty and their effect on mothers and their children also need to be considered. Families of low-SES have limited economic resources due to unemployment, low wages, and minimal public assistance, and are more likely to have mental and physical health problems than middle-SES families (Geronimus, Hicken, Keene, & Bound, 2006; McLoyd & Wilson, 1991). Mothers of low-SES are more likely to be single, which often results in social isolation and limited social support (Mullings, 2001). Low incomes, poor housing, instability of resources, and life in unsafe neighborhoods cause chronic stress. All of these factors can, in turn, impact the resources (i.e., time and material resources) parents provide to their children as well as the parenting practices in which they engage (Coleman, 1988; Conger & Conger, 2002). The purpose of this chapter is to examine circumstances of poverty that impact the lives of mothers of low-SES and that need to be taken into account when serving families.

Learning from The Mothers

The Mothers

Ten Puerto Rican and 10 African American mothers of preschool children took part in the study. I recruited the mothers from Head Start, a federal program that serves low-income families, in a small city in central Pennsylvania. The mothers averaged 26 years of age and ranged in age from 20 to 37 years.

Table 12.1   Characteristics of the Mothers

Mother	Years of Education	Employment	Marital Status
Puerto Rican Mothers			
Linda	11	Unskilled position	Single
Ana	12	Unskilled position	Single
Alicia	10	Homemaker	Married
Bea	12	Unskilled position	Single
Dina	12	Unskilled position	Married
Liz	12	Homemaker	Married
Sylvia	15	Homemaker	Married
Julietta	11	Homemaker	Single
Cristina	12	Semi-skilled	Single
Daniela	12	Homemaker	Single
African American Mothers			
Barbara	16	Unskilled position	Single
Breanna	9	Homemaker	Single
Lisa	12	Skilled position	Single
Cynthia	12	Unskilled position	Married
Julie	13	Unskilled position	Married
Rosemary	12	Skilled position	Single
Tanysha	10	Homemaker	Single
Nicole	12	Homemaker	Single
Camilla	11	Skilled position	Married
Jackie	16	Professional	Married

They had 12 years of education, on average, with the number of years of education varying from 9 to 16 years. Sixty percent of the mothers were single. Fifty percent of the Puerto Rican mothers and 70% of the African American mothers worked outside of the home. The mothers had between one and six children, with the mode of three and two for the Puerto Rican and African American mothers, respectively. Information about the individual mothers, using pseudonyms, is provided in Table 12.1.

The Interviews

The mothers participated in a larger project that focused on the language and literacy experiences mothers provided to their Head Start children. Data were collected over three sessions. During the first two sessions, I conducted semi-structured interviews with the mothers. During the second and third sessions, I observed the mothers sharing four books with their preschoolers. This chapter focuses on a subset of the findings from the semi-structured interviews.

The interviews lasted between 1 to 3 hours, depending on the length of time needed to cover the topics. The interviews, which were audiotaped, were conducted in the mothers' homes. In keeping with qualitative research methods, I developed guide questions (Rubin & Rubin, 2011) that covered topics related to children's language and literacy development, parents' and teachers' roles in supporting children's development, and the mothers' literacy and school experiences. Example questions related to children's language and development included: How do you think children learn to talk?; Describe how you and child look at books together; What do you think are the most important skills a child should have before entering kindergarten? Questions about parents' and teachers' support of children's development involved: What did you do to help your child learn to talk? What are you doing to help your child learn to read? and What do you expect your child's Head Start teachers to do to help your child learn to read? When focusing on mothers' experiences, questions included: What were your experiences with adults reading books to you? Tell about your reading experiences in school.

Guide questions were used to stimulate a conversation on a given topic and were not asked in a preset order. After a question was asked, I posed follow up questions as needed. The interviews were open-ended to allow the mothers the opportunity to share information that was most pertinent to them (Bernard, 2005; Rubin & Rubin, 2011; Reinharz, 1992).

It should be noted that no guide questions targeted on the larger circumstances of life or poverty. The questions were designed to talk about child rearing and child development; however, the mothers shared aspects of their lives that were very salient to them and discussed events that impacted the environment in which they raise their children.

Analysis of the Interviews

The audio recordings of the interviews were transcribed verbatim. I coded the transcripts using codes that represented the ideas shared by the mothers (Miles & Huberman, 1994). Example codes included: assistance from family, isolation, strict parents, left home. Then, the coded segments were grouped into categories. For example, "assistance from family" and "isolation" were combined into the category "supports," and "parental relationships" and "left home" were grouped into the category, "independence early in life." During the coding process, new categories emerged. As a result, previously categorized data were sorted into the new categories as appropriate (Miles & Huberman,

1994; Patton, 2001). After the core categories were finalized, themes were generated (Patton, 2001). For example, the category "independence early in life" and "school drop out" became categories under the theme, "challenges during the teenage years."

Results: "It's Hard But I'm Trying"

As the mothers talked about seemingly benign topics of children's literacy development and mothers' efforts to support their children, many of the mothers discussed the difficult circumstances of their lives, as these life challenges provided the context in which the mothers raised their children. The following section describes significant events in the lives of the mothers.

Separation from Parents

One half of the Puerto Rican mothers and one third of the African American mothers experienced separation from their parents during their childhood. This separation occurred in various forms. Several mothers experienced the death of a parent. Tanysha's father died when she was in ninth grade. Ana's mother passed away when she was 18 years of age. Jennifer experienced the losses of her father and stepfather. When she was in elementary school, a drunk driver killed her stepfather. Her biological passed away when she was in high school. Cynthia's grandfather and grandmother, who were her primary caregivers for a period of time, died when she was 6 and 12 years old, respectively.

Two of the mothers' separations occurred, because their mothers left their fathers. Linda's mother left her family when Linda was 8 years old. Her mother did not maintain a relationship with her children nor was she involved in their lives. Alicia had not seen her father since she was 10 years of age, because her mother left her abusive father. Alicia recounted, "She [her mother] was having a lot of problems with my father. Father was abusing her, hitting her. So she got up one day and she never came back." Her mother came to the United States mainland with the children and her father remained in Puerto Rico.

Two Puerto Rican mothers (Julietta and Daniela) and one African American mother (Cynthia) had mothers who were drug addicts. These women described experiences of neglect and/or abuse as a result. Their mothers' drug abuse led to a separation either because the mothers left home or the children were placed in foster care. Julietta recounted that her mother would hit her repeatedly. "And she used to wrap her hands like that [showing how her mother would wrap her hair around her arms] and just hit away at me ... I have bad memories but I still love my mother."

Challenges During the Teenage Years

Many of the mothers faced significant challenges during their teenage years. Seven of the mothers (five Puerto Rican and two African American) became independent at a young age. This included the three mothers whose mothers abused drugs. All three lived on their own as adolescents. Julietta lived on the streets at age 14 and sold drugs to get by. She recounted, "And, um, since I was 14, I emancipated myself 'cuz my mother didn't act like she wanted to do for me. The only thing I know was the life that she showed us, was to sell the drugs outside. That's exactly what I did. I sold drugs to make a living, so me and my brother would eat."

Daniela lived on her own beginning at age 13, because of her mother's drug use. She recounted, "The school called Children and Youth Services, so I was in foster care. So I was raised by foster parents and then I got my own life." Cynthia lived with various family members after her mother "threw" her out. That caused her to "grow up a lot faster in this real world ... My older sister let me stay down the street with her boyfriend. You know, I stayed there for a while and I got a job. And I worked and I worked and I saved money and um, learned to pay bills, to pay rent at 16 years old."

In addition, three Puerto Rican mothers and one African American mother, who did not report that their parents used drugs, became independent at an early age. The Puerto Rican mothers choose to leave home during their teen years. Linda was on her own at 17. Bea left home because her parents were too strict, and Liz married at 18, when she was 4 months pregnant. Breanna, an African American mother, found herself on her own one morning after returning home from staying at a friend's home over the weekend without permission. She said, "And Sunday, when I decided to go home, my things were already packed and she [her mother] said, 'you're going back where you stayed' ... So she put my stuff in the car and took me back where I stayed at. And that's where I lived at." Breanna's sisters also had left home before reaching the age of 18.

School drop out was another challenge that six mothers faced. These mothers dropped out for a variety of reasons. For example, Breanna and Cynthia reported that they did not like school, so they stopped attending. Breanna left school after she was kicked out of her home. "But I went for like 3 months through tenth grade, and I just, since I moved out of my mom's house, I was just hanging out and stuff and I couldn't make it to school." Cynthia reported that she had a learning disability. One mother, Liz, was raped in eighth grade. She dropped out because school officials protected the boy, and other students defended him. She acted out by fighting her classmates. She recalled, "It was eighth grade. I got raped ... And he was the XX track runner. And I guess they try to blame me for it ... 'Cuz people thought I was trying to mess his reputation up."

Julie graduated from high school, but had a rough time doing so. She described herself as a "troubled teen." "I felt I knew all that stuff … I felt I was too smart for school." She skipped classes. She also "used to fight all the time in school" and got a reputation from hanging out with the wrong crowd. "They [her friends] gave me a reputation. Kinda like, they, you know, got this reputation and throwed it on me. And I had to wear this reputation all the way through school until my 12th-grade year." But in the 11th grade she decided to stop following others, which allowed her to "settle down" and graduate from high school.

Teenage pregnancy was a major factor for three African American and three Puerto Rican mothers. They did not have sufficient supports to stay in school. Daniela, who became pregnant in ninth grade, indicated that the school officials would not let her back in school after her child was born. Sylvia dropped out in 11th grade because she had a child that was very ill. She tried to complete her high school degree but gave up after 3 years of trying. Alicia had a child with multiple disabilities, which complicated her efforts to remain in school. Reflecting on her life, she said, "I can't say I have an education. I dropped out of school in tenth grade, yeah, 'cuz of my daughter … she's had oral surgery done twice. She's had surgery for her ears. She's deaf. She don't sit, she don't talk … It's really hard so I had to drop out."

Limited Support from Children's Fathers

Although some of the mothers received support for raising their children from family members, support from many of the children's fathers was limited. Only 40% of the mothers were married and of those, two specifically mentioned the support they received from their husbands (Dina and Julie). In addition, one unmarried mother, Lisa shared that the fathers of her children helped her take care of her children. "And I got all their dads, everyone's dads, is coming to pick the kids up and my family takes the kids for the weekend."

Some fathers were limited in the support that they could provide as four Puerto Rican fathers and one African American father were in prison. The fathers' incarceration placed additional stresses on the family. For example, Daniela was trying to move to Florida because her child's father was in federal prison and his mother was interfering with her life. His mother wanted him to seek custody and had threatened to call Child Protective Services for no specific reason. As discussed in the next section, Bea's children experienced emotional problems as a result of their father's incarceration.

The Special Needs of Children

The special needs of the children also presented challenges to the eight of the mothers (five Puerto Rican and three African American mothers). These included prematurity, health issues, and disabilities as well as the stress of raising children.

Three mothers (Liz, Julietta, and Julie) had children who were born prematurely and were very sick as newborns. Alicia, Liz, and Camilla had children with chronic health concerns. All three mothers had children with asthma. Liz described her child as follows, "She has bad asthma. She was a sick baby since born. You know, since she was born." Camilla described her child as very frail. Alicia's daughter, who was in Head Start, had lead poisoning. Unfortunately, the level of lead in her daughter's blood was rising at the time of the interview and the source of the lead had not been discovered.

Three mothers had children with disabilities. Nicole's older son had a learning disability and her preschool son was taking Ritalin. Alicia's first child, who was a teenager, had multiple disabilities that included cerebral palsy, an intellectual disability, and a significant hearing loss. Sylvia had a child with autism.

Bea's children were affected by their father's incarceration. "Their dad's upstate in jail. And, um, that really affected my son in his schoolwork and stuff. My oldest son and he had to go through counseling and see some people 'cuz of that. So you know, I try to keep their minds busy, but it's hard. 'Cuz I really don't know what they're thinking." Unfortunately, family life was not much better with the children's father prior to his imprisonment. He used drugs and abused the children.

Several of the mothers were challenged by raising their children. Tanysha stated that her child was "overwhelming" to her. She described his behaviors as follows: "Starts running through the house, tearing up. I send him upstairs, but he can't hear whatever I say really, when really he's like that. Sometime he's worked up, and I gotta go to bed. My mom's like, 'Oh no. You got it rough'."

One Puerto Rican mother and one African American mother were raising a large number of children. Specifically, Sylvia had six children that included 8-month-old twins and a child with autism. She was a stay-at-home mother who devoted her time to raising and caring for her children and husband. Lisa had five children when I interviewed her at the age of 21. She worked hard to raise her children, go to school, and work as a baker. She received assistance in taking care of her children from her mother, her family, and her child's father. "I'm not to pat myself on the back, but I give myself a lot of credit, because for 21, I have my GED. I graduate next week. I'll have three certificates for that. I have a certificate in life skills and then I'll be going to the school of cosmetology so plus I'm still working." The demands of school added stress, because if she had missed too many classes, due to child illnesses, childcare needs, etc., she would be kicked out of the program. She summed up her life by saying, "It's hard, but I'm trying."

Mental and Physical Health

Mental and physical health concerns affected more African American (six) than Puerto Rican mothers (two). Four of the mothers, three African American and one Puerto Rican, had on-going health problems. Jennifer had high blood pressure, Cynthia was on disability, and Nicole had been out sick and could not work. Julietta, who was 20 years of age, had a recent and difficult pregnancy that left lingering complications. "I'm just starting to gain my weight back. I was really sick with myself. I had bad kidney infections. My right kidney collapsed on me. I had three surgeries done. They made me give birth to him early because I was getting no better. I was getting more sicker … My infections were so bad, I couldn't even walk."

Four of the mothers (three African American and one Puerto Rican) discussed that they felt depressed. Julie stated that having three children under the age of 5 made her emotionally stressed. She stated, "They stress me. They stress me out big time … Last night, um, I was so stressed out, I just went up and I got in my bed." Rosemary and Tanysha attributed their depression to their birth control shot. Tanysha said that she felt lazy and depressed and, as a result, "hollered a lot" at her child.

Housing, Danger, and Tragedy

All of the mothers lived in the poorest sections of the city, with the exception of one mother, Sylvia, who lived in a working-class neighborhood. Three mothers, Ana, Cristina, and Lisa, lived in housing projects, and one mother, Julietta, lived on a street that was known as the most dangerous street in the area, even more dangerous than living in housing projects.

The mothers discussed crime, drug and safety issues as well as poor housing conditions. Daniela apologized for yawning frequently during the interview. She explained that her neighbor's son was shot and killed by the police in the middle of the night. She had been up since the shooting.

Others talked about the drug deals and drug use that occurred in their neighborhoods. Liz stated, "This is a bad area. There's always shooting, selling drugs at night." Linda wanted to move, because of the presence of drug deals and usage in her area. The tenants below her used drugs. Her neighbor was arrested for dealing drugs. The police raided his apartment found $50,000 worth of drugs in his unit. She lamented, "I'm trying to find a place to move out. It's just so hard. Everything is so expensive."

Camilla lived in poor housing conditions and experienced a significant tragedy. She lost three children and her father when her house caught on fire. To add to this tragedy, the family had no insurance. She recalled, "Then the house catches fire and burns up. And then couldn't even collect the insurance … The person who owned the house got all the insurance money and then sold the house for $75,000 ... We lost everything. This girl right here [pointing to her older daughter], we ain't have nothing but the clothes we had on our backs. That was it."

Discussion

The stories that the 10 Puerto Rican and 10 African American mothers shared clearly show the challenges that are associated with growing up and living in the poverty. All but one of the mothers recounted significant events or tragedies that impacted their lives. Mothers discussed separations from their parents or primary caregivers that were the result of deaths, placement in foster care, parents leaving the family, and drug abuse. They also told of the challenges they faced during their teenage years. These included being independent at an early age, dropping out of school due to personal struggles or life circumstances, and teenage pregnancy. Many mothers experienced limited support from their children's fathers. Five fathers were incarcerated, thereby making it impossible for them to help support their families. In addition, several of the mothers had children with significant disabilities, chronic health problems, and emotional concerns. Many also experienced physical and mental health problems themselves. All but one lived in dangerous neighborhoods. Many discussed the desire to leave their current neighborhood, but poverty prevented them from moving to safer locations. One mother lost three children, her father, and her possessions in a house fire.

Many times speech-language pathologists and educators overlook these challenging circumstances of poverty when working with parents and children from low-income homes. As a result, parents of low-SES are often expected behave like parents who have economic means and are viewed in a negative light. However, I contend, along with others, that parents with low-incomes should not be compared to middle-SES parents. Living in poverty requires parents to focus on meeting the basic needs of their families, such as providing their children with safe housing, good health, and food, while also dealing with the stresses of their life circumstances. These are challenges that middle-income families do not face to the same extent.

Therefore, it is essential that speech-language pathologists understand the lives of the families they serve to better appreciate the challenges that families face. Applying qualitative methods to their practice is a way that can assist them in doing so. In particular, semi-structured interviews, such as those described in this chapter, are an essential tool. When conducting the interviews, emphasis is placed on having a conversation and creating an environment where families feel comfortable sharing the information that they would like to convey. The goal is to establish a foundation upon which the conversation can continue over time. As a rapport emerges, families develop trust in the relationship and gradually they share more information that will help the speech-language pathologist understand their beliefs and practices, as well as the circumstances in which they raise their children (Hammer, 1998). Through the interviews, speech-language pathologists *learn from* rather than *learn about* the families and children that they serve. As a result, speech language pathologists are better able to understand and work from the families' perspective.

References

Adler, A. (1979). *Poverty children and their language: Implications for teaching and treating.* New York, NY: Grune & Stratton.

Bayley, N. (1965). Comparisons of mental and motor test scores for ages 1–15 months by sex, birth order, race, geographical location and education of parents. *Child Development, 36,* 379–411.

Bereiter, C., & Engelmann, S. (1966). *Teaching disadvantaged children in the preschool.* Englewood Cliffs, NJ: Prentice-Hall.

Bernard, H. (2005). *Research methods in anthropology* (4th ed.). Thousand Oaks, CA: Sage.

Bernstein, B. (1971). *Class, codes and control. Volume 1: Theoretical studies towards a sociology of language.* London, England: Routledge and Kegan Paul.

Coleman, J. (1988). Social capital in the creation of human capital. *American Journal of Sociology, 94*(Suppl.), S95–S120.

Conger, R., & Conger, K. (2002). Resilience in midwestern families: Selected findings from the first decade of a prospective, longitudinal study. *Journal of Marriage and Family, 64,* 361–373.

Corbin, R., & Crosby, M. (1965). *Language programs for the disadvantaged: The report of the NCTE Task Force on teaching English to the disadvantaged.* Champaign, IL: National Council of Teachers of English.

Farran, D. (1982). Mother-child interaction, language development, and the school performance of poverty children. In L. Feagans & D. Farran (Eds.), *The language of children reared in poverty* (pp. 19–52). New York, NY: Academic Press.

Feshbach, N. (1973). Cross-cultural studies of teaching styles in four-year-olds and their mothers. In A. Pick (Ed.), *Minnesota symposia on child psychology Vol. 7* (pp. 87–116). Minneapolis: University of Minnesota Press.

Geronimus, A., Hicken, M., Keene, D., & Bound, J. (2006). "Weathering" and age patterns of allostatic load scores among Blacks and Whites in the United States. *American Journal of Public Health, 96*(5), 826–833.

Hammer, C. S. (1998). Toward a 'thick description' of families: Using ethnography to overcome the obstacles to providing family-centered services. *American Journal of Speech-Language Pathology, 9,* 1–22.

Hart, B., & Risley, T. (1995). *Meaningful differences.* Baltimore, MD: Brookes Publishers.

Hess, R., & Shipman, V. (1965). Early experience and the socialization of cognitive modes in children. *Child Development, 36,* 869–886.

Hoff, E. (2003). The specificity of environmental influence: socioeconomic status affects early vocabulary development via maternal speech. *Child Development, 74,* 1368–1378.

Hoff, E. (2006). How social contexts support and shape language development. *Developmental Review, 26,* 55–78.

McLoyd, V., & Wilson, L. (1991). The strain of living poor: Parenting, social support, and child mental health. In A. Huston (Ed.), *Children in poverty: Child development and public policy* (pp. 105–135). New York, NY: Cambridge University Press.

Miles, M., & Huberman, A. (1994). *Qualitative data analysis*. Thousand Oaks, CA: Sage.

Mullings, L. (2001). Households headed by women: The politics of class, race and gender. In J. Goode & J. Maskovsky (Eds.), *The new poverty studies* (pp. 37–56). New York, NY: New York University Press.

Patton, M. (2001). *Qualitative research and evaluation methods* (3rd ed.). Thousand Oaks, CA: Sage.

Radin, N., & Kamii, C. (1965). The child-rearing attitudes of disadvantaged Negro mothers and some educational implications. *The Journal of Negro Education, 34,* 138–145.

Raph, J. (1965). Language development in socially disadvantaged children. *Review of Educational Research, 35,* 389–400.

Raviv, T., Kessenich, M., & Morrison, F. (2004). A meditational model of the association between socioeconomic status and three-year-old language abilities: The role of parenting factors. *Early Childhood Research Quarterly, 19,* 528–547.

Reinharz, S. (1992). *Feminist methods in social research*. New York, NY: Oxford University Press.

Rubin, H., & Rubin, I. (2011). *Qualitative interviewing: The art of hearing data* (3rd ed.). Thousand Oaks, CA: Sage.

13
Intercultural Health Communication
Why Qualitative Methods Matter

CLAIRE PENN

Introduction

During the past few years my research has expanded beyond the speech language pathology clinic and into the broader domain of health communication. In response to a perceived need at some of the sites of practice in which student clinicians train, I began investigating health care interactions across languages and cultures. Using primarily qualitative methods, this research has explored such interactions in the context of a society which has unique characteristics. Not only is this society multilingual but it carries a very complex history of social inequity and asymmetry. Further it has a high and unique disease burden. It has become increasingly clear that qualitative methods and approaches from my primary discipline have a powerful and effective impact beyond our traditional domain.

Some of this work has involved speech pathology and audiology settings (see, for example, Penn & Jones, 2006; Penn et al., 2010) but a lot of it has been in hospitals and outlying rural clinics in response to the specific disease challenges and expressed concerns of health care practitioners. Our work has included HIV/Aids, focusing inter alia on the role of the interpreter, on barriers to drug adherence, and the informed consent process in research trials (Penn, 2007, 2010; Penn & Evans. 2010; Penn, Watermeyer, & Evans, 2011). Other fields have included cerebral palsy (Barratt & Penn, 2009), stroke (Legg & Penn, 2012) and genetic counseling (Penn, Frankel, Watermeyer, & Muller, 2009). Most of the work has involved extensive ethnography and engagement with the settings involved. Guided by some seminal qualitative work in health interactions in sociology, linguistics and in our own profession (e.g., Collins, Britten, Ruusuvuori, & Thompson, 2007; Damico & Simmons Mackie, 2003; Drew & Heritage, 1992; Maynard & Heritage, 2005; Roberts & Sarangi, 1999), most of our work has involved direct recordings of interactions between patients and health professionals. We have combined this evidence with observations, interviews, focus groups, and narratives.

This chapter will describe and illustrate some of these methods of data collection and analysis and how these have been utilized to gain a deeper insight into facilitators and barriers to care in intercultural practice. Through some illustrations and practical suggestions, I will describe how some of the methods have evolved through the work of our research unit and will highlight some potential pitfalls to the research process as well as some novel solutions.

I will argue that the three essential aspects of qualitative research in this intercultural domain are relevance, rigor and responsibility. These are schematically presented in Figure 13.1. While these should be the cornerstones of any research, qualitative methods bring with them particular challenges which have the potential to erode these principles and it is these challenges which I will highlight here, while suggesting caveats to the new researcher.

Finally, I will argue that some of these findings will be sufficiently compelling to convince our profession to take on an expanded role in the 21st century which is characterized by fluidity, transition, and cultural shift.

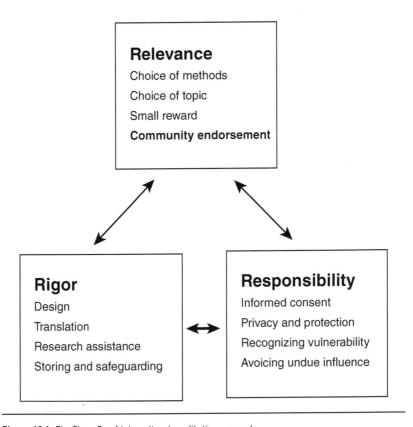

Figure 13.1 The Three Rs of intercultural qualitative research.

Relevance

Certain features of qualitative research make it a preferred framework for the issues we have studied. Some of the medical research that has to be done in South Africa is not easily done using traditional research methods. Questions which might be important for example include:

- Why are patients at a rural hospital non-adherent with antiretroviral drugs?
- What's it like caring for a disabled child in a rural context?
- What's it like living with aphasia in a context of severe poverty?
- Why is the uptake of genetic counseling services so low in this country?
- What is the most effective way to work in a clinic when I do not speak the language of my clients?

Given the focus on social relations and its root in the social sciences and anthropology, qualitative research holds the potential to answer some of these more complex questions we encounter. In its focus on the oral, the particular, and the local it helps bypass the challenges of studying contexts and individuals where there may be limited literacy and education and a legacy of restricted opportunities, lack of agency and access to resources. As Olwen Hufton wrote in 1974 (p. 7), "The approach to the study of poverty must be predominantly qualitative not quantitative. There is no such thing as a graph of human suffering."

In its focus on text as empirical material (derived from talk or observation), it has the potential to use authentic ways of data gathering which are relevant across cultures. Significantly, since a prerequisite of qualitative research is a belief in multiple realities and a commitment to the participant's viewpoint, there is a flexibility not available in more linear structured hypothesis-driven paradigms. Similarly, since qualitative research limits the disruption of natural context, its choice as a method becomes pragmatically compelling especially in a context where a lot of medical services are based in the primary health care setting and in rural areas. Temporal, cultural and spatial features of such contexts vary widely and methods are required which show sensitivity to these aspects. "Every human interaction develops situationally, at a microscopic scale of social structure. Yet, it is always embedded in larger patterns—linguistic, social, cultural, historical—and draws meaning from these larger patterns" (Blommaert, Collins, & Slembrouck, 2005, p. 203).

Types of Research

We have used several types of qualitative research described elsewhere in this volume. I will select a few, illustrate them, provide some examples, and offer some caveats which appear particularly relevant to the intercultural context.

Observation

An ethnography of the context is usually the first step in our research and typically constitutes the pilot and feasibility part of the study. Guided by some useful literature (Erlandson, Harris, Skipper, & Allen, 1993; Spradley 1979, 1980), we focus on relevant dimensions of a particular social situation including: settings and space, actors (participants), events, objects and artifacts, activities and interactions, time factors (frequency and duration), goal, and feeling.

The ideal ethnography is where "the ethnographer participates, overtly or covertly, in people's daily lives for an extended period of time, watching what happens, listening to what is said, asking questions, in fact collecting whatever data available to throw light on the issues with which he or she is concerned" (Hammersley & Atkinson, 1983, p. 2). In reality such sustained engagement is not always feasible but certain important features need to be borne in mind. The first is that observation be regular (and not a once-off) and prolonged and should capture multidimensional aspects. Similarly, as Gobo (2010, p. 17) suggests, there is a difference between non-participant and participant observation and these two aspects may reflect two stages of research. Another helpful distinction to be made is that between "eye-witnessing" where specific features are described and "I-witnessing" in which the observer is encouraged to report not only on physical dimensions but on subtle factors and on the formulation of a personal response to what is being observed. We have found the notion of "hospital ethnography" (Van der Geest & Finkler, 2004) particularly useful in a context of stratified health care, full clinics, and limited resources. Here the hospital setting is seen as extension of the broader societal context "biomedicine and the hospital as its foremost institution is a domain where the core values and beliefs of a culture come into view" (Van der Geest & Finkler, 2004, p. 1996). This view also helps new researchers understand the process of reflection and encourages the description of feelings and interpreting their own experience in relation to the setting, and broader political factors. This self-reflection allows for an interrogation of preconceived ideas. For some of our students, this type of activity provides the opportunity to understand the barriers to clinical practice for the first time (Watermeyer & Barratt, 2013).

There are some potential dangers to observations especially in settings where individuals are employed. In a context of job insecurity and wide unemployment, individuals may view researchers who are on the site as a threat, particularly if access to the site has been via a managerial gatekeeper. For this reason in some settings, online note taking should be avoided or delayed.

From our ethnographic entry into sites derives, in most cases, a model of **action research**, driven by perceived and expressed needs of those working at the sites. For example, on invitation we have been asked to help better integrate and coordinate the use of interpreters at a clinic in a large pediatric hospital and to provide evidence for the effectiveness of a specific and community education program at a rural HIV/Aids clinic (to enable continued funding for that site). This type of investigation, in which researchers work "with and for" people rather than "on" them (Reason & Bradbury 2001, cited in Meyer, 2009, p. 121) has particular advantages of encouraging participation, reinforcing democratic processes and empowering people at that site. Further, hopefully, from such research emerges some potential solutions and the ability to influence policy and practice. In a context of scare resources and historical inequity, this becomes an ethical imperative when gaps are seen, especially when the tools and competence exist to get it measurably right and when there is an appeal from the site of research to do that.

What we have observed at sites has informed training packages, materials video tapes and feedback to sites and participants has resulted in changes of practice and policy. An example is the study of Evans (2010) whose long-term engagement at a site enabled the development of effective new team models for communicating in the context of a pediatric HIV Aids clinic. Similarly, in ongoing research, Seedat has developed a nurse training program for oral care as a precursor to implementing and measuring the effectiveness of a dysphagia protocol in a public hospital. Watermeyer's study of the pharmacy context has influenced communication practices at multiple ARV sites (Watermeyer & Penn, 2009a, 2009b).

Turning the results of this research into such education programs and guidelines for health professionals links to the issue of **knowledge translation** which has been identified by WHO as a global priority. Such research outcomes linked to the local needs of a site are a particular imperative in developing countries and contrasts markedly with what has been termed "helicopter research" where a data and tenure-hungry researcher flies in from another continent to tap into our rich and exotic data base. In the medical field there has been some deep suspicion in developing countries about this, particularly with regard to tissue samples. The obvious pitfalls of this type of approach is the potential for bias of the researcher and also the time commitment required of a long term cyclical engagement at a site.

Narratives and Interviews

Interviews which explore subjective experiences, perceptions, opinions and interpretations of participants require a full understanding of linguistic and cultural barriers. Critical decisions have to be made on which language they should be in, who should conduct them and the terminology and the phrasing of questions.

Properly conducted interviews in a qualitative approach will be open and semi-structured and the focus is likely to be a narrative one. The presence of a cultural broker (interpreter) adds additional layers of complexity which influence spatial and temporal variables as well as perceptions of confidentiality.

The oral narrative is a familiar genre to many indigenous people of South Africa and has proven a particularly fruitful tool in our research. The invitation to tell a story usually elicits a positive and lengthy response and has been a technique which we have encouraged health professionals to take on board in clinical settings (cf. Greenhalgh & Hurwitz, 1998; Charon, 2006). Such narratives are particularly appropriate in situations where literacy might be a challenge and seem to be very sensitive to what Eliot Mishler (1984) calls the "lifeworld." Through this technique we have been able to explore cultural issues, experiences of healthcare, disease, and better understand alternative treatment-seeking paths and barriers to care.

Two of our studies illustrate these points. Both took place in a context of extreme poverty and involved the use of a trained cultural broker. Both yielded rich data which on analysis provided deep insight into the social milieu and some lessons for our profession. While these studies were conducted in very different settings and with a different focus, both studies yield a similar finding.

In the first 27 caregivers of children with cerebral palsy were asked to recount their experience (Barratt & Penn, 2009). The stories highlighted both a universal experience of caring for a child with a disability and also culture-specific features of this experience. The role of hope, acceptance, gender, family structure, and religion emerged in separate narratives. Interestingly, what did not emerge in those narratives was as important as what did. For example, we had expected that the participants would highlight the great hardships imposed by the poverty of the setting and lack of access to basic services such as water, transport and electricity. This did not happen. Similarly as speech-language therapists, we had expected communication to be an important emerging theme or barrier identified by the caregivers, whereas in fact this only emerged as a concern in one of the 27 narratives.

In another study using narratives as a primary technique, Legg (Legg & Penn, 2013) explored the quality of life of individuals with aphasia living in a peri-urban township where challenges of life include financial hardship, limited social and health resources, and high levels of crime. Fieldwork, in the form of regular trips to the area, was carried out over a period of 3 years. Here, observation and interviews took place in local clinics, a day care center, a church group, and an old age home, as well as in the homes and neighborhoods of a small group of adults living with aphasia. As the study progressed, frameworks with which we had been familiar for understanding aphasia became increasingly inadequate. In their narratives, participants did not seem to separate communicative difficulties from the struggles that beset their lives, and conversations about aphasia were woven into wider narratives about gender, generation, family and community, and lack of material and social support. Some participants seemed to show small concerns for language disruption when the physical demands of life seemed all consuming. Such findings reinforce the powerful need for reframing the role of our profession in certain contexts and the power and value of narratives in highlighting this perspective.

We have also found **focus groups** a powerful and efficient method of obtaining data. For example in one study we interviewed three groups of grandmothers about their beliefs and experience regarding some genetic childhood disorders (Penn, Watermeyer, MacDonald, & Moabelo, 2010). Three focus groups were conducted by a trained interviewer with fifteen grandmothers from different cultural backgrounds, in their home languages. The participants represented a wide cultural and geographical mix reflecting the diversity of this particular community.

A semi-structured interview approach was employed. The participants were shown web-based photographs of genetic disorders such as club foot, albinism, Down syndrome, cleft lip and palate, and cerebral palsy. Participants were asked if they were familiar with each disorder and they were asked to provide a name of the disorder in their culture. Questions related to the role of the grandmother in the community, traditional beliefs regarding the causes of various genetic disorders, traditional explanations of heredity, community responses to genetic disorders and methods of prevention and management of disorders. Each focus group lasted for approximately one to one and a half hours. Process notes were taken by three researchers during the interviews and a question and answer opportunity was afforded the participants after the interviews (interpreted by the interviewer).

We found that this method was very effective in producing lively discussion and insights. Hearing others' verbalized experiences appeared to stimulate memories, and ideas in participants. Our participants seemed to enjoy the experience and seemed pleased that their ideas were being valued. Some of the side conversations they had (later transcribed and translated) revealed for example a discussion as to how much they should share. The end product was a negotiated compromise about what was for them clearly a taboo topic. There seemed to be a collective safety in the decision to share this information (in this case, past infanticide of severely disabled children). It was also pleasing that there was a diversity of views in the group and that individuals did not appear to bow to group pressure but kept their voices.

Caveats and pitfalls to this approach should also be recognized: There are limits to confidentiality in a focus group—a factor which should be clearly emphasized when asking participants to consider being part of a study. Sensitive topics may be a cause for concern especially if group participants come from a close-knit community. Such concerns have been expressed at our sites not only about the group members but about the research assistant. Despite assurances from the researchers, and the establishment of ground rules at the beginning of a focus group in the context of stigma, this is an issue of major importance. Recording and transcription of group interactions are very difficult if they are audio recordings only; in our grandmother study participants agreed to be video recorded and each chair was given a number which significantly aided us in transcription and analysis, particularly since the groups were multilingual. This argument, unfortunately, has not convinced institutional review boards (IRBs) evaluating some of our later studies, who have insisted on audio recording only.

Some Methodological Issues

Gaining access to research sites is often a complex and layered process. Given the vulnerability and disease profiles of many populations we study, careful planning and lengthy lead times are required which include gaining permission from institutional, government, as well as multiple ethics authorities. In some cases local community structures (including community advisory boards) are approached and are asked to advise on methods, content and terminology. Much of the research in our project has been driven by an insider perspective—a factor which significantly facilitates access. For example the study on rural attitudes to disability was conducted after Barratt had lived and worked as a speech language pathologist in a poverty-stricken rural community for a year. Solomon's study on hemophilia (2009) came about as a result of years of experience as a genetic counselor. Watermeyer and Penn's (2009b) study on pharmacy interaction in Setswana-speaking patients was triggered by a year's community service in a rural site where there was an active ARV rollout program for HIV/Aids patients. Such familiarity seems to be an important component for credibility and finding a way past a gatekeeper.

Some Thought on Language Diversity: Interpreting and Translation

Critical to intercultural research is effective management of the communication challenges which are inevitable when there is linguistic diversity. In most cases researchers in health sites will have to draw on a third party based at the site or in the community to help with the collection of data. Such individuals have to be very carefully selected and their ability to facilitate the research process depends on a lot more than a level of bilingualism. We need to seek out individuals who are skilled in interviewing and are sensitive to participant distress, should it occur. This research assistance will be needed at each stage of the study—not only in data collection but also data transcription and translation. Though ideally one individual would ensure a level of continuity in a project, in practice often several people may be needed at different stages, and there are indeed different skills and experience levels required, which rarely reside in the same individual. This kind of research thus involves a considerable time commitment and is expensive. It also requires a good understanding of the sociopolitical dimensions of language use and often the input of additional language experts. There are numerous procedural steps and pitfalls. Even in a context where the participants understand well, potential problems occur.

Some lessons learned include the need for very careful training and early monitoring. I have had to discard data because I did not check early enough what was actually happening in the interviews of my research assistant. In a series of interviews with patients in one clinic, I discovered a major threat to validity (after the lengthy transcription and translation process) where the interviewer (who was not the transcriber) had introduced the study in Xhosa (one of the indigenous languages) in the following way: "I am doing some interviews about how doctors communicate with patients. You and I know that doctors in this hospital can't talk properly to patients, so I will ask you some questions about that," thus biasing profoundly the subsequent questions about communication practices at the clinic.

We find it important to transcribe in the language of the interview and then translate into English for analysis purposes. This enables later opportunities for accuracy checking. It is also important to emphasize that whatever is said in an interview or narrative that has been collected should be transcribed. This includes the instructions, the asides and as much as possible what happens before and after the actual formal interview commences. Much of what is said in such asides is very revealing and is sometimes literally "lost in un-translation" (Penn and Watermeyer, in press). Further, a distinction not always understood is that between **translation** (which involves the written adaptation for the purposes of study documents, e.g., letter of invitation or an interview form, or a transcription of an interview) and **interpretation**, which is the verbal/oral adaptation of the material across a linguistic barrier (Javier, 2007, p. 90). We have had difficulties in translating precise novel terminology in some protocols and are often not sure how they are subsequently interpreted by the person interviewing the participant, especially when there are may be differential literacy levels between languages of the researcher and participant.

For example, Solomon (2009) found that, working from a written question sheet, her cultural broker used the English word "genes" in her interviews with Xhosa-speaking participants and that their perception of this term was a different one from that of the researcher. Similarly the terms used will depend on the geographic location and dialectal preferences of the speakers. The process of formal translation is not only highly costly but often takes place at another site (e.g., university or professional translation agency) using established protocols. In practice however, despite the presence of such translated forms, trial enrollers frequently choose the English version as English is considered a language of prestige and there is a perceived erosion of literacy levels in vernacular languages. Further, there are marked differences between written and spoken versions of the language which renders a formally translated version unnatural.

Another example from Solomon's (2009) study is helpful here. She contracted two Xhosa-speaking individuals who were employed to transcribe and translate from the recorded data and check reliability issues through verification. They employed different methods and differed markedly in speed.

Some difference in output was also noted although reassuringly (for the purposes of her analysis) no major differences in the content meaning seemed to emerge:

> Transcriber 1:
> "You know my father is allergic to red meat, but sometimes he eats it and does not react on in. He passed his allergy to everyone at home and I am the only one who does not have allergy."

> Transcriber 2:
> "You know back home in my family, my dad is allergic to red meat but sometimes he would eat it sometimes and nothing would happen to him (health wise). All my siblings inherited dad's allergy. I am the luckiest one. I've never encountered such problem. I am not allergic (to red meat) but my siblings are."

In short, such cultural, linguistic, and sociopolitical factors suggest the need for rigorous control of language issues at research sites including detailed language history taking, careful training and monitoring of research assistants at all stages, possibly a bilingual oral enrolment, and an awareness of potential barriers imposed by terminology, education language profiles, and literacy levels of all the participants.

Setting and Recording Variables

In many clinic sites privacy is difficult to attain as there is limited space for private interviewing. This not only hampers the clarity of recording but the validity of the data. Video-recording presents some unique methodological and ethical challenges (Heath, Hindmarsh, & Luff, 2010). The first relates to the fact that it is invasive and has particular implications in certain disease contexts, where there may be stigma associated with the disease. These threats may be perceived, rather than real, and linked to participants' experience and educational background. For example at one trial site where we were video-recording pharmacy interactions, many of the participants in a rural area indicated deep suspicions about the video camera and declined to participate based on the possibility that they may be on TV.

The second relates to the need for high quality recordings with adequate lighting. The unfortunate results of such a requirement are that it has the potential to interfere with the collection of naturalistic data. The position of the camera is determined by the room lighting and illumination of faces has to be good if one is interested in non-verbal aspects. These technical aspects are not so easy to control especially in rural contexts (where there may be no electricity). Software programs of analysis of facial features do not work well for darker skin colors.

Some would argue that these pitfalls may mitigate against the use of video recording altogether, but our research has consistently highlighted the critical role that non-verbal features play in an understanding of barriers to care and improving communication practice (see Watermeyer & Penn, 2009b) and has been the basis for effective intervention (e.g., using drama techniques) at site. The above discussion on types of research is summarized in Table 13.1.

Rigor

Given some of the methodological challenges described above, steps taken to ensure scientific rigor in design and conduct also have distinct characteristics in the intercultural setting. This pertains to the collection, organization, storage, and management of the data as well as to their analysis. Preparing the data for analysis also includes our case translation, transcription, and back-translation to ensure trustworthiness and grounding of data.

Transcription

Decisions which will need to be made at the transcription phase will include a decision about whether transcription should include verbal and non-verbal aspects, the choice of transcription conventions and how much detail is required. Experience suggests there is often no short cut and nothing is more frustrating than finding transcription flaws late in the process of analysis. What seems critical in any system is capturing the relationship between the verbal and the non-verbal message and ensuring reliability of transcription and where necessary, translation. We have used a number methods for the transcription of non-verbal data., some derived from anthropology, some from conversation analysis (see chapter 5, this volume) and some from the study of sign language and its non- manual accompaniments.

For example in Watermeyer's pharmacy study (Watermeyer & Penn, 2009a) a detailed analysis of non-verbal features enabled an understanding of how props facilitate the vital message in an intercultural context of an anti-retroviral clinic treating patients with HIV/Aids. The following extract illustrates the use of the non-verbal message in reinforcing the verbal message (to a Setswana-speaking patient) and ensuring understanding, as well as the precision of transcription needed for that analysis.

Table 13.1   Some Useful Methods in Intercultural Research

Method	Features and Tips	Advantages	Cautionary axioms
Observation	Sit. Watch, experience, immerse yourself.	Excellent first step.	May be viewed with suspicion in work contexts
	How do you feel? How does this link to your own experience?	Minimally invasive	Gaining trust and access to site may be difficult
	What do your observations tell you about what to do next?	Provides good opportunity for self-reflection	
		Informs nature and direction of more structured observation	
		Flexible, low-cost	
		Powerful teaching tool	
Action research	Long term cyclical engagement	Ethical, democratic, empowering, participatory	Time consuming
	Multiple role-players	Generates solutions	May set up false expectations in site participants
	Highly relevant in many intercultural contexts	Aligns with knowledge transfer imperative	Bias of researcher may be reinforced
			Scope for change may be overestimated
Interviews and narratives	Open ended questions	Culturally relevant method	Require experience and expertise
	Taps critical aspects	May be palliative and cathartic	Analysis methods lengthy and challenging
	Suitable for sensitive topics	Not dependent on literacy	May be distressing for both listener and teller
	Authentic	Yields information about life world	
Focus groups	Generative Supportive	Time efficient	Limits to confidentiality
	Require careful planning of temporal and spatial aspects	Enjoyable and supportive	Large data set
		Stimulates memories and experiences	Difficult to transcribe
Using interpreters	Careful training and monitoring required	Authentic link to community	Time consuming
	Different individuals at each stage	Enhances development of trust	Costly
		Flexible	Requires linguistic expertise
			May threaten confidentiality
			Transcription and translation process lengthy and challenging

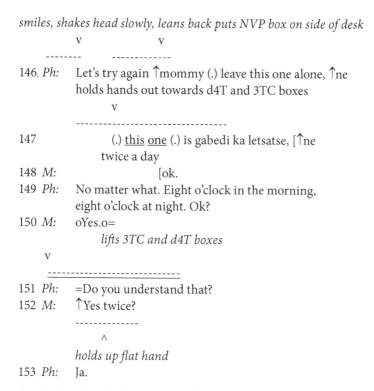

smiles, shakes head slowly, leans back puts NVP box on side of desk

```
           v                v
        --------     -------------
```

146. *Ph:*   Let's try again ↑mommy (.) leave this one alone, ↑ne
             holds hands out towards d4T and 3TC boxes

```
                   v
        ----------------------------------
```

147   (.) this <u>one</u> (.) is gabedi ka letsatse, [↑ne
             twice a day

148 *M:*   [ok.

149 *Ph:*   No matter what. Eight o'clock in the morning,
             eight o'clock at night. Ok?

150 *M:*   oYes.o=
             lifts 3TC and d4T boxes

```
      v
        ----------------------------
```

151 *Ph:*   =Do you understand that?

152 *M:*   ↑Yes twice?

```
        --------------
             ∧
```

             holds up flat hand

153 *Ph:*   Ja.

Similarly, a detailed analysis of the non-verbal behavior of four multiparty intercultural interactions in a pediatric HIV clinic setting between caregivers and medical practitioners, a range of interactive behaviors were identified which taken as a whole appeared to contribute to the success or otherwise of the health interaction (Penn, 2010).

The transcription method used in this study was a multidimensional polyphonic notation system based on CA which included the following elements: vertical mapping of verbal/non-verbal behavior, the inclusion of first language and translations, and the analysis of gestural expression (along a dimension of transparency/opacity; co-speech position and movement), head posturing (sequential and non-sequential, emphasis, speed), body posturing (forward /back), eye gaze (direction), and facial animation based on the methods of Heath (1986) and Damico and Simmons Mackie (2006). Dimensions of measurement included initiation, length, coupling, symmetry, and the search for collaborative moments (moments in the interviews where participants and observers endorsed mutual understanding).

Our findings were linked and triangulated with a detailed analysis of the verbal transcripts as well as with an analysis of the interviews with the participants that were conducted after the health interactions. Our data suggested that patterns of nonverbal behavior linked to communicative efficacy as well as interactional dynamics and content. Further, there was some evidence that practitioner awareness of barriers to communication seemed predictive of embodied aspects emerging in the interactions. Though each interaction had unique characteristics, shaped presumably by the diversity of the participants, there were some commonalities. In the analysis, moments emerged which were judged (by the participants and the researchers) to be critical incidents. These were moments with greater interaction, often informal, personalized, involving more symmetry, coupling and mirroring behaviors. These moments often occurred when non-medical topics were discussed and manifested in increased facial animation, more eye gaze, more forward body posture, increased gesture, and increased participation.

Not surprisingly this type of transcription for these four cases, though highly productive, ran to 104 pages of transcript. For pragmatic reasons (and because of the focus on action research) our thoughts have obviously moved to more efficient and less time-consuming ways of data analysis. In some of our research (especially using thematic content analysis of interviews and narratives), we have used group consensus rating using the recorded data and the joint efforts of a team of judges (Black, 2009).

Some of our ideas about rating have been influenced by the neo-phenomenological work of Langewitz (2007) who has written about the way that physicians are able to make immediate impressions from situations and can make reliable and accurate clinical judgments. This meaning is derived from non-specific atmosphere or impressions which are experienced in authentic ways. Theme-oriented discourse analysis has also proven useful (Roberts & Sarangi, 1999) which involves repeated viewing of recordings, in order to identify the phases of the interactions, examining as content, prosodic cues, non-verbal cues and inferential markers, the outcomes of the whole interaction, and interpreting and comparing interactions in the light of linguistic, sociological, and cultural concepts

This has paved the way to a consideration **of transcription-less analysis.** There are times when recorded text can be analyzed without the benefit of lengthy and time consuming transcription. As shown in the study of Armstrong, Brady, Mackenzie, and Norriel (2007), this will depend on the type of analysis and the purpose of the study. The essential issue is of course ensuring reliability. We have undertaken two studies which suggest that this may be a viable option.

In the first (Frankel, Penn, & Fridjhon, n.d.), which involved an analysis of conversations, global ratings of three dimensions (turn taking, topic management, and repair) based on videotaped material only by an experienced rater were not markedly different from the ratings of a second experienced rater who had access to full transcripts.This finding corroborates Langewitz's

(2007) work and suggests that access to video material allows an external observer to have more complete access to the atmosphere of the interaction than the transcripts alone can convey. A global analysis of the transcripts yielded high degrees of rater concordance, resulting in a confident explication of the data collected.

The second study (ongoing) took place at one of our data sites (a rural HIV/Aids clinic). Following on from experience in the study described above, and constrained by the pressures of time at a site where intervention was planned some two months after our initial data collection, we again explored transcription-free analysis. In this study we had audio recorded interviews from 59 informants in Siswati and English. We transcribed five of these in detail as they were identified as having particular features of interest by the researchers (including laughter), which warranted further micro investigation. For the remaining interviews these were replayed using high-quality speakers to two bilingual researchers (one of whom had conducted the interviews). During the replay, where necessary, there were pauses in the playback and discussion regarding translation issues. Each listener was required to identify main points and themes emerging from the interviews and these were discussed at the end of the playback and merged. Using principles of thematic content analysis, points of consensus were noted and points of dissent shelved for later resolution by a third independent rater. The themes were immediately entered onto a large working space (a wall chart color-coded by category of participant (patient, doctor or counsellor). In addition, during re listening consensus was reached about what we called "juicy" quotes—illuminating verbatim extracts from the interviews which would most appropriately ground the findings with examples. There was no evidence at all that this compromised validity and, in fact, it seems this is more likely to tune into the atmosphere effect described by Langewitz (2007). It is efficient, reliable and probably more ethical, as the absence of written records may protect vulnerable participants better.

Some Thoughts on Triangulation

Investigation that is characterized by multi-method research is considered to be the hallmark of the qualitative paradigm (Denzin & Lincoln, 1994). We have found that this is a particularly important safeguard against **misconception** and bias in our own research.

Thus our methods typically combine observations and field notes, recordings of interactions (video and audio), interviews with multiple participants (e.g., doctors, patients caregivers, interpreters, nurses, hospital managers), review of other sources of data (such as material from case files), and comments gleaned from participants during the review of the tapes or transcriptions (as part of action research).

The richness of data yielded from this process of **triangulation** provides confidence in the analysis but is a point which sometimes has drawn criticism from purists and has presented a challenge to us. When preparing papers for publication a narrowed focus thus becomes difficult. Given these multiple levels of evidence, a narrow analysis for example of turn-taking in a conversational exchange becomes almost impossible without reflecting for example on evidence about gender and power differences at the site—evidence gleaned from other sources. Combining such evidence into a cohesive whole remains a challenge. However it seems to be a highly important feature of our research.

Responsibility

In this final section I will address the notion of responsibility in qualitative research. At the center of this issue is an awareness of ethical issues. Until recently comparatively little has been written about the ethics of qualitative research and there were few guidelines at present for evaluating research ethics in qualitative research, particularly in the medical context (Richards & Schwartz, 2002; Ryen, 2011). However, features of qualitative research have many important ethical implications particularly in intercultural contexts. These include the use of small numbers of participants and the fact that when there are evolving aims in a study which possibly involve several visits and regular collection of material, the relationship with participants becomes sustained. Given the nature of qualitative research, there is often a focus on sensitive information which may elicit powerful responses.

Several assumptions about the nature of qualitative research need to be questioned particularly in a context of historical power inequities such as South Africa. The first is the assumption that there are more balanced and equal power relations between participants. It has become apparent that qualitative research is not as benign as people originally thought. The ideas that participants protect themselves and that if people don't want to talk about themselves, they won't is questionable, particularly in a medical context. The suggestion that telling a story is cathartic or palliative also has questionable validity. While researchers such as Campbell (2002) have found that for certain participants (abused women), the process of telling the story to the researchers is validating and beneficial, this is not always the case, and participants may be profoundly moved by their retell and may require support and follow up.

Similarly, methods such as participant observation, interviewing and focus groups may be regarded as being more stealthy or as we have seen, impose limits to confidentiality. Risks to participants in qualitative research may include: anxiety and distress, exploitation, misrepresentation and loss of self-identity, dependency, stereotyping, and possible identification of the participants in published papers of themselves and others. Identifying details of specific site and systems (through detailed ethnographies) may need to be deliberately masked. Audio and video recording of language samples poses particular challenges as does electronic storing of case material. Interestingly in some studies confidentiality is not always an issue and some of our participants have specifically requested their names to be linked to their viewpoint as they perceive this as an opportunity for a personal voice. A challenge thus ensues and another potential conflict with the research ethics committee!

Qualitative research is also more likely to produce a therapeutic misconception. This refers to the situation in which research participants are unaware of the difference between participating in a study and receiving treatment in a clinical setting. This may happen when there is a close and often sustained relationship between the investigator and the participants (such as between a treating clinician and a patient). Research participants may thus believe that every aspect of a research project to which they consent is designed for them directly and may hence participate out of self-interest and interpret and even distort the information received on the trial to maintain this view (Dresser, 2002).

This has been reinforced by the results of Kerrison, Laws, Cane, and Thompon (2008) in a study of patients' experiences of being part of a number of clinical trials. Qualitative methods revealed that most patients had been channelled into research by the health care professionals treating them and that they perceived the benefits of participation to be extra care and increased surveillance. After the trials had been completed, they expressed disappointment and a frustration with lack of information and reciprocity.

If there is a general lack of access to resources or rehabilitative services in the community in which the research trial takes place, it is just not possible to avoid this issue. Involvement in a research study that offers the potential for any type of treatment may become undue inducement. For example, Tangwa (2004, p. 56) observed "in a situation of general poverty combined with a high burden of disease there is no way to prevent potential victims of a deadly epidemic such as HIV/AIDS from being unduly induced by any type of research participation that hold out the possibility of any type of treatment."

Several guidelines exist as to what constitutes a vulnerable population in clinical research of all types. Council for International Organizations of Medical Sciences (CIOMS, 2002) definition of vulnerable persons, for example, is those who are "relatively/absolutely incapable of protecting own interests—insufficient power, intelligence, education, strength of other needed attributes to protect their own interests" (Guideline 13) (see also NBAC, 2001). In intercultural contexts, the notion of a vulnerable population may take on a different frame. There may be full linguistic and cognitive competence, including educational criteria, but other factors may still render the process of informed consent questionable, particularly in medical contexts. These include historical power imbalances between researcher and participants, a learned "culture of dependency" (Khan, 1991), and roles and attitudes of the nursing profession that are often illness-specific and may inhibit or unduly influence patient participation (Jewkes, Abrahams, & Mvo, 1998). Age and socioeconomic circumstances (including family aspects), home language and gender may also play a part. Characteristics of setting, cultural models of explanation and complications regarding statutory surrogates may further influence the process.

A particularly challenging ethical issue is the role of third party (see above) and the language of informed consent (IC) which may not be fully accessible to research participants. The content, sequence and process of IC may need to be changed from site to site. Many aspects of informed consent components have complex linguistic and cognitive demands and are not easy to convey, even in the situation of a non-vulnerable, healthy, well-educated, and linguistically competent individual (Elbourne, Snowdon, & Garcia, 1997; Dunn, Nowrangi, Palmer, Jeste, & Saks, 2006); and when there are communication problems imposed because of a disorder or a language difference, the difficulties are immense (Barata, Gucciardi, Ahmad, & Stewart, 2006; Emanuel, Wendler, Killen, & Grady, 2004; Molyneux, Peshu, & Marsh, 2004; Russell et al., 2005).

This point has been reinforced by a qualitative investigation of the informed consent process in an aphasia study (Penn et al., 2009). Even though we assumed that our clinical training with communication disorders potentially made us adept at modifying the message, we found flaws in the process. Despite very careful adaptation of materials and language, a detailed conversational analysis of the recorded consent process (long after the study had been completed) showed that not all the elements of the study into which persons with aphasia had agreed to participate, had been fully understood. Further, a paradoxical effect emerged—the use of repetition and visual pictograms (normally clinically helpful tools) in one case seemed to make the understanding of the essential items of the trial even more complex. The results of the study suggested a need for an individual profiling of informed consent and the recognition that this cannot be a static or prescriptive process. It also reinforced the power of qualitative methods (in this case conversation analysis) in exposing such flaws.

Similarly, in a study on the process of informed consent, we found some very disturbing evidence that vaccination trial participants did not understand the language of the trial and had misconceptions about the study and even their own health status (Watermeyer & Penn, 2008).

This point links to an additional concern in this type of research around the safety of the investigators.

Some of our projects have involved long traveling to remote and rural places or to in peri-urban settlement areas where there are high crime rates and threats to personal safety. Some of my work has also taken place in hospital settings where there are infections such as multiple drug resistant Tuberculosis (MDRTB). While a senior researcher may be willing and able to take such risks, a team leader should be cautious about the safety of junior researchers. This concerns not only physical but psychological safety. It is also naïve to expect (a mistake I have made) that, because a person is of the same culture and language as the participants in that site, they will be not be traumatized by its features. In one of the settings in which I worked, my research assistant who spoke the language of the patients at the clinic and lived locally, was traumatized by the site which was full of sick people and was fearful of infection and of being attacked. This reminded me, of course, that one cannot make any assumptions or generalizations about differences between urban/rural or Black/White in a context of diversity and reinforced the need for rigorous training and debrief. This pertains also to the impact of the data we elicit—narratives about death and dying, extreme hardship, gender violence, and hopelessness are traumatic to the listener, and debrief opportunities must be built in as well as practical safety and protection measures (Sikweyiya & Jewkes, 2011).

There are sometimes more subtle and reputational risks to the investigator. In a study on informed consent in a vaccination trial, our finding of poor enrollment practice at a research site antagonized the investigators and was possibly construed as a threat to the trial. This blocked future access to that site. Interestingly, some later qualitative research in the same domain confirmed such inadequacies in the consent process (Newman et al., 2011) and has provided some support for our bruised egos.

For these reason we promote the consideration of a **distress protocol** (Dechesnay, Murphy, Harrison, & Taualii, 2008; Kavanaugh & Ayres, 1998). Acknowledging that there may be some unforeseen psychological harm emanating from qualitative methods, a distress protocol might comprise a set of guidelines (for researchers and ethics committees) which sensitizes the researchers to the possible negative and adverse effects of qualitative methods and includes a demonstration of the awareness by the researchers as to potential harm (to both researchers and participants) and concrete steps to indicate how this will be addressed (e.g., through organizing follow up care or referral).

The use of students as research assistants also poses ethical challenges. An element of coercion may exist in conducting such research especially if that research project is initiated by their supervisor. The same applies for site employees or treating therapists. While on the one hand good ethnography presupposes immersion and familiarity with this site, this very familiarity with the site poses some ethical challenges. We must be aware that some research methods may change the nature of the relationship with the patients they treat. There may also be real or perceived issues of coercion around the need for employees to conduct research (in response to supervisory and managerial pressures.

I similarly became aware of the dangers of such **undue influence** in a study at a mental health clinic, where the method involved review of videotapes by the participants. After transcription and analysis of the sessions, and in search of respondent validation, I had some questions about communication and interactional behaviors which I had prepared and posed to the doctor and her assistant (a cultural broker) during playback of the videos. To my concern, the assistant was rather thrown by my questions and interpreted my search for explanations as a possible criticism of her approach. She expressed concern that her future behavior would become more self-conscious as a consequence of my highlighting them. I reflected after this incident that highlighting specific skills or behaviors in feedback session to any clinicians in training may well not be as effective a teaching method as I had thought, in an asymmetrical power context. I felt that I had unintentionally potentially influenced the individual's natural practice by my comments, an outcome which in clinical training may not always be desirable.

This links to the issue of **remuneration of participants.** The influence of the context on this process is very important. In a context of poverty, there are some compelling reasons why even what researchers would consider to be a modest amount could be perceived as undue incentive. Current legislation in South Africa indicates that there should be no more than R150 (about $20) paid to trial participants. Equally, however, the demonstration for gratitude for time spent, traveling and participation are extremely important, and we have often included food parcels for our participants (provided afterwards and not mentioned in the enrollment process).

Reducing Harm and Getting It Right

The question remains as to how to evaluate the quality of qualitative research and ensure that there is relevance, rigor and responsibility in conduct and design. In recent years a number of guidelines have been put forward particularly in the health field for assessing the quality and relevance of qualitative research. Some criteria are common to both qualitative and quantitative methods while others may be specific (Elliot, Fischer, & Rennie, 1999; Pope & Mays, 2009). Proposals have also been put forward about reducing harm in qualitative research and some guidelines developed for those tasked with evaluating ethical dimensions (Dixon Woods, Shaw, Agarwal, & Smith, 2004). It is probable that most research review and ethics committees need additional expertise on these issues and that humanities disciplines, which are most likely to have experience with qualitative research methods, should be actively involved in such committees.

Table 13.2 Questions for Evaluating the Quality of Qualitative Research

- Is the study worthwhile?
- Will it contribute to new knowledge?
- Is it appropriately designed (and are methods explicit)?
- Is there appropriate training and supervision?
- Who are the participants?
- Is the context explicitly described?
- Does research involve vulnerable groups?
- What process of informed consent will be used?
- Where will research be done?
- How will access to site/s be achieved?
- Who will do research? (consider vulnerability of novice researchers, site employees, students)
- Who else will be involved?
- How will they be trained?
- How will they be monitored?
- How will the participants be interviewed?
- What will happen in interviews? (Expectations in terms of time, self-revelation)
- How will language and culture differences be managed (in recruitment, development of materials, data collection, transcription and analysis)?
- Will participants be paid?
- Is distress (discomfort/embarrassment) anticipated and what steps will be taken to handle this?
- How will knowledge be translated and what feedback will be provided to participants?
- How will data be stored?
- How will data be published?

Drawing on such sources and with reference specifically to intercultural research, Table 13.2 provides a summary of appraisal questions to consider.

Proposed changes to the current rules regarding IRB review (Emanuel & Menikoff, 2011, p. 1145) have implications for the communication specialist. Among the suggestions to "minimize burden and increase effectiveness" in current regulations governing research is the following:

> The goals of change in the treatment of informed consent would be to specify more explicitly the content of consent documents, limit the length of document, simplify and streamline institutional boilerplate, promulgate the use of standardized consent documents and permit the use of oral consent for surveys, focus groups and interviews conducted with competent adults, even if identifiers are retained.

Such recommendations appear to neglect cultural implications and the complexity and relevance of qualitative issues, and we should view this as an important and immediate challenge to pursue.

Conclusions

Shifting to a qualitative framework has not been without difficulties. I have had to learn a new vocabulary and adjust my time frames. I have had to defend myself, find new journals to publish in, new strategies of argument with colleagues and editors, and acquire new ways to challenge the opinions that qualitative research is a soft science, an "add-on," fluffy, subjective, unscientific, anecdotal, and not generalizable.

In truth, qualitative research can be all these things, and I believe that we really have to stay grounded in the cornerstones of relevance, rigor and responsibility to ensure that it does not happen on our watch. It is important to remember that qualitative research is not a substitute for quantitative research. It is not a choice linked to lack of resources, lack of participants, or lack of statistical knowledge. Rather it is linked to type of problem and stage of research and most importantly to its context. It is certainly not easy—either to learn, conduct, analyze or write up and it can be open to a range of criticisms in the same way that quantitative research can. Indeed, I think we have to try harder (like a well-known car hire company) to convince detractors, especially in the medical field, through careful attention to these "Three Rs."

What qualitative research undoubtedly can do is provide an authentic and powerful means of understanding complex human behavior in specific places and temporal contexts. It has particular value in contexts where cultural issues are relevant. Doing qualitative research is the best way of understanding these phenomena, provided that the approach fits the question being asked. While I have highlighted some of the potential pitfalls, I believe that some of these may indeed be less of a burden to researchers who come from a clinical background, particularly a communication disorders background, as they hopefully have the skills and abilities to sustain relationships, handle emotional connections and consequences, and deal with the unexpected. For this reason I would like to see more clinicians doing the work that needs to be done beyond our clinic walls—I think we can (and do) make a significant contribution beyond our scope and probably have a critical role to play in broader society in evaluating qualitative research on research ethics boards, in knowledge translation, and in this global world of facilitating communication across cultures. For this reason I believe increasingly that training programs and text books should include courses on qualitative research and that in health contexts, qualitative methods should be viewed as viable options to biomedical research paradigms.

Qualitative research yields complex, contradictory, and unintended events. It has a role in sensitizing individuals and institutions to a relatively new way of looking at things. It may be viewed not as a technique but a set of attitudes; including a readiness to be surprised.When my qualitative work started, I had some clear ideas about what I would find. I had in my mind some expectations about correlations I would find (to use a positivist term). I had imagined, for example, that there would be a connection between resources and patient satisfaction. I had expected that linguistic mismatch would predict inefficient medical practice in intercultural settings. Neither of these things happened. I found islands of good practice in the poorest settings and complete effective attunement between participants in contexts of huge linguistic disparity. On the other hand, I found power and language struggles impacting adversely on patient satisfaction and adherence, as well as on doctor security in some well-resourced clinics and monolingual settings. I have learned to be prepared to deal with surprises and controversies and I hope to continue in that position of equipoise. The process of discovery has been not just about the phenomena I study, but about myself. In short qualitative research has really allowed me to "stand and stare" and has provided a feast for my curiosity. Most important it has enabled the privilege of engagement with people like Jack Damico, whose holistic view to life is reflected so well in this volume. A journey well lived!

> A poor life this if, full of care,
> We have no time to stand and stare. (W. H. Davies)

Acknowledgments

The work and insights described here reflect the efforts, vision, and energy of a wonderful team of researchers whose lived experience with qualitative research methods, in some very demanding contexts, haa added great texture and understanding to this field. My deep thanks go to Joanne Barratt, Tali Frankel, Mel Evans, Carol Legg, Lesley Nkosi, Dale Ogilvy, Jai Seedat, Samantha Smith, Gabi Solomon, Jennifer Watermeyer, and Tina Wessels for their pioneering work in health communication in South Africa.

The National Research Foundation, South African Netherlands Research Program on Alternatives in Development (SANPAD), the South African Medical Research Council, the Stellenbosch Institute for Advance Studies and Fogarty international are also acknowledged for the funding of some of the research described in this chapter.

References

Armstrong, L., Brady, M., Mackenzie, C., & Norrie, J. (2007). Transcription-less analysis of aphasic discourse: A clinician's dream or a possibility? *Aphasiology, 21*(93/4), 355–374.

Barata, P., Gucciardi, E., Ahmad, F., & Stewart, D. (2006). Cross-cultural perspectives on research participation and informed consent. *Social Science & Medicine, 62*, 479–490.

Barratt, J., & Penn, C. (2009). Listening to the voices of disability: Experiences of caring for children with cerebral palsy in a rural South African setting. In L. Swartz (Ed.), *Disability and international development: Towards inclusive global health* (pp. 191–212). New York, NY: Springer.

Black, N. (2009). Consensus development methods. In C. Pope & N. Mays (Eds.), *Qualitative research in health care* (3rd ed., pp. 132–141). Oxford, England: Blackwell.

Blommaert, J. Collins, J., & Slembrouck, S. (2005). Spaces of multilingualism. *Language and Communication, 25*, 197–216.

Campbell, R. (2002). *Emotionally involved: The impact of researching rape.* London, England: Routledge.

Charon, R. (2006). *Narrative medicine honoring the stories of illness.* Oxford, England: Oxford University Press.

Collins, S., Britten, N., Ruusuvuori, J., & Thompson, J. (2007). *Patient participation in health care consultations.* Maidenhead, England: Open University Press.

Council for International Organizations of Medical Sciences (CIOMS). (2002). *International ethical guidelines for biomedical research involving human subjects.* Geneva, Switzerland: Author.

Damico, J. S., & Simmons Mackie, N. N. (2006). Transcribing gaze and gesture. In N. Müller (Ed.), *Multilayered transcription* (pp. 93–113). San Diego, CA: Plural Publishing.

Damico, J. S., & Simmons-Mackie, N. N. (2003). Qualitative research and speech-language pathology: A tutorial for the clinical realm. *American Journal of Speech-Language Pathology, 12,* 131–143.

DeChesnay, M., Murphy, P., Harrison, L., & Taualii, M. (2008). Methodological and ethical issues in research with vulnerable populations. In M. DeChesnay & B. Anderson (Eds.), *Caring for the vulnerable: Perspectives in nursing theory, practice and research* (pp. 155–170). Sudbury, MA: Jones & Bartlett.

Denzin, N. K., & Lincoln, Y. S. (1994). Introduction: Entering the field of qualitative research. In N. K. Denzin & Y. S. Lincoln (Eds.), *Handbook of qualitative research* (pp. 1–17). Thousand Oaks, CA: Sage.

Dixon-Woods, M., Shaw, R. L., Agarwal, S., & Smith, J. A. (2004). The problems of appraising qualitative research. *Quality and Safety in Health Care, 13,* 223–225.

Dresser, R. (2002). The ubiquity and utility of the therapeutic misconception. *Social Philosophy and Policy, 19,* 271–293.

Drew P., & Heritage J. (1992). *Talk at work: Interaction in institutional settings.* Cambridge, England: Cambridge University Press.

Dunn, L., Nowrangi, M., Palmer, B., Jeste, D., & Saks, E. (2006). Assessing decisional capacity for clinical research or treatment: A review of instruments. *The American Journal of Psychiatry, 163,* 1323–1334.

Elbourne, D., Snowdon, C., & Garcia, J. (1997). Informed consent: Subjects may not understand concept of clinical trials. *British Medical Journal* (Clinical Research Edition), *315,* 248–249.

Elliot, R., Fischer, C.T., & Rennie, D. L. (1999). Evolving guidelines for publication of qualitative research studies in psychology and related fields. *British Journal of Clinical Psychology, 38,* 215–229.

Emanuel, E., & Menikoff, J. (2011). Reforming the regulations governing research with human subjects. *New England Journal of Medicine, 365*(12), 1145–1150.

Emanuel, E., Wendler, D., Killen, J., & Grady, C. (2004). What makes clinical research in developing countries ethical? The benchmarks of ethical research. *Journal of Infectious Diseases, 189,* 930–937

Erlandson, D., Harris, E., Skipper, B., & Allen, S. D. (1993). *Doing naturalistic enquiry: A guide to methods.* Newbury Park, CA: Sage.

Evans, M. (2010). *The impact of communication skills training in the management of paediatric HIV* (unpublished doctoral dissertation). University of the Witwatersrand, Johannesburg, South Africa.

Frankel, T., Penn, C., & Fridjhon, P. (n.d.). *Preserving authenticity of conversation analysis.* Manuscript in preparation.

Greenhalgh, T., & Hurwitz, B. (Eds.). (1998). *Narrative based medicine.* London, England: BMJ Books.

Hammersley, M., & Atkinson, P. (1983). *Ethnography: Principles in practice.* London, England: Tavistock.

Heath, C. (1986). *Body movement and speech in medical interaction.* Cambridge, England: Cambridge University Press.

Heath, C., Hindmarsh, J., & Luff, P. (2010). *Video in qualitative research: Analysing social interaction in everyday life.* London, England: Sage.

Hufton, O. H. (1974). *The poor of eighteenth century France, 1750–1789.* Oxford, England: Clarendon Press.

Javier, R. A. (2007). *The bilingual mind: Thinking, feeling and speaking in two languages.* New York, NY: Springer.

Jewkes, R., Abrahams, N., & Mvo, Z. (1998). Why do nurses abuse patients? Reflections from South African obstetric services. *Social Science and Medicine, 47,* 1781–1795.

Kavanaugh, K., & Ayres, L. (1998). Not as bad as it could have been: Assessing and mitigating harm during research interviews on sensitive topics. *Research in Nursing and Health, 21,* 91–97.

Kerrison. S., Laws, S., Cane, M., & Thompson, A. (2008). The patient's experience of being a human subject. *Journal Royal Society of Medicine, 101,* 416–422.

Khan, K. S. (1991). Epidemiology and ethics: The people's perspective. *Law, Medicine & Health Care, 19,* 202–206.

Langewitz, W. (2007). Beyond content analysis and non-verbal behaviour — What about atmosphere? A phenomenological approach. *Patient Education and Counseling, 67*(3), 319–323.

Legg, C., & Penn, C. (2012). Uncertainty, vulnerability and isolation: Factors framing quality of life in aphasia in a South African township setting. In N. Warren & L. Manderson (Eds.), *Rethinking disability and quality of life: a global perspective.* New York, NY: Springer.

Maynard, D. W., & Heritage, J. (2005). Conversation analysis, doctor-patient interaction and medical communication. *Medical Education, 39*(4), 428–435.

Meyer, J. (2009). Action research. In C. Pope & N. Mays (Eds.), *Qualitative research in health care* (3rd ed., pp. 121–131). London: BMJ Books.

Mishler, E. (1984). *The discourse of medicine: Dialectics of medical interviews.* Norwood, NJ: Ablex.

Molyneux, C. S., Peshu, N., & Marsh, K. (2004). Understanding of informed consent in a low-income setting: three case studies from the Kenyan coast. *Social Science and Medicine, 59,* 2547–2559.

National Bioethics Advisory Commission (NBAC). (2001). *Ethical and policy issues in international research: Clinical trials in developing countries.* Retrieved September 19, 2011 from http://www.georgetown.edu/research/nrcbl/nbac/pubs.html

Newman, P. A., Yim, S., Daly, A., Walisser, R., Halpener, R., Cunningham, W., & Loutfy, M. (2011). Once bitten twice shy: Participant perspectives in the aftermath of an HIV vaccine trial termination. *Vaccine, 29,* 451–458.

Penn, C. (2007). Factors affecting the success of mediated medical interviews in South Africa. *Current Allergy and Clinical Immunology, 20*(2), 65–73.

Penn, C. (2010). Language and power issues in HIV/Aids: Some evidence, challenges and solutions from South African research. In J. Watzke, P. Chamness Miller, & M. Mantero (Eds.), *ISLS readings in language studies, volume 2: Language and power* (pp. 157–182). Lakewood Ranch, FL: International Society for Language Studies.

Penn, C., & Evans, M. (2010). Assessing the impact of a modified informed consent process in a South African HIV/Aids research trial. *Patient Education and Counseling, 80,* 191–199.

Penn, C., Frankel, T., Watermeyer, J., & Muller, M. (2009). Informed consent and aphasia: Evidence of pitfalls in the process. *Aphasiology, 23*(1), 3–32.

Penn, C., & Jones, D. (2006). "We all speak the same language, we all speak aphasic": The evolution of therapy groups within a changing socio-political context. In R. J. Elman (Ed.), *Group treatment of neurogenic disorders: The expert approach* (pp. 195–211). San Diego, CA: Plural Publishers.

Penn, C., & Watermeyer, J. (in press). Cultural brokerage in mediated health consultations in the South African HIV/AIDS context: An analysis of side conversations. In S. Sarangi (Ed), *Interpreter Mediated Healthcare Consultations.* London: Equinox Publishers.

Penn, C., Watermeyer, J., & Evans, M. (2011). Why don't patients take their drugs? The role of communication, context and culture in patient adherence and the work of the pharmacist in HIV/Aids [Special issue]. *Patient Education and Counseling, 83,* 310–318.

Penn, C., Watermeyer, J., Koole, T., de Picciotto, J., Ogilvy, D., & Fisch, M. (2010). Cultural brokerage in mediated health consultations: An analysis of interactional features and participant perceptions in an audiology context. *Journal of Interactional Research in Communication Disorders, 1*(1), 135–156.

Penn, C., Watermeyer, J., MacDonald, C., & Moabelo, C. (2010). Grandmothers as gems of genetic wisdom: exploring South African traditional beliefs about the causes of childhood genetic disorders. *Journal of Genetic Counseling, 19,* 9–21.

Pope, C., & Mays, N. (1999). *Qualitative research in health care* BMJ books (3rd ed.). Oxford, England: Blackwell.

Reason, P., & Bradbury, H. (2001). *Handbook of action research. Participative enquiry and practice.* London, England: Sage.

Richards, H. M., & Schwartz, L. J. (2002). Ethics of qualitative research: are there special issues for health services research? *Family Practice, 19,* 135–139.

Roberts, C., & Sarangi, S. (1999). Introduction: Revisiting different analytic frameworks. In S. Sarangi & C. Roberts (Eds.), *Talk, work, and institutional order discourse in medical, mediation and management settings* (pp. 389–400). Berlin, Germany: Mouton de Gruyter.

Russell, F., Carapetis, J., Liddle, H., Edwards, T., Ruff, T., & Devitt, J. (2005). A pilot study of the quality of informed consent materials for Aboriginal participants in clinical trials. *Journal of Medical Ethics, 31,* 490–494.

Ryen, A. (2011). Ethics and qualitative research. In D. Silverman, *Qualitative research* (3rd ed., pp. 416–438). London, England: Sage.

Sikweyiya, Y., & Jewkes, R. (2011). Perceptions about safety and risks in gender-based violence research: Implications for the ethics review process. *Culture, Health and Sexuality.* doi:10.1080/13691058.2011.604429

Solomon, G. (2009). *An Investigation into the understanding of basic genetic inheritance amongst AmaXhosa caregivers of haemophilia patients* (Unpublished master's thesis). University of Cape Town, South Africa.

Spradley, J. P. (1979). *The ethnographic interview.* New York, NY: Holt, Rinehart, and Winston.

Spradley, J. P. (1980). *Participant observation.* New York, NY: Holt, Rinehart and Winston.

Tangwa, G. (2004). Between universalism and relativism: A conceptual exploration of problems in formulating and applying international biomedical ethical guidelines. *Journal of Medical Ethics, 30,* 63–67.

Van der Geest, S., & Finkler, K. (2004). Hospital ethnography: introduction. *Social Science and Medicine, 59,* 1995–2001.

Watermeyer, J., & Barratt, J. (2013). "I live in a bubble": Speech language therapy and audiology students' expectations and experiences of a rural community work practicum. *Rural and Remote Health, 13,* 2131.

Watermeyer, J., & Penn, C. (2008). "They take positive people": An investigation of communication in the informed consent process of an HIV/Aids vaccine trial in South Africa. *Critical Inquiry in Language Studies, 5*(2), 81–108.

Watermeyer, J., & Penn, C. (2009a). "Come, let me show you": The use of props to facilitate understanding of antiretroviral dosage instructions in multilingual pharmacy interactions. In L. Lagerwerf, H. Boer, & H. Wasserman (Eds.), *Health communication in Southern Africa: Engaging with social and cultural diversity* (pp. 191–216). Amsterdam, The Netherlands: Rozenberg Publishers.

Watermeyer, J., & Penn, C. (2009b). The organization of pharmacist-patient interactions in an HIV/Aids clinic. *Journal of Pragmatics, 41,* 2053–2071.

14
A Narrative Study
on the Onset of Stuttering

JOHN A. TETNOWSKI, SARAH D'AGOSTINO,
AND MITCHELL TRICHON

My privilege as the first author of this chapter is to write the introduction to this chapter. One of the things that I learned from my friend and mentor, Jack Damico, to whom this volume is dedicated, is the importance of stories. As a matter of fact, we traveled to the National Storytelling Festival in Jonesboro, Tennessee, several years ago. The stories, told by the world's best storytellers, were powerful. Many of the stories were fiction, but many others were not. We talked about the power of storytelling and how it can be used as a learning tool. Histories have been passed on through oral tradition in story forms. The power of stories or narratives can be limitless. Narrative research is indeed a classic method of inquiry within the qualitative research paradigm (Creswell, 2009; Damico & Simmons-Mackie, 2003).

When we look at the study of narratives from a child language perspective, narratives reflect what is going on in the child's mind and how the child is making sense of the world around her or him (e.g., Bruner & Lucariello, 1989). In this classic narrative study, the person of interest, Emily, shows her understanding of an event through her personal stories and the interpretation of the "story-teller" (i.e., the authors). Within this narrative, we get an account of what actually happened in the world through Emily's words, but also through hermeneutics, i.e., the understanding of and interpretation of the narrative within its original purpose or context (Patton, 2002). In this way, we get a deeper, richer, and more authentic understanding of an event. This level of understanding is simply not available through more traditional scientific inquiries, such as experiments.

The narrative is appropriate for understanding the human condition. Human behaviors and human thought, communication, and interactions are highly complex and often not appropriate for experiments due to the controls that are required in good experimental designs. As the British psychologist, Don Bannister has noted (cited in Manning, 2002), human beings make for "notoriously nonsensical and unfit subjects for scientific scrutiny" (Bannister,

1966). It is not that human beings cannot be studied scientifically, methodically, or indeed experimentally. It's just that some human communication and behaviors are simply too complex to be investigated with traditional experimental research designs.

Alternate methods of inquiry, including qualitative methods such as narrative research may be more appropriate for understanding human behaviors. There is solid theoretical support for this methodology. For example, the Vygotskyan (1986) principle that thought and language are linked to each other would be extremely difficult to confirm without the benefit of human narratives. Narratives are developed by a researcher studying the lives of individuals or a particular event. The researcher asks the participants to tell their stories. The stories are catalogued and retold by the researcher, often in a chronological order. In this way a picture can be painted, or a story told that reflects the thoughts and actions that surround a person or event. In other words, the thoughts of the participants are consistent with their view of the world as told through their stories. The researcher records the events and stories and meshes them into a representation. In this way, an authentic representation of a person's thoughts and feelings or an event emerge through the narrative retell. This has been widely documented in the study of child language and its development. However, the purpose of this chapter is *not* to concentrate on child narratives, but to get at the narrative of an adult as she encounters a uniquely complex scenario, namely that of her daughter beginning to stutter. The emerging design (with lack of experimental controls) and its systematic process of data collection are what make a qualitative approach, and in particular the narrative research method, suitable for this investigation. In the view of the authors, narrative research was the only way that this important and fascinating information could be brought into the public domain. Without the narrative method, this data would be left to anecdotal evidence or testimonial.

The layout of this chapter will be as follows. A human narrative relating to the onset of stuttering in a very young child will be constructed. Leading up to the narrative will be a short, but relevant background research section that will set the stage for the importance of the study. Following the narrative will be a conclusions and implications section.

Background on Early Stuttering

Much of what we could know about stuttering and specifically its early development is lost because of the temporal sequences surrounding its onset. Most of the data on emerging stuttering in very young children is acquired by soliciting parents to take part in studies after their children have begun to stutter. The most comprehensive of these studies is an ongoing epidemiological study by Yairi and Ambrose that attempts to find the characteristics, causes, and patterns of stuttering very near its time of onset (Ambrose & Yairi, 1999; Yairi & Ambrose, 1999, 2005). The impact of these studies has revealed considerable knowledge about the course of stuttering from near the time of onset, and maps its likelihood of continuance or extinguishment. Unfortunately, this data does not describe in detail the experiences of the parents at the time of onset in a deep or rich fashion. Additionally, the time when participants first entered the study was delayed by some degree. In many cases, the delay was just a matter of days or weeks, but certainly not within the close temporal proximity that the current study provides.

Stuttering typically emerges between the ages of 2 and 5 years, and therefore getting data on stuttering near its onset can be difficult. As children develop speech and language skills, informants have served as primary data sources. Many of the published studies suffer from methodological limitations or simply report on surface features of stuttering only. Almost all of the early research on stuttering has concentrated on counting stuttering, transcribing and analyzing speech behaviors, and other similar surface features. These studies have certainly provided a basis for understanding some aspects of stuttering, but lack the richness, depth, and human insight and thought that can be provided through qualitative methodologies. There have been a few attempts to get these deeper or richer descriptions of stuttering near its onset, such as the early reports by Johnson and associates (1959) and Bloodstein (1960a,b). Unfortunately, their studies were done retrospectively within a descriptive paradigm. In these cases data was hampered by temporal issues and an inability to confirm findings.

Therefore, the purpose of this chapter is to use the narrative as a basis for understanding the complex phenomenon of the onset of stuttering as seen through the eyes and thoughts of the mother. The importance of this study is that the data was collected and catalogued through a series of events that allowed for the narrative to be constructed with data that emerged within a day of when the stuttering was noticed. This method allows for human thought and understanding to be examined through the mother's words.

Stuttering Onset and Its Clinical Importance

Knowledge regarding the onset of stuttering is of great interest to practicing speech-language pathologists and researchers. Speech-language pathologists need to know whether a young person is really stuttering or whether he or she is experiencing increased levels of nonstuttering disfluencies that all children go through. Yairi and Ambrose (Ambrose & Yairi, 1999; Yairi & Ambrose, 1999, 2005) have brought the term "stuttering-like disfluencies" (SLD) into the literature to document the part-word repetitions and dysrhythmic phonations (blocks and prolongations) that are experienced by people who stutter. Still, there are other types of nonfluencies that are produced in the speech of young children that are not stuttering (see Table 14.1 for a summary). It should be noted that some of the speech behaviors considered to be nonfluent, i.e., any type of breakdown in the forward flow of speech, would be considered stuttering or stuttering-like disfluencies, while others would be considered to be nonstuttered disfluncies. Making this distinction is important in gaining a diagnosis of "stutterer" or the preferred term, person who stutters (PWS). Additionally, many children present with SLD for a period of time before they resolve. Research by Yairi and Ambrose (2005) shows that when these stuttering-like disfluencies remain at a constant level or increase in frequency, stuttering is unlikely to resolve spontaneously. However, even if a child presents with significant SLD at one point in time, Yairi and Ambrose have shown that a decline in stuttering-like disfluencies over a period of time is more indicative of the stuttering that will eventually resolve. Thus, accurate assessment of stuttering and its course in the early development of a child at-risk for stuttering are very important clinical data.

Parents are likely to be the first observers to encounter early episodes of stuttering. Although most speech-language pathologists will agree that stuttering typically has its onset in children between the ages of 2 and 5, there is some debate as to what the early symptoms actually look like, and when intervention should be attempted versus when spontaneous recovery is highly likely. Historically, this has been hard to study since most parents do not report the existence of stuttering to a physician or a speech-language pathologist until it has existed for a period of time. Most parents assume that this stuttering is temporary and will go away. The case in point is that early studies of stuttering show that approximately 78% of stuttering will resolve itself before a child reaches adulthood (Andrews & Harris, 1964). In a significant number of

Table 14.1 Speech Behaviors and Their Classification

Nonfluency type	Example	Stuttering/disfluency
Interjections	My *um* dog's name is Sherry.	Disfluency
Part-word repetition	My *d-d-d-d*-dog is a poodle.	Stuttering
Word repetition	*She-she-she* is silver.	Stuttering*
	She is *silver-silver-silver*.	Disfluency*
Phrase repetition	*She likes-she likes* to play.	Disfluency
Revision	*I like-I love* my dog.	Disfluency
Incomplete phrase	*She is-*(oh I forgot how old).	Disfluency
Broken word	The dog is *ru(pause)-nning* fast	Disfluency
Prolonged sounds	*Sssssssssss*ilver is a pretty color.	Stuttering
Tense pause**	*......(pause with tension)*I'm done.	Stuttering

Note: *single syllable words that are repeated are considered stuttering; multi-syllable words are considered disfluency
** Tense pauses are also referred to as blocks, blockages, or stoppages

cases, however, stuttering does not resolve spontaneously, and there are questions as to what the experience of stuttering looks like in its early stages and if there are any clues from a parent's perspective that can add information to help define this dilemma. In addition, it would be interesting to note the feelings and thoughts of a parent as their child begins to show signs of stuttering. Therefore, the purpose of the narrative presented in this chapter is to explore the actual experience of stuttering as it exists very close to its onset. The story will be told through the eyes of a mother who experienced the early onset of stuttering in her own daughter. The mother, who reports and tracks the data is a person who stutters (PWS) herself. It is likely that this is potentially why stuttering was discovered so close to the time of onset.

Development of Stuttering from a Historical Perspective

The pioneers of speech-language pathology were very interested in the onset of stuttering and contributed a great deal of data related to onset, development, and spontaneous recovery of stuttering (Van Riper, 1971). Much of this information is summarized in the writings of Van Riper, who believed that stuttering had a gradual onset in many children who stutter (CWS), although he did note that several cases did also have a sudden onset. His hypothesis was based on several anecdotal reports and case studies. Although Van Riper acknowledged that there was insufficient data to determine whether the onset of stuttering was sudden or gradual, he did develop several "tracks" of stuttering that expressed his findings. In these tracks of stuttering, Van Riper noted that the most predominant track for stuttering, which he referred to as Track I, accounted for nearly 50% of all CWS. Track I stuttering has its onset between 2 and 3 years of age and has easy sound repetitions as its most common early symptom. Eventually, prolongations, observable tension, and emotional reactions develop. According to Van Riper, this group has the best prognosis for successful outcomes in therapy and also has the best chance for spontaneous recovery. Track II accounts for about 25% of CWS in Van Riper's scheme and is marked by a later onset than Track I. It is marked by articulation and language delays with early symptoms of syllable repetitions that appear to be hurried and unorganized. These children show little change in symptoms over time. Track III stuttering has its onset later in childhood (as late as 5–9 years of age) and is also unlikely to change. The children that fit into this track often have severe emotional reactions to stuttering. The stuttering itself is marked by blocks, prolongations and strong reactions to stuttering that are classified as secondary symptoms (facial grimacing, eye blinking, foot tapping, etc.). The individuals in this group develop the most severe form of stuttering symptoms. Track IV CWS also have a sudden and late onset, but symptoms are primarily word and phrase repetitions that show little change over time. There is typically little emotional reaction to stuttering. Van Riper's observations of stuttering development were based up observations and case reviews of 44 PWS.

Although Van Riper's system served as a basis for the understanding of stuttering, many clinicians and researchers reported fluctuations from this classification. Today, we know that variability is one of the hallmarks of early stuttering. For example, Conture (1990) reported that stuttering frequency may vary between 25% and 50% across different clinical settings. Ainsworth and Fraser (1988) further showed that this variation is not necessarily systematic. Clearly, more research is needed.

More recently, our knowledge of the onset of stuttering was greatly enhanced by the epidemiological studies of Yairi and Ambrose (e.g. Ambrose & Yairi, 1999; Yairi & Ambrose, 1999; Yairi & Ambrose, 2005). These studies revolutionized stuttering onset data. These researchers tracked at least 84 children longitudinally over many years. The key to their data was that they began following children very close to the time of onset as a result of intensive recruitment efforts. The results of their ongoing studies have shown that children who will likely continue to stutter will show specific types of nonfluent behaviors. These included part-word repetitions, prolongations, and dysrhthmic phonations, which consisted of broken words and blocks. Their data showed that a threshold of these behaviors was indicative of children who continued to stutter over time, but even more importantly, they showed that children who will recover from stuttering will show a rapid decrease of SLDs over time. This time span may be as little as 6–12 months, but may take as long as 4 years and beyond. Looking at this phenomenon in the opposite direction, children that are likely to continue to stutter, will show much less change in the frequency of SLDs over time. In some cases, the frequency of SLDs over time may even increase in frequency. These findings are summarized in Table 14.2.

In addition to these trends noted in children, there is some evidence that stuttering can occasionally resolve in adults. Finn (1996, 1997; Finn & Felsenfeld, 2004) studied a group of adults who stuttered who claimed that stuttering had resolved without professional intervention. Although many of these participants did not show significant stuttering behaviors, they did report that

Table 14.2 Children That Will Spontaneous Recover from Stuttering Are Likely to Show a Rapid Decrease in the Percentage of Stuttering like Disfluencies (SLD). This is most apparent for Part Word Repetitions (PWR) and Disrhythmic Phonations (DP) (Yairi and Ambrose, 2005).

Type of SLD	Group	Onset – 6 months	6 months – 12 months
PWR	**Recovered**	−63%**	−47%**
PWR	Persistent	−21%	−18%
DP	**Recovered**	−57%**	−51%**
DP	Persistent	−9%	−13%

** indicates significant change $p < .05$

they occasionally continued to stutter in high stress situations. Additionally, the speech of the recovered stutterers was perceptually different from controls. It appears that the development and resolution of stuttering as an adult may be different from the resolution of stuttering that takes place in young children.

In spite of these recent advances in our knowledge about stuttering onset and development, we continue to see variability between individual clients. Fortunately, a relatively recent phenomenon in the social sciences, and more specifically to the field of speech-language pathology and stuttering, has been the incorporation of qualitative data into the research literature (e.g., Tetnowski & Damico, 2001). These methodologies have allowed for greater insights into our knowledge of stuttering through techniques that allow for a richer description of the data, and to look at data sources and data types that were not previously used in an organized fashion. Specifically, one of these methods, and the key methodology used in this study, is the use of the narrative. This method will be used in light of the research questions proposed earlier in this chapter.

The Narrative

Method

In this narrative, the life of a child and her mother is retold by the primary researcher from the onset of stuttering. The child (E) is 1 year, 11 months at the beginning of the data collection. The mother (S) is a person who stutters and the primary supplier of the data. The speech-language pathologist (J) is a stuttering specialist who was contacted by the mother at the onset of stuttering. There are four primary sources of data for this study: (a) e-mail correspondence between S and J, (b) a diary kept by S and shared with J, (c) telephone conversations between S and J, and (d) video segments of E, analyzed by J. This triangulation of data provided a rich source of data for the narrative.

Results

The narrative (in the voice of the mother) is as follows:

> E began to stutter just before her second birthday. She began with easy repetitions. At first I thought she was simply imitating me or mocking me. A few days later it started freaking me out, and I told her, "Don't do that." I soon realized that she could not stop it and I really began to worry.
>
> Since I have some connections with the stuttering community, I contacted some of the "expert" speech-language pathologists that I know. All three of them told me that it was a bit early to be "really scared, but I was nonetheless. My sister mentioned to me that she

heard E stutter and I began to wonder, "Did it just pop up overnight?" I cried almost the whole next day. "How could this stuttering appear so quickly and progress so much in one week?"

I began to question myself. I know it's not my fault, but I wonder what I did? Maybe it's the new vitamins that she has been taking. I know that this didn't make sense, but I began to question everything I did. So did others when I began talking with them. E's babysitter thought it may be her fault because she was really busy and ignored E last week. I called several speech pathologists that I know and asked them what I should do. One of them told me that her daughter stuttered for 18 months and then suddenly stopped. This didn't help much. I would wake up thinking about her speech. It brought me back to my own therapy as a child-it made me a better person. Why wouldn't it be the same for her?

I began to wonder about myself and E. How will this change the way I mother? What do I tell her teachers? People will look to me for answers and how to respond. I wonder what mom's who don't stutter do. I did tell the people at her day care how to respond (patience, model slow talking, etc.). I began to see more signs and others confirmed them. My cousin babysat E last week. She explained to me how she already began substituting words. She wanted m-m-m-m-m-m-m-macaroni, but couldn't finish it, but switched the word to gnocchi (what a good little Italian baby!).

There are still some people that I avoid telling. I do talk to my husband about it. He is less concerned than me, but supports my decisions. After all this thought and effort (worrying, talking to expert speech pathologists, reflecting on my early years, and getting my mother to supply information on how she dealt with my stuttering), I finally had some peace of mind.

The stuttering did begin to get worse. One time I counted about 15 repetitions. I was really worried. From panic to peace, and then back to panic in just a few weeks. It was what I went through for 15 years before I finally accepted my own stuttering. I continue to be "super-tuned-in" to her speech, in spite of my own busy-ness. But then I think, "mom's are really tuned into their kids." If their kid is hurt, they know right away. This is the same gift that I have with stuttering.

Stuttering stopped the week after her second birthday. The only thing I changed was that I stopped giving her the vitamins. Could this be the reason? I know that there will be many ups and downs on this roller coaster ride. The one thing I know is that I will get support. I get great information from the speech pathologists I know and I also regularly log in to the National Stuttering Association's on-line parent group.

E's stuttering stopped as quickly as it started and my motherly concerns for her stuttering stopped there too. I quit journaling and obsessing over the movements of her mouth. I quit being conscious of my unconscious modeling speech behaviors. Every now and again I am reminded of E's stuttering. Sometimes she has an uncharacteristic blip in her speech that brings a flood of thoughts. I have had family member ask, "So what happened with E? How do you feel about that?" Or I email a distant SLP friend of mine and they say, "Whew, I thought you were writing to say that E started stuttering again." I can see how they expect this might happen—it's just a matter of when. So, I am aware, E's stutter may very well start again. If it does, I am confident she will still have a voice. (It might be a Carly Simon type voice.)

Triangulation from Artifactual Data

In addition to the narrative data, some forms of quantitative date were used to verify the results. The speech-language pathologist (J) transcribed and analyzed several "snapshots" of E's stuttering. The results of these analyses are summarized in Table 14.3.

Discussion and Summary

The rich description of the mother's feelings about stuttering show that stuttering, no matter how incipient it is, can be a serious emotional concern for a parent. It is noted on several occasions that the mother is concerned about her own stuttering and uses that as a basis for viewing E's stuttering. S considers that E is just mimicking her by saying, "At first I thought she was simply imitating me or 'mocking me'." This personal account of stuttering may not have been brought forth in other research paradigms. Another key point is how quickly the mother responded to the stuttering and sought the help of others, both family members and professionals. The following excerpts document this finding. "Since I have some connections with the stuttering community, I

Table 14.3 Summary of E's Stuttering Frequency Over Time

Date of Sample	Percentage of Stuttered Syllables	Type of Nonfluency	Weighted Stuttering-Like Disfluency Score*
1-21-2011	17.8%	PWR, SSWR	62.5
2-8-2011	23.5%	PWR	58.75
4-18-2011	3.7%	PWR	7.4
11-14-2011	0.0%	Phrase rep.	0.0
6-2-2012	0.0%	n/a	0.0

* Weighted stuttering-like disfluency score was used by Yairi and Ambrose (2005) in analysis of their longitudinal data for stuttering onset.

contacted some of the 'expert' speech-language pathologists that I know" and "My sister mentioned to me that she heard E stutter and I began to wonder." How S felt about E's stuttering and what she did about it are both important in documenting how parents react to early stuttering.

The most salient finding of this study however are the emotions that the parent goes through. Several key citations document the mother's fear. She says on one occasion, "I cried almost the whole next day" and further goes on to say, "I know that there will be many ups and downs on this roller coaster ride." And finally, the mother's vigilance is noted, even after the stuttering resolved, when she says, "Sometimes she has an uncharacteristic blip in her speech that brings a flood of thoughts."

To summarize some of the key findings, this narrative points out the fear that parents may face when even minor stuttering is noted. Although the stuttering did spontaneously resolve itself, the mother described her fears and anxieties about her daughter's stuttering. These fears are authentic, even though the stuttering resolved.

The fact that this mother is a person who stutters herself may have heightened her awareness. Her connections to local and national self-help organization may have also made her hyper-alert to her daughter's nonfluencies. This support is something that gives her confidence moving forward. Her "connections" to qualified SLPs allowed her to follow a reasonable course of action. In retrospect, the steady decrease in stuttering and weighted stuttering-like disfluency score (WSLD) is consistent with known data and indicates that E will likely continue to spontaneously recover. However, the parent's real-life fear is also documented. At this point, E is still not exhibiting behaviors that would lead a qualified speech-language pathologist to diagnose her as a child who stutters.

In summary, this narrative documents what stuttering looks like from the view of a parent within 1 week of onset and over the next 10 months. The richness of the data can serve as a guide for intervention with children who may stutter and for counseling their parents.

More on Narratives

A narrative creates a representation of the world and of personal experiences so that the reader can understand some component of human existence. It is a way of revealing something about the person from which it came and at the same time it can provide an understanding of the life and culture of those that created it. In the example presented, E's mother talks about the experiences surrounding the onset of stuttering of her daughter. The experience cannot be captured with quantitative measures. It can only be told as her story and her experiences.

Patton (2002) speaks of the numerous types of narratives that exist. These include personal narratives, family stories, life histories, and all types of rhetoric that can fit into the category of narratives. The important point is that narratives "honor" people's stories as valid data that can document a person's experiences (Bochner, 2001). This is a crucial concept in that the human interpretation is personal (Gardner, 1985); human subjects do not come to tasks as "empty slates," but as beings that have well-established schemata for understanding complex material. Thus, the experiences of E's mother shaped her thoughts and behaviors. The experimental researcher is blind to these constructs. Once again, if we consider S, her experiences may be quite different from that of other parents whose child begins to stutter. Her own experiences of stuttering have woven a meaningfulness around the onset of stuttering that may be unknown to other parents. For example, S's experiences with stuttering allowed her to be alert and aware of E's stuttering from day one. This is not typical in the research associated with the onset of stuttering. It is more typical that stuttering is noted by parents several months or even years later.

As of this date, E's stuttering has resolved and she continues to develop without stuttering. The importance of this brief narrative adds several important components to the literature. They shape both the clinical and research implications of this study.

1. Some parents may be "hyper-aware" of stuttering and notice its onset at a very young age. In this case, the mother being a PWS herself was likely the reason for her vigilance.
2. Even though stuttering may resolve spontaneously, parents may go through a significant amount of stress. This was indeed the case of S. Many speech-language pathologists may tell parents to wait for a few months so that we can track development. These same clinicians may not be aware of the stress that this places on parents.
3. Access to qualified professionals can help parents follow the correct course of action.

Thus the clinical implications of this study may argue for the valuable role of professionals following the early detection of stuttering. Without accurate information and tracking, the parent may have spent considerable funds on formal stuttering therapy that was not really needed. This cost saving and efficacy/efficiency of effort are consistent with the ongoing emphasis on evidence-based practice. Evidence of this type has been sparse. The role of self-help is also brought out in this study. A study by Trichon and Tetnowski (2011) found that attendance at even a single self-help conference for people who stutter has significant positive effects on people who stutter. In this case, the support provided to family members was also documented.

There are also some inherent limitations of this study. It should be noted that these findings are not intended to be reproduce-able, nor would they be expected to be generalized to the population at large. This is not the purpose of qualitative research methods, such as this narrative. However, this apparent weakness is made up for by the depth of description and understanding that is developed through this method. It offers insights that only come from personal experiences.

References

Ainsworth, S., & Fraser, J. (1988). *If your child stutters: A guide for parents* (3rd ed.). Memphis, TN: Speech Foundation of America.

Ambrose, N. G., & Yairi, E. (1999). Normative disfluency data for early childhood stuttering. *Journal of Speech, Language, and Hearing Disorders, 42*, 895–909.

Andrews, G., & Harris, M. (1964). The syndrome of stuttering. *Clinics in Developmental Medicine*, No. 17. London, England: Spastics Society Medical Education and Information Unit in association with W. Heinemann Medical Books.

Bannister, D. (1966). Psychology as an exercise in paradox. *Bulletin of the British Psychological Society, 19*(63), 21–26.

Bochner, A. P. (2001). Narrative's virtues. *Qualitative Inquiry, 7*, 131–157.

Bloodstein, O. (1960a). The development of stuttering I: Changes in nine basic features. *Journal of Speech Disorders, 25*, 219–237.

Bloodstein, O. (1960b). The development of stuttering II: Developmental phases. *Journal of Speech Disorders, 25*, 366–376.

Bruner, J., & Lucariello, J. (1989). *Monologue as narrative recreation of the world*. In K. Nelson (Ed,), *Narratives from the crib* (pp. 3–97). Cambridge, MA: Harvard University Press.

Conture, E. G. (1990). Childhood stuttering: What is it and who does it? In J. A. Copper (Ed.), *Research needs in stuttering: Roadblocks and future directions, ASHA Reports 18* (pp. 2–14). Rockville, MD: American Speech-Language-Hearing Association.

Creswell, J. W. (2009). *Research design: Qualitative, quantitative, and mixed methods approaches* (3rd ed.). Thousand Oaks, CA: Sage.

Damico, J. S., & Simmons-Mackie, N. N. (2003). Qualitative research and speech-language pathology: Impact and promise in the clinical realm. *American Journal of Speech Language Pathology, 12*, 131–143.

Finn, P. (1997). Adults recovered from stuttering without formal treatment: Perceptual assessment of speech normalcy. *Journal of Speech, Language, and Hearing Research, 40*, 821–831.

Finn, P. (1996). Establishing the validity of recovery from stuttering without formal treatment. *Journal of Speech and Hearing Research, 39*, 1171–1181.

Finn, P., & Felsenfeld, S. (2004). Recovery from stuttering: The contributions of the qualitative research approach. *Advances in Speech-Language Pathology, 6*, 159–166.

Gardner, H. (1985). *The mind's new science*. New York, NY: Basic Books.

Johnson, W. and Associates (1959). *The onset of stuttering*. Minneapolis: University of Minnesota Press.

Patton, M. Q. (2002). *Qualitative research and evaluation methods* (3rd ed.). Thousand Oaks, CA, Sage.

Tetnowski, J. A., & Damico, J. S. (2001). A demonstration of the advantages of qualitative methodologies in stuttering research. *Journal of Fluency Disorders, 26*(1), 17–42.

Trichon, M., & Tetnowski, J. A. (2011). Self-help conference for people who stutter: A qualitative investigation. *Journal of Fluency Disorders, 39*, 290, 295.

Van Riper, C. (1971). *The nature of stuttering*. Englewood Cliffs, NJ: Prentice-Hall.

Vygotsky, L. S. (1986). *Thought and language*. Cambridge, MA: MIT Press.

Yairi, E., & Ambrose, N. G. (1999). Early childhood stuttering I: Persistency and recovery rates. *Journal of Speech-Langauge-Hearing Research, 42*, 1097–1112.

Yairi, E., & Ambrose, N. G. (2005). *Early childhood stuttering: For clinicians by clinicians*. Austin, TX: PRO-ED.

15

An Investigation of the Processes of Meaning Construction in the Writing Behaviors of a Child with Language Disorder

HOLLY W. DAMICO

Introduction

When focusing on the importance of qualitative research as a clinical tool in speech-language pathology, Jack Damico has contributed a number of crucial publications. Beginning with his well-known case study involving the lack of efficacy in language therapy (1988) while he was a public school clinician, Damico has employed the clinical case study to make important points about service delivery and the state of our clinical practices. Although the case study has not been his primary qualitative methodology when reporting research or making clinical points, he has demonstrated its effectiveness over the years (e.g., Damico, Damico, & Nelson, 2003; Damico, Nelson, Damico, Abendroth, & Scott, 2008; Lynch, Damico, Damico, Tetnowski, & Tetnowski, 2009; Simmons-Mackie & Damico, 1996), and he has continued to advocate for the use of the case study since it "… can have great utility in clinical speech-language pathology" (Damico & Simmons-Mackie, 2003). This chapter is a demonstration of Damico's assertion regarding the utility of this research methodology and it involves a demonstration of the power of this qualitative investigative approach to detail the actual complexity that occurs in the progressive development of writing in a language-disordered child.

Although there has been surprisingly little published research in communicative disorders on the impact of intervention on the writing skills of language disordered children, the process and function of writing has been described as a crucial aspect of overall meaning-making. Indeed, it has been touted as much more than communication in written form. Referred to by Moffett (1968) as "communication within the same nervous system," writing requires a constant rereading of one's own work, constructing meanings for one's self, ordering thinking, and bringing to conscious awareness "ideas, concepts, themes, and ways of organizing thoughts, messages and meanings" (Cambourne, 1988). Many developmental researchers have suggested that of all the language modalities, sustained engagement with writing provides the greatest opportunities for cognitive and linguistic growth (e.g., Avery, 2002; Britton, Burgess, Martin, McLeod, & Rosen, 1975; Cambourne, 1988; Graves, 1994; D. R. Olson, 1992).

Over the last decade, language pathology and applied clinical linguistics have begun to focus more heavily on literacy issues in language-impaired populations. Most often, however, this focus has been on the process of reading while writing has received much less attention in the literature. When writing has been addressed, it has tended to be oriented to experimental investigations and to superficial descriptions of struggling writers when compared with typical developing writers in terms of product analysis (e.g., Cox, Shanahan, & Sulzby, 1990; Graham, Harris, MacArthur, & Schwartz, 1991; Lynch & Jones, 1989). While these studies are revealing, they are also limited in scope. As discussed and demonstrated by Nelson and Damico (2006) in an article on the advantages of qualitative research to the understanding of literacy in language impaired populations, many articles simply focus on the products of literacy and, even then, these products often are based upon test scores and numerical indices that hardly provide sufficient information on the complexity of literacy as a meaning-making manifestation. While a number of studies have examined the effectiveness of a particular instructional strategy designed to work on the improvement of writing skills in this population, most only provide insufficient and superficial data (Berlin & Inkster, 1980; Bridge, Compton-Hall, & Cantrell, 1997; Britton, 1971; Culham, 2005; Hallenbeck, 2002; Langer & Applebee, 1987; Vaughn, Hughes, Schumm, & Klingner, 1998).

Case Study Demonstration

This case study is a further attempt to demonstrate the power of applied qualitative analysis in the clinical setting. It describes some of the writing changes within a 9-year-old male diagnosed with a moderate language learning disability over an 8-month period. In this case, it was demonstrated that while a number of typically employed measures of change did not document change in the participant, a number of crucial changes were occurring. For this clinical investigation, a case study design utilizing video analysis of the intervention sessions, close-in video recording of the pencil in action on the paper, participant observation, writing artifacts and semi-structured interviews as primary data sources and portable eye-tracking technology as a secondary data source were utilized.

Participant

The participant of the case study, Kyle, had just turned 9 years old at the onset of the study and was enrolled in the second grade. Academically, Kyle spent 2 years in a prekindergarten classroom and an additional 2 years in kindergarten. Kyle's mother reported that he was significantly behind the rest of the class in learning colors, numbers, letters, and other concepts. Kyle had an Individualized Education Plan in place during his second kindergarten year. He was receiving accommodations (i.e., repeating directions, modifying directions, and modeling directions) in the regular education classroom with 30 minutes of support daily from the special education teacher, as well as employing a classroom assistant who was available at various times of the day. His classroom teacher reported concerns with his academic progress, stating that he ranked in the bottom 5 out of the 16 students in the class. Among other areas of difficulty, he could only write a few words using invented spelling that was not very comprehensible and he was reluctant to attempt any writing. Table 15.1 provides standardized test data obtained at the time of his last triannual evaluation in the public schools. Kyle received a diagnosis of language-learning disabled when he was between 6½ and 7 years old (which was at the end of his second kindergarten year).

The Context

Kyle began receiving language intervention services through the local university clinic when he was 5 years, 10 months old. His language and literacy intervention sessions centered on a meaning based social constructivist orientation to learning (Bruner, 1983, 1986; Piaget, 1970; Shuell, 1986; Vygotsky, 1978). In

Table 15.1   Kyle's Test Scores at the Beginning of the Case Study (age 6:8)

Measure	Results		
Preschool Language Scale – 4	Auditory Comprehension:	SS: 59	1st %ile
	Expressive Communication:	SS: 61	1st %ile
	Overall:	SS: 56	1st %ile
Peabody Picture Vocabulary Test – 4		SS: 85	16th %ile
Expressive Vocabulary Test – 2		SS: 73	4th %ile
Clinical Evaluation of Language Fundamentals – 4th edition	Receptive language:	SS: 59	<1st %ile
	Expressive language:	SS: 57	<1st %ile
Woodcock-Johnson Tests of Achievement - 3rd edition	Overall Reading:		Age equivalent 5:10
	Spelling:		Age equivalent: 4:60
	Math:		Age equivalent: <5:00

that context, an important component of his intervention involved shared and guided writing activities (Routman, 2005). These activities were conducted daily using a variety of genres including personal narrative, expository, and theme-based writing. Objectives for each session included demonstration and modeling of relevant writing skills and behaviors with Kyle participating as much as he was willing and able. The first half of the investigation documented Kyle's behaviors and strategies in a more "heavily mediated" writing context wherein the clinician took a greater role in the writing process. The objectives for intervention at this stage included supporting the entirety of the writing process. The clinician offered shared effort for every aspect of Kyle's writing. During the second half of the investigation, the objectives shifted to a more "lightly mediated" writing context, during which the clinician expected more independence from Kyle.

Data Collection and Analysis

For the case study, several qualitative data collection procedures were employed to describe the processes and activities performed during Kyle's intervention. These included:

- Video-recording of intervention sessions,
- Over-the-shoulder video-recording while he was writing,
- Collection of his written artifacts during intervention,
- Participant observation,
- Mobile eye tracking while he was writing.

Although behavioral observations from the intervention sessions were included in the analysis, the primary behavioral data set for analysis centered on the actual independent writings that Kyle produced. During the 8 months of the study, Kyle produced a number of independent samples; for the case study seven representative independent writings (two at the onset of the study, three in the middle stage, and two at the conclusion of the study period) were analyzed to determine any changes made during the intervention period. Figures 15.1 and 15.2 are samples taken from the initial and final analysis periods.

Since at least the late 1970s there has been a concerted effort in the discipline of language arts to discuss the evaluation and instruction of writing according to a more holistic cognitive based approach. Based on the early work of several pedagogical researchers (Flower, 1979, 1990; Flower & Hayes, 1981; Graves, 1983, 1994; Graves & Sunstein, 1992), this case study had several alternative descriptive approaches that could be employed. Some were oriented to the description of writing change according to the process and product of actual written artifacts (e.g., Lynch & Jones, 1989), or to process-centered (e.g., Connor, 1987) and various holistic approaches (e.g., Hansen, 1996; Routman, 2005) to description and analysis. Since the purpose of this case study was the investigation of the changes over time, the objective of analysis was to create a rich description of those aspects of writing that serve as indices of growth across as many foci as possible in the developing writer. By employing a "lens" metaphor, a number of the foci necessary for the production of completed writing were utilized to gauge Kyle's progress in this study (Clay, 1975, 1987; Culham, 2005). Seven foci during writing production were detailed in the data analysis to serve as behavioral indices. These were: fluency of writing (including three parameters of topic selection/initiation, composition length, and continuity), voice, ideas/content, organization of ideas, word choice, sentence structure, and other conventions (see Table 15.2 for brief definitions of each index).

In addition to the behavioral indices, the case study also analyzed the data to determine what kinds of writing strategies were employed by Kyle in the process of writing composition. Since we currently view all meaning-making manifestations (including writing) from a constructivist perspective (e.g., Afflerbach, Pearson, & Paris, 2008; Bransford, Brown, & Cocking, 2000; Cook-Gumperz, 1986; Geekie, Cambourne, & Fitzsimmons, 1999; Keene, 2008; Olson, 2007), a focus on the types of cognitive strategies employed by the developing writer is an essential component of progress that should be considered. It is the progressive development and utilization of appropriate

Table 15.2 Brief Definitions for the Writing Analysis Indices (Generally based on Routman, 2005)

Fluency	The ease with which a writer formulates a writing topic and generates ideas to develop into the content for that piece of writing.
Voice	The writer's unique personality made visible on the page. May include a liveliness, passion, and energy as well as involvement in the topic and a capacity to elicit a response from the reader.
Ideas/Content	The ability to include details and facts related to the main idea, to create descriptions to induce mood, time and place, to develop characters, to explain concepts and support judgments. These facets are woven together to create and support the intended meaning of the writing.
Organization of Ideas	The writer's control over his content so that it supports his intended meaning and makes his intentions clear to the reader in a manner that is easy to follow. Placing like information together, staying on topic, formatting words, sentences and paragraphs, and taking the writing from a beginning through to an ending are considered.
Word Choice	Carefully choosing words that will communicate the intended ideas and intensity.
Sentence Structure	The range of sentence structures, logical sentence constructions, and the constructed rhythm and flow of the sentences the writer constructs that will support the reader's experiences and craft lively writing.
Other Conventions	Control of those structural devices that help support the writer's intended meaning and aid the reader's comprehension. Writing conventions include punctuation, spelling, and grammar as well as letter formation, word spacing, and paragraphing.

strategies in context that create the change in the behavioral indices and the final written products (e.g., Brandt, 1990; Flower, 1990; Saddler, 2006).

Results

From the beginning of the investigation, it was evident that Kyle was a reluctant writer who demonstrated significant difficulties with the writing process. Though he participated in discussions and conversations on a potential writing topic from the first, he refused to initiate independent writing activities and avoided the actual writing associated with the topics and activities that he had suggested and discussed. Once he became engaged in a writing context, he would try to complete the writing process as quickly as possible; generally ending the activity after one or two sentences. Even in this situation, the sentences were not always focused on the same topic. At the beginning of the case study, Kyle's independent writing samples were not comprehensible by others due to his initial attempts at invented spelling which relied on first letter cueing with some additional aspects of his intended words represented at times (e.g., "Ir hrs bakwrs" for "I ride horses backwards"). While this was a reasonable strategy for a writer at Kyle's level of functioning (Clarke, 1988; Gentry, 1987), others had difficulty with interpretation. Kyle's strength in writing at this stage was his ability to transcribe the letters he chose to represent his content without significant hesitation or need to consider letter formation, with a few notable exceptions. Figure 15.1 demonstrates Kyle's writing performance at the beginning of the case study.

While less important to the composing process, Kyle also exhibited some motoric difficulty so that his overall mechanical control of the pencil was problematic at times and this exacerbated the text interpretation. While his

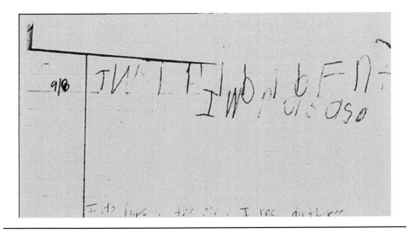

Figure 15.1 Initial independent writing; Kyle reads it as "I do flips in the air. I race."

motoric writing mechanics continued to emerge, he was unable to constrain his writing between the lines of a sheet of lined writing paper.

At the conclusion of the 8-month intervention period, there appeared to be little change in Kyle's writing when overall subjective judgments were applied. The graduate clinician expected significant change in terms of an increase in sentences produced overall and in the application of writing conventions like correct spelling and grammaticality. This did not occur over the 8 months when the actual writing **products** were superficially compared across the pre-mid-post analysis periods. However, when the **processes of writing** were analyzed, a different result was documented. Overall, Kyle had begun to change the dynamic aspects of writing. The **processes** that give rise to significant **product** change were evident.

Changes Across the Writing Behavioral Indices

Based upon careful analysis, while there were no discernible patterns of developmentally positive performance change in the focus categories of Voice, Word Choice, Sentence Structure, and Conventions, a number of process changes were documented that indicated developmental improvement. In two parameters of Fluency (Initiation and length) and in the foci of Ideas/Content and Organization patterns of performance improvements were documented. With regard to Fluency, Kyle changed from needing 3 to 5 clinician probes (and requiring up to 58 seconds) before selecting a topic and then initiating his writing in the initial analysis period at the first of the case study to requiring only 1 probe (and only 9 seconds) before selecting a topic and then initiating his writing in the final analysis period. In the second fluency parameter, length of writing (according to letters written) before terminating, he demonstrated definite change with his last three writing samples consisting of over 40 characters (average 41.33) whereas he had only produced an average of 25.25 characters across his first four samples with a range of 33 to 17 characters. That is, on average, a 40% increase in length across the last three samples. Taken together, these suggest that Kyle did consistently increase his writing fluency (in those two parameters) from the early until the late writing samples. As further indication of positive change in writing production, Kyle's ideas/content and his organization foci both exhibited consistent positive change from the early samples to the later samples collected for this investigation.

With regard to the ideas/content focus, his last three samples exhibited an average content increase of 28% in terms of words that he read back from his writing (11.25 versus 15.33) and a 45% increase in terms of lines produced (2.5 versus 4.5). This indicates not only more fluency in the later writing samples but more actual content. Similarly, his organization increased across the final three writing samples. His longer written products across the last three

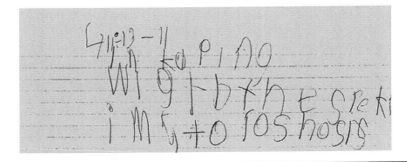

Figure 15.2 Final independent writing; Kyle reads it as "I'm camping. What I'm going to do this weekend. I am going to ride horses."

samples were more cohesive as Kyle more effectively employed sequentialness as a linking device in a quantitatively and qualitatively different way that he did in the first three samples.

Overall, the measures of writing production employed to describe Kyle's writing over the time designated in this investigation shows an interesting set of findings. First, not all production foci did improve. In fact four out of seven of these foci appeared to be stable over the period of the investigation. Second, there were some definite changes that appeared to be emerging. Kyle became more fluent in his writing and produced more content with greater cohesion when the samples were compared progressively over time. Third, the positive changes noted were consistent changes; they appeared to improve over all three of the last writing samples with little range variability. This suggests real improvement over time (Cronbach, 1982). Figure 15.2 provides a demonstration of Kyle's writing performance at the end of the case study in terms of the writing foci.

Changes Across Strategy Usage

From the constructive perspective of meaning-making, active engagement in the composition of written material requires an interaction between one's background resources, one's desire to communicate a message, and the actual message itself. Linguistic, cognitive, and experiential resources are woven together with the aim of meaningful text construction. This weaving together is accomplished through the utilization of numerous strategies that the writer has developed and/or acquired from numerous sources to be able to employ the foci discussed earlier to construct a meaningful message (e.g., Atwell, 1987; Avery, 2002; Bissex, 1980; Britton et al., 1975; Calkins, 1994; Fitzgerald & Markham, 1987; Flower, 1981; Graves, 1983). Basically, a writer employs strategies when undertaking the composition process for writing intended ideas onto the page. These strategies allow a writer to employ a range of skills when writing. Over time and with increased experience, writers gain control over the strategies they employ so that they have a set of constructive "tools adaptable to a variety of situations along with the ability to read contexts well enough to know which tools to employ in a given situation" (Dean, 2005, p. 82). In addition to changes in the writing production foci already described, changes in Kyle's strategies for engaging in writing activities were also described and detailed in this case study

When describing strategies, it is important to stress several points. First, as Graves (1983), Calkins (1994), and others (e.g., Fitzgerald & Markham, 1987; Flower, 1981) have discussed, writing is a cyclical process wherein it is very difficult to tie a particular writing strategy to a specific phase of the writing process (i.e., pre-writing, drafting, editing). The identified strategies are often employed within each of the composition phases. Second, the strategies may overlap so closely that it is difficult to discern a specific function for each strategy. In fact, it can be argued that the strategies may serve multiple functions. For example, when Kyle was actually writing he often employed sub-vocalizing while creating his written product. In one sense the sub-vocalizing can be seen as serving a *focusing* function. That is, the strategy helped him key in to the particular initial sound of the word he was trying to employ. However, this could also be rightly described as *formulation* strategy since the sound is an element of the word he was trying to spell. A third point for consideration is the reality that there are a number of possible strategies that can be employed during writing. Further, these strategies are not always visible to an outside observer. Consequently, even though care has been taken to identify and describe the strategies employed by Kyle during the writing process, this is not intended to be an exhaustive list of his actual writing strategies. Within the confines of this investigation and the samples taken and analyzed, however, those strategies that are most salient are identified and described with the intention of explaining how his (apparently) preferred strategies are employed within these data sets.

The strategies employed by Kyle were identified from the data collected from multiple sources. Careful analysis of videotapes and observations taken while he was writing, linking these data sets with transitory factors derived from his eye gaze patterns and even discussions with Kyle and those significant others interviewed made up the majority of the sources. Additionally, even though the strategies were listed and described separately, many of them tended to co-occur. That is, several strategies might be employed simultaneously to further the goal of meaningful composition. Over all, the investigator was able to identify 13 salient writing strategies employed by Kyle within and across his writing samples: avoidance, invented spelling, sub-vocalizing, rereading, run-up, verbal planning, appropriation, recency preference, reflection, familiarity, verification, response to mediation, and self-editing.

Of these 13 most salient strategies identified and analyzed over time, Kyle exhibited changes in seven of these strategies while writing from the initial to the final stages of the case study. The first kinds of strategic changes involved the ways he focused on the task of encoding (i.e., the actual process of putting thoughts to paper). He demonstrated positive changes in three of the strategies that he used to help him focus on the actual composition process. In terms of his sub-vocalization strategies, he decreased this strategy to focus in on the actual constituents of the words he was trying to spell but he increased this strategy when he had been distracted and was trying to re-establish his composition efforts. That is, he used more word/phrase sub-vocalization rather than letter sub-vocalization to refocus on the task at hand, actively constructing content. Kyle also reduced run-up as a strategy suggesting that as he became more focused on efficient meaning-making that he no longer needed to take a kind of running start to revisit the trouble spot. Consistent with these changes in focus, Kyle's use of rereading simultaneously increased so that when he was composing and lost the thread of the writing rereading previously written material could focus him back upon meaningfulness.

Two other strategies, ones that focused on actual formulation, also changed toward more efficiency in meaning-making. First, his invented spelling strategy changed qualitatively over time. As noted when looking at the behavioral indices (see above), Kyle started using both salient and non-salient sounds as his input for inventing his non-conventional spellings so that his invented spellings become more recognizable. Similarly, his formulation strategies changed in that his self-editing became more accurate and more frequent over time. In fact, his self-edits more than doubled when the beginning and the ending stages were compared.

Finally, as his strategies appeared to become more efficient and more oriented to meaning-making, Kyle appeared to become more confident in his abilities as a writer. Consequently, his avoidance strategies occurred less frequently and, when they did occur in the ending stages, they were more quickly overcome. Similarly, he became less dependent on others as a check on his performance and so the number of verifications that he employed dropped from approximately one every 6.2 characters produced to only about one every 82 characters across the last two analyzed sessions.

Summary of Changes in Writing

Even though the superficial evaluations of Kyle's written product was not viewed as positive by his graduate clinician (and his classroom teacher), he did make important progress when the complexity of the dynamic process of composition for writing purposes was considered. First, there were discernible changes in those aspects of the writing product referred to as foci or traits.

These are the actual productions exhibited in terms of behavior or artifacts and they served as effective indices of change themselves. Over the span of this study, Kyle progressively expanded the amount of content he provided when composing, averaging approximately 33% more content from the beginning stage to the ending stage of the investigation. As the content increased in terms of ideas, his organization was also modified to some extent. From the middle stage of the investigation, he started using his own experience more to generate content and he increased the cohesion of his ideas by using sequential placement of ideas in a logical form. The increased content was also reflected in his writing fluency as he produced more characters in his writing before terminating the writing activity. Additionally, the form of spelling started changing. He progressed from a great reliance on single initial phonemes to spell a word to a more intelligible approach of employing a greater reliance on multiple sounds as the input for word spellings. The percentage of invented spelling per words did not change but this change in the quality of the invented spellings is a noted developmental progression (Gentry, 1987).

Overall, as noted above, Kyle's encoding became more oriented to meaningfulness in his writing, and he became more independent. Additionally, it appears that his most salient strategies (or at least seven of them) became more efficient. This is best documented by analyzing his encoding speed across the three stages of this investigation. Over time, the encoding speed increased significantly. As noted in Table 15.3, focusing on the time from when he put his pencil to the paper to the time he picked it up and ceased active writing, Kyle required an average of 3.87 seconds per letter at the beginning stage of the investigation. This rate decreased to 3.31 seconds per letter in the middle stage and decreased even further to 2.62 letters per second by the end of the data collection period.

Conclusion

As Jack Damico has suggested in a number of his commentaries on qualitative research (e.g., Damico, 1988; Damico, Müller, & Ball, 2004; Damico, Oelschlaeger, & Simmons-Mackie, 1999; Damico & Simmons-Mackie, 2003), the clinical case study can provide significant information that can assist us in

Table 15.3 Summary of Kyle's Encoding Speed Across the Three Stages of the Investigation as Determined by Number of Words and Letters Produced and Average Time Taken to Produce Characters

	Beginning Stage	Middle Stage	Final Stage
Average Number Words Spelled	10.00	11.00	14.00
Average Letters Employed for Spelling	20.00	23.00	32.00
Sec/Letter	3.87	3.31	2.62

gaining a greater understanding in the processes and manifestations of meaning-making that we are working with and the actual practices that we employ in addressing these very complex human skills and abilities.

Specifically in the case of Kyle, this case study demonstrates the value of a qualitative research framework for the investigation of changes in writing behaviors and the strategies needed to create those products. This qualitative investigation has provided a rich and detailed description of the behavioral and strategic developmentally positive changes in this child's writing acquisition and supplanted a more superficial evaluation based upon a focus on simple analysis of the written product that Kyle produced. Above all, this case study demonstrates that if clinical linguists and speech-language pathologists want to become effectively active in the remediation of complex manifestations of meaning making like writing, they must recognize that detailed and rich analysis and description is required. The application of this design and the results provides a possible pathway for furthering clinical understanding of the acquisition of writing in this population.

References

Afflerbach, P., Pearson, P. D., & Paris, S. G. (2008). Clarifying differences between reading skills and reading strategies. *Reading Teacher, 61,* 364–373.

Atwell, N. (1987). *In the middle: Reading, writing, and learning with adolescences.* Portsmouth, NH: Boynton-Cook.

Avery, C. S. (2002). *... and with a light touch. Learning about reading, writing, and teaching with first graders.* Portsmouth, NH: Heinemann.

Berlin, J. A., & Inkster, R. P. (1980). Current-traditional rhetoric: Paradigm and practice. *Freshman English News, 8*(Winter), 1–4, 13–14.

Bissex, G. (1980). *Gnys at wrk: A child learns to red and write.* Cambridge, MA: Harvard University Press.

Brandt, D. (1990). *Literacy as involvement: The acts of writers, readers, and texts.* Carbondale: Southern Illinois University Press.

Bransford, J. D., Brown, A. L., & Cocking, R. R. (Eds.). (2000). *How people learn: Brain, mind, experience, and school.* Washington, DC: National Academy Press.

Bridge, C. A., Compton-Hall, M., & Cantrell, S. C. (1997). Classroom writing practices revisited: The effects of statewide reform on writing instruction. *The Elementary School Journal, 98*(2), 151–170.

Britton, J. (1971). What's the use? A schematic account of language function. *Educational Review, 23,* 205–219.

Britton, J., Burgess, T., Martin, N., McLeod, A., & Rosen, H. (1975). *The development of writing abilities.* Urbana, IL: National Council for Teachers of English.

Bruner, J. S. (1983). *Child's talk. Learning to use language.* New York, NY: W.W. Norton & Company.

Bruner, J. S. (1986). *Actual minds, Possible worlds.* Cambridge, MA: Harvard University Press.

Calkins, L. M. (1994). *The art of teaching writing.* Portsmouth, NH: Heinemann.

Cambourne, B. (1988). *The whole story. Natural learning and the acquisition of literacy in the classroom.* Auckland, NZ: Ashton Scholastic.

Clarke, L. K. (1988). Invented versus traditional spelling in first graders' writings: Effects on learning to spell and read. *Research in the Teaching of English, 22,* 281–309.

Clay, M. M. (1975). *What did I write?* Exeter, NH: Heinemann.

Clay, M. M. (1987). *Writing begins at home.* Portsmouth, NH: Heinemann.

Connor, U. (1987). Research frontiers in writing analysis. *TESOL Quarterly, 21*(4), 677–696.

Cook-Gumperz, J. (Ed.). (1986). *The social construction of literacy.* Cambridge, England: Cambridge University Press.

Cox, B. E., Shanahan, T., & Sulzby, E. (1990). Good and poor elementary readers' use of cohesion in writing. *Reading Research Quarterly, 25*(1), 47–65.

Cronbach, L. J. (1982). *Designing evaluations of educational and social programs.* San Francisco, CA: Jossey-Bass.

Culham, R. (2005). *6+1 traits of writing: The complete guide for the primary grades.* New York, NY: Scholastic.

Damico, J. S. (1988). The lack of efficacy in language therapy: A case study. *Language, Speech, and Hearing Services in Schools, 19*(1), 51–66.

Damico, J. S., Damico, H. L., & Nelson, R. (2003, November). *Impact of mixed instruction on meaning making in literacy.* Paper presented at the Annual meeting of the American Speech-Language-Hearing Association.

Damico, J. S., Müller, N., & Ball, M. J. (2004). Owning up to complexity: A sociocultural orientation to Attention deficit hyperactivity disorder. *Seminars in Speech and Language, 25*, 277–285.

Damico, J. S., Nelson, R. L., Damico, H. L., Abendroth, K., & Scott, J. (2008). Avoidance strategies in an exceptional child during unsuccessful reading performances. *Clinical Linguistics and Phonetics, 22*, 283–291.

Damico, J. S., Oelschlaeger, M., & Simmons-Mackie, N. N. (1999). Qualitative methods in aphasia research: Conversation analysis. *Aphasiology, 13*, 667–680.

Damico, J. S., & Simmons-Mackie, N. N. (2003). Qualitative research and speech-language pathology: A tutorial for the clinical realm. *American Journal of Speech Language Pathology, 12*, 131–143.

Dean, D. (2005). Strategic writing: Moving beyond the classroom assignment. *The English Journal, 95*(2), 82–88.

Fitzgerald, J., & Markham, L. R. (1987). Teaching children about revision in writing. *Cognition and Instruction, 4*(1), 3–24.

Flower, L. (1979). Writer-based prose: A cognitive basis for problems in writing. *College English, 41*, 19–37.

Flower, L. (1981). *Problem-solving strategies for writing.* New York, NY: Harcourt.

Flower, L. (1990). *Reading-to-write: Exploring a cognitive and social process.* New York, NY: Oxford University Press.

Flower, L., & Hayes, J. R. (1981). A cognitive process theory of writing. *College Composition and Communication, 32*, 365–387.

Geekie, P., Cambourne, B., & Fitzsimmons, P. (1999). *Understanding literacy development.* Stoke on Trent, Staffordshire, England: Trentham Books.

Gentry, J. R. (1987). *SPEL ... is a four-letter word.* Portsmouth, NH: Heinemann.

Graham, S., Harris, K. R., MacArthur, C. A., & Schwartz, S. (1991). Writing and writing instruction for students with learning disabilities: Review of a research program. *Learning Disability Quarterly, 14*(2), 89–114.

Graves, D. H. (1983). *Writing: Teachers and children at work.* Portsmouth, NH: Heinemann.

Graves, D. H. (1994). *A fresh look at writing.* Portsmouth, NH: Heinemann.

Graves, D. H., & Sunstein, B. S. (1992). *Portfolio portraits.* Portsmouth, NH: Heinemann.

Hallenbeck, M. J. (2002). Taking charge: Adolescents with learning disabilities assume responsibility for their own writing. *Learning Disability Quarterly, 25*(4), 227–246.

Hansen, J. (1996). Evaluation: the center of writing instruction. *The Reading Teacher, 50*, 188–195.

Keene, E. O. (2008). *To understand: New horizons in reading comprehension.* Portsmouth, NH: Heinemann.

Langer, J. A., & Applebee, A. N. (1987). *How writing shapes thinking.* Urbana, IL: National Council of Teachers of English.

Lynch, E. M., & Jones, S. D. (1989). Process and product: A review of the eesearch on LD children's writing skills. *Learning Disability Quarterly, 12*(2), 74–86.

Lynch, K. E., Damico, J. S., Damico, H. L., Tetnowski, J., & Tetnowski, J. A. (2009). Reading skills in an individual with aphasia: The usefulness of meaning based clinical applications. *Asian Pacific Journal of Speech Language Hearing, 12,* 221–234.

Moffett, J. (1968). *Teaching the universe of discourse.* Boston, MA: Houghton Mifflin.

Nelson, R. L., & Damico, J. S. (2006). Qualitative research in literacy acquisition: A framework for investigating reading in children with language impairment. *Clinical Linguistics & Phonetics, 20*(7), 631–639.

Olson, D. (2007). *Jerome Bruner. The cognitive revolution in educational theory.* New York, NY: Continuum International Publishing Group.

Olson, D. R. (1992). The mind according to Bruner. *Educational Researcher, 21*(4), 29–31.

Piaget, J. (1970). *Genetic Epistemology.* New York: W.W. Norton & Company.

Routman, R. (2005). *Writing essentials. Raising expectations and results while simplifing teaching.* Portsmouth, NH: Heinemann.

Saddler, B. (2006). Increasing story-writing ability through self-regulated strategy development: effects on young writers with learning disabilities. *Learning Disability Quarterly, 29*(4), 291–305.

Shuell, T. J. (1986). Cognitive conceptions of learning. *Review of Educational Research, 56,* 411–436.

Simmons-Mackie, N., & Damico, J. S. (1996). Accounting for handicaps in aphasia: Communicative assessment from an authentic social perspective. *Disability and Rehabilitation: An International, Multidisciplinary Journal, 18*(11), 540–549.

Vaughn, S., Hughes, M. T., Schumm, J. S., & Klingner, J. (1998). A collaborative effort to enhance reading and writing instruction in inclusion classrooms. *Learning Disability Quarterly, 21*(1), 57–74.

Vygotsky, L. S. (1978). *Mind in society: The development of higher psychological processes.* Cambridge, MA: Harvard University Press.

16

A Grounded Theory of Caregiving Based on the Experience of the Daughter of a Woman with Aphasia

MARIE-CHRISTINE HALLÉ AND GUYLAINE LE DORZE

Stroke related changes, and especially aphasia, have a long-term negative impact on family caregivers (Bakas, Kroenke, Plue, Perkins, & Williams, 2006; Draper & Brocklehurst, 2007; White, Mayo, Hanley, & Wood-Dauphinee, 2003). Although caregiving can take on a variety of forms and have a range of repercussions, little is known about the process of caregiving, how it begins, how it changes the relationship with the care receiver and influences both members of the dyad. Answers to these questions will help guide speech-language pathologists who believe family intervention to be a challenge (Johansson, Carlsson, & Sonnander, 2011).

Caregiving takes different forms: protecting or overprotecting; encouraging independence; facilitating communication between the care receiver, the caregiver and others; "speaking for" behaviors; seeking information about aphasia and recovery; and taking responsibilities that the care receiver can no longer assume (Croteau & Le Dorze, 2006; Hallé, Duhamel, & Le Dorze, 2011; Le Dorze & Brassard, 1995; Le Dorze, Tremblay, & Croteau, 2009; Michallet, Tétreault, & Le Dorze, 2003; Purves, 2009). There is evidence that caregivers also undergo a process of adapting to the aphasia and other stroke-related consequences of their partner; they also have needs related to this role (Denman, 1998; Le Dorze & Signori, 2010; Michallet et al., 2003). Caregiving can have a number of negative consequences on the care provider: fatigue, anxiety, burden, depressive symptoms, restrictions in activities and isolation, changes in the relationship with the care receiver due to new roles, as well as some positive consequences: feeling useful and satisfaction (Bakas et al., 2006; Hallé et al., 2011; Le Dorze & Brassard, 1995; Le Dorze et al., 2009; Michallet et al., 2003). Although less explored, the care offered can also have consequences on the care receiver. For example, "speaking for" behaviors may decrease the aphasic person's participation in conversation (Croteau & Le Dorze, 2006).

The influence of gender, age, and type of relationship has not been explored much in the available literature on aphasia as most of it concerns spouses. Yet stroke occurs more frequently in elderly people, who are more likely to be widowed than younger people and cared for by daughters more so than by sons (Bakas et al., 2006). Moreover, widowed women are four times more numerous than their male counterparts (Li, 2004), indicating that more attention should be given to the experience of daughters caring for their aphasic mothers. However, in fields other than aphasiology, the caregiving experience of women and adult daughters helping a parent or their mother has been described.

Daughters' age, work status, marital status, position in the family and their geographical proximity with their mother have been associated with the number of caregiving hours as well as the reason for becoming the mother's caregiver (Lang & Brody, 1983; Pohl, Boyd, & Given, 1997). Changes in the mother's health or death of her spouse often motivated a daughter's decision to become a caregiver (Pohl et al., 1997). Caring for a parent and assuming other roles such as mother or employee is often a source of conflict for a majority of woman and was correlated with depressive symptoms and leisure activity restrictions (Stephens et al., 2001). A central feature of caregiving relates to the characteristics of the caregiver-care receiver relationship. Positive relationships between adult daughters caring for their aging mothers were characterized by experiencing reward when sharing activities, minimal costs, absence of conflict or positive management of conflicts and mutual concerns (McGraw & Walker, 2004; Walker & Allen, 1991). The type of care offered plays a role in the experience. According to Stephens, Townsend, Martire, & Druley (2001), adult daughters who had higher levels of stress due to dealing with their parent's behavioral problems had significantly more depressive symptoms whereas daughters who had higher levels of stress due to helping their parent with instrumental activities of daily living had significantly more restrictions in leisure activity. In adult daughter-aging mother dyads, care that preserved the mother's autonomy or focused on the mother's strengths was associated with positive outcomes (Walker & Allen, 1991; Ward-Griffin, Oudshoorn, Clark, & Bol, 2007). In order to deal with the competing and changing demands of care, women used the strategy of setting boundaries (Wuest, 1998). However, if these boundaries violated the caring ideals of the woman, this could result in guilt, a common feeling experienced by adult daughters caring for their mother and correlated with their sense of burden (Gonyea, Paris, & de Saxe Zerden, 2008; Wuest, 1998).

In sum, these few studies of the caregiving experience of women have revealed how this experience is influenced by a complex and variable interaction of psychological, relational, emotional and social factors and that caregiving involves different kinds of challenges, responsibilities and outcomes. One means of furthering our understanding of the caregiving experience may be to describe single cases within a qualitative framework allowing depth and clarity in the description as well as the identification of the meaningful elements in each case. In order to understand daughters' experiences of caregiving for their aphasic mother, the aim of the present study was to analyze the process of caregiving as described by a single participant in three interviews and identify and relate its various components in a coherent and comprehensive manner.

Methods

Design

We chose qualitative methodology and specifically grounded theory as this method allows conceptualizing and explaining a phenomenon (Damico & Simmons-Mackie, 2003).

Participant

We selected a participant from a larger study on the adaptation of family members of aphasic persons for which other cases have been published (Hallé et al., 2011; Le Dorze et al., 2009). This participant became her mother's main caregiver, but did not live with her, so her experience of caregiving was central but different than those of spouses (Deimling, Bass, Townsend & Noelker, 1989). The participant was a 36-year-old woman, owner of a retail business, and single parent of a pre-school aged child under her care. Her 70-year-old mother, with whom she had a good relationship, lived alone and had an active and independent life. The participant felt the stroke was the result of a medical mistake because when the mother experienced the first symptoms of stroke, she went to the hospital emergency room, but was sent home. A few hours later, she suffered a severe stroke with severe mixed aphasia, right hemiplegia and apraxia. At the hospital, the neurologist told the family she would not recover and would be sent to long-term care. After the family had successfully fought this decision with the hospital team, their mother began in-hospital rehabilitation and then was referred to rehabilitation in an inpatient facility. The participant experienced tension with her siblings because they did not share her opinion regarding her mother's abilities. Following rehabilitation, the mother went to live by herself in a supervised apartment chosen by her children. The mother, however, did not like this facility and missed the city where she lived before the stroke. Later, the daughter helped her mother relocate in another complex of supervised apartments the mother had chosen. The daughter described her mother's aphasia in terms of the number of different words she could say: 3 words at the time of the first interview and 15 words at the last interview. She used a wheelchair, even when in her home and her right arm was not functional.

Data Collection and Analysis

At 6, 11, and 20 months poststroke, a recorded interview was done with the participant at her house or her workplace. Each interview was transcribed. The first analyses, including lists of grouped descriptors also constituted the data (see Le Dorze et al., 2009). First, the interviews were listened to, to get an overall understanding, and commented, as well. Re-occurring ideas were defined as potential categories and supporting descriptors were found. During this process, descriptors illustrating various expressions of a phenomenon, for example, "mother is able to understand" and "mother is able to take decisions," were included in a single subcategory: "daughter thinks mother has abilities." Each category was made up of some or several subcategories that represented facets of the general category. Continuing on with the previous example, the category "daughter recognizes mother's competence," included the following subcategories: "daughter thinks mother has abilities," "daughter disagrees with people who view mother as incompetent," and "daughter sees mother as a 'normal' person."

The creation of the initial categories led to the emergence of new categories. When data was found that negated another category, a new category included those descriptors. For example, while searching for excerpts supporting the category of the "daughter recognizes mother's competence," data pertaining to the participant's perception of her mother's problems were found and joined in the category "confrontation with mother's problems." New categories were also created to fit different recurrent elements. Questions to the data such as how caregiving took place, in what contexts it developed, and what were the impacts, were used throughout the analysis to ensure that the emerging categories completely represented the caregiving experience. Finally, when confronted with seemingly inexplicable data, the primary analyst tried to make sense of them, through a reflective process and discussions between authors. These procedures allowed us to produce an analysis that was theoretically sensitive to the data.

Once the categories and corresponding lists of descriptors were developed, the relationships between categories were searched for by trying to determine how each category was linked to the others by checking potential relationships: cause, consequence, context, condition. From this systematic exploration emerged a series of relationships between categories and then a model which we describe in the results. Several procedures ensured validity and rigor. Discussions took place between authors on all aspects of the analyses: names of categories, relevance, and content. In addition, each author confronted the emerging data to other clinical and research cases and to personal experience, through continuous reflective processes and discussions. After the analytical process was completed, the interviews were read again to ensure that the emerging results reflected fully this participant's caregiving experience. In addition, memos describing what had been accomplished had been written up at every session and these were consulted again to validate the results.

Results

We developed a hypothetical conceptual model representing the experience of a daughter whose mother became aphasic with "goal-oriented selective caregiving" being the core category and attached to other categories conceptualized as triggers, modulators and outcomes (see Figure 16.1). The daughter's caregiving experience was positive overall since the negative consequences experienced at stroke onset and which triggered the caregiving she provided her mother either diminished or disappeared entirely throughout the process of caregiving. The following text details each category, subcategories, and conceptual links between categories.

Goal-Oriented Selective Caregiving

The care offered by the daughter aimed to achieve the two goals of making her mother happy and fostering her independence. In relation to the first goal, the daughter engaged in various activities. The first subcategory was maintaining her mother's dignity, which involved taking care of her mother's hygiene, appearance, and environment's cleanliness. The participant reported caring in this manner mainly when her mother was an inpatient in the acute care

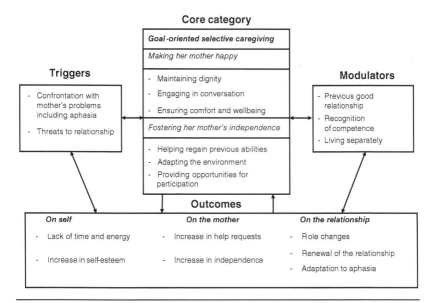

Figure 16.1 Conceptual model of caregiving based on the experience of the daughter of a woman with aphasia.

hospital and rehabilitation and less so during outpatient rehabilitation. The second subcategory was engaging in conversation with her mother in spite of severe aphasia by making efforts to understand her mother's requests and intentions. Over time and beginning when her mother was at the hospital, she reported having telephone conversations with her mother, even with her limited repertoire of one word, and even if this meant taking 20 minutes to find out what her mother was asking for. The third subcategory included activities which ensured her mother's comfort and wellbeing. From the moment her mother was at the hospital to the time she had completed rehabilitation and was living by herself, the participant talked about how she "did things to please her mother," she offered her moral support and made sure her mother had contacts with her friends and other family members. When her mother was out of the hospital environment, the participant also talked about how she ensured her mother's material comfort by taking care of her finances and well-being in her environment and by supporting her mother in all residential issues.

The second goal of caregiving was to foster the mother's independence. The daughter helped her mother regain her previous abilities, and this only when her mother was in the hospital. Afterwards, the participant reported adapting the environment so that her mother could do activities by herself and how she provided opportunities for participation.

In addition to being goal-oriented, caregiving was selective in the sense that it was limited and focused. The participant was not caregiving on a full-time basis; she continued to assume her other roles in running her business and parenting. She also took time for herself by going on vacations. Moreover, even though she was the main caregiver, she involved her siblings in providing assistance. For example, the participant organized a visiting schedule to alleviate her own: "Now what I'm trying to organize is that one of us would go visit her every Sunday." Finally, the participant set limits directly with her mother such as refusing to take some of her mother's phone calls at work.

Triggers and Modulators

One of the triggers to caring was the daughter's confrontation with her mother's problems as a result of the stroke and aphasia. When her mother was in the hospital and in rehabilitation, she was faced with her mother's inability to swallow and to talk and had doubts about her mother's ability to function independently in her new home after rehabilitation. Another caregiving trigger was the threat to their relationship. Indeed, the daughter experienced problems and negative emotions associated to aphasia symptoms. Her mother repeated the same word all the time in most communication situations, "July." "Because you know, 'July' at a certain point it's tough for us too, you know. We're getting impatient." In all three interviews, the participant mentioned difficulties in communicating verbally with her mother: "It remains difficult sometimes, especially when she gets impatient, and I'm busy doing something else," difficulties which decreased over time. In the first interview, the daughter spoke about how she felt she had lost her mother and their previous relationship, in that she could not give her advice and be a grandmother to her son: "just as it was the relationship I've always wanted, she has a stroke and it's over, you know."

In spite of her mother's severe aphasia and stroke related problems, the daughter also had a growing recognition of her mother's competence. She believed her mother had several abilities, such as general understanding, taking decisions about her health, making herself understood. The participant also disagreed with others who perceived and behaved with the mother as if she was incompetent. Furthermore she believed her mother was a "normal" person and behaved accordingly. The daughter's recognition of her mother's competence influenced the care she gave. For example, the participant noted that her mother had difficulty in using the bathroom at her supervised apartment. The type of care she offered was congruent with her mother's ability to learn to say some words: "She really has to make an effort, and when she makes one, sometimes some things come out." The daughter aimed to help her mother become more independent: "We paid the service so they could come, but she had to call the reception with her phone. She had to say 'pee.' So we trained her to say 'pee'."

The participant's caregiving aims fitted in with their previous relationship characterized by mutual independence and help in a spirit of love and respect. It was vital that the mother regain as much of the independence she had so that she could live on her own and mother and daughter could continue to live separately. The daughter initially paid a woman to help her mother to get dressed and undressed, but, over time, the mother did more for herself, especially when the daughter got her clothing that was easy to put on.

Outcomes

On the Daughter. The care the daughter offered was time consuming and it caused her to neglect other aspects of her life such as her work, especially in the first week and at other key moments such as when her mother was moving. She also experienced a lack of energy as a result of the effort required for conversation: "It's something you want to eat? Is it something that you would like us to bring to you? (…) and according to the intonation, we would finally figure it out." This type of communication resulted in fatigue: "So at a certain point for sure we are exhausted at the end of the day (…) because just to dissect what she wants to say." The participant reported these costs and others at every stage of her experience, although less frequently after inpatient rehabilitation when she began to think again about the development of her business. The participant's self-esteem increased throughout the process as she judged her caregiving strategies to be the right ones and felt her competency grow through the care she offered.

On the Mother. The care aiming to ensure comfort and well-being may have encouraged the mother's dependence as shown by increased requests for help. In some areas, the participant chose to act on her mother's behalf. The participant believed the stroke had been caused by high blood pressure and knew financial issues stressed her mother. She withdrew financial responsibilities from her mother, and, as a result, her mother was always in a position where she needed to ask for money. Most of the caregiving, however, increased the mother's independence. After rehabilitation, the mother still required daily assistance, but, over time, she did much more for herself: preparing breakfast, shopping for food, and doing dishes and laundry. Care encouraging her mother's independence played a role in this outcome. The participant explained how she had adapted her mother's apartment: "We put the rail lower, we put the mirrors lower" to allow her to live by herself with minimal supervision. It is possible that the care maintaining her mother's dignity and ensuring her comfort and well-being increased the mother's independence indirectly. In order for the mother to become motivated in rehabilitation, the participant did the mother's hair and nails every week during her hospital stay and encouraged her to "fight" to regain her abilities. When receiving her daughter's encouragements and care, the mother felt empowered and even dared, over time, to make decisions. For example, the mother found a way, in spite of her wheelchair and aphasia, to visit her sister who lived in a neighboring city by hiring a taxi and managing to find the address she didn't have. She had not asked for assistance from her children and spent 3 days enjoying herself with her sister. "She took it as quite an accomplishment. She was so proud yunno, she was gesturing 'I did it' and she was laughing and she was happy yunno."

On the Daughter–Mother Relationship. The participant experienced role changes in her relationship with her mother and reported unpleasant emotions occurring when providing intimate care. For example, she massaged her mother's mouth to stimulate recovery of swallowing: "the fingers in the mouth, I mean it was disgusting ..." When her mother was in her supervised apartment, the participant's negative feelings were due to the necessary limits she had to set. For instance, she had to get angry when telling her mother she didn't have time to help her. Eventually, after rehabilitation and several improvements in her mother's independence, the daughter was satisfied with their relationship. "Even so I think I have a very very close relationship

(...) I'd say the relationship came back almost like before, even an upgraded version." Some aspects of the caring experience played a role in the positive relational outcome. For example, perceiving her mother's competence, she behaved towards her as she did before the stroke: "I try to involve her more and more like before." Also, through the caring process, the daughter adapted to her mother's aphasia and spoke of being able to understand her mother: "She knows that we manage to understand, we have become quite good" at communication with her mother. The daughter's perception of her mother's competence and the conversations she continued to have with her mother facilitated her adaptation to aphasia. These repeated opportunities allowed her to develop strategies to counter the communication problems that initially threatened their relationship.

Discussion

This study aimed to understand the caregiving experience of an adult daughter whose mother became aphasic as a result of a stroke. A model derived from a grounded theory analysis of interview material was constructed with "goal-oriented selective caregiving" as the core concept. Caregiving was triggered by confrontation with the mother's problems and threats to their relationship. Caregiving was modulated by their previous good relationship, the fact that they did not live together, and the daughter's perception of her mother's competence in spite of aphasia. Overall, the outcomes of this experience were positive. These results appear divergent to previous studies of the impact of aphasia in families and of caregiving where positive aspects are not the norm.

The experience of caregiving was in itself positive in its aims as well as in the means used to accomplish the aims, although the participant had moments where she was in conflict with others and felt negative emotions such as anger. However, these were also resolved and led to satisfaction with herself and pride in her mother's accomplishments and happiness in having regained her relationship with her mother. One of the key elements of these positive outcomes was the daughter's perception of her mother's competence in spite of aphasia. This perception of competence was a driving force essential to their continued communication and to the recovery of their relationship. Coupled with goal-oriented selective caregiving the participant in interaction with her mother were both in virtuous cycles of increased competence. The mother's initiatives and the daughter's care reinforced both women's perception of the mother's competence, then, increased opportunities for the mother to be competent and probably enhanced the abilities themselves which reinforced again the perception of competence. Positive caregiving experiences were possible when the care preserved the aging mother's autonomy, focused on her strengths, and was provided in response to her needs, instead of the caregiver's needs (McGraw & Walker, 2004; Ward-Griffin et al., 2007). When the care receiver has aphasia, the daughter's caregiving orientation to strengths or difficulties does not in itself predict whether the outcomes will be satisfactory or not because aphasia acts as a barrier to relationship adjustments (Hallé et al., 2011). In the present study, such a barrier was not present and both women believed the mother was competent and collaborated towards the mother's independence.

The living arrangements of this dyad were also conducive to the mother's continued improvement and increased independence, in that she had daily real opportunities to use her abilities. Elders receiving care in shared residence, either from a spouse or an adult child, may be physically and cognitively more impaired than those receiving care from an adult child in a separate residence (Deimling et al., 1989), in part because the care is more protective and less emancipatory. This cycle has been described as learned helplessness in dementia (Lubinski, 1995) and as the "use it or lose it" principle of neural plasticity (Kleim & Jones, 2008).

The caregiving experience of this participant was initially costly in terms of time and energy, an indication of inter-role conflict (Stephens et al., 2001). She was successful in ordering the various competing demands placed upon her and in providing focused and limited care, a strategy described as determining the legitimacy of the requests and attending to one's voice and personal strengths to contain requests (Wuest, 1998). Our participant exhibited such behaviors which helped decrease requests without violating her caring ideals, protecting her from feelings of guilt and burden (Gonyea et al., 2008; Wuest, 1998).

Validity and Implications

One of the strengths of the longitudinal design was that it allowed us to understand an evolving process which could not have been captured with a single interview. Since the interviews were conducted in real-time, the participant was able to express what was most significant to her without having to rely on her memory of past events. Future studies should develop and validate this model with other dyads.

The present research findings demonstrate far reaching positive consequences on relationships and caregiving when the person with aphasia is assumed to be competent. It is possible that frequent engagement in conversation with her mother fostered the participant's adaptation to aphasia, the mother's independence, and the renewal of their relationship. Consequently, the results of this study should persuade speech-language therapists of the usefulness of teaching supported conversation techniques to caregivers (Kagan, 1995). The participant did not mention she was taught supported conversation techniques, but she understood the principle of preserved competence and applied it throughout her interactions with her mother. Our clinical and research experience shows that not all family members come spontaneously to this conclusion. In fact more often than not, an aphasic person's problems in understanding the meaning of words and his/her word finding difficulties are interpreted incorrectly as difficulties in understanding the world. Speech-language pathologists should therefore explain the concept of competence in the context of aphasia and provide caregivers with positive experiences in conversing with their loved one.

In conclusion, this study of caregiving is an example of how complex social phenomena involving communication can be advantageously studied within a qualitative framework as suggested by Damico and Ball (2010). The essential entities comprising this experience including the role of perception and communication were interpreted within the context of grounded theory methodology; a method well suited to the goal of explaining a complex phenomenon, without direct observation of the phenomena itself. By paying attention to what was significant for this participant at different times, we were able to capture the complexity of the process and interactions between conceptual entities. If our understanding of this phenomena includes the real processes and entities we hypothesized it does, some extrapolation to clinical situations should be possible (Damico & Ball, 2010). Qualitative explorations hold potential to improve outcomes for clients affected by communication disorders.

Acknowledgments

This research was supported by the FQRSC (2003-SGR-94551), by research funds from the CRIR to GLD and by an award from The Scottish Rite Charitable Foundation of Canada (09203) to MCH. We warmly thank the participant for sharing her experience. We also extend our thanks to Marie-Ève Goulet for her assistance. The work presented here is part of MCH's doctoral dissertation. Preliminary analyses were included in MCH's unpublished master's paper.

References

Bakas, T., Kroenke, K., Plue, L. D., Perkins, S. M., & Williams, L. S. (2006). Outcomes among family caregivers of aphasic versus nonaphasic stroke survivors. *Rehabilitation Nursing, 31*, 33–42.

Croteau, C., & Le Dorze, G. (2006). Overprotection, "speaking for," and conversational participation: A study of couples with aphasia. *Aphasiology, 20*, 327–336.

Damico, J. S., & Ball, M. J. (2010). Prolegomenon: Addressing the tyranny of old ideas. *Journal of Interactional Research in Communication Disorders, 1*, 1–29.

Damico, J. S., & Simmons-Mackie, N. N. (2003). Qualitative research and speech-language pathology: A tutorial for the clinical realm. *American Journal of Speech-Language Pathology, 12*, 131–143.

Deimling, G. T., Bass, D. M., Townsend, A. L., & Noelker, L. S. (1989). Care-related stress: A comparison of spouse and adult-child caregivers in shared and separate households. *Journal of Aging and Health, 1,* 67–82.

Denman, A. (1998). Determining the needs of spouses caring for aphasic partner. *Disability and Rehabilitation, 20,* 411–423.

Draper, P., & Brocklehurst, H. (2007). The impact of stroke on the well-being of the patient's spouse: An exploratory study. *Journal of Clinical Nursing, 16,* 264–271.

Gonyea, J. G., Paris, R., & de Saxe Zerden, L. (2008). Adult daughters and aging mothers: The role of guilt in the experience of caregiver burden. *Aging & Mental Health, 12,* 559–567.

Hallé, M.-C., Duhamel, F., Le Dorze, G. (2011). The daughter-mother relationship in the presence of aphasia: How daughters view changes over the first year poststroke. *Qualitative Health Research, 21,* 549–562.

Johansson, M. B., Carlsson, M., & Sonnander, K. (2011). Working with families of persons with aphasia: A survey of Swedish speech and language pathologists. *Disability and Rehabilitation, 33,* 51–62.

Kagan, A. (1995). Revealing the competence of aphasic adults through conversation: A challenge to health professionals. *Topics in Stroke Rehabilitation, 2*(1), 15–28.

Kleim, J. A., & Jones, T. A. (2008). Principles of experience-dependent neuroplasticity: Implications for rehabilitation after brain damage. *Journal of Speech, Language, and Hearing Research, 51,* S225–S239.

Lang, A. M., & Brody, E. M. (1983). Characteristics of middle-aged daughters and help to their elderly mothers. *Journal of Marriage and the Family, 45,* 193–202.

Le Dorze, G., & Brassard, C. (1995). A description of the consequences of aphasia on aphasic persons and their relatives and friends, based on the WHO model of chronic diseases. *Aphasiology, 9,* 239–255.

Le Dorze, G., & Signori, F.-H. (2010). Needs, barriers and facilitators experienced by spouses of people with aphasia. *Disability and Rehabilitation, 32,* 1073–1087.

Le Dorze, G., Tremblay, V., & Croteau, C. (2009). A qualitative longitudinal case study of a daughter's adaptation process to her father's aphasia and stroke. *Aphasiology, 23,* 483–502.

Li, C. (2004). *Widowhood: Consequences on income for senior women.* Retrieved from Statistics Canada website: http://www.statcan.gc.ca/pub/11-621-m/11-621-m2004015-eng.pdf

Lubinski, R. (1995). Learned helplessness: Application to communication of the elderly. In R. Lubinski (Ed.), *Dementia and communication* (pp. 142–149). San Diego, CA: Singular Publishing Group.

McGraw, L. A., & Walker, A. J. (2004). Negotiating care: Ties between aging mothers and their caregiving daughters. *The Journals of Gerontology: Social Sciences, 59B,* S324–S332.

Michallet, B., Tétreault, S., & Le Dorze, G. (2003). The consequences of severe aphasia on the spouses of aphasic people: A description of the adaptation process. *Aphasiology, 17,* 835–859.

Pohl, J. M., Boyd, C., & Given, B. A. (1997). Mother-daughter relationships during the first year of caregiving: A qualitative study. *Journal of Women & Aging, 9*(1–2), 133–149.

Purves, B. A. (2009). The complexities of speaking for another. *Aphasiology, 23,* 914–925.

Stephens, M. A. P., Townsend, A. L., Martire, L. M., & Druley, J. A. (2001). Balancing parent care with other roles: Interrole conflict of adult daughter caregivers. *Journal of Gerontology, 56B,* 24–34.

Walker, A. J., & Allen K. R. (1991). Relationships between caregiving daughters and their elderly mothers. *The Gerontologist, 31,* 389–396.

Ward-Griffin, C., Oudshoorn, A., Clark, K., & Bol, N. (2007). Mother-adult daughter relationships within dementia care. *Journal of Family Nursing, 13,* 13–32.

White, C. L., Mayo, N., Hanley, J. A., & Wood-Dauphinee, S. (2003). Evolution of the caregiving experience in the initial 2 years following stroke. *Research in Nursing & Health, 26,* 177–189.

Wuest, J. (1998). Setting boundaries: A strategy for precarious ordering of women's caring demands. *Research in Nursing & Health, 21,* 39–49.

17

It Was 20 Years Ago Today
What We Can Learn from a 20-Year Case Study

MARTIN FUJIKI AND BONNIE BRINTON

Cody has his car packed and is ready to go. He is about to make the two-and-a half hour trip from his parents' home to a technical college where he has enrolled in a program in car mechanics. Cody has rented a room in an apartment near the college. He will be joining two roommates whom he has not met before. The apartment is located next to a social and educational facility run by the church to which he belongs. Cody is nervous but also excited about his move. He is anxious to be on his own, and he looks forward to the social opportunities that living in a college community can offer.

This scenario is reminiscent of the experience of millions of young adults preparing to become self-sufficient members of their communities. For Cody, however, this move is monumental, and his success in this new setting is by no means certain. He longs for independence, but at the same time, he has relied on his parents to help him negotiate his rental contract, complete his school registration, and contact the religious facility next door. At age 25, Cody cannot yet manage these tasks without support. Why? Cody has language impairment (LI).

Introduction

We initially saw Cody when he was 4:7 years old. He had recently received a comprehensive evaluation by a team at a large children's medical center. Testing had revealed that his verbal IQ was over two standard deviations lower than his non-verbal IQ, which was within the typical range. Standardized tests of receptive and expressive language were consistently one and a half to two standard deviations below the mean. In spontaneous interaction, both his language comprehension and his language production were limited and immature. Cody's hearing and vision were typical, and there were no psychiatric or environmental factors to explain his poor language skills. He was an outgoing, enthusiastic, pleasant child. In short, Cody presented with a textbook case of specific language impairment (SLI).

We have now followed Cody for over 20 years. Aspects of his treatment have been documented in some detail (Brinton & Fujiki, 2004, 2011; Brinton, Fujiki, & Robinson, 2005). When we met Cody, there were few longitudinal studies of children with LI that followed these individuals from childhood to adolescence and adulthood. Since that time, a number of important investigations in Canada, England, and the United States have considered the nature and course of LI over this time period (e.g., Beitchman et al., 2001; Johnson, Beitchman, & Brownlie, 2010; Conti-Ramsden & Botting, 2004; Conti-Ramsden & Durkin, 2008; Lindsay, Dockrell, & Palikara, 2010; Tomblin, 2008). This work has been extremely illuminating in terms of describing the long-term outcomes of LI. Although the importance of this research is unquestioned, it is the case that there is considerable variation within groups, and group results may not characterize individual participants. Additionally, even when group tendencies reflect an individual's experience, they may fail to capture the full richness of that experience. In these situations, a careful examination of an individual can augment group results. This type of investigation may also reveal twists and turns that illustrate complexities of real life that cannot easily be quantified. One of Dr. Jack Damico's many important contributions to the field of speech language pathology has been his emphasis on qualitative research and his insistence that a detailed consideration of an individual's experience can lead us to an understanding of communication disorders that cannot be achieved by group investigations alone.

In this chapter, we consider several findings from large-group longitudinal studies of children with LI. We then describe Cody's experience to "put a face" on these results. We believe that Cody's experience can reveal subtleties that clarify group findings and give us greater insight into the general similarities and differences between individuals with LI and their typically developing peers. We also believe that this more complete understanding will improve our ability to work with these individuals and their families. We do not attempt to provide a comprehensive overview of the longitudinal studies[1] we discuss. Rather we draw on a few important findings and illustrate how these findings have also been evident in Cody's life experience.

Academics

Findings from numerous studies, including large-scale longitudinal investigations, indicate that individuals with LI struggle with academics. Problems with literacy learning are identified early and are persistent. For example, Tomblin (2008) reported that a group of children identified with problematic reading skills in second grade still lagged behind controls at age 16. As might be expected, individuals with LI also have high rates of enrollment in special education throughout their school careers (Durkin, Simkin, Knox, & Conti-Ramsden, 2009; Tomblin, 2008). Johnson et al. (2010) reported that about half of the individuals with LI studied had completed some postsecondary education, but they continued to lag far behind typically developing peers (e.g., 53% compared to 81%).

Cody's academic experience resonates with these findings. In a nutshell, LI has had a serious impact on Cody's academic performance, and we can only offer a brief synopsis of his academic journey. Initially, we were concerned about his aversion to print, and we focused on his understanding of basic story grammar and on his telling his own story through journaling. This was motivating, and he learned to love stories and books. He had difficulty learning to read, however, and he did not thrive in the phonics-based instruction offered in his school. He responded best to a more holistic approach to literacy, and he required considerable intervention utilizing a variety of strategies over a number of years.

Happily, Cody became an avid reader, even though his understanding of text lagged behind that of his peers. When he was young, Cody relied heavily on his knowledge of basic story structure to understand fiction, but he had difficulty with more complex plots. He enjoyed informational text if he was interested in the topic, and he read to increase his knowledge. He had difficulty with abstract and figurative language, however, and was often unable to infer information when reading. To this day, these difficulties reduce the depth of his reading comprehension.

Motivational factors have been very important to Cody's academic performance. Even when things were difficult, Cody attended school consistently and demonstrated a strong work ethic. In addition, he benefited from ongoing intervention from special service providers, careful support from his parents at home, and periodic adjustments and accommodations from his school. With these supports in place, he graduated from high school with a regular diploma, a significant accomplishment.

In summary, many facets of Cody's academic career resemble the findings of longitudinal group studies. His struggle to learn to read and general difficulty with academics were predictable considering his language deficits. The fact that he responded more favorably to particular instructional methods was of interest, but again, not unexpected. What is more surprising, and also encouraging, is the fact that he eventually learned to enjoy reading and writing (albeit a rather specific genre of writing) and to pursue these activities enthusiastically. It is also heartening that the concentrated levels of support from his family, teachers, and special service providers facilitated his passing his classes and graduating from high school. It was extremely important to address Cody's academic needs, but as he matured, other aspects of development became even more concerning. As Cody's mother commented, "We can handle the academics, it's the social stuff we need help with." We spend the remainder of this paper focusing on the "social stuff."

Socioemotional Difficulties

There is a great deal of evidence that individuals with LI have higher rates of socioemotional problems than their typically developing peers. Conti-Ramsden and Botting (2008) reported higher rates of anxiety and depression in 16-year-olds with SLI than in a same age peer group with typical language skills. Tomblin (2008) also reported higher levels of depression in 16-year-olds with SLI, but found these levels linked to nonverbal IQ. Beitchman et al. (2001) reported that at age 19, individuals with LI were more likely than typical peers to suffer from anxiety disorder or antisocial personality disorder. Wadman, Durkin, and Conti-Ramsden (2008) reported high levels of shyness in 16-year-olds with SLI. These individuals did not differ from their typical peers in their desire for social interaction, however. It is of note that in these and similar studies, groups with LI have high rates of problems in a variety of areas, but not all individuals with LI have socioemotional problems.

In preschool and early elementary school, Cody was a gregarious, outgoing child, and we did not expect that he would develop the range of social and emotional issues that would impact his life in significant ways. One of the first indications of these difficulties emerged when Cody was about 7 years old. He began to tug repeatedly at his hair, often pulling strands out. His parents watched for times when Cody was likely to do this, and they tried to reduce stress in these situations and to give him something that he could do with his hands (e.g., manipulate a stress ball or toy). The hair pulling (trichotillomania) abated, but returned from time to time as Cody grew older, occasionally becoming quite severe. Although trichotillomania is often associated with impulse control disorder or compulsive disorder, Cody's hair pulling was associated with stress and anxiety. As Cody entered middle school and junior high, he began to show more anxious behaviors. During this time, Cody felt stressed and threatened in classroom situations where he perceived that students were unruly or that the teacher was not in control. He had limited tolerance for noisy or chaotic learning contexts. He sometimes became frustrated and agitated if he did not know where he was supposed to be at a given time or if there were mix-ups in his schedule or plans. There were incidents in which he melted down (became unable to work) and on rare occasions even became aggressive in stressful contexts.

As he entered high school, Cody was formally identified with an anxiety disorder and was followed by a psychologist and a psychiatrist. He has received both pharmacological treatment and counseling since that time. Various physical manifestations of anxiety have emerged at different times. In his teenage years, Cody developed irritating skin rashes that took several years of treatment to resolve. Cody's dermatologist felt that his rashes were exacerbated—if not caused by—anxiety. It seemed that as one symptom abated, another arose. As he grew older, the hair pulling ceased to be such a significant issue and the skin rashes cleared. Cody then developed migraine headaches and severe intermittent tinnitus that continue to trouble him. Whether they are symptoms or causes of anxiety, these issues compromise Cody's ability to function and sabotage his quality of life.

It is of interest that, as a child, Cody clearly met the diagnostic criteria for LI. His intelligence and language testing, as well as his gregarious personality, suggested that he did not have psychological issues. Seen later in life, Cody's anxiety might have ruled out the exclusionary diagnosis of LI (or SLI). From a traditional point of view, he would still have been eligible for intervention services due to his linguistic limitations. The anxiety disorder, however, might well have been considered as co-occurring with LI, but outside the purview of those who treat LI. Given the broader perspective gained from watching Cody's case evolve, it is of interest to see how he has crossed the categorical boundaries of his diagnoses from time to time. A narrow perspective at any of these points in treatment may have seriously limited the comprehensive, coordinated treatment that he required.

For Cody, as for many individuals with LI, social and emotional factors have demanded consideration in an intervention plan. It has also been critical for his speech-language pathologists (SLPs) to be involved in the treatment of these issues both directly and as consultants. For example, it has been important to work with Cody's psychologist and psychiatrist to help them adjust their treatments to take into account his language limitations. At the same time, Cody has depended on his SLPs to help him acquire and use the language of emotion to express himself and to formulate strategies to deal with stressful situations. Only a holistic perspective and a coordinated team approach could facilitate the comprehensive intervention program needed.

Peer Interactions and Social Relationships

Individuals with LI have difficulty with peer interactions that persist from childhood through adolescence. Tomblin (2008) examined parent and teacher ratings of adolescents (age 16) with LI. Both groups rated these individuals as less socially involved with others than their typical peers. Analyzing data collected from age 7 to age 16, St. Clair, Pickles, Durkin, and Conti-Ramsden (2011) found that individuals with SLI experienced increasing numbers of social problems during this time period. The same group of individuals reported higher levels of victimization at age 11 (Conti-Ramsden & Botting, 2004) and fewer friends (Durkin & Conti-Ramsden, 2007) than typical peers at age 16. Lindsay, Dockrell, and Mackie (2008) did not report a higher level of victimization in adolescents with LI. They did find, however, that these individuals were rated as having poorer prosocial skills than typically developing peers, and that level of prosocial behavior was linked to victimization.

Cody was always an affable person; he valued interaction and enjoyed being around others. Throughout elementary school, Cody's teachers and administrators provided strong support, and Cody seemed generally happy. As a 24-year-old reflecting back, Cody commented, "Elementary school, I consider that the golden years. I had the best elementary school I ever had. Ah, I miss those glory days." Even though Cody was quite well accepted by his peers during elementary school, he struggled with social interaction. He had difficulty entering peer conversations, and he sometimes had problems working and playing cooperatively with others. When we observed Cody in a triad with other boys his age, he was often excluded. Sometimes he disrupted the play, other times he withdrew from it, and occasionally he was rejected. Most concerning, however, was the fact that Cody very rarely formed close reciprocal friendships even though he longed for such relationships. Looking back, he remembered only one such friendship during his fourth grade year, and that ended when the boy moved away.

Cody's social experience in his supportive elementary school context did not extend into middle school. Middle school was a particularly difficult time, and he felt lonely and isolated from his peers. Even though Cody lived in a relatively small community where civility was highly valued, his middle school tolerated a high level of student aggression. Cody did not have reciprocal friends in middle school, and this put him at risk, particularly during gym class and lunch breaks. He was often victimized by peers. Since Cody was unable to describe and explain the incidents clearly (and his more verbal aggressors were able to provide alternate explanations), the school administration took no action. His parents made every effort to work with the school, but the administration remained apathetic. Finally, school personnel observed some boys hitting Cody in the hall, and one perpetrator was suspended. The next day, however, the perpetrator's brother threatened Cody. The victimization abated somewhat when the school counselor offered Cody a "safe place" in her office where he could come between classes or after lunch.

Cody's experience in middle school provides a dramatic example of the nature and effects of victimization of children with LI. Looking back 10 years later, Cody described his middle school experience saying, "That was hell. There were bullies. I got picked on. I got bullied, picked on, threatened. Middle school, that was the time I wanted to curl up in a ball and cry. That was the time we discovered I had this thing called stress. Every day was torture" (Brinton & Fujiki, 2011, p. 155). He concluded, "If I had things my way, I would never see that school again. Those particular buildings would be a crater."

When Cody entered junior high school, his social situation improved. The school administration was more sensitive to victimization, and bullying was not tolerated. Still, Cody was lonely and isolated. His problems with language comprehension and production limited his ability to keep up with the fast-paced conversations of his peers. He lacked the pro-social strategies he needed to engage peers in the kinds of conversations that build relationships. At times he was reticent. At other times he monopolized the conversational floor and talked on and on about topics that were not interesting to his peers. He was sometimes unsuccessful in engaging others in interaction, and he was often unresponsive to the needs of his conversational partners. Throughout junior high and high school, Cody participated in Boy Scouts and in religious activities with peers. He earned an Eagle Scout award, but he did not form reciprocal friendships within his social circle.

Cody's main concern about his communication was interacting with peers and making friends. He was highly motivated to improve his conversational skill, and we focused on helping him understand the reciprocal nature of conversation. We compared conversation to a game where a ball must be passed back and forth, and Cody learned strategies to attend to his conversational partner and to gear his own contributions to his listener's needs. When he employed these strategies, he was much more successful in engaging his peers, and this increased his motivation. Employing these strategies required concentration, however, and when he did not use these strategies, he reverted to an unresponsive conversational style.

Cody continued to work on his interactional skill during his high school years, and he showed gradual improvement. Anticipating the reactions and meeting the needs of his conversational partners continued to be a challenge, however, and he did not form reciprocal friendships. During this time he was part of a neighborhood group of students who gathered to eat lunch at each other's homes every day. Cody enjoyed this interaction and occasionally participated in social activities with this group outside of school. Sometimes, however, the group would make plans in which Cody was not included, and they talked about these plans while Cody was present. The other boys did not intend to insult Cody when they did this. Rather, they did not seem to notice that he was there.

Cody's high school curriculum—typically 3 years—was extended to 4 years to allow him to take a lighter course load and work part time at a neighbor's business. During his super-senior year, Cody participated in several activities that he had previously felt unable to handle. He acted in the school play, traveled on a class trip, and went to the prom. Cody felt part of a group in each of these activities, and he greatly enjoyed both the events and the social interaction involved.

After he graduated from high school, Cody lived at home and enrolled in some special classes in a local university. He did not have a great deal of interaction at school, however, and his social world largely revolved around his family and his church. He wanted to make friends and to begin dating, and he continued intervention focused on improving his interactional skills. Even so, peer relationships were slow in coming, and he reflected, "I've never had a true friend."

When he was about 21, Cody gradually began to establish a reciprocal friendship with Alex, a young man who lived next door. Alex was a few years younger than Cody, but they shared interests including adventure stories, movies, and video games. Cody and Alex began to spend time together regularly. Cody's mother reported that much of their interaction was "parallel." That is, they played video games together or watched each other play games. Cody and Alex enjoyed being together, and Cody recently acted as best man at Alex's wedding.

When he was 23, Cody moved into an apartment with two roommates, one of whom knew Cody and was familiar with his challenges. Cody was part of a church congregation made up entirely of young adults. During the next year, Cody had many opportunities to interact with peers at his apartment, at church, and at neighborhood social activities. Surprisingly, Cody did not always take full advantage of these opportunities even when his roommate and others made efforts to include him. He seemed to experience considerable approach-avoidance where social activities were concerned. On one hand, he longed for relationships with his peers. When he was around other young people and he concentrated on responsive conversational strategies, he was pleased with his interactions. On the other hand, these interactions required considerable effort. Rather than attend social events with his neighbors, he often chose to visit a local bookstore or drive 30 minutes to spend the evening playing video games at Alex's home.

At 25, Cody recently reflected on his social world and expressed a desire to move to a student community farther from his home. His greatest desire is to establish close peer relationships, date, and eventually marry. He feels that increased distance will "force" him to interact more with other young adults in his neighborhood and church group and thus bring him closer to his goal. The challenge for Cody's parents, for his SLP, and for the other professionals who follow him is to encourage his move toward independence while providing enough support, from a distance, to help him succeed.

Emotion Understanding

Cody's difficulty with language production and language comprehension has compromised his ability to interact with his peers, but his LI per se has not been the only inhibiting factor. His inability to read the emotions of his peers and to appreciate their feelings in a given situation has been just as problematic.

Considering that he seemed so interested in others, it was surprising that Cody so often misjudged the emotions of other people. There was evidence of this problem relatively early, but we appreciated it fully only in hindsight. As a

5-year-old, he had trouble anticipating how others might react to his input in interaction. An early indication of his difficulty was evident when, as a kinder-gartener, Cody identified as a friend a classmate who evidently did not like to play with him. In another particularly memorable incident, 6-year-old Cody proudly presented Ann, his student clinician, with a hand-made card. Cody's mother warned, "Remember, this is a child with language impairment, and his favorite animals are pigs." When the clinician opened the card, it contained the greeting, *Ann is a pig*, complete with illustration. We were highly amused at the time. We were less amused 13 years later when we heard 19-year-old Cody converse with a peer about Christmas presents:

"What did you get?" asked Cody.

"Mostly clothes," replied Rob.

"Loser!" shouted Cody.

Cody was unable to read Rob's deflated expression and remained unaware that he had said anything that might offend him. Cody has always been quick to notice and utilize visual information in books, pictures, and movies, but this ability has not extended to recognizing facial expression or other physical manifestations of emotion. Cody has had ongoing difficulty with various aspects of emotion understanding from recognizing facial expressions of emotion to anticipating the effects of his words and actions on others.

Cody's difficulty understanding emotion has had far-reaching effects per-meating virtually all aspects of his communication. Most problematic, his lack of awareness of the emotional reactions of others has seriously under-mined his ability to establish and maintain relationships. When he was in elementary school, he was often unable to read the emotional and social cues of his peers. As an adolescent, he often misjudged his peers' emotions and intents in conversation. Not only did he struggle to connect with others, he sometimes unintentionally offended them. As a young adult, he still must make a conscious effort to attend to, understand, and respond appropriately to the emotion cues of others. Difficulty with emotion understanding has been particularly problematic in that it has hindered Cody's ability to build rela-tionships by commiserating, empathizing, and sharing emotional experience with others.

Cody's difficulty with emotion understanding has also affected his reading comprehension. When he initially learned to read literature, he could under-stand the events that transpired, but he struggled to grasp the characters' per-spectives and emotional reactions regarding those events. It was, therefore, very difficult for him to draw social and emotional inferences when reading. As a young adult, Cody prefers straightforward adventure stories and infor-mational texts that require minimal emotional inferencing. Even now, Cody loves to write fantasy fiction, but his stories rarely describe the emotional experience of his characters.

When we initially saw Cody, we did not anticipate that emotion understanding would be an issue we would address. As it turned out, this aspect of development has been absolutely critical to his social communication. Facilitating Cody's ability to understand the emotions of others has been a significant treatment focus over the years, and it has required ongoing intervention to help him respond appropriately to the emotion cues of his conversational partners. He has made steady progress over the years, but this learning has required considerable effort, and it remains an ongoing challenge.

The Importance of Family Support

Johnson et al. (2010) reported outcomes for a group of young adults with LI who were initially identified at age 5. These researchers reported that at age 25, the individuals with LI reported poorer outcomes than young adults with typical development in several behavioral domains (e.g., educational, occupational). Despite lower ratings, the groups did not differ in the perceptions of quality of life. These perceptions, however, were largely linked to strong social support from family, friends, and other individuals.

This finding underscores the importance of a social support system, and Cody's case provides a vivid example of how strong family support facilitates opportunity, experience, and growth. Cody's mother is a gentle, accommodating individual who is not inclined to make demands on others. Nevertheless, she became a tireless advocate for him, tactfully pressing for resources and actively coordinating services in his behalf for 20 years and counting. Before each school year began, Cody's mother met with school personnel, observed available classrooms, and chose Cody's teachers. She communicated with each teacher regularly from preschool through high school. She attended planning meetings and negotiated appropriate special services. She helped Cody manage his assignments and schedule, and she coordinated additional language intervention, medical and psychiatric care, and psychological counseling outside of school. Cody's father is an outgoing, affable individual who has been effective in marshaling neighborhood support and promoting Cody's welfare. Cody's parents have always been on the lookout for opportunities for him to pursue his interests and develop his talents. Cody's older brothers have looked out for him, advising him on personal issues, and training him to work in their business. Grandparents and extended family members have also been active in Cody's social circle and support system.

On more than one occasion, extraordinary networks of support have fallen into place to allow Cody to participate in activities that would not have been possible otherwise. Two experiences Cody has had as a young adult provide vivid illustrations of the amount of family support that Cody requires.

The first example is specific to Cody's social culture, the serving of a full-time proselyting mission for his church. Cody and his family are members of the Church of Jesus Christ of Latter Day Saints (Mormons). In this church, young men between 18 and 21 years of age frequently serve as full-time religious missionaries away from their homes (almost always in another state or country) for a 2-year period. During this time, they contact their families only through weekly e-mails or letters and phone calls twice a year. In Cody's community, a *mission* is considered an important demonstration of religious commitment. Cody's older brothers all served as missionaries, and Cody wanted desperately to do so as well. At 19, however, Cody was ill equipped to handle the demands of living away from home and proselytizing among strangers. Interestingly enough, his anxiety posed a more significant barrier to this endeavor than did his difficulty communicating. When Cody was 20, his grandfather was unexpectedly assigned to administrate a mission area within the United States. Through a series of special arrangements, Cody successfully served as a full-time missionary for a shortened assignment of 6 months under his grandfather's supervision. During this time, Cody lived and worked with other missionaries, participating in proselytizing and service activities daily. His grandfather monitored his situation, arranging for him to work with other missionaries who would be sensitive to his needs and providing assistance when difficulties arose. With this level of support, Cody performed well, and he found this experience both rewarding and personally validating.

The second example is an experience common to many young people, moving from home into an apartment. Following Cody's service as a missionary, he again lived at home. He then moved to a residential facility designed especially for young men with language-learning disabilities. He participated in a curriculum designed to facilitate academics, vocational skills, and independent living. This setting was helpful, but after several months, Cody wanted to move on. He was not able to negotiate this transition by himself, however. His parents located an apartment fairly close to their home where Cody could live with two roommates. A network of support helped Cody manage this situation. His brothers hired him to work in their car business and counseled him on workplace behavior and social interaction. His parents monitored (but did not manage) his financial accounts and provided assistance as needed. His roommate introduced him to other young people, made sure that Cody's ecclesiastical leaders were aware of him, and saw that Cody was apprised of church meetings and social activities. Cody continued to receive language intervention during this time focusing on social communication skills pertinent to his living situation. Cody's parents, brothers, and roommate and SLP communicated with each other, directly or indirectly, to coordinate their efforts and to monitor Cody's functioning. This impressive level of support helped Cody manage the demands of holding a job and living in an apartment.

Cody's extraordinary level of family involvement has encouraged and allowed him to move toward the quality of life he desires. It has been vital, and extremely rewarding, for Cody's SLPs and other service providers to work with Cody's family to capitalize on their support and enhance their effectiveness.

Conclusion

When Cody was a young child, traditional views of LI emphasized the specificity of the disorder. We expected that the development of skills dependent on language, such as literacy and academics, would be affected. It was less obvious that deficits associated with LI might extend into social and emotional domains. Recent longitudinal group studies report that many adolescents and young adults with LI experience persistent academic, social, and emotional difficulties, and these findings are congruent with Cody's experience. Like all individuals with LI, however, Cody has a unique story that group investigations cannot describe. Considering Cody's journey over the last 20 years provides a poignant illustration of what life has been like for one child growing up with LI.

At 25, Cody has achieved many important milestones. He has graduated from high school, received some vocational training, served as a missionary for his church, lived in an apartment with roommates, managed his finances, and held a job. He enjoys reading, writing, and talking with others. Viewed from the surface, Cody has developed his communicative skills and is compensating for his residual communicative deficits.

Closer examination reveals that Cody continues to face a range of challenges across multiple domains. Despite the improvement he has shown over the years, he still struggles with receptive and expressive language. He notes, "Cause I have both receiving and giving. I need to constantly ask for a person, to constantly ask for a person to ask that question again. Trip on my own tongue to get the words out." At this point, however, language deficits are not the only significant limitation to Cody's quality of life. Symptoms of anxiety, including headaches and tinnitus, decrease his comfort and reduce his ability to function. Non-responsive interactional skills limit his connection with peers. Poor emotion understanding hinders his establishing close reciprocal relationships. A strong system of family support has allowed Cody to achieve considerable independence, but his social and emotional challenges limit his ability to achieve what he wants most—to be liked, to make friends, to marry, to have a family of his own.

The move Cody is about to make to the technical college away from his home is a big step. If he can complete the course in car mechanics, he will increase his earning potential. He hopes that moving out of his current social circle will force him to meet new people and make friends. Cody is putting some distance between himself and his support system, however, and it remains to be seen how that will play out for him.

Following Cody for 20 years has challenged our assumptions and increased our understanding of the nature and course of LI. The extent to which Cody's experience reflects that of others with LI is not clear. Nevertheless, Cody's story illustrates the importance of adopting a holistic approach in considering the multiple factors that may be associated with LI. Cody has taught us that planning and implementing intervention requires a perspective that is broad enough to appreciate the complex nature of LI and individualized enough to focus on the needs of each child.

In closing we wish to acknowledge Dr. Jack Damico's influence in our work. His writings have emphasized the importance of focusing on interventions and intervention goals that will make the greatest difference. He has also helped focused our attention on the complex details of communicative interactions. Both lines of thinking have enriched our research and made the treatments we provide better for the children, adolescents, and adults whom we serve.

Note

1. More complete descriptions of these projects may be found in the studies cited. These individual articles provide a beginning point to learn more about the projects they represent.

References

Beitchman, J. H., Wilson, B., Johnson, C. J., Atkinson, L., Young, A., Adlaf, E., … Douglas, L. (2001). Fourteen-year follow-up of speech/language-impaired and control children: Psychiatric outcome. *Journal of the American Academy of Child and Adolescent Psychiatry, 40*, 75–82.

Brinton, B., & Fujiki, M. (2004). Social and affective factors in language impairments and literacy learning. In C. A. Stone, E. R. Silliman, B. J. Ehren, & K. Apel (Eds.), *Handbook of language and literacy: Development and disorders* (pp. 130–153). New York, NY: Guilford.

Brinton, B., & Fujiki, M. (2011). Listening to individuals with language impairment. In S. Roulstone & S. McLeod (Eds.), *Listening to children and young people with speech language and communication needs* (pp. 155–160). Albury, Guildford, England: J & R Press.

Brinton, B., Fujiki, M., & Robinson, L. (2005). Life on a tricycle: A case study of language impairment from 4 to 19. *Topics in Language Disorders, 25*, 338–352.

Conti-Ramsden, G., & Botting, N. (2004). Social difficulties and victimization in children with SLI at 11 years of age. *Journal of Speech, Language, and Hearing Research, 47*, 145–161. doi:10.1044/1092-4388(2004/013)

Conti-Ramsden, G., & Botting, N. (2008). Emotional health in adolescents with and without a history of specific language impairment (SLI). *Journal of Child Psychology and Psychiatry, 2008*(49), 516–525. doi:10.1111/j.1469-7610.2007.01858.x

Conti-Ramsden, G., & Durkin, K. (2008). Language and independence in adolescents with and without a history of specific language impairment. *Journal of Speech, Language, and Hearing Research, 51*, 70–83. doi:10.1044/1092-4388(2008/005)

Durkin, K., & Conti-Ramsden, G. (2007). Language, social behavior, and the quality of friendships in adolescents with and without a history of specific language impairment. *Child Development, 78*, 1441–1457.

Durkin, K., Simkin, Z., Knox, E., & Conti-Ramsden, G. (2009). Specific language impairment and school outcomes. II: Educational context, student satisfaction, and post-compulsory progress. *International Journal of Language & Communication Disorders, 44*(1), 36–55.

Johnson, C. J., Beitchman, J. H., & Brownlie, E. B. (2010). Twenty-year follow-up of children with and without speech-language impairments: Family, educational, occupational, and quality of life outcomes. *American Journal of Speech-Language Pathology, 19*(1), 51–65. doi:10.1044/1058-0360(2009/08-0083)

Lindsay, G., Dockrell, J., & Mackie, C. (2008). Vulnerability to bullying in children with a history of specific speech and language difficulties. *European Journal of Special Needs Education, 23*, 1–16. doi:10.1080/08856250701791203

Lindsay, G., Dockrell, J., & Palikara, O. (2010). Self-esteem of adolescents with specific language impairment as they move from compulsory education. *International Journal of Language & Communication Disorders, 45*, 561–571. doi:10.3109/13682820903324910

St. Clair, M. C., Pickles, A., Durkin, K., & Conti-Ramsden, G. (2011). A longitudinal study of behavioral, emotional and social difficulties in individuals with a history of specific language impairment (SLI). *Journal of Communication Disorders, 44*, 186–199. doi:10.1016/j.jcomdis.2010.09.004

Tomblin, J. B. (2008). Validating diagnostic standards for specific language impairment using adolescent outcomes. In C. F. Norbury, J. B. Tomblin, & D. V. M. Bishop (Eds.), *Understanding developmental language disorders* (pp. 93–114). New York, NY: Psychology Press.

Wadman, R., Durkin, K., & Conti-Ramsden, G. (2008). Self-esteem, shyness, and sociability in adolescents with specific language impairment. *Journal of Speech, Language, and Hearing Research, 51*, 938–952. doi:10.1044/1092-4388(2008/069)

18
Using Thematic Network Analysis

An Example Using Interview Data from Parents of Children Who Use AAC

JULIET GOLDBART AND JULIE MARSHALL

Introduction

In this chapter we will introduce a method of qualitative data analysis, Thematic Network Analysis (TNA; Attride-Stirling, 2001), and illustrate it with reference to a study we have undertaken which explores some of the salient issues in parenting a child who is acquiring language through augmented means.

Augmentative and alternative communication (AAC) is "any method of communicating that supplements (augments) or replaces (provides an alternative to) the usual methods of speech and/or writing where these are impaired or insufficient to meet the individual's needs" (Murray & Goldbart, 2009, p. 464). Unsurprisingly, given the role of parents in language acquisition, the involvement of parents, and indeed the wider family, in AAC interventions with children is widely supported (e.g., Cress, 2004; Mathisen, Arthur-Kelly, Kidd, & Nissen, 2009). Granlund, Bjorck-Akesson, Olsson, and Rydeman (2001) describe the multiple roles of these families as: *family as **decision maker**, family as **communication environment**, family as consumers, family in crisis, and family as **trainers***. McCord and Soto (2004), however, caution that some families find the demands of these multiple roles overwhelming. Research relating to the roles highlighted in bold will be illustrated below.

Parette, VanBiervliet, and Hourcade (2000) promote the involvement of parents in *decision-making* in all aspects of assistive technology. This, they argue, is essential from the outset since involving families in decision-making ensures consideration of cultural factors and other issues of individual concern. In a review of studies up to 2003, however, Snell, Chen, and Hoover (2006) found only limited evidence of collaborative decision making. In their study, McCord and Soto (2004) found that the Mexican American parents felt distanced from decision making and that their children's AAC systems lacked vocabulary critical for home use, for example, the names of daily visitors and their home language.

Parents in McNaughton, Rackensperger, Benedek-Wood, Krezman, and Williams' (2008) focus group study identified what they needed to embed AAC in the child's *communication environment* as: opportunities for individual exploration, use of the technology in role play activities, organized instruction, and opportunities for functional use in the community. Support for parents' more formal role in what McNaughton et al. describe as "organized instruction" and Granlund et al. (2001) call *trainers*, delivering home-based AAC interventions, comes from a number of studies (e.g., Binger, Kent-Walsh, Berens, del Campo, & Rivera, 2008; Sevcik Romski, Adamson, 2004; Sigafoos et al, 2004; Tait, Sigafoos, Woodyatt, O'Reilly, & Lancioni, 2004; Thunberg, Dahlgren Sandberg, & Ahlsén, 2009).

Granlund, Björck-Akesson, Wilder, and Ylvén (2008) identify the many accommodations families make when a child uses AAC and argue that for AAC interventions to be sustainable they must fit with these accommodations. Cress (2004, p. 55) adds, "It is more important to influence the child's routine communication (i.e., with parents) than to influence a few moments 'best' communication" (e.g., in the clinical setting). "Thick descriptions" (Hammer, 1998) of families' daily lives and views are therefore critical for professionals aiming to embed AAC into families' unique routines. A greater understanding of families' contribution and involvement would also help professionals, as recent studies (Iacono & Cameron, 2009; Lindsay, 2010) suggest that professionals involved in AAC service delivery sometimes find aspects of collaboration with parents challenging.

There are several ways through which greater understanding of family life could be achieved, including questionnaires, interviews and ethnographies. Although Granlund et al. (2001) argue for ethnographic studies, using, for example, video recording, we know of only one in AAC; Wickenden's (2011) exploration of identity in adolescents who use AAC. Questionnaires have been used effectively to elicit feedback on participation in home based interventions (Jonsson, Kristoffersson, Ferm, & Thunberg, 2011) and to establish parents' priorities in AAC intervention (Calculator & Black, 2010). We suggest, however, that family members are better able to describe in detail ("thick description") the issues of importance to their lives in an interview. Previous interview studies with families of children with disabilities include Rodger and Mandich (2005) on mothers' experiences of their child's occupational therapy, Sleigh (2005) on feeding children with cerebral palsy, Leiter (2004) on early intervention, and Piggot, Paterson, and Hocking (2002) on home therapy for children with cerebral palsy.

Several ways of analyzing interview data have been described in this book. In this chapter we use TNA (Attride-Stirling, 2001). TNA has been used to analyze data from a diverse range of recent studies in health, for example, parents' experience of early language intervention (Lyons, O'Malley, O'Connor, & Monaghan, 2010), clinicians' experience of automatic external defibrillators (Hancock, Roebuck, Farrer, & Campbell, 2006), and nutrition and chronic obstructive pulmonary disease (Dickenson, 2009). It is also being used in social care research, for example, clothing choices made by people with rheumatoid arthritis (Goodacre & Candy, 2011), resilience of refugees in Nepal (Thomas, Roberts, Luitel, Upadhaya, & Tol, 2011), and the lives of child carers in rural Kenya (Skovdal, 2011).

The data presented in this chapter comprise an exploration of the ways in which parents talk about their children's communication in various aspects of everyday life. Some data from this study have been published elsewhere (Goldbart & Marshall, 2004; Marshall & Goldbart, 2008).

Method

Methodological Considerations

Design: A qualitative design involving data collection using in-depth semi-structured interviews was used to explore communication from the informants' perspectives. This study involved interviews with a small number of participants; the exploration of social phenomena rather than hypothesis testing and the interpretation of the meanings of people's actions (Atkinson & Hammersley, 1994).

As is common in ethnographic research (Langdridge, 2004), thematic analysis was used in order to organize and make sense of the data. As we wished to feed findings back to families in an accessible form, an approach which offers techniques for the "systematization and presentation of qualitative analyses" was adopted (Attride-Stirling, 2001, p. 385), namely TNA. This tool for analysis emphasizes the avoidance of predetermined coding schemes. Attride-Stirling (2001) reports that TNA has much in common with other techniques such as Grounded Theory and also developed from aspects of argumentation theory. The analytical process is described in more detail below.

Procedure

Preparing for the Interviews: The initial proposal was presented and discussed at a conference which included key stakeholders; people who use AAC, parents/carers, and professionals. Ethical approval was obtained from the authors' employing university.

Recruiting Participants: Participants were recruited through schools in North West England and though family support groups. Potential participants were approached with information about the study via an intermediary. The criteria for inclusion were: speech was not the child's primary mode of communication;

the child was aged 3 to 11 years; the cause of the communication disability was congenital and non-progressive; the child was either using, or expected to need, a formal AAC system; intermediaries considered that families would be able to cope with the potentially emotive questions and, because of financial constraints, participants could speak and understand English sufficiently to participate in an interview without an interpreter.

Participants

The participants were 13 Caucasian, English-speaking, parents or carers, living in single- or two-parent families, with 0 to 5 other children. The children were 3 to 10 years old and had communication impairments and associated physical and/or intellectual impairments that had necessitated the introduction of AAC. They attended a range of state funded mainstream and special education schools and parents reported that they used between two and five modes of communication. Limited data are presented about the families to maintain anonymity.

Data Collection

Data collection was by semi-structured interviews. The interviewer was a teacher with experience of working with families of children who have disabilities. Participants were mainly interviewed at home, in some cases with the child present and, if appropriate, involved. Interviews commenced with basic biographic questions. In order to address the aims of the research, the topic guide for the interview was very open: "Tell me about a typical day with (child's name)," and participants were encouraged to raise and discuss any and all issues that they considered to be relevant. Interviews lasted 45–120 minutes, were recorded onto minidisk and transcribed verbatim. Transcripts were sent to interviewees for respondent validation.

Data Analysis

Data analysis followed the six-stage procedure described by Attride-Stirling (2001, p. 391). The first stage involved open coding of the transcripts. All transcripts were entered onto ATLAS.ti (1997), a qualitative data analysis software package, and coded using this package. The coding scheme was derived from repeated reading of the transcripts and represented recurrent and salient issues within the text. The codes were applied to meaningful segments of the textual data.

The second stage involved moving from these codes to themes. This requires the rereading of all text segments, or quotes, within each code, identifying the underlying pattern that has resulted in them being coded in the same way and, from this, abstracting themes. These rather specific themes are known as Basic Themes (BT) (Attride-Stirling, 2001, p. 388). The third step involved developing the thematic networks. This is itself a six step procedure involving bringing together the Basic Themes and grouping them into Organizing Themes (OTs) "according to the underlying story they are telling" (Attride-Stirling, 2001, p. 389). OTs summarize the main assumptions of a group of BTs and are thus more abstract. They also divide up and reflect the main assumptions of the super-ordinate Global Themes, which represent the major points in the interviews. The result is web-like network/s.

Attride-Stirling's (2001) fourth stage involves describing and exploring the networks generated. The themes were presented at a second conference, to an audience of people who use AAC, carers and professionals, to enhance the trustworthiness of the findings. There is no claim that findings are generalizable to other participants or settings, but by allowing a larger group of people who share the participants' experience, to consider and discuss the findings, some support for credibility and transferability (Lincoln & Guba, 1985) might be obtained. This forum also enabled the consideration of rival explanations (Miles & Huberman, 1994). In stage five, presented below, the network is summarized and the principal issues which characterize it are described. Stage six (in the Discussion section) involves using the significant themes to discuss the research questions and their theoretical underpinnings.

Findings

Three global themes were developed (reported in more depth in Marshall & Goldbart, 2008): parents' views and experiences (see also Goldbart & Marshall, 2004), wider societal issues, and parents' perspectives on their child's communication or interaction. In this chapter we will focus on the six organizing themes (OTs) and the associated basic themes that relate to parents' perspectives on their child's communication or interaction (see Figure 18.1).

Organizing Theme 1. How and About What Do Parents Communicate with Their Child?

This theme, perhaps unsurprisingly given the nature of the interview, was discussed extensively by parents. It is comprised of four Basic Themes each relating to parents' accounts of the ways in which they and their child communicate.

(i) Input and Output Modes: Parents gave clear descriptions of the communication modes that their children used, with parents of children who sign more likely to describe input modes than those using symbol based systems.

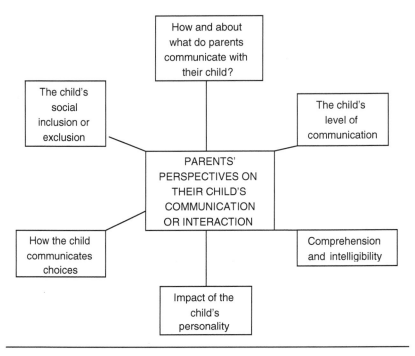

Figure 18.1 Global Theme: Parents' perspectives on their child's communication or interaction.

I do use some of the signs when he is reading his book at school … but most of the time I just talk to him.

If he is actually looking at me and I know the sign I will do the sign as well and I will speak…. it helps him to pick the signs up.

They were very aware of the multimodal nature of their child's communication, and gave detailed descriptions of how their child uses his/her AAC system.

At the moment … she would probably ask for her symbol book before her Dynavox because that's been around longer.

Some of these quotes also demonstrated the role parents had played in introducing or developing the child's communication system.

I taught Hannah to sign and myself to sign from the book.

The clarity of many parents' descriptions suggests that they were knowledgeable about their children's modes of communication and confident in this knowledge. It also suggests that AAC systems were being used at home as well as at school.

(ii) Content: Parents identified a diversity of topics about which they and their children communicated. Foremost were the child's wants and needs, which tended to relate to concrete, everyday items such as food, clothes, and toilet needs.

She will use colors quite a lot so she will point to the red and I will know she wants to wear red trousers.

She has signs for food and toilet and things like that.

School or nursery was also a common topic, although when children were reporting on something parents had not experienced, this could be more difficult.

What she has done at school is quite difficult. Obviously that's where the book comes in.

Play was a less complicated topic.

that's where we first started using symbols just very very simply in play really you know do you want to play with the dolls or do you want to brush the doll's hair.

Some parents described conversation about family activities and interests.

We talk about where we're going on holiday and we get holiday brochures out.

Where children had greater access to complex language parents reported that they were able to talk about their thoughts and feelings.

One cold dark winter night she didn't want to go, and I said what's the matter Rachel and I put the symbol book in front of her to tell me and she went to the feelings page and told me that she felt frightened and tired and she didn't want to go horse riding.

There was recognition, however, that these more abstract topics can be more difficult for children using AAC.

Easy stuff's what she needs, what she wants to do. Less easy, how she feels. We often try and say how're you feeling today? … she's always open to suggestion of what we put forward … so you never know whether you're suggesting it to her or whether she truly feels it herself.

Parents' accounts of what their children talk about have a significant contribution to make to decisions regarding vocabulary selection and organization, providing complementary perspectives to those of teachers. These parents seemed to be sensitive to the kinds of words and concepts their son or daughter could readily assimilate into their communication system and those which, although desirable, were more abstract and, hence, more difficult.

(iii) Communication Strategies: It was clear that parents had developed by themselves, or learned from professionals, a wide range of strategies for supporting their children's communication. These strategies give insight not only into parents' knowledge of their children, but also into their understanding of the nature of communication.

We've been working on him asking with "please" because he knows "please," and say if you'd start by saying "please," then we know it's a question.

Some parents were very realistic about the extent to which they could apply optimal strategies in daily life, supporting McCord and Soto's (2004) finding that parents prized rate over complexity in everyday family settings.

Actually we constantly ask closed questions, which is what you're not supposed to do.

It is important that parents and professionals share this information and make it available to other communication partners. This might involve working with children to develop their strategic and social competence (Light, 1989) or developing a communication passport (Millar, 2003) to guide partners towards successful strategies.

(iv) Interaction: This theme tells us something of the contexts within which parents are communicating with their children. Again, parents demonstrate the extent to which they have thought about the process of communication.

I've realized that when I feed Andrew sometimes I don't talk to him at all and other times I do talk to him. Yesterday I said I'm not talking to you (am I) is that OK? By nodding and shaking his head he made it quite clear that he was quite happy to not have me talking to him. There are other times now when he will actually point to his mouth because he wants you to talk about something.

Of particular concern was inclusion of the child in family conversation.

We communicate with all our kids and Nina was no different we just communicate we talked with her did the same sorts of things with all the other kids.

Within this Organizing Theme a range of issues emerged of considerable relevance to the dialogue between parents and professionals supporting children's developing use of AAC.

Organizing Theme 2. The Child's Level of Communication

The parents gave detailed and insightful descriptions of their children's communicative strengths and needs, in terms of their current abilities and the demands on these abilities occasioned by the social and educational settings they encounter. We did not aim to evaluate the accuracy of their comments.

(i) Describing the child's current skills: Parents' descriptions of all 11 children addressed both comprehension and expression. They often related current skills to earlier ways of communicating, typically before a formal AAC system was introduced. This suggests an awareness of developmental progression that would support discussion with speech-language pathologists and educators.

Her expressive communication is at one word level.

If you showed her a picture of, say, cheese, she would know to go into food and then you know within the food category where exactly where that one is.

(ii) Commenting on the child's skills: These quotes suggest that, despite the acknowledged limitations, parents are encouraged by their children's achievements.

Given her needs she is a good communicator.

She says things to a degree and in her own way.

(iii) Current difficulties: Some parents contrasted their child's abilities and difficulties in ways that seemed realistic, although they sometimes appeared to sound regretful.

He won't ask, he can't ask, so that's the hard thing. He could be wondering anything at all, he could be wondering and thinking one thing and I'm standing there wittering on.

As a whole, comments within this Organizing Theme confirm the impression gained in the first theme; that parents are actively observing and trying to make sense of their child's development of communication through AAC. The quotes suggest that parents have a good understanding of their child's skills, a realistic appreciation of the difficulties their child experiences and a positive view of what has already been achieved. This level of insight is a valuable resource that parents have to offer professionals.

Organizing Theme 3. Comprehension and Intelligibility Difficulties

This theme contains parents' accounts of external factors that act as supports or barriers to their children's communication. Some parents described their own limitations either in acquiring AAC skills or in understanding their child's output, and how they have tried to address these.

I had been doing it completely wrong it is my signing that gets in the way of our communication but my signing isn't at the level that she is at, she is way beyond my level.

Others talked of the technical difficulties they experienced, particularly with high tech systems, or the limitations of AAC systems.

By the time he was 4 I was starting to panic that I was going to carry the Encyclopaedia Britannica around with me because he's got a fantastic memory.

Whilst this theme contained fewer quotes than others, these kinds of difficulty were mentioned by all but one of the parents. As these frustrations may affect parents' motivation and hence their continued support for AAC (e.g., Angelo, Jones, & Kokoska, 1995), it is important that professionals are aware of them.

Organizing Theme 4: How the Child Communicates Choices

The opportunity and ability to make choices is an important aspect of communication. Almost all parents identified systematic approaches that allowed their children to express preferences.

Not so long ago we got on to the fingers on the hands and give him 5 choices and he'd remember them and the interesting thing is that you might give 3 choices ... and immediately he'd use his thumb/index/middle finger.

She has got a tight hand fist for yes and an open hand for no and that is very obvious to everybody.

Interestingly, choice making tended not to involve the child's formal AAC system, but, rather, either eye pointing or simple conventions that could be used at any time. Furthermore, choices tend to involve selection from a set range of options, even when that child has a wider range available within their AAC vocabulary. This may be a pragmatic solution reflecting the demands of everyday life, again supporting McCord and Soto's (2004) finding of the importance of rapid rather than complex exchanges. However, it may be that professionals could discuss with parents contexts where their children could initiate choices in a less constrained manner.

Two further themes emerged from the interview data that might not seem, in the first instance, to relate directly to AAC. However, they were clearly related by parents to their children's communication strengths and difficulties. These were the impact of the child's personality and the child's social inclusion or exclusion.

Organizing Theme 5: Impact of the Child's Personality

This was mentioned by all of the parents, in common with findings from a study by Marshall, Goldbart, and Phillips (2007), relating to children with delayed speech and language. For parents, their child's personality affected many aspects of communication, particularly their persistence in getting their messages across, and was seen as influencing the extent to which they engaged with others, particularly those outside the immediate family.

She's very persistent she never gives up easily so if people don't understand her straight away she will keep making the same gestures until they eventually they get through.

There's still many occasions when he tries to say something and no one knows what it is but when you get it right he's delighted he's quite patient.

Whilst generally seen as an asset, some aspects of a child's personality were seen as a disadvantage.

She is very easily distracted I suppose and gets bored very easy.

The significance to parents of personality in children's learning to communicate through AAC suggests that it should be included routinely by AAC professionals within the endogenous factors they discuss with parents.

Organizing Theme 6: Child's Social Inclusion or Exclusion

Whatever the strengths of the children's personalities, their social inclusion or exclusion was seen as greatly influenced by their communication skills. Difficulties in making themselves understood were seen as particularly significant in the extent to which children who use AAC were included or excluded at home, at school and in other social situations.

Sometimes he gets frustrated and sometimes this is going to sound awful and I think he resigns himself to the fact that he can't communicate fully to some of the younger members of the family.

She is sort of is very much a passive observer really.

There were no comments suggesting that AAC had increased the children's social inclusion. This may be because all were at relatively early stages of using AAC, but may suggest that professionals could offer strategies for home and school.

Discussion

The extent and depth of these parents' observations of their children's communication confirm Cress' (2004) confidence in parents' ability to contribute significantly to AAC intervention. If these parents are typical (bearing in mind the limited claims regarding representativeness and generalizability in qualitative research), then discussion eliciting the type of data gained in this study would assist professionals in developing approaches that are consistent with families' views, priorities, routines, and activities. Furthermore, the awareness of both the limitations of AAC, as well as the advantages to their children, suggest that parents have much to contribute to effective collaboration with professionals in AAC implementation.

The semi-structured interview format seemed to afford parents a comfortable context within which to provide information on the family as a communication environment. Unlike McCord and Soto's interviewees, those parents whose children had access to high tech speech generating (voice output) devices valued them highly, perhaps because, as English speakers, they did not experience language barriers, or because "cultural preferences for speed and intimacy" (McCord & Soto, 2004) are different for these U.K., Anglophone families. Professionals should consider that such views may not be universal. In many situations, families in this study used light tech, often highly individualized, systems to facilitate rapid communication. This would support McCord and Soto's (2004) finding that families find speed more important than complexity.

For these parents, the child's individual personality was an important factor which does not seem to have received a great deal of attention in the literature. Parents demonstrated their awareness of the need for multiple modes of communication and the need for communicative creativity. Their comments (perhaps guided by the interview structure) focused more on past and current communication, and there was little discussion of the child's likely future communication needs. Professionals should be aware that they may need to lead on this agenda.

Thematic Network Analysis provides a transparent, step-wise process for researchers to follow. Furthermore, for studies such as this, the resulting thematic networks could provide professionals with an evidence-based, visual structure for discussions with parents.

References

Angelo, D., Jones, S., & Kokoska, S. (1995). Family perspective on augmentative and alternative communication: Families of young children. *Augmentative and Alternative Communication, 11,* 193–201.

Atkinson, P., & Hammersley, M. (1994). Ethnography and participant observation. In N. Denzin & Y. Lincoln (Eds.), *Handbook of qualitative research* (pp. 248–261). Thousand Oaks, CA: Sage.

ATLAS.ti. (1997). *Visual qualitative data analysis management model building.* Berlin, Germany: Thomas Muhr Scientific Software Development.

Attride-Stirling, J. (2001). Thematic networks: an analytic tool for qualitative research. *Qualitative Research, 1*(3), 385–405.

Binger, C., Kent-Walsh, J., Berens, J., del Campo, S., & Rivera, D. (2008). Teaching Latino parents to support the multi-symbol message productions of their children who require AAC. *Augmentative and Alternative Communication, 24*(4), 323–338.

Calculator, S., & Black, T. (2010). Parents' priorities for AAC and related instruction for their children with Angelman Syndrome. *Augmentative and Alternative Communication, 26*(1), 30–40.

Cress, C. (2004). Augmentative and alternative communication and language: Understanding and responding to parents' perspectives. *Topics in Language Disorders, 24*(1), 51–61.

Dickenson, J. (2009). An exploratory study of patient interventions and nutritional advice for patients with chronic obstructive pulmonary disorder, living in the community. *International Journal on Disability and Human Development, 8*(1), 43–49.

Goldbart. J., & Marshall, J. (2004). "Pushes and pulls" on the parents of children using AAC. *Augmentative and Alternative Communication, 20*(4), 194–208.

Goodacre, L., & Candy, F. (2011). 'If I didn't have RA I wouldn't give them house room': The relationship between RA, footwear and clothing choices. *Rheumatology, 50*(3), 513–517.

Granlund, M., Bjorck-Akesson, E., Olsson, C., & Rydeman, B. (2001). Working with families to introduce augmentative and alternative communication systems. In H. Cockerill & L. Carroll-Few (Eds.), *Communicating without speech: Practical augmentative & alternative communication. Clinics in development medicine No. 156* (pp. 88–102). New York, NY: Cambridge University Press.

Granlund, M., Björck-Akesson, E., Wilder, J., & Ylvén, R. (2008). AAC interventions for children in a family environment: Implementing evidence in practice. *Augmentative and Alternative Communication, 24*(3), 207–219.

Hammer, C. (1998). Toward a "thick description" of families: Using ethnography to overcome the obstacles to providing family-centered early intervention services. *American Journal of Speech-Language Pathology, 7*(1), 5–22.

Hancock, H., Roebuck, A., Farrer, M., & Campbell, S. (2006). Fully automatic external defibrillators in acute care: Clinicians' experiences and perceptions. *European Journal of Cardiovascular Nursing, 5*(3), 214–221.

Iacono, T., & Cameron, M. (2009). Australian speech-language pathologists' perceptions and experiences of augmentative and alternative communication in early childhood intervention. *Augmentative and Alternative Communication, 25*(4), 236–249.

Jonsson, A., Kristoffersson, L., Ferm, U., & Thunberg, G. (2011). The ComAlong communication boards: Parents' use and experiences of aided language stimulation. *Augmentative and Alternative Communication, 27*(2), 103–116.

Langdridge, D. (2004). *Introduction to research methods and data analysis in psychology.* Harlow, England: Pearson.

Leiter, V. (2004). Dilemmas in sharing care: maternal provision of professionally driven therapy for children with disabilities. *Social Science & Medicine, 58*(4), 837–849.

Light, J. (1989). Toward a definition of communicative competence for individuals using augmentative and alternative communication systems. *Augmentative and Alternative Communication, 5,* 137–143.

Lincoln, Y., & Guba, E. (1985). *Naturalistic inquiry.* Beverly Hills, CA: Sage.

Lindsay, S. (2010). Perceptions of health care workers prescribing augmentative and alternative communication devices to children. *Disability and Rehabilitation: Assistive Technology, 5*(3), 209–222

Lyons, R., O'Malley, M. P., O'Connor, P., & Monaghan, U. (2010). 'It's just so lovely to hear him talking': Exploring the early-intervention expectations and experiences of parents. *Child Language Teaching & Therapy, 26*(1), 61–76.

Marshall, J., & Goldbart, J. (2008). 'Communication is everything I think': Parenting a child who needs augmentative and alternative communication. *International Journal of Language and Communication Disorders, 43*(1), 77–98.

Marshall, J., Goldbart, J., & Phillips, J. (2007). Parents' and speech and language therapists' explanatory models of language development, language delay and intervention. *International Journal of Language and Communication Disorders, 42*(5), 533–555.

Mathisen, B., Arthur-Kelly, M., Kidd, J., & Nissen, C. (2009). Using MINSPEAK: A case study of a preschool child with complex communication needs. *Disability and Rehabilitation: Assistive Technology, 4*(5), 376–383.

McCord, M. S., & Soto, G. (2004). Perceptions of AAC: An ethnographic investigation of Mexican-American families. *Augmentative and Alternative Communication, 20*(4), 209–227.

McNaughton, D., Rackensperger, T., Benedek-Wood, E., Krezman, K., & Williams, M. (2008). "A child needs to be given a chance to succeed": Parents of individuals who use AAC describe the benefits and challenges of learning AAC technologies. *Augmentative and Alternative Communication, 24*(1), 43–55.

Miles, M., & Huberman, A. (1994). *Qualitative data analysis.* London, England: Sage.

Millar, S. with Aitken, S. (2003). *Personal communication passports: Guidelines for good practice.* Edinburgh, Scotland: CALL Centre.

Murray, J., & Goldbart, J. (2009). Augmentative and alternative communication: A review of current issues. *Paediatrics and Child Health, 19*(10), 464–468.

Parette, Jr., H. P., VanBiervliet, A., & Hourcade, J. J. (2000). Family centered decision-making in assistive technology. *Journal of Special Education Technology, 15*(1), 45–55.

Piggot, J., Paterson, J., & Hocking, C. (2002). Participation in Home programmes for children with cerebral palsy: A compelling challenge. *Qualitative Health Research, 12*(8), 1109–1126.

Rodger, S., & Mandich, A. (2005). Getting the run around: accessing services for children with developmental co-ordination disorder. *Child: Care, Health and Development, 31*(4), 449–457.

Sevcik, R., Romski, M., & Adamson, L. (2004). Research directions in augmentative and alternative communication for preschool children. *Disability and Rehabilitation, 26* (21–22), 1323–1329.

Sigafoos, J., O'Reilly, M., Seely-York, S., Weru, J., Son, H., Green, V., & Lancioni, G. (2004). Transferring AAC intervention to the home. *Disability and Rehabilitation, 26*(21–22), 1330–1334.

Skovdal, M. (2011). Examining the trajectories of children providing care for adults in rural Kenya. *Children and Youth Services Review, 33*(7), 1262–1269.

Sleigh, G. (2005). Mothers' voice: A qualitative study on feeding children with cerebral palsy. *Child: Care, Health and Development, 31*(4), 373–383.

Snell, M., Chen, L., & Hoover, K. (2006). Teaching augmentative and alternative communication to students with severe disabilities: A review of intervention research 1997–2003. *Research and Practices for Persons with Severe Disabilities, 31*, 203–214.

Tait, K., Sigafoos, J., Woodyatt, G., O'Reilly M., & Lancioni, G. (2004). Evaluating parent use of functional communication training to replace and enhance prelinguistic behaviours in six children with developmental and physical disabilities. *Disability and Rehabilitation, 26*(21–22), 1241–1254.

Thomas, F., Roberts, B., Luitel, N., Upadhaya, N., & Tol, W. (2011). Resilience of refugees displaced in the developing world: A qualitative analysis of strengths and struggles of urban refugees in Nepal. *Conflict and Health, 5*(1), 20. Retrieved November 18, 2011 from http://www.conflictandhealth.com/content/5/1/20

Thunberg, G., Dahlgren Sandberg, A., & Ahlsén, E. (2009). Speech-generating devices used at home by children with autism spectrum disorders: A preliminary assessment. *Focus on Autism and Other Developmental Disabilities, 24*(2), 104–114.

Wickenden, M. (2011). Talking to teenagers: Using anthropological methods to explore identity and the lifeworlds of disabled young people who use AAC. *Communication Disorders Quarterly, 32*(3), 151–163.

19

Interactional Phonetics
Background and Clinical Application

BEN RUTTER, MARTIN J. BALL, AND TOBIAS KROLL

The preceding chapters in this volume have focused on qualitative research in the area of language, and, at first consideration, it might seem that applying qualitative approaches to the study of speech would not be successful. However, as has been shown elsewhere in this book, qualitative research in communication disorders is mainly concerned with characterizing interactions between speakers; as these interactions are commonly mediated through the medium of speech, it then becomes clear that a study of interactional phonetics will have much to add to this research approach.

Indeed, interactional linguistics in general can be considered as a movement away from the laboratory and into settings where language use really happens thus as a reaction against the study of language as a behavior of the individual.

Methodologies in Language Research

The question of what constitute appropriate data and data collection techniques is a central issue in language research (Yuan, 2001). It has been a tradition in linguistic, especially phonetic, research to take a controlled environment approach to data collection. This usually entails a researcher eliciting utterances from a participant, usually in a laboratory setting, and usually without the presence of a conversational partner. Material such as word lists and written sentences/passages may be used, or the participant may be asked to engage in a monologue. The researcher will record the utterances and conduct analysis on the specific aspect of the participant's linguistic repertoire that happens to be of relevance to the project in hand. Methods of this kind are researcher driven.[1] The motivation for such research is usually two-fold: first, elicitation material allows the researcher to control the extent to which a target token is used, and second, creating ideal recording conditions for the purposes of thorough analysis is of some difficulty in the field, and hence a laboratory setting is preferred. In the case of the first reason, it is assumed that overly large amounts of data would have to be collected in naturalistic settings in order to collect sufficient tokens of interest in sufficiently varying contexts.

Research in speech pathology has been similarly influenced by such concerns. In, for example, the acoustic analysis of dysarthria, there is abundant evidence that conversational speech is more likely to exhibit the symptoms of the disorder than elicited lab talk (e.g., Tjaden & Watling, 2003). Spontaneous, natural speech remains, however, far less studied than read sentences, individual words, or even repeated consonant-vowel syllables. Kent, Weismer, Kent, Vorperian, and Duffy (1999, p. 166) summarize the drawbacks of using conversational speech as stemming from "... the lack of control over properties of the utterances, including length, syntactic structure, and phonetic composition." Furthermore, many of the acoustic hallmarks of speech segments are derived from the analysis of citation form pronunciation. In connected speech, many of these hallmarks are rendered undiscoverable by the tendency for assimilation, coarticulation, and other connected speech processes (Ball & Lowry, 2001, p. 71). The tendency, therefore, is to revert to the analysis of lab speech so as to maintain the traditional methods, rather than adjust the methods to fit with the complexities of natural speech.

The shortcomings of such researcher-driven, laboratory-based speech research have been well documented (Abercrombie, 1965, p. 4; Local & Kelly, 1986; Shriberg, 1994). Chiefly, the question arises as to what extent laboratory artifacts are truly representative of the participant's productions outside the lab. To what extent does the analysis of citation form productions provide useful information about the everyday production of words? Second, to what extent can we deem these lab productions true examples of language use? They are, at the very least, not prototypical, to borrow Levinson's (1983) terminology. An over reliance on individual words and sentences as divorced from interactional context also runs the risk of drawing attention away from the use of linguistic material for communication (e.g., variation in the release of word-final stop closure as related to turn-sequence location) and instead creating a lexicon-centric approach to linguistic analysis. Finally, it is likely that speech perception works rather differently when presented with single words as it does for connected speech (Stevens, 2002) with the detection of word boundaries being paramount in the perception of connected speech yet redundant in isolated word recognition.

An alternative to the controlled environment approach involves collecting data in as naturalistic a setting as possible, with the participant asked to do no more than they would do on a daily basis. This is the approach of Conversation Analysis (CA; see chapter 5, this volume) and more generally of interactional linguistics. Conversation analysts broke trend and collected data that was both conversational in nature, and that was frequently recorded outside of the lab and in natural settings. CA was able to use such an approach to do research for two major reasons. First, in CA, rather than eliciting tokens that the researcher has identified a priori as the subject of the research, conversation analysts seek to discover the order of conversation as it unfolds naturally (Heritage & Atkinson, 1984). Second, because CA only requires data of sufficient enough quality to make written transcriptions, not conduct detailed acoustic-phonetic analysis, it was possible to collect this data in the field. Psathas (1995, p. 9) notes that a "… tape recorder (and later the video recorder), which could be taken into the field or connected to a telephone, was capable of collecting numerous instances of interaction." He goes on to say that large amounts of data could be collected with "… minimal expenditure of funds, time, and other recourses." In short, CA's design meant the two motivations for controlled environment research identified above were non-applicable.

CA's transcriptions do involve some attempts to encode phonetic detail (Psathas, 1995, p. 12; Psathas & Anderson, 1990). Durational effects, for example, are shown with colons (as in so:::::), emphasis with an underscore, pauses by seconds in brackets and intonation with a system of symbols corresponding to a rise, fall and continuation. However, both the method with which such acoustic detail is transcribed and elicited, and the quality of the recordings from which such detail is taken would be considered wholly inadequate compared to the standards of laboratory based acoustic research. In order to conduct detailed, reliable phonetic (especially acoustic) analysis of naturally occurring data, then, a more sophisticated arsenal of data collection techniques are required. With the huge technological advances in field recording equipment and digital signal processing methods, this has been tested and proved possible (Campbell, 2002). As a result we have seen the incorporation of acoustic analysis[2] and detailed phonetic transcription into the naturalistic approaches of CA. Such a merger has given rise to interactional phonetics, discussed in detail below.

Interactional Phonetics

In a series of publications by Local and colleagues (French & Local, 1983; Local & Kelly, 1986; Local, Kelly, & Wells, 1986) the idea that phonetic variation might best be understood when studied in the context of natural, spontaneous conversation was gradually introduced. The researchers involved argued that so called talk-in-interaction should be the true venue in which to study phonetic variability and to formalize theories of phonological representation. They opposed, explicitly, the controlled environment approach to linguistic/phonetic research outlined above.

Equally, they advocated the incorporation of detailed phonetic analysis into the analysis of conversation, a move considered by Gumperz (1996, p. 12) to be "… a major and in many respects controversial move, which raises fundamental questions of theory and method."

Because interactional phonetics[3] is carried out using the formal techniques of CA, much research in the area links phonetic events to observable social actions. Terms like "repair," "assessment," and "compliments" are used in interactional phonetics, as in CA, as technical terms to refer to "observable details of the talk" (Curl, Local, & Walker, 2006). This is a departure from traditional phonetic analysis, which usually seeks the phonetic correlates of phonological contrasts; of those elements of the speech signal that seem to correspond to distinctions between lexical items. The phonetics of language in use, however, must by necessity be "... set in relation to empirically discoverable tasks which participants can be shown to be addressing" (Ford & Couper-Kuhlen, 2004, p. 12). In essence, these two endeavors are not completely divorced from one another. They are both concerned with contrast and both seek acoustic exponents of meaningful information in the speech signal. For interactional linguists, though, what is meaningful reaches far beyond lexical meaning and what may be contrasted are not just words, but different types of task; different types of questions formation, for example, or the question/statement distinction. Therefore we find work detailing the systematic phonetic variation associated with, amongst other things, the projection of an upcoming turn completion point (Wells & MacFarlane, 1998), repair initiation (Selting, 1996), repair execution (Curl, 2004), interactive (i.e., collaborative) repair (Couper-Kuhlen, 1992), and the displaying of continuation at a potential turn-transition point (Local, 1992).

The Phonetics of Social Action

There has been a great deal of concentration in interactional phonetics around long-domain phonetic events such as pitch, tempo, loudness, duration, and even voice quality (see Ogden, 2001). These are challenging theoretically for a number of reasons. Traditionally, such phonetic features have been dealt with as pertaining to 'paralinguistic' meaning only (Laver, 1994) and have not generally been incorporated in to phonology proper. If they are dealt with as being phonological, it is on a different plane to segmental phonology, often termed "intonational phonology" (Ladd, 1996). However, when intonation is studied in the context of natural conversation, not read speech, such long domain phonetic features are shown to contribute greatly to meaning, both linguistic and paralinguistic. This was argued by Abercrombie (1965, p. 6) when he observed that intonation contributes very little to "read prose" but in conversation it "... contributes more independently to the meaning." More recently French and Local (1983) considered the covariation of both high pitch and increased loudness to achieve certain conversational acts, and Curl (2004) looks at loudness, duration, and pitch in combination with articulatory settings in the context of repetitions.

Interactional phoneticians (e.g., Local, 2004) have also been keen to emphasize that what have been traditionally dealt with as segment sized phonetic events must also be considered in the context of conversation and highlighted the role of sub-phonemic detail in shaping conversation and in serving interactional function. Sub-phonemic detail is often treated as noise in the signal, as being in free variation. However, Local (2003, p. 325) uses the case of the degree of glottal closure found in word final plosives and argues that there is "lawful" variation found amongst the plosives, determined by whether they appear utterance finally or not. Such a suggestion raises interesting questions for the treatment of sub-phonemic detail. If speakers are controlling it, as suggested by Pierrehumbert (2002, p. 102), and indeed using it productively to convey "meaning," then the question arises as to what extent this sub-phonemic, or allophonic, detail is actually extra-phonological.

In sum, interactional phoneticians argue that phonetic features that mark particular social actions are seemingly systematic and must thus form some part of both speaker and listener's linguistic knowledge. The term "fine phonetic detail" is widely used to refer to these phonetic features that are "… systematically distributed but not systematically treated in conventional approaches" (Hawkins & Local, 2007). "Conventional approaches," here, refers to mainstream phonology where the distinction between phonetics and phonology is based largely on lexical contrast, with grammatical, indexical, and conversational meaning ignored.

Some Implications for Linguistic Theory

The study of conversational speech has generated an abundance of implications for the way in which the domain of phonology should be conceptualized. Some of these are discussed in Local (2003), Hawkins (2003), and Couper-Kuhlen (2007). In this section we will focus on one particular topic, the phonetics/phonology interface. Of particular interest is the amount of phonetic variability deemed to be phonological.

The Phonetics/Phonology Interface

Few topics in linguistics cause such deliberation as when the boundary between two distinct sub-fields of the discipline is disputed. As well as helping shape the architecture of linguistic theory, such disputes can often have serious implications for the way in which more applied areas of linguistics are carried out, with clinical linguistics being a prime example.[4] In recent years studies in interactional phonetics, and of spontaneous conversational speech in general,[5] have been particularly important in highlighting the need for some serious inspection of the location of the boundary between phonetics and phonology. Researchers in interactional phonetics, and in phonetics in phonology = discrete, categorical

≠

phonetics = continuous, gradient

Figure 19.1 A schema of the phonetics/phonology distinction adapted from Cohn (2006, p. 26).

general, have been both implicit and explicit in their suggestion that phonology may be lacking in phonetics detail.

The traditional view of the phonetics/phonology interface is that of the generative approach to phonology (Scobbie, 2007). Here phonology recognizes abstract categories which comprise phonetically distinct but functionally equivalent places along a phonetic continuum. Phonetics is the study of these categories as they are actually realized in speech. Cohn (2006, p. 25) sketches this in Figure 19.1.

Studying the phonology of a language, then, is the business of studying abstract categorical units that can be shown to serve some (lexical) function, while phoneticians are concerned with the continuous and the gradient. Research into conversational speech has provided a number of findings, however, that are difficult to incorporate into such a modular system. Among the most important are the following observations

1. A single lexical item has numerous phonetic realizations associated with it, many varying considerably from its citation form pronunciation (Johnson, 2004).
2. Much of the variation noted in item 1 is used productively to achieve multiple functions in conversation, many simultaneously (Local, 2003). It is not noise.

Both of these points rely upon the rather simple observation that words vary in their phonetic realization. If a single speaker produces several repetitions of the same word, there will be some variability. If multiple speakers from the same speech community produce the same word, there will likely be even more variability. More importantly, however, as the word is used in different grammatical, interactional and social contexts, it will vary as a function of the context it appears in. Variation of this kind is studied under the term fine phonetic detail.[6]

Fine Phonetic Detail

Traditionally, it has been understood and assumed in phonology that meaning simply refers to lexical meaning; if some aspect of the speech stream contributes to contrasting one lexical item from another, it should be regarded as being phonological. Phonetic information that does not do this, the nasality in vowels in English, for example, or more gradient properties of speech such as pitch, are not considered to fall inside the domain of phonology proper, much less be encoded in phonological representations. Such arguments that phonological representations should be stripped of a certain amount of phonetic information (e.g., Keating, 1984, p. 289) are centered around the notion that only those contrastive details should be stored, so as to maintain phonological representations that include all possible linguistic contrasts but not all possible phonetic contrasts. Local (2003, p. 322), however, argues that meaning "… is much more than lexical meaning" and that systematic fine phonetic detail should not be dismissed a priori as noise in the signal.

An increasing amount of research seems to support Local's (2003) claim that fine phonetic detail is indeed perceived and stored by listeners. Findings reported by, amongst many others, Goldinger (1996, 1998), Pisoni (1997), West (1997), and Coleman (2002) are all suggestive of the fact that speech perception involves the detection and recollection of a vast amount of the phonetic detail. This points to the fact that listeners are sensitive to a great amount of the variability that is observable in the speech stream. Traditional abstractionist approaches to the problem of noise in the speech signal have posited a system by which this detail is filtered out and speaker normalization occurs (cf. Pisoni, 1997). However, Goldinger (1996), for example, demonstrates that the voice characteristics of a speaker are retained in memory by a listener for at least a week, and prior familiarity with a voice actually aids in word recognition tasks when compared to an unfamiliar voice. Goldinger concludes that "speech is not a noisy vehicle of linguistic content; the medium may be an integral dimension of later representation" (1996, p. 1180).

Such findings are often interpreted as meaning that listeners attend to unimportant (or non-linguistic) variation in the speech stream. That is, both linguistic and non-linguistic information is seemingly perceived and stored by listeners. Local (2003, p. 323), however, stresses that "fine phonetic detail simultaneously provides interactional, grammatical and lexical information." Thus Hawkins and Local (2007) insist that if the definition of the possible roles phonetic detail could potentially play is broadened, then much of this variability may not be unimportant, but rather may just have been ignored by approaches that have previously focused entirely on lexical contrasts. Then "… the term fine phonetic detail can be replaced, once more, by phonetic information" (p. 181).

Exemplar Theory

If knowledge of fine phonetic detail forms part of a speaker's knowledge of a language, it must be modeled appropriately. Although not talking about fine phonetic detail by name, this point is made forcibly by Bod, Hay, and

Jannedy (2003): "Within individuals, production patterns differ on the basis of stylistic factors such as addressee, context, and topic, and the stylistic variation to a large degree echoes the variation present across members of society. Knowledge of variation, then, must form part of linguistic competence, since individuals can manipulate their implementation of phonetic variants to portray linguistic and extralinguistic information" (pp. 2–3). One possible way to handle fine phonetic detail is using the development of Exemplar Theory and multiple trace, probabilistic phonology (Johnson, 1997; Pierrehumbert, 2003; Scobbie, 2007). This is based on the notion of episodic memory and the idea that language learning is intertwined with experience. As exposure to language increases, so too does the build up of stored recollections of linguistic material. It is from here that grammatical knowledge emerges. This basic architecture of the theory is summarized particularly well by Scobbie (2007): "Multiple detailed exemplars or traces of every lexeme are stored: but in storing such an enormous number of only subtly different tokens of real world productions, abstraction, and coalescence occur by necessity. This happens automatically by virtue of encountering 'different' tokens of the 'same' word. Memories are contextualized to the situation of use, so sound patterns are associated or labeled with a contextual meaning" (p. 42).

Using such a model, phonetic detail can be used and retained by listeners during the course of spoken interaction. Abstraction occurs, thus satisfying the fact that language is combinational, but only after distributional patterns emerge. Using such a system, fine phonetic detail can be used and maintained by listeners because lexically non-contrastive phonetic information is not stripped away at the point of perception (as implied by theories of categorical perception). The advantages of such an approach to phonology are numerous. In particular, phonology would be system of concrete forms, each related to individual speakers, social contexts, and interactional functions. This is summarized unequivocally by Coleman (2003): "I like to think of such representations as simply memories of heard or spoken words; memories which, like others, are not encoded in some abstract system of symbols or graphs, but are at root episodic and in their form closely related to the different modalities of sensory and motor experience" (p. 99).

Interactional Phonetics in the Speech Clinic

The use of interactional phonetics for the purposes of analyzing disordered speech has rarely been exploited. One area of research that has emerged is the study of echolalia from an interactional phonetic perspective. Often found in children with autism and aphasic adults, echolalia is the repetition of an utterance previously used by another speaker. Papers by Local and Wootton (1995) and Tarplee and Barrow (1999) both consider the potential for assigning interactional function to echoing in an autistic child. While neither paper takes discovering the phonetic characteristics of echolalia as its primary aim, both augment the CA presented with impressionistic and, in the case of the first paper, acoustic phonetic analysis. Both use phonetic detail to add weight to the arguments put forward; essentially that echolalia can serve some form of interactive function.

In the area of dysarthria, for example, interactional phonetics could represent a potentially major change from the assessment of the severity and type of the condition using the elicitation of sounds, words and sentences or the use of non-speech, oromotor tasks (see Ballard, Robin, & Folkins, 2003). Non-speech, oromotor tasks in particular represent the complete decontextualization of speech-like sounds (typically syllables) from any linguistic or social context. Their use is motivated by the assumptions that (a) the composite movements (or gestures) of speech can be studied in isolation of each other and in isolation of phonation (the subsystems assumptions), and that (b) speech behavior can be studied outside the context of some linguistic task. While they are popular as an assessment tool in speech-language therapy, they have also been heavily criticized (see Weismer, 2006, for a review). When considering the alternatives to the study of oromotor tasks in dysarthria study, Weismer (2006) claims: "Because it is difficult to assemble large groups of subjects with dysarthria, consortiums should be formed, equipment and measurement approaches standardised (within reason), and data pooled to learn about speech in these patients. An empirically grounded theory of speech production phenomena in motor speech disorders should lead to the right hypothesis concerning underlying mechanisms. Moreover, it would be the first step to identifying the variables, such as rate and loudness manipulation, that change speech motions in such a way as to improve or depress speech intelligibility" (p. 343).

The theoretical underpinnings of interactional phonetics are far removed from those that motivate the analysis of non-speech oromotor tasks, and studying speech production in the context of natural conversation provides an opportune departure for studies in motor speech disorders. It would offer a method for assessing the impact of a speech deficit in conversation, rather than simply labeling repeated words as erroneous due to some omission, distortion, substitution, or addition. The study of fine phonetic detail in dysarthria could also illuminate the impact of speech disorders on communicative functions, not just on the ability to contrast minimal pairs.

There exists already a pool of data regarding the acoustic properties of speech produced by normal speakers during specific conversational tasks, and a similar data set could be developed for a variety of speech disorders. In interactional phonetics speech is studied in context, and in concert with the full repertoire of the linguistic system. If speakers with speech disorders are studied as they try to achieve social action, then the effects of intelligibility problems on the functional aspect of language can be sought. In the following sections, we look at fine phonetic details in the spoken interaction of an adult with dysarthria and a child with speech sound disorder.

Repair in Dysarthric Speech[7]

Repair in conversation (an organized set of principles used to overcome problems with individual conversation involving speaking or hearing) comes with a range of phonetic cues which have not often been described in the main CA literature until recently. The examples included in this section come from an investigation by the first author into the interactional phonetics of speakers with dysarthria (see Rutter 2008). The first extract is an example of "other initiated repair," and the second is of "self-initiated repair."

The first fragment to be discussed, from a conversation between Teddy and the researcher, R, is complex, both in terms of its sequential organization and its phonetic design. The fragment is *ground meat* and the conversation is about Teddy's history of working with meat.

ground meat_6 192.48 to 204.49
```
1    T:     when I was working at Maxi Pierce's (←h(.))
2→          {he had} ground m- when I worked at Maxi=
3    R:     {where?}
4→   T:     =Pierce's in the store? (0.8) he would get
5           ((1 syll))orders and we had to fulfill them (.)
6           so I'd make ground meat
```

In terms of its organization, this repair is complex for a number of reasons. First, the repair initiated by R ("where?") overlaps Teddy's ongoing talk at a point subsequent to the trouble source. Teddy has to halt his ongoing talk to deal with the repair request. He does so using a cut-off during "ground meat." Second, it is impossible to tell whether R initiates repair due to some intelligibility problem with the structure "Maxi Pierce's" or because he lacks some background knowledge about the individual Maxi Pierce and where Teddy used to work. It is clear, however, that "Maxi Pierce's" is the trouble source, as opposed to anything else on 1, because R uses a category-specific repair initiator (Schegloff, 2007, p. 101). Teddy seems to interpret the repair request as being due to a lack of background knowledge, because he executes his repair not by simply reproducing "Maxi Pearce" (perhaps with some phonetic modifications) but rather by using expansion, or addition (see Most, 2002). That is, he provides more contextual information the second time around. Additionally, phonetically the repair request is interesting; it is executed with the acoustic hallmarks of a question, and it drops in intensity relative to the prior talk. The interrogative nature of the utterance is conveyed primarily by an

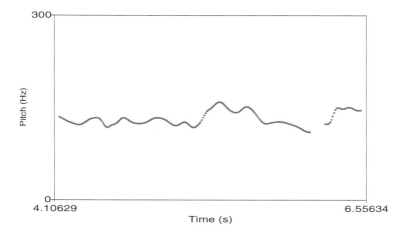

Figure 19.2 f0 plot of Teddy's utterance "when I worked at Maxi Pierce's in the store?"

upwards shift in f0 at the end of the utterance, and major pitch peaks on the first and second syllables of the word "Pierce's." Figure 19.2 shows the f0 contour, and Figure 19.3 shows a nonlinear curve fit over the numeric values of the contour.

Measurements of the mean intensity (dB) before and after the repair reveal that it is lower than the surrounding talk. The repair turn has an average

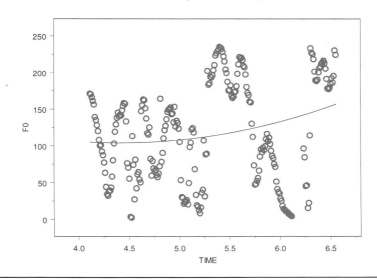

Figure 19.3 A Nonlinear curve fit for "when I worked at Maxi Pierce's in the store." Circles represent the values for f0 at specific time points. Note the terminal rise that is typically associated with question turns in English.

intensity of 70.76 dB. The mean intensity of the talk immediately prior to the interruption point is 75.67, and the talk immediately following it is 74.61.

The repair in "ground meat," then, is phonetically distinct to others described in Rutter (2008). This is seemingly because Teddy does not interpret the cause of the trouble source as being related to intelligibility but rather being due to a lack of shared speaker-hearer knowledge. This suggests a relationship between the cause of the repair request and the phonetic design of the repair itself. Specifically, a loudness increase, something often associated with repaired speech, is associated primarily with intelligibility repairs.

The majority of the self-repairs discussed in Rutter (2008) involve modifications of the phonetic structure of some trouble source because it has been shown to be, or could potentially be, unintelligible. In this fragment, repair is carried out in a way that is very sensitive to the interactional environment in which the trouble source occurs. The example comes from a conversation between Teddy and the researcher about the U.S. economy, and the politics of Louisiana in particular. Teddy is stating an opinion about taxation in Louisiana.

crooks_9 28 to 63

```
1   T:    yeah round here they they crooks they don't
2         wan- they're so greedy they don't want to help
3         nobody (←h(.)) that's why you gotta pay so high
4         (.) 'cause all them rich people they try
5→        to do their best not t-   ↑not to pay tax
```

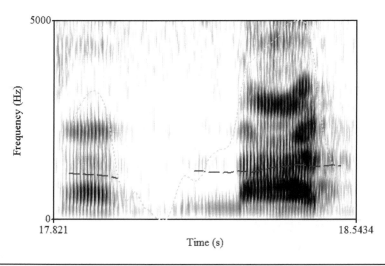

Figure 19.4 Spectrogram showing the first and second forms of the word "not." Note the difference in duration, intensity (marked with a doted line) and the differences in direction of the pitch contours (marked with a dashed line).

The repair of interest comes on line 5 when Teddy produces a cut-off in the word "to" and goes back to repair the word "not." The repair involves modifying the phonetic parameters responsible for stress assignment; specifically, loudness, pitch, and duration. Figure 19.4 is spectrogram showing the first and second versions of "not" side by side, and Table 19.1 summarizes the measurements of the two sayings.

Taken together, these phonetic changes give the second saying of "not" the linguistic function of contrastive stress, bringing about contextually appropriate focus.

Affective Signalling in a Child with a Speech Sound Disorder

M, a 5-year old male, presented with multiple articulation problems and prosodic anomalies, with productions ranging from near-typical to fully unintelligible. Able to correctly produce most problem sounds, he scored only in the 'mild' range on a single-word articulation assessment (Goldman & Fristoe, 2000). A qualitative study (Kroll & Müller, 2011) that used methodologies from CA, Systemic-Functional Linguistics, and Grounded Theory revealed that variations in M's productions were intertwined with interactional context, and that they could be read as indicators of affective changes. The discussion here will focus on previously unpublished examples of phonetic and prosodic variation that functioned as signals of negative affect.

The first pattern to emerge in the prior study was that M's productions deteriorated during word drills, being accurate first and subsequently becoming distorted. The following fragment shows this phenomenon for the session dated 7/16, minutes 00:24–00:40 of the audio recording. The target sound is [s]. (C = clinician; /slash brackets\ indicate overlap.)

1   *C*   alright let's see what words we have today (.) what about these (.) Huskie
2   *M*   Huskie
3   *C*   that was a great Huskie. Ice-skate.
4   *M*   [ˈaɪçˌkeːt]
5   *C*   good ice-skate. Mosquito.
           /(clatter of game chip)\
6   *M*   \[ˌmʌç{V! ˈkɪːdʌo V!}]/

Table 19.1 Comparison of Acoustic Measures for the First and Second Saying of 'Not' from the Fragment 'Crooks'.

Measure	Trouble Source	Repair Attempt
Duration (secs.)	0.14	0.33
Mean intensity (Hz)	69.14	76.85
f0 mean (Hz)	113.57	127.21

M produces an accurate target in his first response, palatalises it in the second one, and in the third adds a harsh voice quality on the second and third syllables of the target word while clattering with a chip of the game that served as incentive activity.

The next fragment stems from the same word drill, minutes 1:40–1:53 of the recording. It shows inaccurate target sounds paired with phonetic alterations.

1   C   alright. Let's go for some more words=
2   M   =[h↓ hî̞ː]
3   C   bus stop
4   M   [ˈbʌç̥ˌtap̬ˈ]
5   C   fiesta
6   M   [fiˈɛçˈ(.)ta̋]
7   C   footstep
8   M   [ˈfʊçˈˌtɛpˈ]

In turns 4 and 8, M produces the word-final plosives as ejectives; in turn 4, the preceding vowel is rendered voicelessly. In turn 6, he inserts a brief pause after the first syllable of the word and produces the second syllable with rising intonation.

The analysis of this data raises some methodological issues. Interactional phonetics, with its CA origin, assumes that phonetic and prosodic detail is relevant to the on-going interaction. However, the nature of its relevance can only be determined through participant actions (Damico, Oelschlaeger, & Simmons-Mackie, 1999; Goodwin & Heritage, 1990). None of the clinician's actions in the fragments above suggest that he treats M's productions as meaningful. How, then, can they be relevant?

The answer is twofold. First, CA studies have found that sequential organization differs between contexts; the collaborative nature of conversation may be suspended (e.g., in formats restricted to question-answer sequences; Goodwin & Heritage, 1990). It can be argued that the same applies to word drills, where sequences are restricted to model and repetition. This would explain the lack of local responses to M's actions. Second, the audio data for the session in question reveals a considerable amount of negative affect on M's part. Three minutes further into the drill, he refused to participate; the remainder of the session is laced with avoidance of target words, more refusal, and requests for the session to be terminated. Together, these observations provide a basis for analysis. Note that in the fragments above, M uses two signals conventionally associated with negative affect: The harsh voice quality in fragment 1, turn 6 and the "sigh" (audible in-outbreath) in fragment 2, turn 2. The inference that they are, in fact, meant to convey negative affect, is consistent with M's behaviour later in the session.

Are M's phonetic alterations relevant signals as well? If so, other reasons for their occurrence would need to be excluded. Specifically, the palatalization might be due to lack of focus on his output. This seems unlikely, however, since changes in voice quality and the production of ejectives require articulatory effort (the devoicing may be a result of gestural configuration). They are therefore clearly intentional. Likewise, M's hesitation and "questioning" intonation on the uncommon word *fiesta* indicate that he is attending to what he saying. In sum, his alterations do not appear to be unintentional. Note also that since the goal of the interaction is articulatory accuracy, they effectively defeat its purpose. Together with the conventional signals of negative affect, and in line with his subsequent behaviour, they can thus be understood as expressions of resistance towards the exercise. The case history indicates that the clinician adopted this reading and discontinued the use of word drills.

Conclusion

The methodology adopted in the study of normal or disordered language has the potential to greatly shape the results obtained. In experimental studies, variables can be constrained so as to facilitate tests of statistical significance, and in studies of speech in context, the phonetic properties of spontaneous social action can be discovered. It is most likely in unison, however, that the best approach will be found, as observations made in the field are tested in the lab, and the validity of experimental results are checked in the field, to ensure that theories of language are not built upon laboratory artifacts.

Notes

1. Labov (1984) described his "sociolinguistic" interview technique, a method which was intended as a compromise between research driven approaches to data collection and the participant driven methods.
2. With the advent, and relatively low cost, of portable digital audio tape (DAT) recorders (Tatham & Morton, 1997), Mini Disc (MD) recorders (especially the recent Hi-MD devices; Campbell & Mokhtari, 2002), and, more recently, solid state portable compact flash based recorders, it is now possible to make recordings in the field suitable for acoustic-phonetic analysis.
3. Referred to also as conversational phonetics by Local (1996) and interactional phonology by Couper-Kuhlen (2007).
4. The distinction between a phonetic and phonological disorder, for example, has evolved from the notion that phonology is concerned with categories of sounds capable of contrasting lexical items, while phonetics is concerned with acoustic variability that cannot serve such a function.
5. See, for example, work on the Buckeye corpus (Pitt, Johnson, Hume, Kiesling, & Raymond, 2005) and some of the theoretical discussions arising from its study (e.g., Johnson, 2004) as well as the work of Kohler (2007) on speech communication.
6. See, for example, the "Sound 2 Sense" project described in Carlson and Hawkins (2007) and Hawkins and Local (2007).
7. These examples derive from Rutter (2008).

References

Abercrombie, D. (1965). *Studies in phonetics and linguistics*. London, England: Oxford University Press.

Ball, M. J., & Lowry, O. (2001). *Methods in clinical phonetics*. London, England: Whurr.

Ballard, K. J., Robin, D. A., & Folkins, J. W. (2003). An integrative model of speech motor control: A response to Ziegler. *Aphasiology, 17*(1), 37–48.

Bod, R., Hay, J., & Jannedy, S. (Eds.). (2003). *Probalistic linguistics*. Cambridge, MA: MIT Press.

Campbell, N., (2002, May). *Recording techniques for capturing natural everyday speech*. Paper presented at the Proceedings of the Language Resources and Evaluation Conference, Las Palmas, Spain.

Campbell, N., and Mokhtari, P., (2002). DAT vs. Minidisc: Is MD recording quality good enough for prosodic analysis? (Paper1-P-27). *Proceedings of the Acoustical Society of Japan, Spring Meeting*, 405–406.

Carlson, R., & Hawkins, S. (2007). When is fine phonetic detail a detail? In J. Trouvain & W. Barry (Eds.), *Proceedings of the 16th International Congress of the Phonetic Sciences* (pp. 211–214). Saarbrücken, Germany: ICPS.

Cohn, A. (2006). Is there gradient phonology? In G. Fanselow, C. Fery, R. Vogel, & M. Schlesewsky (Eds.), *Gradience in grammar: Generative perspectives* (pp. 25–44). Oxford, England: Oxford University Press.

Coleman, J. (2002). Phonetic representations in the mental lexicon. In J. Durand & B. Laks (Eds.), *Phonetics, phonology, and cognition* (pp. 96–130). Oxford, England: Oxford University Press.

Coleman, J. (2003). Commentary: Probability, detail and experience. In J. Local, R. Ogden, & R. A. M. Temple (Eds.), *Papers laboratory phonology 6*. Cambridge, England: Cambridge University Press.

Couper-Kuhlen, E. (1992). The prosody of interactive repair. In P. Auer & A. D. Luzio (Eds.), *The contextualization of language* (pp. 337–364). Amsterdam, The Netherlands: John Benjamins.

Couper-Kuhlen, E. (2007). Situated phonologies: patterns of phonology in discourse contexts. In M. C. Pennington (Ed.), *Phonology in context* (pp. 186–218). Basingstoke, England: Palgrave Macmillan.

Curl, T. (2004). 'Repetition' repairs: The relationship of phonetic structure and sequence organization. In E. Couper-Kuhlen & C. E. Ford (Eds.), *Sound patterns in interaction* (pp. 273–298). Amsterdam, The Netherlands: John Benjamins.

Curl, T., Local, J., & Walker, G. (2006). Repetition and the prosody-pragmatics interface. *Journal of Pragmatics, 30*, 1721–1751.

Damico, J. S., Oelschlaeger, M., & Simmons-Mackie, N. (1999). Qualitative methods in aphasia research: conversation analysis. *Aphasiology, 13*, 667–679.

Ford, C. E., & Couper-Kuhlen, E. (2004). Conversation and phonetics: Essential connections. In E. Couper-Kuhlen & C. E. Ford (Eds.), *Sound patterns in interaction: cross-linguistic studies of phonetics and prosody for conversation* (pp. 377–400). Amsterdam, The Netherlands: John Benjamins.

French, P., & Local, J. (1983). Turn-competitive incomings. *Journal of Pragmatics, 7*, 701–715.

Goldinger, S. D. (1996). Words and voices: Episodic traces in spoken word identification and recognition memory. *Journal of Experimental Psychology: Learning, Memory and Cognition, 22*, 1166–1183.

Goldinger, S. D. (1998). Echoes of echoes? An episodic theory of lexical access. *Psychological Review, 105*, 251–279.

Goldman, R., & Fristoe, M. (2000). *Goldman-Fristoe test of articulation — Second edition (GRTA2)*. Circle Pines, MN: American Guidance Service.

Goodwin, C., & Heritage, J. (1990). Conversation analysis. *Annual Review of Anthropology, 19,* 283–307.

Gumperz, J. J. (1996). Foreword. In E. Couper-Kuhlen & M. Setting (Eds.), *Prosody and conversation* (pp. 10–12). Cambridge, England: Cambridge University Press.

Hawkins, S. (2003). Roles & representations of systematic fine phonetic detail in speech understanding. *Journal of Phonetics, 31,* 373–405.

Hawkins, S., & Local, J. (2007). Sound to sense: An introduction. In J. Trouvain & W. Barry (Eds.), *Proceedings of the 16th International Congress of the Phonetic Sciences* (pp. 181–184). Saarbrücken, Germany: ICPS.

Heritage, J., & Atkinson, J. M. (Eds.). (1984). *Structures of social action: studies in conversation analysis.* Cambridge, England: Cambridge University Press.

Johnson, K. (1997). Speech perception without speaker normalization: An exemplar model. In K. Johnson & J. W. Mullennix (Eds.), *Talker variability in speech processing* (pp. 145–165). San Diego, CA: Academic Press.

Johnson, K. (2004). Massive reduction in conversational American English. In K. Yoneyama & K. Maekawa (Eds.), *Spontaneous speech: Data and analysis. Proceedings of the 1st Session of the 10th International Symposium* (pp. 29–54). Tokyo, Japan: The National International Institute for Japanese Language.

Keating, P. (1984). Phonetic and phonological representations of stop consonant voicing. *Language 60,* 286–319.

Kent, R. D., Weismer, G, Kent, I. F., Vorperian, H. K., & Duffy, J. R. (1999). Acoustic studies of dysarthric speech: Methods, progress, and potential. *Journal of Communication Disorders, 32,* 141–186.

Kohler, K. J. (2007). Beyond laboratory phonology: The phonetics of speech communication. In M-J. Solé, P. S. Beddor, & M. Ohala (Eds.), *Experimental approaches to phonology* (pp. 41–53). Oxford, England: Oxford University Press.

Kroll, T. A., & Müller, N. (2011). The impact of contextual, conversational, and affective factors on a child's speech intelligibility. *Journal of Interactional Research in Communication Disorders, 2.2,* 293–319.

Labov, W. (1984). Research methods of the project on linguistic change and variation. In J. Baugh & J. Sherzer (Eds.), *Language in use: Readings in sociolinguistics* (pp. 28–53). Englewood Cliffs, NJ: Prentice Hall.

Ladd, R. D. (1996). *Intonational phonology.* Cambridge, England: Cambridge University Press

Laver, J. (1994). *Principles of phonetics.* Cambridge, England: Cambridge University Press.

Levinson, S. C. (1983). *Pragmatics.* Cambridge, England: Cambridge University Press.

Local, J. (1992). Continuing and restarting. In P. Auer & A. D. Luzio (Eds.), *The contextualization of language* (pp. 273–296). Amsterdam, The Netherlands: John Benjamins.

Local, J. (1996). Conversational phonetics: some aspects of news receipts in everyday talk. In E. Couper-Kuhlen & M. Selting (Eds.), *Prosody in conversation* (pp. 177–230). Cambridge, England: Cambridge University Press.

Local, J. K. (2003). Variable domains and variable relevance: Interpreting phonetic exponents. *Journal of Phonetics, 31,* 321–339.

Local, J. (2004). Getting back to prior talk: and-uh(m) as a back-connecting device. In E. Couper-Kuhlen & C. E. Ford (Eds.), *Sound patterns in interaction: Cross-linguistic studies of phonetics and prosody for conversation* (pp. 377–400). Amsterdam, The Netherlands: John Benjamins.

Local, J., & Kelly, J. (1986). *Doing phonology.* Manchester, England: Manchester University Press.

Local, J. K., Kelly, J., & Wells, W. H. G. (1986). Towards a phonology of conversation: Turntaking in Tyneside English. *Journal of Linguistics, 22*(2), 411–437.

Local, J., & Wootton, T. (1995). Interactional and phonetic aspects of immediate echolalia in autism: a case study. *Clinical Linguistics & Phonetics, 9*(2), 155–194.

Most, T. (2002). The use of repair strategies by children with and without hearing impairment. *Language, Speech, and Hearing Services in Schools, 33,* 112–123.

Ogden, R. (2001). Turn transition, creak and glottal stop in Finnish talk-in-interaction. *Journal of the International Phonetics Association, 31,* 139–152.

Pierrehumbert, J. (2002). Word-specific phonetics. In C. Gussenhoven & N. Warner (Eds.), *Laboratory phonology 7* (pp. 101–139). Berlin, Germany: Mouton de Gruyter.

Pierrehumbert, J. (2003). Probabilistic theories of phonology. In R. Bod, J. B. Hay, & S. Jannedy (Eds.), *Probability theory in linguistics* (pp. 177–228). Cambridge, MA: MIT Press.

Pisoni, D. B. (1997). Some thoughts on 'normalization' in speech perception. In K. Johnson & J. Mullennix (Eds.), *Talker variability in speech processing* (pp. 9–32). San Diego, CA: Academic Press.

Pitt, M. A., Johnson, K., Hume, E., Kiesling, S., & Raymond W. (2005). The Buckeye corpus of conversational speech: Labelling conventions and a test of transcriber reliability. *Speech Communication, 45,* 89–95.

Psathas, G. (1995). *Conversation analysis: The study of talk-in-interaction.* Thousand Oaks, CA: Sage.

Psathas, G., & Anderson, T. (1990). The 'practices' of transcription in conversation analysis. *Semiotica, 78,* 75–99.

Rutter, B. (2008). Acoustic properties of repair sequences in dysarthric conversational speech : an interactional phonetic study (Unpublished doctoral dissertation). University of Louisiana at Lafayette.

Schegloff, E. A. (2007). *Sequence organization in interaction.* Cambridge, England: Cambridge University Press.

Scobbie, J. (2007). Interface and overlap in phonetics and phonology. In G. Ramchand & C. Reiss (Eds.), *The Oxford handbook of linguistic interfaces* (pp. 17–52). Oxford, England: Oxford University Press.

Selting, M. (1996). Prosody as an activity type distinctive cue in conversation: the case of so called 'astonished' questions in repair initiation. In E. Couper-Kuhlen & M. Selting (Eds.), *Prosody and conversation* (pp. 231–270). Cambridge, England: Cambridge University Press.

Shriberg, E. (1994). Preliminaries to a theory of speech disfluencies (Unpublished doctoral dissertation). University of California at Berkeley.

Stevens K. N. (2002). Toward a model for lexical access based on acoustic landmarks and distinctive features. *Journal of the Acoustical Society of America, 111*(4), 1872–1891.

Tarplee, C., & Barrow, E. (1999). Delayed echoing as an interactional resource: a case study of a three year old child on the autistic spectrum. *Clinical Linguistics and Phonetics, 13*(6), 449–482.

Tatham, M., & Morton, K. (1997). Recording and displaying speech. In M. J. Ball & C. Code (Eds.), *Instrumental clinical phonetics* (pp. 1–21). London, England: Whurr.

Tjaden, K., & Watling, E. (2003). Characteristics of diadochokinesis in multiple sclerosis and Parkinson disease. *Folia Phoniatrica Logopaedica, 55,* 241–259.

Weismer, G. (2006). Philosophy of research in motor speech disorders. *Clinical Linguistics and Phonetics, 20,* 315–349.

Wells, B., & MacFarlane, S. (1998). Prosody as an interactional resource: turn projection and overlap. *Language and Speech, 41*(3–4), 265–294.

West, P. (1997). Perception of distributed co-articulatory properties of English /l/ and /r/. *Journal of Phonetics, 27,* 405–426.

Yuan, Y. (2001). An inquiry into empirical pragmatics data-gathering methods: written DCTs, oral DCTs, field notes, and natural conversations. *Journal of Pragmatics,33*(2), 271–292.

III
Epilogue

20
Qualitative Research Revisited

JACQUELINE GUENDOUZI

Introduction

As the chapters in this book demonstrate, qualitative research has for some time now been a valuable addition to the field of communication disorders, yet, as a discipline, it is given less scientific status than quantitative or experimental research. Indeed, it is often difficult to obtain external funding for clinical research projects that propose qualitative methods. As Packer (2011) has pointed out, it is the randomized blind trial that has set the *gold standard* for health and medical research. Studies that use experimental paradigms are typically preferred in the more prestigious journals within the field of communication disorders, and given that obtaining external grants and publishing in highly ranked journals are requirements for faculty seeking tenure, it is not surprising that pursuing qualitative research may seem a less appealing career choice for new researchers.

As the extensive work of Damico (and colleagues) has shown, it is often the case that when writing articles reporting on qualitative studies the authors not only report their findings but are also forced to explain or make a case for the acceptability of using qualitative methods (e.g., Tetnowski & Damico, 2001). Although qualitative methods have been more readily accepted in other disciplines (e.g., anthropology, linguistics, sociology, etc.), they are still deemed more circumspect in the field of communication disorders. It appears that despite being widely used, qualitative methods represent an *idea* that has not yet acquired the scientific respect that empirical research carries. To understand why researchers have had to argue the case for using qualitative methods we need to consider what makes an idea both successful and transmittable.

Experimental Research: A Selfish Meme?

Ideas can be discussed in relation to the notion of a *meme*. A meme is a successful idea or element of culture (Blackmore, 1999; Dawkins, 1976) that is passed on by non-genetic means. Memetic theory suggests that the social transmission of ideas depends on whether or not they are easy to understand, remember, copy, and communicate to others. Kamhi (2004) drew on meme theory to suggest that certain terms and theories have dominated the field of communication disorders, further he suggests that some explanations of particular disorders have been passed on in meme-like fashion, so that they are now often viewed as having *a priori* status, that is, they are accepted as having an ontological reality. As Kamhi has pointed out, successful memes are not necessarily those ideas, theories or paradigms that are the most useful (or even accurate); rather, they are ideas that are easy to replicate and communicate. The dominance of experimental empirical research in the field of communication sciences and disorders represents the transmission of a successful meme. This is due, in part, to the fact that this type of empirical research answers specific hypotheses, presents results in terms of significance, and is easier to replicate. Empirical research in communication disorders draws on well-established paradigms used in the hard sciences and traditional medical research; thus it is associated with an already successful meme. In some respects, much like Dawkins' selfish gene (1976), the hypothesis-testing model has, within the scientific community, become a *selfish meme*.

The Hypothesis-Testing Model

Packer suggested that the "roots of the hypothesis testing model of science" (2011, p. 21) began with the ideas of the Vienna Circle, a group of scientists, mathematicians, and philosophers under the leadership of Morris Schlick (1882–1936), who met informally near the University of Vienna during the years of 1924 to 1936 to discuss science and philosophy. They used the term "logical positivism" to reflect their connection to the ideas of French philosopher Auguste Compte (1798–1857). The word "logical" signaled a focus on formal logic in the deductive process of scientific investigation. The Vienna Circle attempted to address a divide in both thinking and scientific enquiry by synthesizing the empirical approaches of John Locke (1632–1704) and David Hume (1711–1776), both of whom argued that *experience* was the basis of knowledge, and the Cartesian rationalists who based knowledge on the human ability to reason. For logical positivists, logic and mathematics provided the form, and observations the content of scientific enquiry.

The logical positivists of the 20th century and indeed, much of the general academic community had been shocked by the implications of Einstein's theories on established knowledge. Newtonian laws, a system that had seemed to provide an explanation that was complete, had been brought into question by Einstein's new physics. The logical positivists concluded that Newtonian physicists had included metaphysical assumptions rather than scientific assumptions in their work. In order to place science back on a solid path the Vienna Circle began to define principles of scientific enquiry that would avoid this type of problem arising again. Among these principles was the notion that only statements that could be empirically tested were valid questions of science. For example, we could investigate an *a priori* statement like *the sun is hot* by measuring its temperature but not a statement like *the sun feels good* because it is a *post priori* statement reflecting a subjective value judgment. This emphasis on measurement and observable phenomena is still the focus of research today, particularly within the world of communication disorders. Yet qualitative research often investigates *post priori* questions in order to explore what it means to experience a particular communication disorder, or to establish what is specifically breaking down in a particular individual's communicative ability. Thus, by its very nature, qualitative research, unlike empirical research, is by necessity more subjective and open to interpretation.

Indeed, some of the criticisms directed at qualitative research are that (a) its methods are too subjective, (b) its findings can't be measured, and (c) data is typically collected from individual case studies or small participant groups and can't be generalized to the larger population under scrutiny. Furthermore, qualitative research is often seen as less theoretically grounded than quantitative methods which have emerged from the traditions of hard science and empiricism (Packer, 2011). However, it is important to be aware that qualitative research does in fact have theoretical roots going back centuries and draws on work stemming from early Greek philosophy through to the modern disciplines of critical theory, pragmatics, linguistics, anthropology, and sociology.

The Roots of Qualitative Research

One of the reasons that qualitative research has found it difficult to establish a strong methodological base in communication disorders is because there is no academic tradition of studying the epistemological roots that underpin this method. Research, and to some extent teaching, in communication disorders has historically drawn on the medical model, an approach that is firmly rooted in empirical positivist methods. Anthropology and linguistics, on the other hand, have not only drawn on philosophy and critical theory, they also had a long tradition of carrying out ethnographic and observational research studies. Therefore it is not surprising that within these disciplines, qualitative research was more readily accepted. A second factor is that many of these disciplines had other resources to draw on; resources that helped to establish more descriptively acceptable methodologies. For example, discourse analysis (e.g., Schiffrin, Tannen, & Hamilton, 2001), a method that emerged from linguistic programs, had a rich tradition of descriptive linguistic devices (e.g., phonetic, semantic and syntactic tokens) available to describe data (furthermore, linguistic tokens, could actually be quantified). In addition grammatical approaches to language such as systemic-functional linguistics (Halliday, 1987) have attempted to explore the ideational aspect of communication through detailed analyses of the lexico-grammar. Discourse analysis also had a well-established body of research involving textual analysis that grew from both narrative studies (e.g., Labov & Fanshel, 1977; Labov & Waletzky, 1967) and the early hermeneutic schools of thought in the philosophy of language.

Qualitative research thus has drawn on a rich tradition of work stemming from a wide range of critical perspectives, for example, hermeneutics (e.g., Dilthey, 1964; Gadamer, 1960; Schleiermacher, 1810/1990), phenomenology (e.g., Heidegger, 1975; Merleau-Ponty, 1945/1962), linguistic semiotics (e.g., Levi-Strauss, 1958/1963; Peirce, 1958; Saussure, 1915), and the structural linguistics associated with the Russian formalist movement (1910–1928) and its successor the Prague circle (1928–1939). The ideas of both the Russian formalists and the Prague circle (Eagleton, 1992), which included the linguists Roman Jakobson (1896–1982), Nikolai Trubetsky (1890–1938), and the literary scholar Jan Mukarovsky (1891–1975), were highly influential in the work of later researchers such as Dell Hymes. Hymes commented that his essay *The Ethnography of Speaking* (1962) was an introduction of the ideas of the Prague circle to American linguistic anthropology.

Work by post-modernist critical theorists (e.g., Derrida, 1976; Foucault, 1966) has further added to the knowledge base of qualitative research. Derrida's (1976) notion that there is nothing beyond the text, no truly objective non-textual referent from which we can interpret a cognitive reality, is an idea that has influenced qualitative methods such as conversational analysis (e.g., Sacks, Schegloff, and Jefferson, 1974). Work in the philosophy of language changed the way meaning was interpreted (e.g., semantic holism cf. Quine, 1953; Wittgenstein, 1953), and gave rise to speech act theory (e.g., Austin, 1957; Searle, 1969) and Gricean pragmatics (Grice, 1975). Speech act theory and Gricean pragmatics have both been highly influential approaches in qualitative research that examines interactional data. Although their approaches may have been different, all of these philosophers and researchers have been concerned with the role of language in categorizing both individual and socially negotiated experience; they have explored how meaning is interpreted within the local context of the dialogue itself, and within the global context of social and cultural meanings.

Qualitative researchers have also drawn on anthropological traditions (e.g., Bateson, 1979; Malinowski, 1967; Mead, 1961) of embedded observation, in order to situate speech events (Hymes, 1972) within the socio-cultural context of the group under scrutiny (e.g., Geertz, 1973; Guendouzi & Müller, 2006). The ethnographic interview is often the starting point in a clinical diagnosis and therefore, it is important to understand that context (e.g., Duranti & Goodwin, 1992) and participant roles (Goffman, 1981) are dynamic elements that may affect an interaction. More recently, critical ethnographers have incorporated the ideas of sociologist Anthony Giddens (1984) and developed the notion of a critical ethnographic study (Heller, 2008, p. 253), a method that situates its analyses within the ideology of institutional discourses. In the field of communication disorders, the social construction of institutional ideologies and the terms we use to differentiate disorders are major issues. Similarly, critical linguistics (e.g., Fairclough, 1992; Fowler, 1990), discursive psychology (e.g., Edwards & Potter, 1992, 1995; Harré & Stearns, 1995; Potter & Wetherell, 1987), and positioning theory (e.g., Davies & Harré, 2007; Harré & van Langenhove, 1999) have provided methods to explore questions such as what it means to have dementia or to experience a fluency disorder (Guendouzi & Müller, 2006; Guendouzi & Williams, 2011; Sabat, 2001) and how these disorders are portrayed in the media and social milieu of institutional discourses. Indeed investigating how discourses of disorder function in the public domain is a very important aspect of qualitative research in this field.

A connecting thread that has emerged from the work of all these scholars is that they have grappled with questions, such as what it means to use language, what it means to be a language user, and what the role of language is in constructing our social world. That is, how do we, as subjective beings, make sense of our interactions with others and communicate shared meanings? The "hallmark of the linguistic revolution of the twentieth century ... is the recognition that meaning" is not something that is a simple reflection or expression of language, but rather, "it is actually produced by it" (Eagleton, 1992, p. 60). The belief that it was possible to have an objective science of subjectivity started in the 19th century with the writings of William Dilthey (1833–1911). Dilthey drew on the work of Schleiermacher (1768–1834) in an attempt to define the human sciences in a way that was distinct from the natural sciences. He referred to this science as *Geisteswissenschften,* or science of the mind. It contained two central ideas that remain in the standard practice of qualitative research today, namely (a) the reconstruction of subjectivity (subject positions) underlying or expressed in a text (verbal or written), and (b) the recovery of this subjectivity in an objective manner. Dilthey's program was not ultimately a success (Packer, 2011), but the ideas underpinning hermeneutics (or the art of interpretation) were further developed in the work of Hans-Georg Gadamer (1900–2002) and Martin Heidegger (1889–1976).

Heidegger (1975/1982) introduced the notion of the "hermeneutic circle" that operates between the act of understanding and the act of interpretation. Understanding is a "pre-reflective comprehension one has of a text or situation" whereas interpretation is the "working out ... of this understanding" (Packer, 2011, p. 87); it is how we articulate how we arrived at our understanding. The hermeneutic circle is a dynamic relationship between a person (researcher) and the world (the interaction under scrutiny) and not unlike the cyclical approach of some current qualitative research. However, in the "process of articulating ... understanding, inconsistencies and confusion become evident" (Packer, 2011, p. 87), therefore interpretation has to be modified throughout the cyclical layers of analysis.

It is this process of hermeneutic interpretation, that is, the continual modifying of both the questions asked, and the conclusions drawn as the researcher goes through a cyclical process of analysis and re-analysis, that is one of the strengths of qualitative research. However, it is also an aspect of this research paradigm that has led to many of the criticisms leveled against qualitative research, thus before discussing the value of qualitative research and the hermeneutic process it is first necessary to consider its potential limitations.

Limitations and Constraints of Qualitative Methods

Qualitative research has had a somewhat checkered history in the field of communication disorders. In some areas, for example in the study of aphasia, qualitative approaches have made considerable progress and produced well-grounded research (e.g., Damico & Simmons-Mackie, 2003; Damico, Simmons-Mackie, Oelschlaeger, Elman, & Armstrong, 1999). However, it is has also been the case that researchers have plunged into this emerging area of research without a thorough grounding in the disciplines (e.g., linguistics) and/or theoretical background (e.g., philosophy) that underpin the methods they are applying. This is particularly true in the case of studies claiming to draw on "phenomenology" and "grounded theory." Graduate students and new researchers often use these two terms as evidence to support the analyses used to identify particular themes drawn from conversations and research interviews. These themes are then presented as representing a cognitive reality in relation to a particular communication disorder. While thematic analyses can be useful in identifying issues that present challenges for individuals with communication impairments (e.g., Daniels & Gabel, 2004; Daniels, Hagstrom, & Gabel, 2006), they are also vulnerable to subjective unsubstantiated conclusions.

Some researchers cite grounded theory as justification for what are often mere paraphrased interpretations. Ironically, they misinterpret the notion of allowing meaning to be generated from the data and often draw conclusions that are biased by their own preconceived perceptions of an interaction. Grounded theory (Glaser & Strauss, 1967) has had a mixed history: its goals were admirable, to eliminate the analyst's subjective experience. However, as Packer has pointed out, grounded theory does at times "ignore the influence of the researcher" (2011, p. 8). Grounded theory suggests that through cycles of abstraction and generalization the analyst can find common elements or patterns. The analyst should break down the data into units, remove the unit from the context, identify general categories, abstract the content from the categories, and then describe the content in technical or formal terms (Packer,

2011). Indeed, this is, to some extent, the way all qualitative research goes about the business of interpreting data.

Grounded theory intended to move social science research away from the hypothesis-testing model and fill this gap by offering a systematic way of producing theory from empirical data. In other words, it reversed the traditional model of using data to prove a theory or answer a question; rather, in the case of grounded theory, the data would produce the theory. So research moved away from the deductive model to a more inductive method. The basis of grounded theory is the "explicit coding" (Packer, 2011, p. 61) of the data and the use of triangulation of sources. Herein lies the problem: explicit coding relies on the researcher breaking down the data into units (be they turn-constructional units, as in conversation analysis, or grammatical categories, such as modal verbs), and that requires the researcher to decide what those units represent. As Mischler pointed out,

> [t]he central problem for coding may be stated as follows[:] because meaning is contextually grounded, inherently and irremediably, coding depended on the competence of the coders as ordinary language users. (1986, p. 3)

Thus grounded theory relies on the ability of the coder to abstract recognizable units or frequently occurring patterns in a dataset, and then use these units to infer what is general and also attempt to interpret what these commonalities mean. As Wittgenstein (1953) noted, language is polymorphous and has exemplars of concepts that have family resemblances. A son may have his father's hair but his mother's mouth, and so forth. So, although concepts or exemplars of a theme (as abstracted by a researcher) may share features, they are also "a complicated network ... overlapping and crisscrossing" (Packer, 2011, p. 67). Coding data is not easy and relies on the researcher having a reasonable knowledge of both a range of qualitative methods and the philosophical and theoretical underpinnings of these methods.

It is the latter point above that results in qualitative research being vulnerable to what is paradoxically ungrounded theory, that is, the analysis is reduced to a mere paraphrasing of what the participants reported, or said, in an interaction. One of the contributing authors of this collection recently noted "students often choose qualitative research as the soft option" (Perkins, 2011, personal correspondence). Qualitative research may at first sight appear an easier option when faced with formulating a specific hypothesis, constructing a clean experimental condition, and running numerous statistical measures, but qualitative research requires as much rigor as quantitative research. It calls for considerable background reading, and the delineation of precise parameters and/or descriptions of the analytical units the researcher is abstracting from the dataset. It also requires a sound knowledge of the method chosen for analyzing the data (e.g., speech act theory, conversation analysis, narrative theory, or textual linguistic analysis, etc.). After this initial process, the researcher then needs to interpret the analytical units she or he has identified. This involves a hermeneutic process of drawing inferences from the description of a dynamic speech event.

It is at this stage of the process that the researcher needs to be both aware of, and sensitive to their own personal and academic biases. Interpretation of data is always carried out through the filter of the researcher's own perspective. As critical linguistic studies (Kress & Hodge, 1979) have shown, there is no such thing as neutral text or unbiased interpretation. This is not necessarily a negative aspect of qualitative methods, but researchers should be aware of potential other interpretations and be wary of generalizing explanations of small datasets. Furthermore, they need to be cautious of positing their interpretations as if they have an *a priori* status or ontological reality.

Physicist Leonard Mlodinow recently stated that just because there are gaps in science we can't fill them with any explanation (Chopra & Mlodinow, 2011). Mlodinow's comment is highly relevant to the case of qualitative research. If we collect data and don't find anything noteworthy or novel, what do we write up? Unlike quantitative researchers, we don't have the option of accepting a null hypothesis or redesigning our experiment. Collecting, transcribing, and analyzing data is a substantial investment of time and effort and the temptation for the inexperienced researcher might be to fill in the gaps with subjective opinions, or mere descriptive narratives of what occurred in an interaction. Qualitative research in the social and psychological sciences bridges a difficult divide between the hard sciences and openly subjective disciplines such as philosophy. In the latter field the aim is to understand subjectivity and explore issues of consciousness and meaning; in the former the aim is to understand the laws and principles of how the universe works. Newton did not need to worry about how the apple felt as it fell to the floor; he simply had to describe its (observable) motion, direction, and velocity to deduce how the force of gravity was at work. When we carry out qualitative analyses we cannot simply reiterate what an individual said or describe their behaviors in the way a physicist can; rather we have to suggest possible interpretations and outcomes for behaviors that are affected by (nonobservable) internal cognitive processes to which the researcher has no access. Furthermore, we have to make decisions about whether we view a behavior as volitional or a simply an artifact of the interactional event. How we interpret or label certain behaviors affects clinical decisions and diagnoses. For example, if, after transcribing an interaction involving a person with dementia, we decide their habitual use of fixed phrases (van Lancker-Sidtis, 2011) is a deliberate compensatory strategy we might suggest in our conclusion that this is a phenomenon that could be used clinically; yet this assumption is based on purely subjective speculation.

The use of fixed phrases might equally be the result of reduced cognitive resources and a reflexive product of a processing route that is more procedural in nature. As researchers we can only note that the person with dementia used a great deal of fixed phrases and suggest that one explanation (of two possible theories) might be that it is a volitional compensatory strategy reflecting a social need to participate in the interaction. In contrast, a physicist, based on previous observations, can conclude that if you drop an object of a certain size and weight from a specific height, it will fall to earth at a particular speed and be accurate in his predictions. Thus the problem for qualitative researchers is that conclusions have to be posited tentatively and are based on a process of induction rather than deduction.

As mentioned above, within the field of communication disorders, qualitative researchers have had to defend their choice of methods and rationalize their reasons for drawing specific conclusions. Therefore, it is not surprising that we may be less than comfortable pointing out the weaknesses inherent in qualitative research. Admission of limitations does not detract from the strengths of qualitative research; indeed it has much to offer the field of communication disorders. However, it needs to be acknowledged that the inductive nature of qualitative research has, in some cases, resulted in subjective or biased conclusions, and this in turn has resulted in criticism that qualitative methods are not as scientifically robust as hypothesis-driven experimental research. However, as the chapters in Part II of this volume demonstrate, the inductive process, when carried out rigorously, can make valuable contributions to the field of communication disorders.

Qualitative research represents a paradigm shift within the research world of communication disorders. As Kuhn has suggested, a change in paradigm is seen as "a transformation of the world in which science is done" (Packer, 2011, p. 32). Kuhn (1970) described these paradigm shifts in terms of practical and tacit knowledge that is shared by the research community. He proposed that a "tacit mode of knowing makes possible a way of seeing the world" (Packer, 2011, p. 33). Thus, for Kuhn, interpretation was reasoning that applied explicit rules or criteria, tacit knowledge that was not individual but was "the tested and shared possessions of the members of a successful group" (i.e., scientists) who "learn to see the same things ... by being shown examples" (Kuhn, 1970, p. 193). As Mlodinow (Chopra & Mlodinow, 2011) warned, this does not mean that researchers can posit any conclusions for their data as long as they agree that certain ways of perceiving the world are correct; indeed several centuries ago all scientists and thinkers agreed the earth was the center of the universe. Yet this is often the way that successful (but unsubstantiated) memes have been disseminated in communication disorders (Kamhi, 2004). Kuhn was not positing epistemological relativism but rather suggesting that "we learn how to see as we learn how to talk about what we see" (Packer, 2011, p. 35), and this idea can be applied to qualitative methods of analysis; as experienced researchers expose a wider audience of scientists to this paradigm they begin to learn how to do it, and ultimately, how to do it well.

The Strengths of Qualitative Research

One of the strengths of qualitative research is that it allows the analyst access to a wide range of analytical tools with which to examine their data. For example, methods such as conversation analysis and discourse analysis aid the researcher to identify analytical units such as sequential conversational turns, functional speech acts or narrative elements to examine how communication is negotiated over large stretches of discourse. Methods such as systemic functional linguistics can help show how specific lexico-grammatical choices help construct ideational and interpersonal meanings within interactions. Qualitative research may utilize smaller participant groups, or report on individual case studies, but this is appropriate for its goals—exploring and understanding the complexities of interactional communication. Case studies qualitatively describe the individuals who comprise the mean of quantitative studies, a collective numerical group with homogenized characteristics. Qualitative research helps us define and understand the individual embedded within both the label of a disorder, and the statistics of the hypothesis-testing model of research.

Future Directions of Qualitative Research

It will not escape the reader's notice that the section above, on the strengths of qualitative research, is considerably shorter in length than the section on its limitations. This is because qualitative research no longer needs to argue for its credibility; as a research paradigm it incorporates systematic and rigorous methods that provide a great deal of insight into communication disorders. To put it in colloquial terms qualitative research *is what it is*; the most appropriate way to examine the subjective and individual experience of what it means to be a person who has a communication disorder.

This book is dedicated to the work of Jack Damico who, for more than two decades, has persuasively argued for greater use of qualitative methods within the field of communication disorders. However, this text is more than just a collection of studies reflecting the methodological approaches Damico has used in his work. It is also a milestone in the history of qualitative research within the field of communication disorders. Qualitative research is like the elephant in the room that nobody noticed, it has always been there waiting to be acknowledged. The chapters in this book exemplify the significance of qualitative research in extending the knowledge base of this field; they represent rigorous analyses that are framed within methodological paradigms that incorporate the theoretical roots necessary to produce a *successful meme* in communication disorders.

References

Austin, J. L. (1957). *How to do things with words* (2nd ed.). Cambridge, MA: Harvard University Press.

Bateson, G. (1979). *Mind and nature: A necessary unity (advances in systems theory, complexity, and the human sciences.* New York, NY: Hampton Press.

Blackmore, S. (1999). *The meme machine.* Oxford, England: Oxford University Press.

Chopra, D. & Mlodinow, L. (2011). *War of worldviews: Science versus spirituality.* New York, NY: Harmony Books.

Damico, J. S., & Simmons-Mackie, N. (2003). Qualitative research and speech-language pathology. *American Journal of Speech Language Pathology, 12,* 131–143.

Damico, J. S., Simmons-Mackie, N.N., Oelschlaeger, M., Elman, R., & Armstrong, E. (1999). Qualitative methods in aphasia research: Basic issues. *Aphasiology, 13,* 651–666.

Daniels, D., & Gabel, R. (2004). The impact of stuttering on identity construction. *Topics in Language Disorders, 24*(5), 200–215.

Daniels, D., Hagstrom, F., & Gabel, R. (2006). A qualitative study of how African American men who stutter attribute meaning to life choices and identity. *Journal of Fluency Disorders, 31*(3), 200–215.

Davies, B., & Harré, R. (2007). Positioning: The discursive production of selves. *Journal for the Theory of the Social Behaviour, 20*(1), 43–63.

Dawkins R. (1976). *The selfish gene.* Oxford, England: Oxford University Press.

Derrida, J. (1976). *Of grammatology* (Gayatri Chakravorty Spivak, Trans.). Baltimore, MD: Johns Hopkins University Press.

Dilthey, W. (1964/1990). The rise of hermeneutics. In G. L. Ormiston & A. D. Schrift (Eds.), *The hermeneutic tradition from Ast to Ricoeur* (pp. 101–114). Albany: State of University of New York Press.

Duranti, A., & Goodwin, C. (1992). *Rethinking context: An introduction.* Cambridge, England: Cambridge University Press.

Eagleton, T. (1992). *Literary theory: An introduction.* Oxford, England: Blackwell.

Edwards, D., & Potter, J. (1992). *Discursive psychology.* London, England: Sage.

Edwards, D., & Potter, J. (1995). Attrition. In R. Harré & Stearns, P. (Eds.), *Discursive psychology in practice* (pp. 87–119). London, England: Sage.

Fairclough, N. (1992). *Discourse and social change.* Cambridge, England: Polity Press.

Foucault, M. (1966/1973). *The order of things: An archaeology of the human sciences.* New York, NY: Vintage Books.

Fowler, R. (1990). *Critical Linguistics.* Oxford, England: Oxford University Press.

Gadamer, H. G. (1960/1976). *Philosophical hermeneutics.* Berkeley: University of California Press.

Geertz, C. (1973). *The interpretation of cultures.* New York, NY: Harper & Row.

Giddens, A. (1984). *Positivism and sociology.* London, England: Heinemann.

Glaser, B. G., & Strauss, A. L. (1967). *The discovery of grounded theory: Strategies for qualitative research.* Chicago, IL: Aldine.

Goffman, E. (1981). *Forms of talk.* Philadelphia: University of Pennsylvania Press.

Grice, H. P. (1975). Logic and conversation. In D. Davison & G. Harman (Eds.), *The logic of grammar* (pp. 64–75). Encino, Ca: Dickenson.

Guendouzi, J., & Müller, N. (2006). *Approaches to discourse in dementia.* Mahwah, NJ: Erlbaum.

Guendouzi, J., & Williams, M. J. (2011). Discursive resources in clinical interviews with people who stutter. *Communication & Medicine, 7*(2), 119–129.

Halliday, M. A. K. (1987). *An introduction to systemic functional linguistics.* Seven Oaks, Kent, England: Edward Arnold.

Harré, R., & Stearns, P. (1995). *Discursive psychology in practice.* London, England: Sage.

Harré, R., & van Langenhove, L. (1999). *Positioning theory: Moral contexts of intentional action.* Oxford , England: Blackwell.

Heidegger, M. (1975/1982). *The basic problems of phenomenology* (A. Hofstadter, Trans.). Bloomington: Indiana University Press.

Heller, M. (2008). Doing ethnography. In L. Wei & M. G. Moyer (Eds.), *The Blackwell guide to research methods in bilingualism and multilingualism* (pp. 249–262). Oxford, England: Blackwell.

Hymes, D. H. (1962). The ethnography of speaking. In T. Gladwin & W. C. Sturtevant (Eds.), *Anthropology and human behavior* (pp. 13–53), Washington, DC: Anthropological Society of Washington.

Hymes, D. (1972). The use of anthropology: Critical, political, personal. In D. Hymes (Ed.), *Reinventing anthropology* (pp. 3–79). New York, NY: Pantheon Books.

Kamhi A. (2004). A meme's eye view of speech-language pathology. *Language, Speech and Hearing Services in Schools, 35*, 105–112.

Kress, G., & Hodge, R. (1979). *Language as ideology.* London, England: Routledge & Kegan Paul.

Kuhn, T. S. (1970). *The structure of scientific revolutions* (2nd ed.). Chicago, IL: University of Chicago Press.

Labov, W., & Fanshel, D. (1977). *Therapeutic discourse: Psychotherapy as conversation.* New York, NY: Academic Press.

Labov, W., & Waletzky, J. (1967). Narrative analysis. In J. Helm (Ed.), *Essays on the verbal and visual arts* (pp. 12–44). Seattle: University of Washington Press.

Levi-Strauss, C. (1958/1963). *Structural anthropology.* New York, NY: Basic Books.

Malinowski, B. (1967). *A diary in the strict sense of the term.* London, England: Routledge & Kegan Paul.

Mead, M. (1961). *Coming of age in Samoa.* New York, NY: William Morrow.

Merleau-Ponty, M. (1945/1962). *Phenomenology of perception.* London, England: Routledge & Kegan Paul.

Mischler, E. G. (1986). *Research interviewing: Context and narrative.* Cambridge, MA: Harvard University Press.

Packer, M. (2011). *The science of qualitative research.* Cambridge, England: Cambridge University Press.

Peirce, C. S. (1958). *The collected papers. Volumes 7 & 8* (A. Burks, Ed.). Cambridge MA: Harvard University Press.

Potter, J., & Wetherell, M. (1987). *Discourse and social psychology: Beyond attitudes to behaviour.* London, England: Sage.

Quine, W. V. (1953). *From a logical point of view.* Cambridge, MA: Harvard University Press.

Sabat, S. R. (2001). *The experience of Alzheimer's disease: Life through the tangled veil.* Oxford, England: Blackwell.

Sacks, H., Schegloff, E. A., & Jefferson, G. (1974). A simplest systematics for the organization of turn-taking in conversation. *Language, 50*, 696–735.

Saussure, F. de (1915/1959). *A course in general linguistics* (W. Baskins, Trans.). New York, NY: Philosophical Library.

Schleiermacher, F. D. E. (1810/1990). The aphorisms on hermeneutics from 1805 and 1809/10. In G. L. Ormiston & A. D. Schrift (Eds.), *The hermeneutic tradition from Ast to Ricoeur* (pp. 57–84). Albany: State of University of New York Press.

Schiffrin, D., Tannen, D., & Hamilton, H. E. (Eds.). (2001). *The handbook of discourse analysis* Oxford, England: Blackwell.

Searle, J. (1969). *Speech acts: an essay in the philosophy of language.* Cambridge , England: Cambridge University Press.

Tetnowski, J. A., & Damico, J. S. (2001). A demonstration of the advantages of qualitative methodologies in stuttering research. *Journal of Fluency Disorders, 26,* 17–42.

van Lancker-Sidtis, D. (2011). Formulaic language. In J. Guendouzi, F. Loncke, & M. J. Williams (Eds.), *The handbook of psycholinguistic & cognitive processes: Perspectives in communication disorders* (pp. 247–272). Hove, England: Psychology Press.

Wittgenstein, L. (1953). *Philosophical investigations* (G.E.M. Anscombe, Trans.). Oxford, England: Basil Blackwell.

21

Aiming for Explication
Reflections on the Qualitative Research Process

JACK S. DAMICO

The chapters contained in this book effectively accomplish the task of discussing the qualitative approach to research in the areas of human communicative sciences and disorders. Linking my work to a number of the authors of these chapters and the issues that they describe is a great honor for me. Whether I deserve the recognition and kindness afforded me in this handbook is a judgment best left to the reader. However, I can say with complete candor that I have been fortunate, over an approximately 35-year career, to have had contact with a number of the contributors here and have benefitted greatly from their knowledge and practice. Each of the authors in this text (and a number of others who are not included) has contributed to the progressive development and utilization of qualitative research in our discipline. It has not been an easy enterprise. As has been rightly discussed in a previous chapter, the "meme" for research in communicative sciences and disorders has been more quantitative-experimental than qualitative, and this has delayed the acceptance of the qualitative research process.

When the editors of this handbook informed me of its production and then asked me to contribute a piece at the end of the volume expressing a few thoughts that I might have about the qualitative research enterprise in our discipline, I was delighted to agree. My typical contributions to edited volumes are generally data-based studies or more theoretical pieces, but here I will present several reflections upon the process of conducting qualitative research in our discipline. Perhaps some of the experiences that I have had and the time I have spent trying to figure out our roles as theorists, researchers, and practitioners may be of interest.

Explication as the Goal of Qualitative Research

The starting point for any set of reflections should appropriately begin with a discussion of the primary goal of qualitative research in our discipline. Practically speaking, *why do qualitative research? What's in it for us?* Over the previous 30 years, those of us working to advance the qualitative enterprise in our field have had to address this issue for various reasons. First, we had to determine why we chose to employ such a different research paradigm when investigating human communication sciences and disorders—why we sought methods and procedures that were different from the experimental status quo. Second, once we determined for ourselves a rationale for our efforts, we had to defend ourselves from claims (about our research decisions) made by others in the discipline. For example, at various times, fellow professionals have suggested that I employ qualitative methods due to a lack of knowledge of experimental research design, in order to avoid having to use predictive statistical analyses, to avoid employing the rigor that experimental research demands, because I was more interested in clinical activism than genuine research, or because I was simply iconoclastic and obstinate. Without a solid rationale, one is placed in the position of defending against such unsubstantiated ad hominem challenges rather than stating one's reasons. Third, in a more formal way, we have had to develop a concise rationale for our qualitative efforts when preparing research grants, tenure documents, responses to institutional review boards, answering editorial reviews, and even when asked by interested students why we approach research differently.

While I cannot answer for the other qualitative researchers who operate within our discipline, I do know that my primary reason for turning to qualitative research approaches was because these approaches best met my needs—to understand how (and sometimes even why) social action is accomplished through communicative interactions in both ordered and disordered populations. As with many speech-language pathologists of my generation, I was trained within a behavioristic perspective that valued experimental research and encouraged the fragmentation of the complex social phenomena known as language and communication into convenient types of positive and negative behaviors governed by formulated laws of learning and the stimulus-response-reinforcement paradigm. Upon graduation with a master of science degree in communicative disorders and having spent the early portion of my career as a clinician in the public schools, I recognized that much that I read in the archival journals of our discipline was not really very relevant to my needs or to the needs of my clients in the actual social contexts within which I worked. Consequently, I was driven to find better ways to meet the demands of my clinical life and to re-establish my intellectual equilibrium. I eventually turned to the qualitative paradigm. As I reviewed my decontextualized clinical practices and read the experimental research in the literature, I recalled a few research studies that I had read that took a different route. In the late 1970s, while casting around for research findings that were more pertinent to my needs, I came across a chapter by Ray McDermott and Kenneth Gospodinoff (1979) dealing with how constant miscommunications and the identification of children from diversity backgrounds as disabled is actually an interactional accomplishment based upon collusion of all parties involved. This chapter and a few other publications (Abkarian, 1977; Bruner, 1975; Muma, 1975; Rees & Shulman, 1978) had a profound impact on me in terms of recognizing that language and communication were far more social and far more complex than we had been led to believe at that time in our profession, and I realized that more appropriate approaches to addressing this complexity were required. Consequently, I started reading in the social sciences (e.g., Denzin, 1978; Rabinow & Sullivan, 1979; Spradley, 1979, 1980; Stake, 1978) and in areas dealing with development from a more qualitative perspective (e.g., Bissex, 1980; Bruner, 1981; Halliday, 1978; Rogoff & Lave, 1984). I then employed this research to inform my appreciation of the complexity of social action and guide my efforts in addressing that complexity. My early article on the lack of efficacy in my own language therapy (Damico, 1988) was my first attempt in 1979–80 to employ more qualitative approaches (although published nearly 10 years later, a first version of this paper was finished in 1980 as a personal exercise and stored away).

Stated directly, I believe the primary reason for engaging in qualitative research is because it enables us to accomplish a special form of *explication*. That is, an attempt to try and work out the extent to which both unremarkable and remarkable descriptions of an individual's communication are based upon a set of social-intentional elements that systematically and predictably drive social action. This explication certainly involves construction of rich or detailed descriptions of what is occurring; however, even more is involved. Specifically, there is the additional facet of contextualizing communication within the social-cognitive fabric that defines our lives so that we can achieve a deeper understanding of the actions individuals produce and how these actions are accomplished. In a sense, this form of explication strives for interpretive sufficiency; we attempt to determine not only *what* is happening but *how* (and sometimes, even *why*) it is happening.

When reflecting on this form of explication, Gilbert Ryle's (1949) distinction between "thin" and "thick description" may be beneficial. This philosopher discussed the difference between formulating a behavioral description of an action as if taking a picture (thin description) versus characterizing the action with references to its social context—its intentions, circumstances, history, and hoped for future (thick description). In other words, thick description is the creation of a discussion of targeted behavioral acts relative to their social action. Consequently, this description of a social action is thick not only with intentionality but also with social-organizational matters (Sharrock & Button, 1993, p. 169). The anthropologist Clifford Geertz (1973) was aware of these distinctions. He stated that various forms of qualitative research should not be assessed according to the amount of information that they contain but by the clarification they provide about the social/cultural actions observed within the targeted context. In fact, Geertz used Ryle's example of a boy winking, recognizing that to appropriately unravel the wink's significance as (alternatively) a parody, an imitation of a parody, a conspiratory gesture, flirting, or something else, interpretation based upon the contextual constraints was necessary.

This goal of achieving explication when studying some phenomenon of communication can lead to a greater understanding of the phenomenon and the intentions, mechanisms, and constraints by which it operates. Emanuel Schegloff has described the value of such explication. He implied that conversation analysis has the potential to provide a clear depiction and exemplars of "... how the prima facie, observable embodiment of sociality—action, activity, and conduct in interaction—as effectuated through the deployment of language and the body can be put at the center of theorizing about the social and can be grounded and elaborated in detailed, empirical analysis of that conduct" (1996, p. 162). While Schegloff was positioning conversation analysis as a necessary contribution to sociological theory when he wrote that statement, I believe that his depiction of explication can be extended, to some extent, to all qualitative research methodologies, since the focus of such qualitative studies is on *how* social-communicative experience is created and given meaning. In contrast, quantitative-experimental studies emphasize the measurement and analysis of causal relationships between variables—not processes—and these studies are typically de-contextualized (Maxwell, 2012).

So then, this is why we employ qualitative research as our preferred paradigm. Because we recognize qualitative research as a situated activity that locates the researcher in the targeted world by using a set of interpretative practices that make that world visible to us (Denzin & Lincoln, 2008). Consequently, we can investigate the complexity of language and communication as social action, and we can strive to embrace that complexity through this research paradigm since it is best suited to accomplish our goal of explication in all of its potential.

The Foundations of Qualitative Research

A second issue of importance when we employ qualitative research in our discipline involves how well we actually understand the foundations of this paradigm. When I became interested in this research perspective, it was important to me that I understood the warrants for qualitative research. That is, *how is the qualitative paradigm handled from a theoretical perspective? Is there support in science for this paradigm?* I reasoned that if I did not understand the foundations of this research, then I had to operate from a position of faith, a dangerous strategy for a researcher. I further reasoned that when I looked for support, if there were only weak or minimal support for qualitative research within the enterprise of science, then I would have to carefully reconsider this as a viable research paradigm.

When investigating these foundational questions, it soon became apparent that there is great support for qualitative research both from a theoretical perspective and as a viable component of the great intellectual enterprise we refer to as science. Work in the philosophy of science (e.g., Bhaskar, 1978; Cartwright, 1999; Chalmers, 1999; Harré & Secord, 1972; Putnam, 1999; Salmon, 1998), scholarship involving social theory in the twentieth century (e.g., Baert, 1998; Gergen, 1985; Lin, 1976; Mackenzie, 1977; Manicas, 1983; Phillips, 2000), and some excellent writings about qualitative research (e.g., Alasuutari, 2010; Becker, 1996; Hammersley, 1992; House, 1991; Huberman & Miles, 1985; Maxwell, 1996, 2012) supply sufficient discussion and strong support for the foundations of this research paradigm.

As practioners in the social and psychological sciences, we often view research from a methodological perspective (Hornstein, 1988). That is, when we consider the scientific enterprise, we tend to think about the scientific method, our hypotheses or questions, and the design and implementation of our research. Doubtless, these are important components of the enterprise. Science, however, is more than a set of methods; what we believe and how we use those beliefs to act upon the world through science is actually directed by the various theoretical orientations that we possess. While there are a number of theoretical ideas linked within science in general (e.g., Kuhn, 1962; Olby, Cantor, Christie, & Hodge, 1990; Salmon, 1989), the most pervasive ideas involve how we view reality and how we can come to know that reality. These two questions often give rise to what we consider the nature of science and how it is employed and benefits us.

The philosophic investigation of the first question, how we view reality or what is the actual nature of reality, is referred to as *ontology*. Since the latter part of the 20th century, the dominant ontological position in the philosophy of science has been one of realism. D.C. Phillips, in the glossary of his book, *Philosophy, Science, and Social Inquiry*, defined realism as "the view that entities exist independently of being perceived, or independently of our theories about them" (1987, p. 205). That is, there is a reality outside of our human experiences made up of atoms and objects, worlds and stars, along with ideas and processes that have existence regardless of how (or how accurately) we conceptualize or identify them. In science we struggle to understand this reality to the best of our abilities, but we realize that our best may not be sufficient to actually discern the true nature of reality (Bhaskar, 1978; Cartwright, 1999). Consequently, it is the task of science to assume an attitude of striving to create as functional and accurate an approximation of reality as is possible; one that is sufficiently accurate to enable us to create technologies and knowledge bases that ultimately have given rise to our modern world, but one that is tentative rather than dogmatic so that our ideas are open to continual modification as we move closer to accurate understanding of reality. This brand of philosophical realism has a number of versions, all very complex. However, as discussed by Maxwell, "A distinctive feature of all of these forms of realism is that they deny that we can have any 'objective' or certain knowledge of the world, and accept the possibility of alternative valid accounts of any phenomenon" (2012, p. 5). Whether considering the physical or social sciences, this view of the necessity for the tentative nature of science should govern our perceptions and practices.

The second question, how we can come to know that reality (if we can, in fact, know it), is referred to in philosophy as *epistemology*. In the psychological and social sciences, constructivism has been the dominant epistemological position for nearly 50 years. As a response to positivism and its descendant, behaviorism, this position has asserted that human knowledge is constructed rather than directly perceived via our sensorial experiences (see Damico & Ball, 2010; Mills, 1998; Phillips, 2000; Shuell, 1986, for further discussion). Whether we are discussing the acquisition and use of cognitive structures in individuals (*psychological constructivism*) or the knowledge bases that are obtained and employed in the various social and cultural disciplines and realms (*social constructivism*), our knowledge of reality is constructed from a specific vantage point dependent primarily upon the minds of the knower(s) and whatever set of sociocultural influences are present when the individual or community is in the process of active construction. Jean Piaget, a genetic epistemologist and foundational figure in constructivism, put it succinctly for psychological constructivism:

> Fifty years of experience have taught us that knowledge does not result from a mere recording of observations without a structuring activity on the part of the subject. Nor do any a priori or innate cognitive structures exist in man; the functioning of intelligence alone is hereditary and creates structures only through an organization of successive actions performed on objects. Consequently, an epistemology conforming to the data of psychogenesis could be neither empiricist nor preformationist, but could consist only of a constructivism. (1980, p. 23)

Given the theoretical and empirical support for it, as we investigate the human psychological and symbolic processes and as we look to research paradigms to aid in these investigations, the constructivist stand on human knowledge acquisition and use should be paramount in our considerations.

The work of Joseph Maxwell is especially pertinent to the weaving together of these two philosophical stances regarding qualitative research. His most recent book, *A Realist Approach for Qualitative Research* (2012), argues for "critical realism" (the combination of ontological realism and epistemological constructivism) as a most useful and important resource for the qualitative paradigm. Since his version of critical realism adopts ontological realism as a starting point, and this paradigm asserts that reality is both complex and multi-layered, and that it is likely beyond our capacity to obtain certain knowledge of it, research as an activity must be considered a difficult enterprise that requires systematic and interpretive practices designed to seek answers to questions that stress how actions and experiences within this complexity are created and sustained (Damico & Ball, 2010). Qualitative research is designed to accomplish this enterprise in social science via a set of descriptive analytic procedures oriented toward providing a detailed view of the procedural affairs underlying observable social phenomena in order to explain how social actions are accomplished.

In terms of critical realism serving as a resource for the qualitative research paradigm, ontological realism enables qualitative researchers to operate from the belief that there is an actual reality (even if we may never objectively know it). Consequently, we can organize our research efforts to try and seek this reality (social reality in our case) and this gives us a genuine goal or objective. We can strive to understand as best we can and, in doing so, we can try to derive a progressively improved or more approximate knowledge base about the objects of our research efforts. Additionally, unlike versions of positivism or empiricism that reject theoretical terms and concepts (causality, mental states and attributes) as fictions that might be predictably useful but that don't have any reality themselves (they are considered logical constructions based on observational data of the real world), critical realism enables an ontological perspective to be applied to less concrete objects. That is, the meanings that individuals construct and hold, their cultural conceptions, intentions, and feelings, are also aspects of reality, especially since we employ them to help guide our everyday lives. These meanings and ideas are real because we use them to act upon the world in systematic fashion and they have consequences in the same way that more physical objects and events do. Although physical and mental/social entities may be conceptualized differently (see Maxwell, 2012, Chapter 3), they both have reality. Consequently, mental/social entities are central to our understanding of the social world and, since they are seen as real phenomena, they are available for investigation. This is a powerful resource for qualitative research since a research paradigm that enables the investigation of social processes and social action is a dynamic resource for understanding symbolic and social realities.

Finally, since critical realism employs a constructivist epistemology, it suggests that all explanation and conceptions of the world are grounded in a particular worldview or perspective dependent on the contexts and experiences of the knower(s). While this view does not allow for the idea that there are multiple realities, it does recognize that there are different but valid perspectives on reality that are based upon context and experience. If one hopes to investigate and interpret these perspectives (including how they operate and influence individuals and societies), one must have a flexible enough methodology to deal with the complexities of social action and experience as well as the interpretations of these actions and experiences. Since qualitative research is designed to employ systematic research techniques in naturalistic settings that are oriented to accounting for the complexity of social action instead of controlling it, this paradigm is well suited for constructivist operations in the real world. The strengths of qualitative methodologies revolve around studying social phenomena within their natural contexts and from the perspective of the participants so that the variables that make up the events and structures of social action can be accounted for within the actual contexts rather than controlled through experimental designs. Based upon these points, qualitative research appears ideally suited to critical realism and it is a means to implement research in this complex social reality.

As philosophy of science has changed over the past 50 years and moved theory and research away from positivism, behaviorism, and experimentalism, we find that qualitative research does offer a more open and flexible approach to the systematic investigation of the social world, one consistent with the changes noted in the physical and social sciences in the latter half of the 20th and in the 21st centuries. Based upon these changes, there are philosophic and scientific foundations for qualitative research. Of course, this discussion of critical realism is our current best approximation of these philosophical issues. Some qualitative researchers have produced different interpretations (e.g., Denzin & Lincoln, 2008; Smith & Deemer, 2000), and this type of debate is in keeping with the best operational tenets of science. To suggest that this version of critical realism is the ultimate correct paradigm would be inconsistent with its basic premises. However, along with numerous other theorists and researchers, I believe that it is our best current theoretical position, and it has great utility for qualitative research.

Some Practical Realities

Once we recognize and understand the goal and the foundations of qualitative research, we should be better oriented to this investigatory paradigm in terms of our practices and our confidence concerning its utilization. However, even given the theoretical and pragmatic support for qualitative research, there is still much concern about the actual applications and implementation of this research perspective. To say otherwise would be disingenuous. There are practical realities that qualitative researchers have to face in human communication sciences and disorders. While the list of such realities is long, I will mention only two that should be addressed.

Getting Started and Sustaining Qualitative Research Practices

For both the neophyte and the experienced qualitative researcher there is the reality that one can only conduct quality research if one has a sufficient knowledge base about this research paradigm. Obtaining this knowledge base is dependent on several strategies. First, *selecting and reading well-written qualitative research* is important—especially for the beginning researcher. There are a number of excellent books, chapters, and articles that can provide this knowledge. Of course, a number of the chapters in this handbook represent a fine start to that endeavor. However, there are other texts that I believe are also very effective. In terms of the overall framework there are several places where one could begin. As mentioned previously, the work of Maxwell (e.g., 1996, 2012) is well written and well defended, as is the work of Silverman (e.g., 2011), Creswell (1998), Duranti and Goodwin (1992), and Denzin and Lincoln (1994, 2008). For more methodological instruction across the various qualitative traditions of inquiry, I believe that the work of Spradley (1979, 1980), Agar (1986), Smith (2003), Schegloff (2007), and several others (e.g., Button & Lee, 1987; Charmaz, 2006; Ochs, Schegloff, & Thompson, 1996) present clear demonstrations of how many qualitative research methods are employed. The journals *Education Researcher, Journal of Interactional Research in Communicative Disorders, Qualitative Inquiry,* and *Qualitative Researcher* are primarily dedicated to the publication of qualitative studies. Of course, there are also excellent chapters and articles produced in human communicative sciences and disorders, and many of these have been cited throughout this handbook.

A second strategy for improving one's knowledge base is *gaining actual experience* in conducting qualitative research; in-depth reading on the subject will not suffice. Once the researcher is informed via reading and study, practice with data collection, analysis and interpretation is essential. One benefit of such practice is that the researcher realizes that actual research is more complicated than what is often presented in the texts. Consequently, the methods discussed in the texts are not intended to be followed exactly. Rather, they may be viewed as guidelines. Since there is so much variation in real research contexts, good research is improvisational—but that improvisation is based upon one's knowledge and understanding in order that the principles of the qualitative enterprise are not violated. The result of this type of informed practice is improved qualitative research, not methodological anarchy. A third strategy that I have found necessary is that the researcher should strive to *collaborate with like-minded researchers*. Regardless of how much each of us learns through reading, coursework, and practical experience, it is important to check your beliefs and practices with other researchers. I was fortunate to collaborate early in my qualitative work with Dana Kovarsky, Nina Simmons-Mackie, and Madeline Maxwell, all professionals in our discipline who enabled me to greatly improve my methods. Eventually, I also took coursework and informally learned from well-established qualitative researchers like Chuck and Candy Goodwin, Miles Richardson, and Keith Basso. However, it was my struggling and discussions with Nina and Dana that primarily improved my research understanding and skills.

Finally, to progress and improve as a qualitative researcher it is important to *be systematic in your applications and bold in your interpretations.* I think that many qualitative researchers—especially less experienced ones—are not as systematic in their applications of the principles that they have learned or as willing to follow their data and analyses to the logical interpretations as they might be. Such implementation difficulty often results in methodological mistakes and in conclusions that are little better than commonsense notions. Qualitative research is a powerful paradigm that has great potential to help us understand social action in all of its forms. Qualitative researchers in our field have to possess the discipline to systematically employ the appropriate principles and the courage to write and extend the interpretations of their findings.

Dealing with Uncertainty

Another reality faced by qualitative researchers in human communicative sciences and disorders is that we are not always comfortable with our efforts in qualitative research—and the skepticism of our colleagues doesn't help—so it is easy to second guess ourselves; we develop a form of methodological perplexity. Such is the fate of those who are not part of the "master narrative" (Stanley, 2007) in some research disciplines. But the history of establishing the qualitative paradigm in other social sciences suggests that we in human communication sciences and disorders are not alone. Even in the disciplines that are now well established as having strong qualitative research traditions, similar concerns and acceptance issues have been part of the inclusion process. For example, a number of researchers have discussed their difficulties in getting their results published (e.g., Ceglowski, Bacigalupa, & Peck, 2011; Dahlberg, 2006) when first trying to break into journals that are more experimentally oriented; at the 2006 International Congress of Qualitative Inquiry held in Champaign-Urbana, Illinois there was a panel of seven distinguished qualitative researchers who discussed their own uncertainty and the vexations they had to deal with in their own careers. They finally gained acceptance for their research methods and agendas but not without some initial barriers that had to be overcome (Ellis et al., 2008).

Fortunately, many of these more experienced qualitative researchers not only provide us with conflict narratives, they also provide us with suggestions, guidelines, and encouragement to continue working toward greater acceptance of qualitative methodologies. Texts have been published that provide beneficial suggestions for achieving greater publishing success (e.g., Becker, 1986; Ceglowski et al., 2011; Dahlberg, 2006; Gage, 1991; Hess, 1989; Stanley, 2007), for evaluating the quality of various qualitative methods (e.g., Ambert, Adler, Adler, & Detzner, 1995; Bryman, 1988; Chapelle & Duff, 2003; Creswell & Miller, 2000; Flyvbjerg, 2006; Gilgun, 2006; Horsburgh, 2003; Howe & Eisenhart, 1990; Morse, 2006; Tracy, 2010), and for providing support of the essentialness of qualitative research in human social action (e.g., Alasuutari, 2010; Bunniss & Kelly, 2010; Simmons-Mackie & Damico, 2003). These texts can serve as resources for each of us. If the perplexity that we struggle with results in keen circumspection of our research efforts and in personal declarations that we are committed to advancing the agenda for qualitative research, then we can continue to advance our efforts in the field.

Conclusion

Despite the difficulties that we might have faced individually in advancing qualitative research in our discipline, we have made great strides. Even after confronting the most recent barriers based upon the ill-conceived scientifically based research (SBR) movement connected to the No Child Left Behind Act of 2001 and initiated by the National Research Council (e.g., Lather, 2004a, 2004b; Ryan & Hood, 2004), qualitative research endures. The reason it endures is that qualitative research incorporates the same kinds of intellectual endeavors that all effective science employs: a problem or question is identified and clarified, potential solutions or answers are discussed and advanced, there is some type of testing of these solutions or answers to determine which best fit the data at hand, and then there is an extension or a reformulation of the solution that has been sustained until we find even better ways of addressing the original problems. Whether we refer to this as the scientific method or the hypothetico-deductive method, this is the process that is used in all good science, including within the qualitative paradigm. Without question, there has been an evolution of acceptance for qualitative research in applied social science over the past 40 years, and we are seeing this trend in human communicative sciences and disorders. As detailed by Howe (1988), qualitative research has evolved from unacceptable, to being viewed as exploratory, to being accepted as an alternative approach, to being a valuable research paradigm in its own right. I join with all the other authors in this handbook to continue to advance its power and potential.

References

Abkarian, G. G. (1977). The changing face of a discipline: Isn't it "romantic"? *Journal of Speech and Hearing Disorders, 42*, 422–435.

Agar, M. (1986). *Speaking of ethnography*. Newbury Park, CA: Sage.

Alasuutari, P. (2010). The rise and relevance of qualitative research. *International Journal of Social Research Methodology, 13*(2), 139–155.

Ambert, A.-M., Adler, P. A., Adler, P., & Detzner, D. F. (1995). Understanding and evaluating qualitative research. *Journal of Marriage and Family, 57*(4), 879–893.

Baert, P. (1998). *Social theory in the twentieth century*. New York, NY: New York University Press.

Becker, H. S. (1986). *Writing for the social scientist*. Chicago, IL: Chicago University Press.

Becker, H. S. (1996). The epistemology of qualitative research. In R. Jessor, A. Colby, & R. A. Shweder (Eds.), *Ethnography and human development: Context and meaning in social inquiry* (pp. 205–216). Cambridge, England: Cambridge University Press.

Bhaskar, R. (1978). *A realist theory of science* (2nd ed.). Brighton, England: Harvester Press.

Bissex, G. (1980). *Gnys at wrk: A child learns to red and write*. Cambridge, MA: Harvard University Press.

Bruner, J. S. (1975). From communication to language — a psychological perspective. *Cognition, 3*, 255–288.

Bruner, J. S. (1981). The social context of language acquisition. *Language and Communication, 1*, 155–178.

Bryman, A. (1988). *Quantity and quality in social research*. London, England: Unwin Hyman.

Bunniss, S., & Kelly, D. R. (2010). Research paradigms in medical education research. *Medical Education, 44*(4), 358–366.

Button, G., & Lee, J. R. E. (Eds.). (1987). *Talk and social organisation*. Clevedon, England: Multilingual Matters.

Cartwright, N. (1999). *The dappled world: A study of the boundaries of science*. Cambridge, England: Cambridge University Press.

Ceglowski, D., Bacigalupa, C., & Peck, E. (2011). Aced out: Censorship of qualitative research in the age of "scientifically based research." *Qualitative Inquiry, 17*, 679–686.

Chalmers, A. (1999). *What is this thing called science?* (3rd ed.). Indianapolis, IN: Hackett.

Chapelle, C. A., & Duff, P. A. (2003). Some guidelines for conducting quantitative and qualitative research in TESOL. *TESOL Quarterly, 37*(1), 157–178.

Charmaz, K. (2006). *Constructing grounded theory. A practical guide through qualitative analysis*. Thousand Oaks, CA: Sage.

Creswell, J. W. (1998). *Qualitative inquiry and research design: Choosing among five traditions*. Thousand Oaks, CA: Sage.

Creswell, J. W., & Miller, D. L. (2000). Determining validity in qualitative inquiry. *Theory into Practice, 39*(3), 124–130.

Dahlberg, K. (2006). The publication of qualitative research findings. *Qualitative Health Research, 16*, 444–446.

Damico, J. S. (1988). The lack of efficacy in language therapy: A case study. *Language, Speech, and Hearing Services in Schools, 19*(1), 51–66.

Damico, J. S., & Ball, M. J. (2010). Prolegomenon: Addressing the tyranny of old ideas. *Journal of Interactional Research in Communication Disorders, 1*, 1–29.

Denzin, N. K. (1978). *The research act: A theoretical introduction to sociological methods* (2nd ed.). New York, NY: McGraw-Hill.

Denzin, N. K., & Lincoln, Y. S. (Eds.). (1994). *Handbook of qualitative research*. Thousand Oaks, CA: Sage.

Denzin, N. K., & Lincoln, Y. S. (Eds.). (2008). *The landscape of qualitative research* (3rd ed.). Thousand Oaks, CA: Sage.

Duranti, A., & Goodwin, C. (Eds.). (1992). *Rethinking context: Language as an interactive phenomenon*. Cambridge, England: Cambridge University Press.

Ellis, C., Bochner, A., Denzin, N., Lincoln, Y. S., Morse, J., Pelisa, R., & Richardson, L. (2008). Talking and thinking about qualitative research. *Qualitative Inquiry, 14*, 254–284.

Flyvbjerg, B. (2006). Five misunderstandings about case-study research. *Qualitative Inquiry, 12*, 219–245.

Gage, N. L. (1991). The obviousness of social and educational research results. *Educational Researcher, 20*(1), 10–16.

Geertz, C. (1973). *The interpretation of cultures*. New York, NY: Basic Books.

Gergen, K. J. (1985). The social constructivist movement in modern psychology. *American Psychologist, 40*, 266–273.

Gilgun, J. F. (2006). The four cornerstones of qualitative research. *Qualitative Health Research, 16*(3), 436–443.

Halliday, M. A. K. (1978). *Language as social semiotic: The social interpretation of language and meaning*. London, England: Arnold.

Hammersley, M. (1992). Ethnography and realism. In M. Hammersley (Ed.), *What's wrong with ethnography? Methodological explorations* (pp. 43–56). London, England: Routledge.

Harré, R., & Secord, P. (1972). *Explanation of social behaviour*. Oxford, England: Blackwell.

Hess, D. J. (1989). Teaching ethnographic writing: A review essay. *Anthropology & Education Quarterly, 20*(3), 163–176.

Hornstein, G. A. (1988). Quantifying psychological phenomena: Debates, dilemmas, and implications. In J. G. Morawski (Ed.), *The rise of experimentation in American psychology* (pp. 1–34). New Haven, CT: Yale University Press.

Horsburgh, D. (2003). Evaluation of qualitative research. *Journal of Clinical Nursing, 12*, 307–312.

House, E. R. (1991). Realism in research. *Educational Researcher, 20*(6), 2–9, 25.

Howe, K. R. (1988). Against the quantitative-qualitative incompatibility thesis or dogmas die hard. *Educational Researcher, 17*(8), 10–16.

Howe, K. R., & Eisenhart, M. (1990). Standards for qualitative (and quantitative) research: A prolegomenon. *Educational Researcher, 19*(4), 2–9.

Huberman, A. M., & Miles, M. B. (1985). Assessing local causality in qualitative research. In D. N. Berg & K. K. Smith (Eds.), *Exploring clinical methods for social research*. (pp. 351–382). Beverly Hills, CA: Sage.

Kuhn, T. S. (1962). *The structure of scientific revolutions*. Chicago, IL: University of Chicago Press.

Lather, P. (2004a). Scientific research in education: A critical perspective. *British Educational Research Journal, 30*, 759–772.

Lather, P. (2004b). This IS your father's paradigm: Government intrusion and the case for qualitative research in education. *Qualitative Inquiry, 10*(1), 15–34.

Lin, N. (1976). *Foundations of social research*. New York, NY: McGraw-Hill.

Mackenzie, B. D. (1977). *Behaviourism and the limits of scientific method*. Atlantic Highlands, NJ: Humanities Press.

Manicas, P. T. (1983). *A history and philosophy of the social sciences*. Oxford, England: Blackwell.

Maxwell, J. A. (1996). *Qualitative research design: An interactive approach*. Thousand Oaks, CA: Sage.

Maxwell, J. A. (2012). *A realist approach for qualitative research*. Thousand Oaks, CA: Sage.

McDermott, R. P., & Gospodinoff, K. (1979). Social contexts for ethnic borders and school failure. In A. Wolfgang (Ed.), *Nonverbal behavior* (pp. 175–195). New York, NY: AcademicPress.

Mills, J. A. (1998). *Control: A history of behavioral psychology*. New York, NY: New York University Press.

Morse, J. M. (2006). Reconceptualizing qualitative evidence. *Qualitative Health Research, 16*(3), 415–422.

Muma, J. R. (1975). The communication game: dump and play. *Journal of Speech and Hearing Disorders, 40*, 296–309.

Ochs, E., Schegloff, E. A., & Thompson, S. A. (Eds.). (1996). *Interaction and grammar*. Cambridge, England: Cambridge University Press.

Olby, R. C., Cantor, G. N., Christie, J. R. R., & Hodge, M. J. S. (Eds.). (1990). *Companion to the history of modern science*. New York, NY: Routledge.

Phillips, D. C. (1987). *Philosophy, science, and social inquiry: Comtemporary methodological controversies in social science and related applied fields of research*. Oxford, England: Pergamon.

Phillips, D. C. (2000). *The expanded social scientist's bestiary*. Lantham, MD: Row & Littlefield.

Piaget, J. (1980). The psychogenesis of knowledge and its epistemological significance. In M. Piattelli-Palmarini (Ed.), *Language and learning: The debate between Jean Piaget and Noam Chomsky* (pp. 23–34). Cambridge, MA: Harvard University Press.

Putnam, H. (1999). *The three-fold cord: Mind, body, and world*. New York, NY: Columbia University Press.

Rabinow, P., & Sullivan, W. (Eds.). (1979). *Interpretive social science: A reader*. Berkeley, CA: University of California Press.

Rees, N. S., & Shulman, M. (1978). I don't understand what you mean by comprehension. *Journal of Speech and Hearing Disorders, 43*, 208–219.

Rogoff, B., & Lave, J. (Eds.). (1984). *Everyday cognition: Development in the social context*. Cambridge, MA: Harvard University Press.

Ryan, K. E., & Hood, L. K. (2004). Guarding the castle and opening the gates. *Qualitative Inquiry, 10*, 79–95.

Ryle, G. (1949). *The concept of mind*. Chicago, IL: Chicago University Press.

Salmon, W. C. (1989). Four decades of scientific explanation. In P. Kitcher & W. C. Salmon (Eds.), *Scientific explanation* (pp. 3–219). Minneapolis: University of Minnesota Press.

Salmon, W. C. (1998). *Causality and explanation*. New York, NY: Oxford University Press.

Schegloff, E. A. (1996). Confirming allusions: Toward an empirical account of action. *The American Journal of Sociology, 102*(1), 161–216.

Schegloff, E. A. (2007). *Sequence organization in interaction. A primer in conversation analysis*. Cambridge, England: Cambridge University Press.

Sharrock, W., & Button, G. (1993). The social actor: Social action in real time. In G. Button (Ed.), *Ethnomethodology and the human sciences* (pp. 137–175). Cambridge, England: Cambridge University Press.

Shuell, T. J. (1986). Cognitive conceptions of learning. *Review of Educational Research, 56*, 411–436.

Silverman, D. (Ed.). (2011). *Qualitative research* (3rd ed.). Thousand Oaks, CA: Sage.

Simmons-Mackie, N. N., & Damico, J. S. (2003). Contributions of qualitative research to the knowledge base of normal communication. *American Journal of Speech-Language Pathology, 12*(2), 144–154.

Smith, J. K., & Deemer, D. K. (2000). The problem of criteria in the age of relativism. In N. K. Denzin & Y. S. Lincoln (Eds.), *SAGE handbook of qualitative research* (2nd ed., pp. 877–896). Thousand Oaks, CA: Sage.

Smith, J. S. (Ed.). (2003). *Qualitative psychology. A practical guide to research methods*. Thousand Oaks, CA: Sage.

Spradley, J. (1979). *The ethnographic interview*. New York, NY: Holt, Rinehart and Winston,

Spradley, J. (1980). *Participant observation*. New York, NY: Holt, Rinehart and Winston.

Stake, R. E. (1978). The case study method of social inquiry. *Educational Researcher, 7*(2), 5–7.

Stanley, C. A. (2007). When counter narratives meet master narratives in the journal editorial-review process. *Educational Researcher, 36*, 14–24.

Tracy, S. J. (2010). Qualitative quality: Eight "big-tent" criteria for excellent qualitative research. *Qualitative Inquiry, 16*, 837–851.

Author Index

Subject Index